THE **Building Christian English** SERIES

Building

Christian English

Beginning Wisely

Grade 3

Teacher's Manual

Rod and Staff Publishers, Inc.

Hwy. 172, Crockett, Kentucky 41413

Telephone: (606) 522-4348

11   12   13   14   15   —   21   20   19   18   17   16   15   14   13   12

Acknowledgments

We are thankful to God for the opportunities of our day to provide sound textbooks for Christian schools. He has given a vision to many of His people to produce school materials that will encourage right living and an understanding of God's will.

The original edition was written by Lela Birky, and the revision by Rachel Christopher and Verna Mast. Marvin Eicher edited the material, and Lester Miller illustrated it.

A number of other Christian persons have reviewed the manuscripts. We are grateful for the time they have given to this and for their helpful criticisms, as well as to various teachers who tested it in a classroom setting.

Various reference works were consulted in the production of this textbook, such as dictionaries and English handbooks. We have chosen to favor the more conservative schools of thought that are considered authoritative in correct English usage.

Great effort has been put forth to produce a high-quality work in every way. We trust it will be a blessing to all who use it.

—*The Publishers*

Table of Contents

Unit 1

Building with Sentences

Unit 2

Building With Nouns and Pronouns

Unit 3

Building With Verbs

Unit 4

Building With Adjectives and Adverbs

Unit 5

Building With Our Language

Worksheets

Unit 1

Unit 2

Unit 3

Unit 4

Unit 5

Tests

To the Teacher

This English course is designed for approximately 120 minutes of class time per week. There is a pupil's book, a teacher's guide, a booklet of worksheets, and a test booklet.

The Pupil's Book

The lesson text explains and illustrates the new concepts. The exercises may be divided into several parts, with the first one or two parts based on the present lesson. Then there is often a part called Review and Practice, which has exercises on concepts taught previously. Each part may be further divided into several parts.

The average class should usually do all the written exercises in each lesson. If this is not feasible, you should assign at least the odd or even numbers in each part, including Review and Practice. An occasional challenge exercise called **Can You Do This?** provides optional work, which may be done for extra credit or assigned to more able students.

Review lessons occur every five lessons or so, and there are also two reviews at the end of each unit. The test booklet has a test for each unit.

The Teacher's Guide

Each lesson in the teacher's guide begins with **Aim,** which states the purpose of the lesson. The next part, called **Class,** gives suggestions for teaching the lesson.

Beginning in Lesson 3, a part called **Oral Review** comes after Aim. The review questions in this part are intended for use at the beginning of the class period, both to review concepts already taught and to get the pupils' minds "in gear" for the new English lesson. Sometimes there is an Oral Drill in the pupil's book (usually in a review lesson); and if so, the Oral Review is omitted from the teacher's guide.

Every half unit or so, there is a **Written Quiz** instead of an Oral Review. These quizzes may be given orally, or they may be reproduced if the teacher so desires. Both the Oral Reviews and the Written Quizzes are optional; see the following section for further explanation.

Pattern of Drill and Review

This course is designed to provide sufficient drill and review of all the English concepts taught. If the written exercises (including Review and Practice) are used as indicated above, the average pupil's mastery of the concepts should be satisfactory for this grade level.

However, for a thorough mastery of the material (especially for slow students), it is helpful to drill and review until the concepts are "overlearned." This is the purpose of the Oral Reviews and Written Quizzes in the teacher's guide, and it is also one purpose of the worksheets. If there is enough time, or if the pupils seem to need it, the teacher is strongly encouraged to use the extra materials. But they may be omitted if time is limited. *The worksheets, the Oral Reviews, and the Written Quizzes are not required for successful teaching of this English course.*

Teaching Suggestions

Use the chalkboard frequently to illustrate ideas. Keep a brisk pace, and do not waste precious class time to "major on minors." Students should follow along with open books during class discussion.

Use a grading system that provides an accurate picture of the children's progress, yet does not bog you down with time-consuming work. Do not give full credit if students fail to do neat work or follow directions.

It is also a good policy to take grades on class participation. Students need to pay attention, follow along in their books, show interest in what is being said, and participate in giving answers during oral drill.

The worksheets may be used for remedial practice or simply for extra drill on various concepts. They may be reproduced as needed in teaching this course.

Unit 1

Building Sentences

Lines must be drawn in certain ways
   To make the letters right,
And letters must in order stand
   To make a word spelled right.

Each word is put in proper place
   To give a sentence sense;
No one could ever understand
   "By tree the was the fence."

We need some knowledge how to build
   A sentence that is right;
So we will study Unit One,
   And study with our might!

Whatsoever thy hand findeth to do,
do it with thy might.
Ecclesiastes 9:10

Building
With Sentences

1. An Introduction to Your English Book

God wants us to make good friendships. This English textbook is to become one of your good friends. It was written to help you understand and use the English language.

Treat this book as a friend. Since it is not a workbook, you should not write in the book. Write on your paper instead. The following rules will help you treat your textbook as a friend.

1. Always handle the book with clean hands.
2. Quietly turn the pages from the top outside corner of the book.
3. Use a strip of paper or a ribbon as a marker. Never dog-ear the pages by turning down the corners.
4. Keep the book dry so that it does not warp.

English
Ruth Book   September 1, 20—
page 21

1. Handle the book with clean hands.
2. Turn the pages quietly and carefully so that they do not become "dog-eared."
3. Do not write anything in the textbook.
4. Use a strip of paper as a marker. Do not fold the page or use pencils.
5. Eagerly read every word in each lesson.
6. Follow directions carefully and cheerfully.
7. Check your work when you finish to see that you did everything neatly and correctly.

Prepare your English papers according to the pattern shown at the right. Remember to do the following things.

1. Use capital letters, periods, and commas where they belong.
2. Keep a good margin along both edges of your paper.
3. Write your name at the proper place.
4. In the upper right corner of your paper, write the date on which you do the lesson. Your teacher can help you.

Lesson 1

Aim: (1) To introduce the children to their English textbooks, and to encourage a wholesome attitude toward the study of English. (2) To give a good pattern for preparing English papers.

Class: Tell the children, "The Bible tells us what we must do if we want to have friends." (Read Proverbs 18:24.) "This English book will be a friend if we show ourselves friendly to it."

If the textbooks are new, demonstrate how to break them in. A new book should be set on its spine, and both covers should be gently opened and creased. Then the pages should be folded out a few at a time, from both front and back, until the center of the book is reached.

Discuss the first set of rules in class. You may need to explain what is meant by dog-earing—marking a place in a book by folding down the upper corner of a page. "Books naturally become dog-eared as they get older. We

do not need to make this happen sooner by purposel[y] folding down corners."

Also discuss the pattern for preparing Englis[h] papers. For margins (point 2): "It is helpful to dra[w] light pencil lines until we are in the habit of leavin[g] good margins. Draw the lines about an inch fro[m] each edge of your paper."

Note: The pattern shown is only one of several pos[-] sibilities. The most important thing is to have a goo[d] pattern and follow it consistently. Here is an alte[r] nate pattern for those teachers who may prefer it.

Subject	Name
Page (or Lesson)	Date

Do some exploring of the English textbook i[n] class. Show how the table of contents gives an ove[r] all picture of what the book contains. Also turn t[o] the index and point out that it has an alphabetic[al] listing of the things taught in the book.

5. Write the page numbers of your lesson in the proper place.

6. Write your lesson neatly.

Make a good start in English by carefully and cheerfully reading and following directions. Then keep up the good work. Best wishes!

> Writing an English Lesson >

A. Prepare an English paper according to the pattern shown in the lesson. Then copy neatly and carefully the four rules for treating your textbook as a friend.

B. The following sentences review some things you studied in Grade 2. You will study them again in Grade 3.

Copy the correct words in parentheses ( ). The lesson numbers tell you the lessons in this book where you can find the answers.

1. A group of words with a complete thought is a (phrase, sentence, contraction). Lesson 4

2. Words like **run** and **sing** show action. They are called (nouns, verbs, adjectives). Lesson 51

3. Words like **man, town,** and **pencil** name people, places, or things. They are called (nouns, verbs, adjectives). Lesson 26

4. Words like **green** and **large** describe nouns. They are called (verbs, pronouns, adjectives). Lesson 76

5. A word that takes the place of a noun is called a (verb, pronoun, adjective). Lesson 36

6. If a noun tells about more than one, it is (singular, plural, past). Lesson 32

7. A sentence usually ends with a (comma, question mark, period). Lesson 4

Lesson 1 Answers
Writing an English Lesson

A. (Check to see that pupils' English papers follow the pattern that you gave them. The first set of rules in the lesson is to be copied neatly.)

B. 1. sentence
   2. verbs
   3. nouns
   4. adjectives
   5. pronoun
   6. plural
   7. period

2. Using the Dictionary

The dictionary is a book about words. It gives information about many thousands of words. Then how can you find the one word you want?

Finding a word in the dictionary is not hard because the words are listed in **alphabetical order.** In the lists below, the letters in bold print show how the words have been put in alphabetical order.

bread	**ca**bbage	**ea**ch
carrot	**ce**lery	**ea**ger
fish	**ch**eese	**ea**rn
green	**co**le slaw	**ea**sy
meat	**cr**acker	**ea**t

The letter **b** comes before **c,** so **bread** comes before **carrot.** If the first letters are the same, look at the second letter, the third letter, and so on until you find a letter that is different. **Cabbage** comes before **celery** because **ca** comes before **ce. Each** comes before **eager** because **eac** comes before **eag.**

Lesson 2

Aim: To give practice with alphabetical order in preparation for dictionary use.

Class: Explain alphabetical order. "Alphabetical order is A-B-C order. Words beginning with *a* come first, then words beginning with *b,* and so on. Also words beginning with *ab* come before those beginning with *ac.*" Illustrate with the alphabetized word lists in the lesson. At this level, all the words in a given list are alphabetized by the same letter (first, second, and so forth). The pupils are not required to work with lists such as *believe, before, bring, because.*

The amount of instruction you need to give will depend on how much the pupils have studied alphabetical order in other classes, such as spelling. Here are some lists that you could write on the board for more practice with alphabetical order.

rain	mitten	inside
wind	music	invent
cloud	more	index
storm	match	intend
hail	mean	infant

★ **EXTRA PRACTICE**
Worksheet 1 (*Alphabetical Order*)

> Practice With Alphabetical Order >

A. Write the words in each column in alphabetical order.
Look at the letters in bold print.

1. **d**amp	2. **b**ook	3. **st**op	4. **wh**en
find	ball	stir	why
bring	bridge	stand	what
elbow	bite	stray	whose
cover	bend	steel	which

B. Each column has one word that is not in alphabetical
order. Copy that word on your paper.

1. lever	2. dry	3. pack	4. teach
month	dash	pause	teapot
oven	decide	pad	tear
grain	dime	palm	tease
round	dove	paw	team

> Can You Do This? >

After each word you wrote for Part B above, write a
number to show where that word **should** come in its column.
If it should be the first word, write 1 after it. If it should be
the second word, write 2, and so on.

●━●━●━●━●━●━●━●━●

3. More About the Dictionary

Where would you go if you wanted to know
   a. how to spell a word correctly?
   b. how to pronounce a word?
   c. what a word means?

Lesson 2 Answers
Practice With Alphabetical Order

A. 1.	bring	3.	stand
	cover		steel
	damp		stir
	elbow		stop
	find		stray
2.	ball	4.	what
	bend		when
	bite		which
	book		whose
	bridge		why

B. (Number answers are for Can You Do This?)
   1. grain, 1
   2. dry, 5
   3. pause, 4
   4. team, 2

Can You Do This?
(Answers are included with Part B.)

Lesson 3

Aim: To introduce the dictionary, and to practice dictionary use.

Oral Review:

(These questions are intended to be asked orally at
the beginning of the class period. The pupils should usually give oral answers, though you may sometimes want
them to answer on paper. About every half unit there is
a Written Quiz, which is designed to review some of the
more important concepts.)

1. Why is it not hard to find a word in the dictionary? (The words are listed in alphabetical order.)
2. If two words begin with the same letter, how can
   you tell which word comes first in the dictionary?
   (Look at the second letter.)
3. Why does *march* come before *market* in the dictionary? (The letter *c* in *march* comes before *k* in
   market.)

Class: Each pupil should have a dictionary to use
while you present this lesson. Say, "A dictionary tells
us many things about words. It shows us how to spell
words, how to pronounce words, what words mean,
and other things." Work together in finding some
simple words, and show how spellings, pronunciations, and other information are given. Examples:
mouse (point out the plural *mice*), *lead* (show the
past form *led*), and *big* (show *bigger* and *biggest*).
Have the students read several definitions aloud.

For Can You Do This? you will need to have a
dictionary available that is advance enough to list
the words indicated.

A dictionary will answer all three questions for you. Look at the dictionary **entry** below. The word in bold print is called an **entry word.** It is the word you are looking up.

The entry word shows you the correct spelling of **bouquet.** The letters in parentheses ( ) show you how to pronounce **bouquet.** Then there is a phrase that tells you what **bouquet** means.

bou·quet (bō·kā′) A bunch of flowers.

> Using the Dictionary >

A. Use the dictionary to help you find which of the spellings in parentheses ( ) is correct. Copy the correct spelling on your paper.
1. Write your answers on a clean (peice, piece, piese) of paper.
2. Be careful not to do (sloppy, sloppie, slopy) work.
3. Have a good (marjin, margin, margen) along both edges of your paper.
4. If you make a mistake, (erace, errase, erase) it carefully.

B. Write **a** or **b** to tell which is the correct pronunciation of each word in bold print. Use a dictionary if you are not sure.
1. **humor**   a. hyü′·mər   b. hum′·ər
2. **mechanic**   a. mə·chan′·ik   b. mə·kan′·ik
3. **vague**   a. vā′·gü   b. vāg
4. **ridicule**   a. rid′·ə·kyül   b. rē·dik′·əl

C. Use this entry to answer the questions.

   re·ceipt (ri·sēt′) A note showing that one has paid a bill.

Lesson 3 Answers
Using the Dictionary

A. 1. piece
   2. sloppy
   3. margin
   4. erase

B. 1. a
   2. b
   3. b
   4. a

1. What is the entry word?
2. How many syllables does the word have?
3. Does the word rhyme with **kept** or with **neat?**
4. When might someone give you a receipt?

SMITH & HESS, INC.
Bernville, PA 19506

Received from Harry Graber   April 4 2008

nine hundred sixty and °⁰/₁₀₀   Dollars

For   mower (# 44681)

$ 960.00   Carl Smith

> **Can You Do This?**

Find and write the following words. You may need to use a dictionary for older pupils.
1. The name of an animal beginning with **aa.**
2. The name of a squash beginning with **zu.**
3. The name of a bird beginning with **tou.**

●━●━●━●━●━●━●━●━●

4. What Is a Sentence?

Not every group of words written like a sentence is a sentence. In the following list, all the groups of words begin with a capital letter. They all end with a period. But only two of them are really sentences. Do you know which ones they are?

1. Jesus walked on the water.
2. The disciples in the boat.
3. Cried out in fear.
4. Jesus called to them.
5. Stilled the storm.

Every sentence must have a complete thought. In the groups of words above, only numbers 1 and 4 have

C. 1. receipt
   2. two
   3. neat
   4. After you pay a bill.

Can You Do This?
1. aardvark *or* aardwolf
2. zucchini
3. toucan *or* touraco

Lesson 4

Aim: (1) To teach the recognition of sentences. (2) To teach that a sentence must have a subject and a predicate.

Oral Review:
1. Words in bold print in a dictionary are called ——— words. (entry)
2. Why is it not hard to find a word in the dictionary? (The words are in alphabetical order.)
3. If two words have the same first letter, how can you tell which word comes first in the dictionary? (Look at the second letter.)
4. Which word comes first in the dictionary: *paste* or *paint*? Why? (*Paint* comes first. The letter *i* in *paint* comes before *s* in *paste.*)
5. What three things does a dictionary tell you? (how to spell words, how to pronounce words, and what words mean)

Class: In order to answer the question in the lesson title, children need a "sentence sense." This lesson should help to develop that sense.

Emphasize: "Every sentence has a complete thought. To express that thought, a sentence must have two parts: a subject and a predicate." This lesson focuses only on complete subjects and predicates, so you need not get into nouns and verbs at this point. Just make it clear that every complete sentence has two main parts.

Say, "I will write some sentences on the board. You tell me where to divide them between the subject and the predicate." Then write the following sentences. To show how important both parts are, you could give just the subject or predicate and point out the lack of meaning without the other part. You could

complete thoughts. They are the only two sentences.

To have a complete thought, a sentence must have a part that tells **who** or **what** the sentence is about. This part is called the **subject.** In sentences 1 and 4, **Jesus** tells **who** the sentence is about. The subject is **Jesus.**

A sentence must also have a part that tells what the subject **does** or **is.** This part is called the **predicate.** In sentences 1 and 4, the predicates are **walked on the water** and **called to them.** These predicates tell what Jesus **did.**

Look at the other groups of words above. Can you tell which part is missing from each group that is not a sentence?

Remember: A sentence is a group of words with a complete thought. It must have a **subject** that tells who or what the sentence is about and a **predicate** that tells what the subject does or is.

All sentences begin with a capital letter, and most sentences end with a period.

> Recognizing and Writing Sentences >

A. Read each group of words. If it is a complete sentence, write **complete.** If it is not a complete sentence, write whether it is a **subject** or a **predicate.**
   1. The rain pattered softly on the roof.
   2. Mother hummed a tune.
   3. Galloped across the field.
   4. The tall pine trees.
   5. The girl spoke softly.
   6. A great crowd of people.
   7. Was bright and cheery.
   8. Grandmother's old rocking chair.

Lesson 4 Answers
Recognizing and Writing Sentences
A. 1. complete
    2. complete
    3. predicate
    4. subject
    5. complete
    6. subject
    7. predicate
    8. subject

also show how the meanings can be changed by using different subjects and predicates.

   1. A strong wind | blew fiercely.
   2. The great oak tree | crashed to the ground.
   3. Father and the boys | sawed the tree into firewood.
   4. The next winter | was very cold.
   5. The stacks of firewood | kept the house warm all winter.

★ **EXTRA PRACTICE**
Worksheet 2 (*Recognizing Sentences*)

9. David won a great victory for Israel.
10. Was splashing through the creek.
11. The beautiful morning.
12. The carpenters were busy.
13. Healed many sick people.
14. Patches of beautiful flowers.

B. Make a complete sentence with each group of words in Part A that is not complete.

> **Review and Practice**

Write each column of words in alphabetical order.

1. orange	2. pheasant	3. Abihu
grapes	pelican	Abiathar
apple	plover	Abishai
banana	puffin	Abijah
pear	parrot	Abigail
cherry	pigeon	Abiram

●━━━━━━━━━●

5. Telling Sentences

Every day we say many things about the world around us. We hear others say many things too. Here are some things we may say or we may hear others say.

It is very warm today.
I am hungry.
Your pencil is on the floor.
It is time for family worship.

All these sentences are **telling**

---

9. complete
10. predicate
11. subject
12. complete
13. predicate
14. subject

B. (Individual answers.)

Review and Practice

1. apple	2. parrot	3. Abiathar
banana	pelican	Abigail
cherry	pheasant	Abihu
grapes	pigeon	Abijah
orange	plover	Abiram
pear	puffin	Abishai

Lesson 5

Aim: To teach pupils about sentences that state a fact.

Oral Review:
1. Words in bold print in a dictionary are called —— words. (entry)
2. If two words each begin with the same two letters, how can you tell which word comes first in the dictionary? (Look at the third letter.)
3. Give these words in alphabetical order: *trust, truck, truth*. (truck, trust, truth)
4. What three things does a dictionary tell you? (how to spell words, how to pronounce words, and what words mean)
5. A sentence must have a —— and a ——. (subject, predicate)

Class: Not all sentences do the same work. Some sentences give information. Others ask for information.

Still others give a command or express strong feeling.

"Today we will study sentences that state a fact. That means they tell us something." Illustrate with statements of truth from the Bible, such as the following.

1. In the beginning God created the heaven and the earth.
2. God so loved the world, that he gave his only begotten Son.
3. The Lord is my shepherd.
4. The Word was made flesh, and dwelt among us.

Ask the pupils for statements that they have heard others make. Write them (or the sentences in the lesson) on the board without capital letters and periods. Ask the pupils to help correct them. Give sufficient drill before assigning the written work.

sentences. They are called telling sentences because they tell something. Each sentence states a fact.

Look carefully at each sentence. What do you notice about the beginning and ending of a telling sentence?

Remember: Every sentence begins with a capital letter. A telling sentence states a fact, and it ends with a period.

> Practice With Telling Sentences >

A. Decide which groups of words are complete telling sentences. Write those groups correctly, as sentences should be written.
  1. beautiful flowers of many colors
  2. the children's letter cheered Grandmother
  3. God made light on the first day
  4. brought a chair for Mother
  5. the boys raked the lawn
  6. the animals went into the ark
  7. Jesus raised the dead man to life
  8. baked bread for Elijah
  9. fuzzy baby ducks
  10. spoke from heaven
  11. kindness has cheered many hearts
  12. God opened the prison doors for Peter

B. Think of two people in the Bible. Then think of a sentence beginning with **He** or **She** that tells about something each person did. Write your sentences correctly. The others in your class will guess the name of the person who did each thing.

Lesson 5 Answers
Practice With Telling Sentences

A. (Check for initial capitalization and en punctuation.)
  2. The children's letter cheered Grandmother
  3. God made light on the first day.
  5. The boys raked the lawn.
  6. The animals went into the ark.
  7. Jesus raised the dead man to life.
  11. Kindness has cheered many hearts.
  12. God opened the prison doors for Peter.

B. (Individual answers.)

★ **EXTRA PRACTICE**
  Worksheet 3 (*Telling Sentences*)

6. The Two Sentence Parts

Every sentence has two main parts. The one part tells **who** or **what** the sentence is about. This part is called the **subject** of the sentence. The other part tells what the subject **does** or **is.** That part is called the **predicate** of the sentence.

Subject + Predicate = Sentence
birds   fly   Birds fly

Every subject has a **noun** or **pronoun** that tells who or what the sentence is about. This noun or pronoun is called the **simple subject** of the sentence.

Every predicate has a **verb** that tells what the subject does or is. This verb is called the **simple predicate** of the sentence.

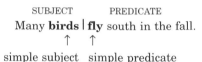

SUBJECT   PREDICATE
Many **birds** | **fly** south in the fall.
↑   ↑

simple subject   simple predicate

A diagram can be used to show the parts of a sentence. To diagram a sentence, start with a long line divided in half.

On the left half of the line, write the simple subject. The simple subject is the noun or pronoun that tells who or what the sentence is about.

Birds

Lesson 6

Aim: (1) To teach that the subject of a sentence has a noun or pronoun called the simple subject, and that the predicate has a verb called the simple predicate. (2) To introduce the sentence diagram.

Oral Review:

1. Why is it not hard to find a word in the dictionary? (The words are in alphabetical order.)
2. If two words each begin with the same three letters, how can you tell which word comes first in the dictionary? (Look at the fourth letter.)
3. What three things does a dictionary tell you? (how to spell words, how to pronounce words, and what words mean)
4. What two parts must a sentence have? (a subject and a predicate)
5. How should a telling sentence begin and end? (It should begin with a capital letter and end with a period.)

Class: Ask the children, "What are the two main parts of a sentence?" (They are the subject and the predicate.) "What does the subject do?" (It tells who or what the sentence is about.) "What does the predicate do?" (It tells what the subject does or is.)

Say, "The subject part of a sentence has a noun that tells *who* or *what.* That noun is called the simple subject. The predicate part has a verb that tells what the subject *does* or *is.* The verb is called the simple predicate." Illustrate with the following sentence, or use the one in the pupil's text.

SUBJECT   PREDICATE
The <u>robins</u> in the maple tree | <u>sing</u> cheerily every day.
↑   ↑
simple subject   simple predicate

Note that when *subject* and *predicate* are used

On the right half of the line, write the simple predicate. The simple predicate is the verb that tells what the simple subject does or is.

| Birds | fly |

> Diagraming Sentence Parts >

Diagram these sentences.

1. Sarah giggled.
2. We hurried.
3. Jonathan came.
4. Lightning flashed.
5. They prayed.
6. Flowers bloomed.
7. Leaves rustled.
8. Grandmother sang.

> Writing Sentences >

A. Name the people and the dog in the picture. Then write a complete sentence to answer each question.
1. Who came?
2. Who ran?
3. What barked?

B. Decide what each person in the picture is doing. Then write a complete sentence to answer each question.

Lesson 6 Answers
Diagraming Sentence Parts

1. | Sarah | giggled |

2. | We | hurried |

3. | Jonathan | came |

4. | Lightning | flashed |

5. | They | prayed |

6. | Flowers | bloomed |

7. | Leaves | rustled |

8. | Grandmother | sang |

Writing Sentences

A. (Possible answers. Underlining is for Part C.)
1. Grandfather <u>came</u>.
2. James <u>ran</u>.
3. Rover <u>barked</u>.

alone, they generally refer to the complete subject or predicate.

Give drill as needed on nouns, pronouns, and verbs. Emphasize that nouns are *naming words;* they name people, places, and things. The subject pronouns are *I, you, he, she, it, we, they.* (List them on the board.) Most verbs are words of *action.*

Describe a diagram as a drawing which helps us to understand how something is made. Explain where the simple subject and simple predicate are placed on a sentence diagram, and practice diagraming on the board. These sentences may be used for drill.

1. Stars twinkled.
2. Winds blew.
3. Waves roared.
4. Rain fell.

1. What did Mother do?
2. What did Father do?
3. What did Jason do?

C. In each sentence you wrote for Parts A and B, draw two lines under the simple predicate (the verb).

●◆●◆●◆●◆●◆●

7. Subjects and Predicates

The simple subject of a sentence tells **who** or **what** the sentence is about. But sometimes there is more than one noun or pronoun that tells who or what. Then the sentence has more than one simple subject.

> Paul and Silas sang.
> **Birds, bats,** and **insects** fly.

Who sang? Both **Paul** and **Silas** tell **who.** What creatures fly? **Birds, bats,** and **insects** all tell **what.**

The simple predicate of a sentence tells what the subject **does** or **is.** But sometimes there is more than one verb. Then the sentence has more than one simple predicate.

> The disciples **sang** and **prayed.**
> Mother **baked, washed,** and **sewed.**

When you look for the simple subject of a sentence, be careful to find all the nouns or pronouns that tell **who** or **what** the sentence is about.

B. (Possible answers. Underlining is for Part C.)
1. Mother <u>sewed</u>.
2. Father <u>read</u>.
3. Jason <u>listened</u>.

C. (Answers are included in Parts A and B.)

Lesson 7

Aim: (1) To teach that some sentences have more than one simple subject or simple predicate. (2) To teach how to diagram these sentences.

Oral Review:
1. Words in bold print in a dictionary are called ——— words. (entry)
2. What three things does a dictionary tell you? (how to spell words, how to pronounce words, and what words mean)
3. What two parts must a sentence have? (a subject and a predicate)
4. How should a telling sentence begin and end? (It should begin with a capital letter and end with a period.)
5. On the left half of a sentence diagram, we write the ———. On the right half, we write the ———.

(simple subject, simple predicate)

Class: On the board write pairs of sentences such as the following.

> Paul sang. Silas sang.
> They sang. They prayed.

Ask, "Is this the way we usually talk? No, we would combine the sentences. Why?" (They are too short and choppy. It is tiresome to repeat so many words.) Have the pupils help to combine the sentences as follows.

> Paul and Silas sang.
> They sang and prayed.

Say, "When we combine the first pair of sentences, we have one sentence with two simple subjects. It has a *compound subject.* When we combine the second pair of sentences, we have one sentence with two simple predicates. It has a *compound predicate.*"

When you look for the simple predicate of a sentence, be careful to find all the verbs that tell what the subject **does** or **is**.

A sentence with two simple subjects is diagramed like this.

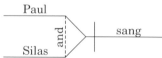

A sentence with two simple predicates is diagramed like this.

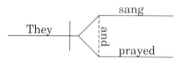

> Diagraming Sentences >

Diagram these sentences. Follow the examples given in the lesson.

1. Paul and Barnabas traveled.
2. They worked and preached.
3. Men and women listened.
4. They believed and rejoiced.

> Working With Sentences >

A. Copy each sentence, using correct capitalization and punctuation.
1. cardinals like sunflower seeds
2. lilacs and lilies bloomed
3. waterfalls splashed and sparkled in the sunlight

Draw one line under each simple subject in the first sentence, and two lines under each simple predicate in the second sentence. (This will help to establish the pattern followed in this book.)

Emphasize the importance of finding all the nouns that tell who or what the sentence is about, and all the verbs that tell what the subject does or is.

Use these sentences for practice with diagraming compound parts. Be sure to point out where *and* is placed on the diagram.

1. Peter and John preached.
2. Men and women heard.
3. They believed and repented.
4. Others scoffed and mocked.

Lesson 7 Answers
Diagraming Sentences

1.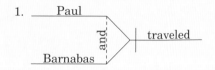

2.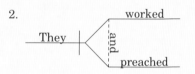

3.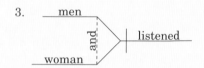

4.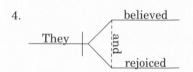

Working With Sentences

A. (Check for initial capitalization and end punctuation. Underlining is for Part B.)
1. <u>Cardinals</u> like sunflower seeds.
2. <u>Lilacs</u> and <u>lilies</u> bloomed.
3. <u>Waterfalls</u> splashed and sparkled in th sunlight.

Note: A sentence with three subjects is diagrame as follows.

Peter, James, and John obeyed.

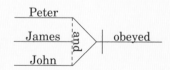

★ **EXTRA PRACTICE**
Worksheet 4   (*Simple Subjects and Simple Predicates*)

4. boys and girls jump, skip, and run
5. the wind whistled and howled around the house
6. cows and horses ate grass in the meadow
7. butterflies and moths fluttered about
8. snow and rain fell from the sky
9. God made the sun and the moon

B. In the sentences you copied, draw one line under each simple subject. Then draw two lines under each simple predicate.

 Can You Do This?

See if you can diagram this sentence.

Paul and Silas sang and prayed.

8. Reviewing What You Have Learned

Oral Drill

A. Answer these questions.
1. How should you treat your English textbook?
2. How should you turn the pages of your book?
3. What should you use to mark the place you are studying in your book?
4. What things should you write at the top of your English papers?

B. Look at each group of words. If it is a sentence, read it aloud. If it is not a sentence, read it and add what is needed to make it a sentence.

4. Boys and girls jump, skip, and run.
5. The wind whistled and howled around the house.
6. Cows and horses ate grass in the meadow.
7. Butterflies and moths fluttered about.
8. Snow and rain fell from the sky.
9. God made the sun and the moon.

B. (Answers are included in Part A.)

Can You Do This?

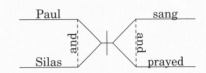

Lesson 8 Answers
Oral Drill
A. 1. You should treat your English textbook as a friend.
2. You should turn the pages quietly from the top outside corner.
3. You should use a strip of paper or a ribbon to mark the place.
4. You should write the word *English,* the page number of the lesson, your name, and the date.

Lesson 8

Aim: To review the things learned in Lessons 1–7.

Class: Point out the importance of remembering things we learn. Tell the pupils, "This lesson will give you a chance to see how well you remember what you have learned in English class."

Instead of an Oral Review in the teacher's guide, use the Oral Drill in the pupil's book for class discussion. It would also be good to look at Written Practice with the pupils and answer any questions they may have about it.

1. Trees and flowers
2. Jesus is coming again
3. Were moaning and crying
4. A big black bear
5. God protected Daniel
6. Rose from the dead
7. Father brought food from the garden

C. What mark should be added at the end of each sentence in Part B?

D. Tell where to divide each sentence between the subject and predicate.
   1. Her baby sister walks now.
   2. We saw the ocean last summer.
   3. Spring is a lovely time.
   4. My grandmother makes delicious homemade bread.
   5. Your green pencil is on the floor.

> Written Practice

A. Write answers to these questions.
   1. What three things does a dictionary tell you?
   2. Why is it not hard to find words in a dictionary?
   3. How many syllables does the word **material** have? Use the dictionary to find out.
   4. What is a telling sentence?
   5. What does the subject of a sentence do?
   6. What does the predicate do?

B. Write each column of words in alphabetical order.
1. camel	2. swallow	3. earnest
monkey	sparrow	ears
bear	sunbird	earache
giraffe	starling	early

B. (Numbers 2, 5, and 7 are sentences to be read a[s] they are. The others are to be completed orall[y] by the students.)

C. A period should be added to the end of each sen[-]tence.

D. 1. Her baby sister | walks now.
   2. We | saw the ocean last summer.
   3. Spring | is a lovely time.
   4. My grandmother | makes delicious home[-]made bread.
   5. Your green pencil | is on the floor.

Written Practice

A. 1. A dictionary tells you how to spell words, how to pronounce words, and what words mean.
   2. It is not hard to find words in a dictionary because they are listed in alphabetical order[.]
   3. The word *material* has four syllables.
   4. A telling sentence is a sentence that states a[ ]fact.
   5. The subject tells *who* or *what* the sentence i[s] about.
   6. The predicate tells what the subject *does* or *is*[.]

B. | 1. bear | 2. sparrow | 3. earache |
   | --- | --- | --- |
   | camel | starling | early |
   | giraffe | sunbird | earnest |
   | monkey | swallow | ears |

Use these sentences to do Parts C, D, and E.

1. Ostriches and rheas run.
2. Penguins swim.
3. Geese swim and fly.
4. Robins and orioles built nests in our trees.
5. A woodchuck lived under our porch.

C. Copy the simple subjects of the sentences above. Watch for compound subjects.

D. Copy the simple predicates of the sentences above. Watch for compound predicates.

E. Diagram the simple subjects and simple predicates.

●━●━●━●━●━●━●━●

9. Asking Sentences

In Lesson 5 you learned about sentences that state a fact. They are called telling sentences, and they end with a period.

Today you will learn about sentences that ask a question. Below are three **asking sentences.** Look at each one carefully.

Where is the red ball?
Have you watered the flowers?
Is everyone ready for church?

Asking sentences begin just like telling sentences. But they end with a question mark, not with a period.

> **Remember:** An asking sentence asks a question, and it ends with a question mark.

C. 1. Ostriches, rheas
2. Penguins
3. Geese
4. Robins, orioles
5. woodchuck

D. 1. run
2. swim
3. swim, fly
4. built
5. lived

E. 1.
2.
3.
4.
5.

Lesson 9

Aim: (1) To show the difference between asking and telling sentences. (2) To teach pupils how to write asking sentences.

Oral Review:

1. Why is it not hard to find a word in the dictionary? (The words are in alphabetical order.)
2. A sentence must have a —— and a ——. (subject, predicate)
3. How must a telling sentence begin and end? (It must begin with a capital letter and end with a period.)
4. On the left half of a sentence diagram, we write the ——. On the right half, we write the ——. (simple subject, simple predicate)
5. Give the simple subjects in this sentence: *Father and Mother went on a trip.* (Father, Mother)

Class: Write an asking and a telling sentence on the board, such as the following.

Where is the red ball?
The red ball is there.

Ask, "Which is a telling sentence? Which is an asking sentence?" Point out that whereas a telling sentence states a fact, an asking sentence asks for a fact.

You could also call attention to the different word order in asking sentences. In the sentences above, the asking sentence ends with *the red ball* and the telling sentence begins with *The red ball.*

Discuss the asking sentences in the lesson, and have pupils give other examples orally. Drill question marks by having the students write questions such as the following on the board.

1. What is your name?
2. Where do you live?

> **Practice With Asking Sentences**

A. Find each asking sentence, and write it correctly.
1. do you know what the sequoias are
2. they are huge trees
3. can you guess where they are found
4. what color is the wood of the tree
5. one large sequoia is called the Grizzly Giant
6. do most sequoias have leaves or needles
7. do these trees have cones as pine trees do
8. some sequoias are a thousand years old
9. did you know that none of these trees has ever died from disease
10. the trees were named for Sequoya, a Cherokee Indian

B. Write correctly five asking sentences of your own.

> **Review and Practice**

Write the correct spelling to be used in each sentence. Use a dictionary if you need help.
1. All the children in the first grade knew the (alphabet, alphebet, alphabett) well.
2. The poor children had (niether, nether, neither) coats nor shoes.

3. How old are you?
4. When did you come?
5. Who is your teacher?

★ **EXTRA PRACTICE**
Worksheet 5 (*Asking Sentences*)

Lesson 9 Answers
Practice With Asking Sentences
A. (Check for initial capitalization and end punctuation.)
1. Do you know what the sequoias are?
3. Can you guess where they are found?
4. What color is the wood of the tree?
6. Do most sequoias have leaves or needles?
7. Do these trees have cones as pine trees do?
9. Did you know that none of these trees has ever died from disease?

B. (Individual answers.)

Review and Practice
1. alphabet
2. neither

3. We will (separate, seperate, sepurate) the old books from the new ones.

4. Abraham and Isaac went up the (mountian, mountain, mountin).

5. Mother used a (patern, pattren, pattern) to make the shirt.

3. separate
4. mountain
5. pattern

●━━━━━━━━━●

10. Subjects and Predicates in Asking Sentences

You have learned that a telling sentence has two parts. Today you will see that an asking sentence also has two parts.

Can butterflies hear?

To find the two parts of this sentence, change the word order so that it is a telling sentence.

Butterflies can hear.

The simple subject of the sentence is **Butterflies.** The simple predicate is **can hear.** This simple predicate is a **verb phrase.** A verb phrase is two or more verbs that work together.

The sentence **Can butterflies hear?** is diagramed like this.

| butterflies | can hear |

Lesson 10

Aim: To teach that a question has a subject and predicate, and that it must be inverted in order to identify these basic parts.

Oral Review:

1. A sentence must have a ——— and a ———. (subject, predicate)

2. What does a telling sentence do? (It states a fact.)

3. On a sentence diagram, where do we write the simple subject? Where do we write the simple predicate? (on the left half; on the right half)

4. Give the simple predicates in this sentence: *Paul preached and wrote.* (preached, wrote)

5. What should we put at the end of an asking sentence? (a question mark)

Class: Use these sentences to review subjects and predicates in telling sentences.

Mark | worked hard.
Janet | reads well.
Mother | cleaned the house.

Tell the pupils, "In today's lesson you will learn how to find the subject and the predicate in asking sentences." On the board write simple asking sentences that are related to the telling sentences.

Did Mark work?
Can Janet read?
Has Mother cleaned?

Say, "In an asking sentence, the simple predicate is a verb phrase instead of just one word. In order to find the phrase, we need to change the asking sentence into a telling sentence." Illustrate with the examples on the board.

You need not say much about helping verbs at this point, and neither should you try to explain how

Below are two more asking sentences that have been diagramed.

Did Jesus rise?	Jesus	Did rise

Has Father come?	Father	Has come

> Working With Asking Sentences >

A. Change the word order of each asking sentence so that it becomes a telling sentence.
1. Can robins fly?
2. Do babies sleep?
3. Do children sing?
4. Do flowers bloom?
5. Do trains whistle?
6. Will bees sting?
7. Have people prayed?
8. Are farmers working?
9. Could Peter preach?
10. May Rhoda go?

B. Diagram sentences 1–5 in Part A.

> Review and Practice >

Write each list of words in alphabetical order.

1. baby	2. keys	3. quarter
dinner	greyhound	mice
elephant	igloo	rooster
alligator	haystack	oatmeal
calf	leader	peacock
figs	January	nephew

a verb phrase is different from a compound predicate as taught in Lesson 7. The difference should be explained only if a pupil asks about it.

The sentences on the board can also be used for instruction and drill on the diagraming of asking sentences.

★ **EXTRA PRACTICE**
Worksheet 6 (*Subjects and Predicates in Asking Sentences*)

Lesson 10 Answers
Working With Asking Sentences
A. 1. Robins can fly.
    2. Babies do sleep.
    3. Children do sing.
    4. Flowers do bloom.
    5. Trains do whistle.
    6. Bees will sting.
    7. People have prayed.
    8. Farmers are working.
    9. Peter could preach.
    10. Rhoda may go.

B. (On a sentence diagram, the most important thing is to put the words in the right places. Capitalization of the first word is of secondary importance. For this reason, the diagrams in the answer keys do not show initial capitalization for any sentences that must be reworded before diagraming.)

1.	robins	can fly

2.	babies	do sleep

3.	children	do sing

4.	flowers	do bloom

5.	trains	do whistle

Review and Practice

1. alligator	2. greyhound	3. mice
baby	haystack	nephew
calf	igloo	oatmeal
dinner	January	peacock
elephant	keys	quarter
figs	leader	rooster

11. Commanding Sentences and Exclaiming Sentences

The Ten Commandments are found in Exodus 20. Here are some of them.

> Remember the sabbath day, to keep it holy.
> Thou shalt not steal.
> Thou shalt not kill.

These are called commandments because God tells us to do some things. Sentences like these are **commanding sentences,** and they end with a period. Here are two more commanding sentences.

> Close the door, please.
> Pick up the toys.

When we are surprised or excited, our voices show strong feeling. Sentences showing strong feeling are called **exclaiming sentences.** Here are some examples of exclaiming sentences.

> What a beautiful sunset that is!
> The cows are in the cornfield!

Lesson 11

Aim: (1) To introduce the word *command,* and to give practice in recognizing commands. (2) To teach what exclamatory sentences are, and how they are punctuated.

Oral Review:

1. How should we begin and end a telling sentence? (Begin with a capital letter and end with a period.)
2. How should we begin and end an asking sentence? (Begin with a capital letter and end with a question mark.)
3. On a sentence diagram, which sentence part belongs on the left half? Which part belongs on the right half? (left—the subject; right—the predicate)
4. Give the simple subject of this sentence: *Did Grandmother come?* (Grandmother)
5. Diagram the simple subject and simple predicate of this sentence: *Peas and carrots grow in the garden.* [Teacher: Answers may be given at the board or on paper.]

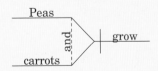

Class: Begin class by issuing commands to a few of your pupils. For example: "Thomas, write your name on the board. Richard, get a pen from my desk."

Tell the class that these sentences are *commands.* Mention that the Bible contains commands for us, such as the Ten Commandments. Other examples are "Love one another" (subject understood) and "Be ye kind" (subject expressed).

Remember: A commanding sentence tells someone to do something. A commanding sentence ends with a period.

An exclaiming sentence shows strong feeling. An exclaiming sentence ends with an exclamation mark.

> Practice With Commanding and Exclaiming Sentences

A. All of these are commanding or exclaiming sentences. Copy each one and put a period or an exclamation mark after it.

1. Pass the bread, please
2. Do not touch the wet paint
3. What a beautiful morning it is
4. Run to the mailbox
5. The barn is on fire
6. Martha tore her best dress
7. Do not feed the bears
8. Feed the dog, James
9. The baby has Mother's scissors
10. Run to the field and tell Father

B. Write **exclaiming** or **commanding** to tell what kind of sentence you would write about each picture. Then write an exclaiming or commanding sentence to go with each picture.

1.    2.

Lesson 11 Answers
Practice With Commanding and Exclaiming Sentences

A. 1. Pass the bread, please.
    2. Do not touch the wet paint. *or* !
    3. What a beautiful morning it is!
    4. Run to the mailbox. *or* !
    5. The barn is on fire!
    6. Martha tore her best dress!
    7. Do not feed the bears. *or* !
    8. Feed the dog, James.
    9. The baby has Mother's scissors!
    10. Run to the field and tell Father. *or* !

B. 1. Commanding
   2. Exclaiming
      (Possible answers.)
   1. Pick up the toys.
   2. The goat is eating the apples!

To introduce exclamatory sentences, ask for statements people make when they are surprised. Write these on the board, and call attention to the mark that is put at the end. It may be good to point out that many exclaiming sentences would be called telling sentences if they did not express strong feeling.

★ **EXTRA PRACTICE**
   Worksheet 7 (*Commanding and Exclaiming Sentences*)

> **Review and Practice** >

Write **telling, asking, commanding,** or **exclaiming**
for each sentence. Write the correct end punctuation for
each one.

1. We came home from our trip last night
2. What a beautiful tail that peacock has
3. Please get a drink for Grandmother
4. May I use your eraser
5. Father bought a new wheelbarrow
6. Do not wake the baby

Review and Practice

1. telling (.)
2. exclaiming (!)
3. commanding (.)
4. asking (?)
5. telling (.)
6. commanding (.)

●━●━●━●━●━●━●━●━●

12. Subjects and Predicates
in Commanding Sentences

A command tells someone to do something. If I give you
a command, you know that I want **you** to do something.

Hurry!

Who is to hurry? **You** are to hurry.

The simple subject of a command is usually not written,
because it is understood to be **you.** A command can be
written by using the verb alone, or the verb with some other
words.

Listen.
Do your lessons.

Sometimes a speaker does say **you** when he gives a
command.

Lesson 12

Aim: To teach that in a commanding sentence the subject is *you* even though it may not be stated.

Oral Review:

1. Give the simple predicates in this sentence:
   Abraham worshiped and traveled. (worshiped,
   traveled)
2. How should we end an asking sentence? (with a
   question mark)
3. Give the simple predicate in this sentence: *Did
   Timothy work?* (did work)
4. How should we end a commanding sentence?
   (with a period)
5. What should we put at the end of an exclaiming
   sentence? (an exclamation mark).

Class: Begin by writing several commands on the
board, such as the following.

Get out your books.
Close the door.

Ask, "What is the simple subject of each command?" Since this is a new concept, probably no one
will be able to find it. You may wish to have the
pupils read the lesson silently and raise their hands
when they find the answer to the question.

For more examples of commands in which *you*
is expressed, use the Ten Commandments. Some of
them have *Thou* and some do not.

Remember the sabbath day, to keep it holy.
Thou shalt not steal.

Discuss the diagraming of commands. Tell the

Mother is busy kneading bread dough. When the telephone rings, she looks at Esther and says, "**You** answer it."

Sometimes **you** and someone else are to do something.
Then the command has two simple subjects.

Grandfather tells Father that he would like some help
with raking leaves. Father looks at Luke and says, "**You**
and **Daniel** go with Grandfather."

If the subject **you** is understood, a command is diagramed
with parentheses ( ) around **you.** If **you** is stated, the subject
is diagramed without parentheses.

Go.   You and Daniel go.

> Working With Commands >

A. Write the **simple predicates** (the verbs) in these
   commands. Watch for compound predicates.
   1. Study well.   6. Obey your parents.
   2. Try harder.   7. Wash and dry the dishes.
   3. Come here.   8. You and Joy sweep.
   4. You hide.   9. Look both ways.
   5. Run!   10. Watch and pray.

Lesson 12 Answers
Working With Commands
A. 1. Study   6. Obey
   2. Try   7. Wash, dry
   3. Come   8. sweep
   4. hide   9. Look
   5. Run   10. Watch, pray

---

class, "Every sentence diagram shows what the simple
subject is. But often the simple subject of a command is
not given. To show that it is understood, parentheses are
put around *you* on the diagram." Illustrate by diagraming some of the commands in the lesson.

(you) | Hurry

(you) | Listen

(you) | answer

Note especially the two simple subjects in *You and
Daniel go with Grandfather.*

★ **EXTRA PRACTICE**
   Worksheet 8 (*Subjects and Predicates in Com-
                  manding Sentences*)

B. Diagram sentences 4, 5, 8, and 10 in Part A. Remember to put parentheses ( ) around **you** if it is not written but understood.

C. Write a **command** that the parent in each picture might be giving.

1.

3.

2.

4.

> Can You Do This?

In 1 Thessalonians 5:14–26, there are many commands. Read the verses, and copy the verbs that are used as commands. There are sixteen in all. How many can you find?

⬥⬥⬥⬥⬥⬥⬥⬥⬥

B. 4.
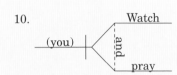

| You | hide |

5.

| (you) | Run |

8.

You
Joy and sweep

10.

Watch
(you) and
pray

C. (Possible answers.)
1. Don't touch it!
2. Come down!
3. Open the door, please.
4. Go to sleep.

Can You Do This?
v. 14—warn, comfort, support, be
v. 15—See, follow
v. 16—Rejoice
v. 17—Pray
v. 18—give
v. 19—Quench
v. 20—Despise
v. 21—Prove, hold
v. 22—Abstain
v. 25—pray
v. 26—Greet

13. Telling, Asking, Commanding, and Exclaiming Sentences

You have learned about four kinds of sentences. They are telling sentences, asking sentences, commanding sentences, and exclaiming sentences. We use these different kinds of sentences because we have different reasons for making sentences.

Read these four sentences, and answer the questions about them.

> a. God created the earth.
> b. How dark those storm clouds are!
> c. Please close the window.
> d. Is that dog yours?

1. How are the sentences alike? How are they different?
2. Which sentence asks a question?
3. Which sentence states a fact?
4. Which sentence tells someone to do something?
5. Which sentence shows strong feeling?
6. Would it be right to put a period at the end of each sentence? Why not?
7. Look at the end punctuation of sentence **b.** What does it show about the way this sentence should be read? How would you read the sentence if it ended with a period?

> Working With Sentences

A. Write the correct word or phrase for each blank.
1. A ——— sentence states a fact. It ends with a ———.
2. An ——— sentence asks a question. It ends with a ———.

Lesson 13

Aim: To study the four kinds of sentences together for the sake of comparing them.

Written Quiz:

(A Written Quiz reviews major concepts that have been taught over the past half unit or so. You may write the word lists on the board and read the questions orally, or reproduce the quiz for distribution to the pupils.)

Write the correct word or phrase for each blank.

subject	exclamation mark
spelling	alphabetical order
you	question mark
meaning	capital letter
phrase	predicate
compound	pronunciation

1. Words are not hard to find in a dictionary, because they are in ———.

2. Three things a dictionary shows are ——— ———, and ———.
3. Every sentence should begin with a ———.
4. The sentence part that tells **who** or **what** the ———.
5. The sentence part that has the verb is t| ———.
6. An asking sentence ends with a ———.
7. An exclaiming sentence ends with an ———
8. In a commanding sentence, the subject ———.
9. A sentence with two subjects has ——— subject.

Lesson 13 Answers
Working With Sentences

A. 1. telling, period
   2. asking, question mark

Quiz Answers:
1. alphabetical order
2. spelling, meaning, pronunciation
3. capital letter
4. subject
5. predicate
6. question mark
7. exclamation ma|
8. you
9. compound

3. A —— sentence tells someone to do something. It ends with a ——.

4. An —— sentence shows strong feeling. It ends with an ——.

B. Write **telling, asking, commanding,** or **exclaiming** to tell what kind of sentence each one is. There are only three exclaiming sentences.

1. grasshoppers do not live at the north and south poles
2. what big leaps they can take
3. be careful when you handle a grasshopper
4. you might get brown juice on your hands from the grasshopper's mouth
5. what are the three main parts of a grasshopper
6. they are the head, the thorax, and the abdomen
7. did you know that some people eat grasshoppers
8. what a different meal that would be
9. do you know how many eyes a grasshopper has
10. it has five eyes
11. how strange it would be to have five eyes
12. some grasshoppers' ears are on their front legs

C. After each answer in Part B, write correctly the word in that sentence which needs a capital letter. Also write the correct end mark for that sentence. Be sure each end mark is right for its kind of sentence.

3. commanding, period
4. exclaiming, exclamation mark

B. (Answers for Part C are also included.)
   1. telling; Grasshoppers (.)
   2. exclaiming; What (!)
   3. commanding; Be (.)
   4. telling; You (.)
   5. asking; What (?)
   6. telling; They (.)
   7. asking; Did (?)
   8. exclaiming; What (!)
   9. asking; Do (?)
   10. telling; It (.)
   11. exclaiming; How (!)
   12. telling; Some (.)

C. (Answers are included in Part B.)

Class: Ask the pupils to give the four kinds of sentences. Then say, "You have learned that all four kinds of sentences begin with a capital letter. You also know that the end punctuation may be different. But it is more than end punctuation that makes different kinds of sentences. Each kind of sentence has a different *purpose*. The purpose of a sentence is what makes it a telling, asking, commanding, or exclaiming sentence."

Use the sentences and questions in the pupil's text to discuss the four kinds of sentences and the purpose of each. The answers to the questions are as follows.

1. (alike) They all begin with a capital letter.
   (different) They end with different kinds of punctuation. They are used for different purposes.
2. sentence *d*
3. sentence *a*
4. sentence *c*
5. sentence *b*
6. No; An asking or exclaiming sentence should end

with a question mark or an exclamation mark.
7. It shows that the sentence should be read with strong feeling. If it ended with a period, you would read it like a telling sentence (in a normal tone of voice).

14. Reviewing What You Have Learned

> Oral Drill

Use these sentences to do Parts A, B, and C.
1. Amanda waved.
2. Has Roy arrived?
3. Margaret read the book.
4. Whisper.
5. May I try?
6. Hornets and wasps sting.
7. Snakes slither and crawl.
8. Ducks fly, swim, and waddle.
9. You and Simon play outside.
10. Will Father and Mother sing?
11. Should men and women pray?
12. Hurry and finish.
13. Carl, Steven, and I finished our work.
14. Have Ella and John left?

A. Tell which part of each sentence is the subject, and which part is the predicate.

B. Tell whether each sentence is a **telling, asking,** or **commanding** sentence.

C. Which sentences have a compound subject? Which ones have a compound predicate?

> Written Practice

A. Diagram these sentences.
1. Dorcas sewed.
2. Have people left?

Lesson 14 Answers
Oral Drill

A. (Sentences are divided between subjects and predicates.)
1. Amanda | waved.
2. Roy | has arrived.
3. Margaret | read the book.
4. (you) | Whisper.
5. I | may try.
6. Hornets and wasps | sting.
7. Snakes | slither and crawl.
8. Ducks | fly, swim, and waddle.
9. You and Simon | play outside.
10. Father and Mother | will sing.
11. Men and women | should pray.
12. (you) | Hurry and finish.
13. Carl, Steven, and I | finished our work.
14. Ella and John | have left.

B.
1. telling	8. telling
2. asking	9. commanding
3. telling	10. asking
4. commanding	11. asking
5. asking	12. commanding
6. telling	13. telling
7. telling	14. asking

C. *Compound subjects:* 6, 9, 10, 11, 13, 14
Compound predicates: 7, 8, 12

Written Practice

A. 1. ___Dorcas___ | ___sewed___

2. ___People___ | ___have left___

Lesson 14

Aim: To review concepts taught in the last five lessons.

Class: Do the Oral Drill in class. Give extra practice with anything the pupils had difficulty mastering.

3. Karen stayed.
4. Watch.
5. Mark and Betty helped.
6. Grandmother worked and sang.
7. Should Susan and I wait?
8. Listen and learn.
9. Have Philip and Peter finished?
10. Lester sat and thought.

B. Write a question for each picture. Use the verbs given. Underline the simple subjects in your questions.

1. has gone

3. can walk

2. does help

4. will fall

> Can You Do This? >

Can you find the simple subject of this sentence? Can you find the simple predicate?

Up on a branch, high above me, a little squirrel sat alone in the tree.

3.   Karen | stayed

4.   (you) | Watch

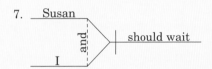

5.   Mark ... and ... Betty > helped

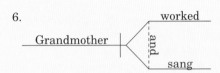

6.   Grandmother — worked ... and ... sang

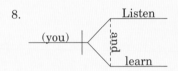

7.   Susan ... and ... I > should wait

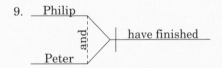

8.   (you) — Listen ... and ... learn

9.   Philip ... and ... Peter > have finished

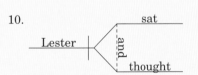

10.   Lester — sat ... and ... thought

B. (Possible answers.)
1. Has <u>Father</u> gone?
2. Does <u>Carol</u> help?
3. Can <u>Sharon</u> walk?
4. Will Edward and <u>Dale</u> fall?

Can You Do This?
Simple subject: squirrel
Simple predicate: sat

15. Capitalization and Punctuation in Names and Initials

Have you read the book *A Home for Grandma?* It is an interesting story about the Metzler family.

The children are Lois Ann, William, Jean, Arvin, and Merle, and they have many pleasant times as they work together with their parents. When a boy name Joseph Dancey comes from the city to spend two weeks with them, many exciting things happen.

There are six names in the paragraph above. Do you see that the first letter of each name is capitalized? People's names always begin with capital letters.

Sometimes people write only the first letters of their names. These letters are called **initials.** Lois Ann Metzler would write her initials this way: L. A. M. Which one of the children would write his initials A. M.? Which one is W. Metzler?

Initials must be capitalized because they take the place of names. You must also put a period after each initial.

> Writing Names and Initials >

A. Write each name correctly.

1. lester miller	7. matthew m hartzler
2. lisa a smith	8. maria ann patterson
3. mary r zook	9. leah anderson
4. robert l martin	10. carol mae stevens
5. sandra white	11. thomas n yoder
6. john b howe	12. david edward baker

Lesson 15 Answers
Writing Names and Initials

A. 1. Lester Miller
2. Lisa A. Smith
3. Mary R. Zook
4. Robert L. Martin
5. Sandra White
6. John B. Howe
7. Matthew M. Hartzler
8. Maria Ann Patterson
9. Leah Anderson
10. Carol Mae Stevens
11. Thomas N. Yoder
12. David Edward Baker

Lesson 15

Aim: To teach that names and initials must always be capitalized and periods must follow initials.

Oral Review:

1. Name the four different kinds of sentences, and tell how each one should end. (telling sentence—period; asking sentence—question mark; commanding sentence—period; exclaiming sentence—exclamation mark)
2. What is the simple predicate in this sentence: *Does Gloria sing?* (does sing)
3. How should a commanding sentence end? Give an example of one. (with a period; Individual sentences.)
4. What is the subject in a commanding sentence? (you)
5. What kind of sentence shows strong feeling? (an exclaiming sentence)

Class: Write several names on the board without capitalizing them, such as *isaac watts, charles wesley,* and *john newton.* When the pupils discover the errors, they may make corrections.

Have the pupils go to the board and write their own names correctly. Then they could change places and write their classmates' initials below their names.

For Part C of the exercises, tell the pupils to make up names if they do not have a brother or sister.

★ **EXTRA PRACTICE**
Worksheet 9 (*Names and Initials*)

B. Write initials for the names in Part A. Remember to follow the rules you learned for writing initials.

C. Write correctly the names and initials of these people.
1. Your mother
2. Your teacher
3. Your brother
4. Your minister
5. Your uncle
6. Your sister
7. Your friend
8. Yourself

B. 1. L. M.
    2. L. A. S.
    3. M. R. Z.
    4. R. L. M.
    5. S. W.
    6. J. B. H.
    7. M. M. H.
    8. M. A. P.
    9. L. A.
   10. C. M. S.
   11. T. N. Y.
   12. D. E. B.

C. (Individual answers.)

---

16. Quotations and Quotation Marks

When you use a **quotation,** you are repeating the exact words that someone said. The sentences below contain quotations.

> Abraham said, "God will provide himself a lamb for a burnt offering."
> "I will come again," Jesus promised.

When a quotation is written, **quotation marks** are placed before and after the words of the speaker. The quotation marks show that the writer is repeating someone's exact words.

> The woman said, "Sir, give me this water."

Sometimes a sentence tells you what someone said without repeating his exact words. Quotation marks are not used in such a sentence. Quotation marks are used only when a speaker's exact words are repeated.

esson 16

im: To introduce quotations, and to teach the correct
se of quotation marks with quotations.

ral Review:
1. Give the simple subject of this sentence: *Did Joseph go?* (Joseph)
2. What is a commanding sentence? (a sentence that tells you to do something)
3. If the subject of a command is understood, how should we write it on a sentence diagram? (Put *you* in parentheses.)
4. How should an exclaiming sentence end? (with an exclamation mark)
5. What kind of letter should be used for names and initials? What should be put after each initial? (a capital letter; a period)

Class: On the board write sentences with statements that pupils have made recently. Use commas but no quotation marks in them. Say, "These sentences contain *quotations.* In today's lesson we will start learning how to write quotations."

Use the examples in the text to discuss and illustrate quotations. Then ask the pupils to correct the quotations on the board. Have them suggest a few others for you to write, and let them provide the quotation marks. (Do not teach capitalization or other punctuation at this point.) Use some sentences with the quotation coming first, and some with the quotation coming last.

Emphasize: "A quotation is the exact words of a speaker. Sometimes we simply write what someone said without repeating his exact words. But that is not a quotation, so we should not use quotation marks." (The former is a direct quotation; the latter is an indirect quotation.)

Exact words repeated:
Jesus said, "I am the good shepherd."

Exact words not repeated:
Jesus said that He is the good shepherd.

Remember: A quotation is the exact words that someone has said. Quotation marks are used to show the exact words of a speaker.

> Working With Quotations >

A. Read each sentence. Write **yes** if it repeats the exact words of a speaker. Write **no** if it does not repeat the exact words of a speaker.
  1. God said, Let the earth bring forth grass.
  2. God told Adam that he would eat bread in the sweat of his face.
  3. God said that His Spirit would not always strive with man.
  4. Make thee an ark of gopher wood, the Lord told Noah.
  5. Jesus said to the disciples, It is I; be not afraid.
  6. John told Herod that it was not lawful for him to have his brother's wife.
  7. Lord, if thou wilt, thou canst make me clean, the leper said.
  8. Peter said that even if he had to die, he would not deny Jesus.

B. In Part A, copy each sentence that repeats the exact words of a speaker. Put in quotation marks where they belong.

Lesson 16 Answers
Working With Quotations
A. 1. yes
   2. no
   3. no
   4. yes
   5. yes
   6. no
   7. yes
   8. no

B. 1. God said, "Let the earth bring forth grass."
   4. "Make thee an ark of gopher wood," the Lord told Noah.
   5. Jesus said to the disciples, "It is I; be not afraid."
   7. "Lord, if thou wilt, thou canst make me clean," the leper said.

Compare the two examples in the text. Show that in the second example, *I* is changed to *He,* and *am* is changed to *is.* For further teaching, change some of the direct quotations in the lesson (or on the board) to indirect quotations.

★ **EXTRA PRACTICE**
Worksheet 10 (*Quotation Marks*)

> Can You Do This? >

Rewrite each sentence so that it tells what a speaker said without repeating his exact words.
1. Anna said, "I lost my pencil."
2. "I saw a pencil under the table," said Mother.

•——•——•——•——•——•——•——•——•

17. Writing Quotations

A sentence containing a quotation always begins with a capital letter. The first word in the quotation is also capitalized.

Two of the following sentences have a quotation at the beginning of the sentence. The other two sentences have a quotation at the end. In both kinds, the first word in the quotation is capitalized.

> Steven said, "**W**e went to Kansas."
> "**T**hat state is in the West," Sister Anna told him.
> "**M**y cousin lives in Iowa," said Betty.
> Sister Anna said, "**M**y grandmother lives in Iowa."

> **Remember:** The first word in a quotation begins with a capital letter.

> Practice With Quotations >

Copy each sentence, and put in capital letters and quotation marks where they are needed.
1. one morning ralph said, it is as hot as summer.

Can You Do This?
(Wording may vary slightly.)
1. Anna said that she lost her pencil.
2. Mother said that she saw a pencil under the table.

Lesson 17 Answers
Practice With Quotations
(Corrected items are underlined.)
1. <u>One</u> morning <u>Ralph</u> said, "<u>It</u> is as hot as summer."

Lesson 17
Aim: To give more practice with quotations, and to teach the correct use of capital letters with quotations.

Oral Review:
1. Give the simple predicate in this sentence: *Do cardinals sing?* (do sing)
2. Name the four different kinds of sentences, and tell how each one should end. (telling sentence—period; asking sentence—question mark; commanding sentence—period; exclaiming sentence—exclamation mark)
3. What is the subject of a commanding sentence? (you)
4. How should we write names and initials? (with capital letters, and with a period after each initial)
5. When do we use quotation marks in a sentence? (to show the exact words of a speaker)

Class: Ask one of the pupils to answer this question in a complete sentence: What day is today? Write his answer on the board as a direct quotation in two ways: —— said, "Today is ——." and "Today is ——," said ——. Have pupils supply quotation marks.

Point out that *Today* is capitalized in both sentences. This is done because *Today* is the first word in the quotation. Emphasize: The first word of every sentence is capitalized, and the first word of every quotation is also capitalized.

★ **EXTRA PRACTICE**
Worksheet 11 (*Capitalization in Quotations*)

2. it is too hot to do anything, mark agreed.
3. ralph said, i wish we could go swimming.
4. the water would be too cold, rachel told him.
5. mark said, we can go to the creek even if we don't swim.
6. you must stay in bed till your clothes dry, Aunt Maude said later.
7. i have some better things for you to do this afternoon, she told the boys.

> Review and Practice

Diagram the simple subjects and simple predicates of these sentences.
1. Men work.
2. Water gurgled and splashed.
3. Did farmers plow?
4. Run fast.
5. Mark and Merlin played.

━━━━━━━━━━

18. More About Quotations

Here are two rules that you have already learned for writing quotations.

1. Place quotation marks before and after the exact words of the speaker.
2. Capitalize the first word of the quotation.

Today you will learn another rule for writing quotations. Sometimes the quotation is an asking sentence or an

2. "It is too hot to do anything," Mark agreed.
3. Ralph said, "I wish we could go swimming."
4. "The water would be too cold," Rachel told him
5. Mark said, "We can go to the creek even if w don't swim."
6. "You must stay in bed till your clothes dry Aunt Maude said later.
7. "I have some better things for you to do thi afternoon," she told the boys.

Review and Practice

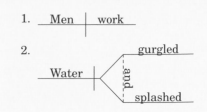

1.   Men | work

2.   Water gurgled and splashed

3.   farmers | did plow

4.   (you) | Run

5.   Mark and Merlin | played

Lesson 18

Aim: To teach pupils to place question marks and exclamation marks correctly at the end of quotations.

Oral Review:
1. What two parts does every sentence have? (a subject and a predicate)
2. What should we put after an initial? (a period)
3. What is a quotation? (the exact words of a speaker)
4. What punctuation do we use to show a quotation? (quotation marks)
5. How should we write the first word in a quotation? (with a capital letter)

Class: Call attention to the two rules taught in the preceding lessons. Then tell the children, "This lesson teaches more about quotation. If a quotation is an asking sentence, it should end with a question mark.

If it is an exclaiming sentence, it should end wit an exclamation mark. These end marks should b placed *before* the quotation marks."

Discuss the examples in the pupil's text, then d Oral Practice With Quotations in class. You may als wish to give some chalkboard practice with sentence containing quotations. The following sentences dri all the concepts that have been taught so far.

1. God called from the bush, "Moses, Moses
2. Moses answered, "Here am I."
3. The jailer asked, "What must I do to b saved?"
4. "Oh that my words were now written cried Job.

Note again that the use of commas is not drille it is simply mentioned in passing. Also note th instruction that the pupils are to always put th end marks before the quotation marks. There a

exclaiming sentence. Then it should end with a question mark or an exclamation mark.

God said to Adam, "Where art thou?"
"Look at the deer!" exclaimed Marvin.

When a question mark or exclamation mark is used, it takes the place of a comma or a period. Also, the mark at the end of a quotation is put **before** the quotation marks. When you write a quotation, always put the end marks there.

Remember: If a quotation is an asking sentence, it ends with a question mark. If a quotation is an exclaiming sentence, it ends with an exclamation mark. The end mark comes before the quotation marks.

> Oral Practice With Quotations >

Read each word in bold print, and say what punctuation mark should be used after it.

Example: "Behold the **Man**" cried **Pilate**
Answer: Man—exclamation mark; Pilate—period

1. The crowd shouted, "Crucify **Him**"
2. Rhoda said, "Peter is at the **gate**"
3. "Believest thou the **prophets**" Paul **asked**
4. The children shouted, "Look at the **snow**"
5. "What do I **hear**" Samuel asked **Saul**
6. "Where does the smoke come **from**" asked **John**
7. "Please pick some corn," said **Mother**
8. When Father came inside, all the children cried, "**Surprise**"
9. "Children, have ye any **meat**" asked **Jesus**

Lesson 18 Answers
Oral Practice With Quotations

1. Him—exclamation mark
2. gate—period *or* exclamation mark
3. prophets—question mark; asked—period
4. snow—exclamation mark
5. hear—question mark; Saul—period
6. from—question mark; John—period
7. Mother—period
8. Surprise—exclamation mark
9. meat—question mark; Jesus—period

entences in which end marks come after quotation
 arks, as in this example. *Did he say, "Come in"?* So
 void saying that quotation marks are *always* put after
 he end marks. Emphasize only that the children are
  do it this way.

EXTRA PRACTICE
Worksheet 12 (*End Marks in Quotations*)

10. "Let's eat outside today," Sister Ann **said**
11. "**Good**" exclaimed the **children**
12. "How long have you been **sick**" asked the **doctor**

10. said—period
11. Good—exclamation mark; children—period
12. sick—question mark; doctor—period

> Writing Quotations >

A. Copy these sentences, adding capital letters, quotation marks, and end marks where they are needed. In sentence 6, change the comma to a better punctuation mark.
   1. we are going to do a few jobs, Aunt Maude told the children
   2. she said to ralph, i want you to mow the lawn
   3. rachel may help Grandmother peel apples, Aunt Maude continued
   4. that evening Aunt Maude said, you have been very good helpers today
   5. we will eat supper on the lawn tonight, she said
   6. good, cried the children

B. Copy and add quotations to the following.
   1. Jesus said, ——.
   2. Mother said, ——.
   3. —— asked the teacher.
   4. —— yelled Father above the noise.

Written Quotations
A. (Corrected items are underlined.)
   1. "We are going to do a few jobs," Aunt Maude told the children.
   2. She said to Ralph, "I want you to mow the lawn."
   3. "Rachel may help Grandmother peel apples," Aunt Maude continued.
   4. That evening Aunt Maude said, "You have been very good helpers today."
   5. "We will eat supper on the lawn tonight," she said.
   6. "Good!" cried the children.

B. (Individual answers.)

19. Using Apostrophes

Suppose you were using a pencil that belonged to your friend. If someone asked whose pencil you were using, you might say, "It is Deborah's pencil" or "It is Harold's pencil." You would not say, "It is the pencil of Deborah" or "It is the pencil of Harold."

The little mark before the **s** in **Deborah's** is an **apostrophe** (ə·pos′·trə·fē). The apostrophe is used to show **possession** (ownership). Do you see that it is easier to show possession by using an apostrophe and **s**? It is easier because it takes less time and less space.

Here are some more possessive phrases.

Mark's boots	the dog's foot
someone's cap	Anna's home
Daniel's bicycle	a doll's dress

> Working With Possessive Phrases >

A. Write these possessive phrases correctly.
1. Fathers shovel
2. Donnas covering
3. Rogers puppy
4. Ruths garden
5. Marks hammer
6. Janets doll
7. Davids sheep
8. Mothers dishes

B. Make each sentence shorter by using a possessive phrase with an apostrophe.

Example: The skin of a fish is tough.
Answer: A fish's skin is tough.

1. The tail of a fox is bushy.
2. Look at the huge mane of that lion.
3. Three eyelids protect the eye of a camel.

Lesson 19 Answers
Working With Possessive Phrases
A. 1. Father's shovel
   2. Donna's covering
   3. Roger's puppy
   4. Ruth's garden
   5. Mark's hammer
   6. Janet's doll
   7. David's sheep
   8. Mother's dishes

B. (Wording may vary slightly.)
   1. A fox's tail is bushy.
   2. Look at that lion's huge mane.
   3. Three eyelids protect a camel's eye.

Lesson 19

Aim: To teach the use of apostrophes to show possession.

Oral Review:
1. What is the subject of a command if it is not stated? (you)
2. When do we use quotation marks in a sentence? (to show the exact words of a speaker)
3. How do we write the first word in a quotation? (with a capital letter)
4. What end mark should come after a quotation that is an asking sentence? an exclaiming sentence? (a question mark; an exclamation mark)
5. Should the end mark be put before or after the quotation marks? (before the quotation marks)

Class: On the board write examples like the following,

using pupils' names if you wish.

the shoes of Edward	the notebook of Mary
the sled of John	the mittens of Susan

Ask, "Is this our usual way of showing that something belongs to someone?" Introduce the little punctuation mark called the apostrophe. "We use this little mark with s to show possession. The apostrophe helps to save time and space." Illustrate with the examples in the lesson.

Have pupils go to the board and write the normal way of showing possession under each phrase you wrote. You could also have them write a possessive phrase about the teacher.

Note that the possessive form of names ending with s (such as *Moses*) is not taught at this level.

4. The egg of an ostrich weighs about three pounds.
5. The front teeth of a beaver grow constantly.
6. There are no bones in the trunk of an elephant.
7. The tongue of a giraffe is seventeen inches long.
8. The skin of a zebra is used to make leather.
9. The hand of God made all these wonderful things.

4. An ostrich's egg weighs about three pounds.
5. A beaver's front teeth grow constantly.
6. There are no bones in an elephant's trunk.
7. A giraffe's tongue is seventeen inches long.
8. The zebra's skin is used to make leather.
9. God's hand made all these wonderful things.

C. Make sentences of your own with four of the possessive phrases that you wrote for Part A.

C. (Individual answers.)

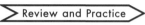

> Review and Practice >

Write three exclaiming sentences.

Review and Practice

(Individual answers.)

20. More About Apostrophes

In the following sentences, look at the words in bold print.

1. Ralph **is not** in the garden.
   Ralph **isn't** in the garden.
2. We **are not** ready to go.
   We **aren't** ready to go.
3. I **have not** seen the other girls.
   I **haven't** seen the other girls.
4. Carol **has not** come.
   Carol **hasn't** come.

Lesson 20

Aim: To teach the use of apostrophes in contractions.

Oral Review:

1. Name the four different kinds of sentences, and tell how each one should end. (telling sentence—period; asking sentence—question mark; commanding sentence—period; exclaiming sentence—exclamation mark)
2. What kind of punctuation shows the exact words of a speaker? (quotation marks)
3. How do we write the first word in a quotation? (with a capital letter)
4. What do we put after a quotation that is an asking sentence? an exclaiming sentence? (a question mark; an exclamation mark)
5. What do we add to a word to make it show possession? (an apostrophe and *s*)

Class: Say, "We have learned that apostrophe are used in possessive phrases to show ownership Today we will study another way that apostrophe are used."

Use the examples in the pupil's text to show con tractions formed by combining words with *not,* an other contractions. The main point of this lesson i that the apostrophe is used to replace omitted let ters, so you should teach it from that angle. Con tractions are taught again in Unit 3 (Working Wit Verbs).

You may wish to mention that some contraction can stand for more than one pair of words. Their us in a sentence tells us which one is meant. Example he's—he is *or* he has; you'd—you had *or* you would

The second sentence in each pair is shorter because it has a **contraction** (kən·trak′·shən). In each contraction, the word **not** is joined with another word. The letter **o** in **not** is left out, and an apostrophe is used instead of the missing letter.

Other contractions can also be made by joining pairs of words. Look at the lists below. Do you know what two words are used to make each contraction? Can you tell what letter or letters are replaced by the apostrophe?

| I'm | he's | we'll | I'll |
| you're | they're | we've | they've |

> Using Apostrophes in Contractions >

A. For each sentence, write a contraction that could be used instead of the words in bold print. Be careful to use apostrophes correctly.
1. The farmer **is not** finished with his harvest.
2. King Herod **did not** give God the glory.
3. The disciples **were not** fishing.
4. Mother said **she is** planning to come early.
5. **We will** try to be ready on time.
6. I hope **you are** going with us.
7. Thomas **was not** with the other disciples.
8. He **would not** see Jesus until later.

B. These contractions are not written as they should be. Write them correctly.
1. have'nt
2. wasnt
3. wer'ent
4. theyr'e
5. Im
6. has'nt
7. yo'uve
8. shel'l

Lesson 20 Answers
Using Apostrophes in Contractions
A. 1. isn't
2. didn't
3. weren't
4. she's
5. We'll
6. you're
7. wasn't
8. wouldn't

B. 1. haven't
2. wasn't
3. weren't
4. they're
5. I'm
6. hasn't
7. you've
8. she'll

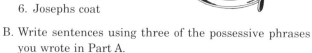

A. Write each possessive phrase correctly.
1. Aunt Sarahs cookies
2. Hannahs son
3. Grandmothers flowers
4. The doctors office
5. Esaus pottage
6. Josephs coat

B. Write sentences using three of the possessive phrases you wrote in Part A.

Practice With Possessive Phrases
A. 1. Aunt Sarah's cookies
2. Hannah's son
3. Grandmother's flowers
4. The doctor's office
5. Esau's pottage
6. Joseph's coat

B. (Individual answers.)

21. Reviewing What You Have Learned

> Oral Drill >

A. Say what is wrong with each name or initial.
1. George washington
2. h. A Hoyt
3. Timothy ray Hostetler
4. H. r simpson

B. Say the exact words of the speaker in each sentence.
1. Joyce said, the clock stopped.
2. is supper ready, asked John.
3. Mother said, please sweep the floor.
4. Oh, look at the bright star, exclaimed rachel.
5. the teacher asked, do you know your verses
6. I cannot find my mittens, said Alice.
7. what a pleasant surprise, said Grandmother.

Lesson 21 Answers
Oral Drill
A. (Corrected items are underlined.)
1. George <u>W</u>ashington
2. <u>H</u>. A<u>.</u> Hoyt
3. Timothy <u>R</u>ay Hostetler
4. H. <u>R</u>. <u>S</u>impson

B. 1. the clock stopped
2. is supper ready
3. please sweep the floor
4. Oh, look at the bright star
5. do you know your verses
6. I cannot find my mittens
7. what a pleasant surprise

Lesson 21

Aim: To review concepts taught in the last six lessons, and to evaluate pupils' mastery of these concepts.

Class: By doing Oral Drill first, determine which pupils need extra practice in certain concepts. Drill these before assigning the written work.

C. Now say what is wrong with each sentence in Part B.

D. Change these to possessive phrases that need apostrophes. Say where the apostrophe belongs in each of your phrases.
1. the doll of Gloria
2. the pet of Miriam
3. the coat of a man
4. the bill of the hawk

E. Say where the apostrophe belongs in each contraction.
1. cant
2. Ive
3. dont
4. shes
5. youre
6. wouldnt

> **Written Practice**

A. Copy only the names and initials that are written correctly.
1. M. A. Howard
2. Julia mae Smith
3. Roger L Nolt
4. M. R. A.
5. Monica Kay Roberts
6. H. T. R.
7. L. M. T
8. Barbara Ann Byler
9. Samuel m. Thompson
10. Anna W Martin

B. These sentences have three mistakes each. Copy each sentence correctly, and underline your corrections.

Example: Mother asked, why is there mud on the floor"

Answer: Mother asked, "Why is there mud on the floor?"

1. The doctor said, "you wont need to come back anymore.
2. The robins eggs have hatched, announced Father.
3. "We arent having English class today, said the teacher

C. (Corrected items are underlined.)
1. Joyce said, "The clock stopped."
2. "Is supper ready?" asked John.
3. Mother said, "Please sweep the floor."
4. "Oh, look at the bright star!" exclaimed Rachel.
5. The teacher asked, "Do you know your verses?"
6. "I cannot find my mittens," said Alice.
7. "What a pleasant surprise!" said Grandmother.

D. 1. Gloria's doll
2. Miriam's pet
3. a man's coat
4. the hawk's bill

E. 1. can't
2. I've
3. don't
4. she's
5. you're
6. wouldn't

Written Practice
A. 1. M. A. Howard
4. M. R. A.
5. Monica Kay Roberts
6. H. T. R.
8. Barbara Ann Byler

B. 1. The doctor said, "You won't need to come back anymore."
2. "The robin's eggs have hatched," announced Father.
3. "We aren't having English class today," said the teacher.

4. Andrew asked the postman, "did Fathers package come yet"
5. I am so excited about my trip" exclaimed Martha

C. Read each phrase in bold print. Rewrite it as a possessive phrase with an apostrophe in it.
   1. **The wash of Mother** fluttered in the breeze.
   2. Today we got **a letter of Aunt Mary.**
   3. **The call of the mockingbird** was clear and loud.
   4. **The voice of the nurse** was kind and gentle.
   5. There are many promises in **the Word of God.**

━◆━◆━◆━◆━◆━◆━

22. Checking for Capitalization

Here are three rules for capitalization that you have studied.

   1. Capitalize the first word of every sentence.
   2. Capitalize the names and initials of people.
   3. Capitalize the first word of a quotation.

Below is an example of what a story would look like if not enough capital letters were used. See if you can find sixteen mistakes in these paragraphs.

> Long ago an Indian bought some things at the store of a white man named john. when the Indian got home, he found some money inside the package. "good!" he said to himself. "I will keep this money. it will buy many things."
>
> But the next morning the Indian took the money back. "why didn't you keep it?" asked john.

Lesson 22

Aim: To give extended practice with capitalization as taught in previous lessons.

Oral Review:
   1. What are the two main parts of a sentence? (subject and predicate)
   2. What are two rules for writing every quotation? (Put quotation marks before and after the quotation. Capitalize the first word of the quotation.)
   3. If a quotation is an asking or an exclaiming sentence, do we put the end mark before or after the quotation marks? (before the quotation marks)
   4. How do we make a word show possession? (Add an apostrophe and *s.*)
   5. In a contraction, what is used to replace the letters that are dropped? (an apostrophe)

---

4. Andrew asked the postman, "Did Father's package come yet?"
5. "I am so excited about my trip!" exclaimed Martha.

C. 1. Mother's wash
   2. Aunt Mary's letter
   3. The mockingbird's call
   4. The nurse's voice
   5. God's Word

Class: Call attention to the rules for capitalization in the text, and then discuss the story. Each time someone points out a mistake, ask why a capital letter should be there. The mistakes are as follows:

   Paragraph 1: John, When , Good, It
   Paragraph 2: Why, John
   Paragraph 3: There, One, John, Keep, The Take, Those, They
   Paragraph 4: Now, Tonight

★ **EXTRA PRACTICE**
Worksheet 13 (*Capitalization*)

The Indian replied, "there are two men inside of me. one man says john will never know what happened. keep the money! the other man says that would be wrong. take it back! those two men talked all night. they would not let me sleep."

"I have brought the money back," said the Indian. "now the two men will stop talking. tonight I shall sleep."

> Practice With Capitalization >

Some words in these sentences begin with small letters, but they need capital letters. Write those words correctly.

Example: the disciple who betrayed Jesus was judas.
Answer: The, Judas

1. there was a man named jesse.
2. this man had eight sons.
3. the oldest son was eliab and the youngest was david.
4. david was anointed king by samuel.
5. one day jesse told David, "please take some food to your brothers."
6. as david talked with his brothers, a giant named goliath came up.
7. david told saul, "I will go and fight with this giant."
8. he said, "once I killed a lion and a bear because God helped me."
9. God helped david, and he killed goliath.
10. saul's son jonathan became David's good friend.
11. his daughter michal became David's wife.
12. three of David's sons were amnon, absalom, and solomon.

Lesson 22 Answers
Practice With Capitalization
1. There, Jesse
2. This
3. The, Eliab, David
4. David, Samuel
5. One, Jesse, Please
6. As, David, Goliath
7. David, Saul
8. He, Once
9. David, Goliath
10. Saul's, Jonathan
11. His, Michal
12. Three, Amnon, Absalom, Solomon

> Review and Practice >

Diagram the simple subjects and simple predicates of these sentences.

1. Does water freeze?
2. Hoe faster.
3. Pigs grunted and squealed.
4. Leaves and acorns fell.
5. Scrub hard.

●━━●━━●━━●━━●━━●━━●

23. Proofreading for Punctuation

Punctuation marks are very small, but they are very important. Did you know that many years ago people did not use periods, commas, and other punctuation marks? They did not even leave a space between the words. Sometimes they used all capital letters.

NOWWEHAVERULESFORBEGINNINGANDENDING
SENTENCESCORRECTLYWEUSEPERIODSWEUSEQUESTION
MARKSANDCOMMASFOLLOWINGTHERULESMAKES
READINGEASIER

Do you see how important it is that we use correct punctuation?

Tell what kind of punctuation should be used to
    a. end a telling sentence.
    b. end an asking sentence.
    c. end a sentence that shows strong feeling.
    d. show that someone owns something.
    e. show the exact words of a speaker.
    f. show where letters are missing in a contraction.

Review and Practice

1. ___water___ | ___does freeze___

2. ___(you)___ | ___Hoe___

3. Pigs ———< grunted / and / squealed

4. Leaves / and / acorns ——> fell

5. ___(you)___ | ___Scrub___

Lesson 23

Aim: To review and reinforce the rules of punctuation.

Oral Review:
1. What is a quotation? (the exact words of a speaker)
2. Spell the possessive form of *girl*. (girl's)
3. What is a contraction? (A contraction is two words written together with some letters missing. An apostrophe takes the place of the missing letters.)
4. Give the three rules for capitalization that you have learned. (Capitalize the first word of every sentence. Capitalize the names and initials of people. Capitalize the first word of a quotation.)

Class: Call attention to the paragraph in all capital letters. Ask, "Would you enjoy reading a whole book written like this? Aren't you glad that we have punctuation marks today, and spaces between words?" In today's

standard form, the paragraph would read as follows:

Now we have rules for beginning and ending sentences correctly. We use periods. We use question marks and commas. Following the rules makes reading easier.

The word *legible* (whose root means "choose") gives a hint of how hard it was to read writing without spaces between the words. The reader had to "pick out" the words as he went along.

Give additional review of punctuation rules by writing these sentences on the board and asking the children what punctuation is missing.

1. The sun is shining brightly (period)
2. Isnt it time to go (apostrophe, question mark)
3. Please set the table (period)
4. How glad the disciples were (exclamation mark)

> Using Punctuation in Sentences

A. Each set of words contains three sentences. Write the sentences correctly.
1. do you know who Paul was he was a Christian he took the Gospel to many lands
2. Timothy was only a young man do you know what he did he helped Paul tell about Jesus
3. Christians still take God's Word to other places some ministers went to Mexico do you know why they went there

B. Two words in each sentence need an apostrophe. Find the words and write them correctly.
1. Pauls shirt isnt dry yet.
2. Sarahs art and Marys handwriting have improved.
3. Jasons blocks werent brought inside.
4. Theyre glad the accident wasnt any worse.
5. The orioles song and the doves cooing filled the air.

C. Write a sentence using a quotation to tell what you think Keith said in each picture.
1.   2.

5. My mothers brother is my cousins father (apostrophes, period)
6. Didn't you find the answer asked the teacher (quotation marks, apostrophe, question mark, period)

You may wish to have the pupils scan the exercises to see if they can find some of the mistakes.

★ **EXTRA PRACTICE**
Worksheet 14 (*Punctuation*)

Lesson 23 Answers
Using Punctuation in Sentences

A. 1. Do you know who Paul was? He was a Christian. He took the Gospel to many lands.
2. Timothy was only a young man. Do you know what he did? He helped Paul tell about Jesus.
3. Christians still take God's Word to other places. Some ministers went to Mexico. Do you know why they went there?

B. 1. Paul's, isn't
2. Sarah's, Mary's
3. Jason's, weren't
4. They're, wasn't
5. oriole's, dove's

C. (Possible answers.)
1. "Fetch it," said Keith.
2. "Good dog," said Keith.

24. Checking Our Spelling

Do you remember the story in John 5 about the sick man at the Pool of Bethesda? Jesus was right there to help him, and the man was healed because he accepted Jesus' help. If that man had not allowed Jesus to heal him, he probably would have stayed by the pool the rest of his life.

If we do not accept the help available to us, we also will stay where we are in our understanding. Our minds will not grow.

One of the ways to receive help is by using the dictionary. This will help our minds to grow and will help us to avoid many mistakes.

In Lesson 3 you learned that the dictionary is helpful in three ways. Do you remember what they are? If you do not, go back and review Lesson 3.

It is not courteous to spell words wrong, because this makes it hard for others to read what we have written. In this lesson you will practice using the dictionary to spell words correctly.

Lesson 24

Aim: To teach the importance and helpfulness of using the dictionary to check the proper spelling of words.

Oral Review:

1. Give three rules for capitalization that you have learned. (Capitalize the first word of every sentence. Capitalize the names and initials of people. Capitalize the first word of a quotation.)
2. Why is it important to use punctuation marks? (Reading is made easier if correct punctuation marks are used.)
3. What kind of punctuation should be used
   a. after telling and commanding sentences? (a period)
   b. after an asking sentence? (a question mark)
   c. after a sentence with strong feeling? (an exclamation mark)
   d. with the exact words of a speaker? (quotation marks)
   e. in contractions and possessive words? (a apostrophe)

Class: Tell the pupils, "It is good to sound out new words when we read. But when we write, it is better to check the dictionary if we are not sure of a spelling. Who can remember why it is not hard to find words in the dictionary?" (The words are listed in alphabetical order.)

But the pupils may wonder how they can find a word in the dictionary if they cannot spell it. Give them this hint? "Try to think of how the word is probably spelled, and find a word in the dictionary which looks like that word. If the definition matches the meaning of the word you want, it is probably the right one." Give practice with frequently misspelled

> Practice With Spelling >

A. One word in each list is misspelled. Write each misspelled word correctly, using a dictionary if you need help. Hint: First look up the word that you **think** is probably misspelled.

1. autum
   anything
   accident

2. envalope
   eternity
   eastward

3. beautiful
   becuase
   between

4. factory
   faithfull
   feather

5. cannot
   continue
   chiken

6. guiltie
   guard
   groaning

7. dauhter
   daytime
   depend

8. headache
   hessitate
   hopefully

B. For each sentence, choose the correct spelling from the ones in parentheses. Check your answers with the dictionary.

1. Mother looked at the (calender, calendar, calandar) to see when Grandmother would arrive.

2. Jerry had an appointment with the (dentest, dennist, dentist) to have his tooth filled.

3. Mother stood on a step stool to change the light bulb on the (cieling, ceiling, seiling).

4. The squirrels were gathering (hickory, hichory, hickery) nuts that had fallen from the tree.

5. After you swallow your food, it goes down to your (stomack, stumach, stomach).

6. The mob wanted Pilate to (crusify, crucify, cruicify) Jesus.

Lesson 24 Answers
Practice With Spelling

A. 1. autumn
   2. envelope
   3. because
   4. faithful
   5. chicken
   6. guilty
   7. daughter
   8. hesitate

B. 1. calendar
   2. dentist
   3. ceiling
   4. hickory
   5. stomach
   6. crucify

words such as the following.

| beggar | familiar | reign |
| cemetery | muscle | vacuum |

This method *must* be used if one is not sure about pairs like *angel—angle, altar—alter,* and other commonly confused words.

★ **EXTRA PRACTICE**
Worksheet 15 (*Spelling Correctly*)

25. Reviewing What You Have Learned

Can you name some stories you have enjoyed reading? Perhaps one reason you enjoyed reading these stories was that they were easy to read. What makes a story easy to read? Would you enjoy reading this story?

Careless Kathy

"Saturday cleaning, ugh," Kathy muttered. She pulled her bedroom door shut. *Swish, swish,* the dust cloth flew across the top of her dresser. She grabbed the bed covers and tossed them up over the pillow.

then kathy pulled the vacuum cleaner from the closet. she pushed the cleaner arm recklessly around the furniture, chanting, "zoom, zoom, around the room."

"Their, that should do," said Kathy. She swiched off the cleaner and skiped downstiars. "May I read for a while?" she quesoined.

Are you finished already Mother asked She turned from the sink to make sure it was Kathy

Mothers emphasis on **already** sent little shivers down Kathys back Yes, Im all done, she said.

Lets go see Mother started for the stairs. Kathy had no choice but to follow Mother.

> **For You to Do**

Write a story about something that happened to you or someone else in your family. Be sure your story looks better than "Careless Kathy."

Lesson 25

Aim: (1) To rivet the concepts taught in the last three lessons. (2) To review subjects and predicates.

Written Quiz:

1. Write this name correctly: **richard m nixon.**
2. Write this sentence correctly: **where are you going, asked james**
3. Write the possessive form of **boy** and **girl.**
4. Write the two words that each contraction stands for: **I'm, doesn't.**
5. What are two places that capital letters are used?
6. What should we use for help with our spelling?

Quiz Answers:

1. Richard M. Nixon
2. "Where are you going?" asked James.
3. boy's, girl's
4. I am, does not

Lesson 25 Answers
For You to Do

(Individual stories. Be sure they used correc♦ capitalization, punctuation, and spelling.)

5. (any two) at the beginning of a sentence, at th♦ beginning of a quotation, in names and initial♦
6. the dictionary

Class: Use the story about Kathy for oral drill. Fo♦ the sake of simplicity, the different kinds of mistake♦ are in groups as follows.

Paragraph 1: No mistakes
Paragraph 2: Mistakes in capitalization♦ (then, kathy, she, zoom)
Paragraph 3: Mistakes in spelling (Their♦ swiched, skiped, downstiars♦ quesoined)
Paragraphs 4–6: Mistakes in punctuation

Point out how the mistakes make the story unpleasant to read. In paragraph 3, *There* is con♦ fusing, and the other spelling mistakes are distract♦ ing. In paragraph 4, is *already* part of the quotation♦ or does it belong to the rest of the sentence? I♦

Write the simple subject and the simple predicate of each sentence. If it is a commanding sentence and the subject is understood, write **(you)** for the simple subject.

1. The Lord smote all the firstborn in the land of Egypt.
2. Pharaoh rose in the night.
3. The Israelites sang unto the Lord.
4. Gather manna every day except the seventh day.
5. Did they gather manna?
6. They journeyed through the wilderness.
7. The Israelites complained to Moses.
8. Give us water.
9. Did God give them the Ten Commandments?
10. Did they worship a golden calf?

Review and Practice

1. Lord smote
2. Pharaoh rose
3. Israelites sang
4. (you) Gather
5. They did gather
6. They journeyed
7. Israelites complained
8. (you) Give
9. God did give
10. They did worship

aragraph 5, is *Mothers* a plural form? In paragraph , does the first sentence mean, "Let's go see Mother"?

After discussing the mistakes, you may wish to ask he pupils to identify the kind of mistake found in different parts of the story. For example, "What kind of mistakes do you see in the second paragraph?" The more ble students may enjoy rewriting the story correctly.

For Review and Practice, point out that the simplest ay is to first find the verb and then ask *who* or *what* ith it. You could use this sentence to illustrate.

The people of Egypt suffered from ten terrible plagues.

Which word is the verb? suffered

Who suffered? people (not Egypt)

The simple subject and simple predicate is people suffered.

Review One

> Oral Drill >

A. Answer these questions.
1. What is a sentence?
2. How should you begin all sentences?
3. What is a command?
4. What is an exclaiming sentence?
5. How can you find the subject and the predicate in an asking sentence?

B. Find the simple subject in each of these sentences.
1. Some Indians lived in tepees
2. Were the snowbanks melting fast
3. Ronald rode his new bicycle
4. Lucy picked some flowers for Mother
5. We saw many fish in the water
6. Did Mother go to the sewing

C. Tell whether each sentence in Part B tells or asks. Then tell what mark you would put at the end of each sentence.

D. Find the simple predicate of each sentence in Part B.

Review One

Aim: To review and strengthen concepts taught in previous lessons in preparation for a test.

Class: Do the Oral Drill in class. Be alert to any areas that need extra drill. Pupils may want to scan the written exercises and ask questions about any part they do not understand.

Review One Answers
Oral Drill

A. 1. A sentence is a group of words with a complete thought. It has a subject that tells who or what and a predicate that tells what the subject does or is.
2. You should begin all sentences with a capital letter.
3. A command is a sentence that tells someone to do something.
4. An exclaiming sentence is a sentence that shows strong feeling.
5. First change the word order so that it is a telling sentence. Then find the word that tells *who* or *what* the sentence is about, and the word that tells what the subject *does* or *is*.

B. 1. Indians
2. snowbanks
3. Ronald
4. Lucy
5. We
6. Mother

C. 1. tells; period
2. asks; question mark
3. tells; period
4. tells; period
5. tells, period
6. asks; question mark

D. 1. lived
2. were melting
3. rode
4. picked
5. saw
6. did go

> Written Practice

A. Put each list of words in alphabetical order.
   1. king   2. fishermen   3. sky
      crown   nets   sling
      throne   boat   staff
      queen   hunters   sheep
      law   water   sudden
      palace   shore   spear

B. Write the numbers of the groups of words below that
   are sentences. Beside each number put the correct end
   mark for that sentence.
   1. Some farms raise flowers
   2. Acres and acres of flowers
   3. What a beautiful sight that is
   4. To go there
   5. Do not pick the flowers
   6. The work of many people
   7. How pretty the flowers are
   8. Would you like to visit a flower farm

C. Diagram these sentences.
   1. Do children work?
   2. Dogs and cats doze.
   3. Run and play.
   4. Babies eat and grow.
   5. Will Jesus come?

Written Practice

A. 1. crown   2. boat   3. sheep
      king   fishermen   sky
      law   hunters   sling
      palace   nets   spear
      queen   shore   staff
      throne   water   sudden

B. 1. .
   3. !
   5. .
   7. !
   8. ?

C. 1.  Children | do work

   2. 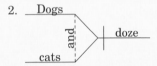 Dogs and cats doze

   3. 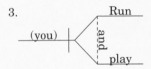 (you) Run and play

   4. 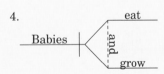 Babies eat and grow

   5.  Jesus | will come

Review Two

> **Oral Drill**

A. Tell what is wrong with each name or initial.
1. Caleb L Miller
2. susie Mae Finch
3. R. T. M
4. Marian L Brown
5. Roberta Ann fox
6. T. M Leslie
7. Anna Mae martin
8. H J M

B. Tell what is missing in each quotation below.
1. "Do you like the new song" asked the teacher.
2. "How are they increased that trouble me! said the psalmist David.
3. We have run into a storm, announced the pilot.
4. Father said, "you may start the chores early tonight"
5. "Look at the big snow-flakes" exclaimed Betty.
6. Jesus said, let not your heart be troubled.

C. Say where the apostrophe belongs in each phrase or contraction.
1. Howards horse
2. Carols pen
3. Davids letter
4. Wilburs truck
5. doesnt
6. hes
7. youve
8. shouldnt

> **Written Practice**

A. Each set of words contains three sentences. Write each sentence correctly.

Review Two Answers
Oral Drill
A. (Corrected items are underlined.)
1. Caleb L. Miller
2. Susie Mae Finch
3. R. T. M.
4. Marian L. Brown
5. Roberta Ann Fox
6. T. M. Leslie
7. Anna Mae Martin
8. H. J. M.

B. (Corrected items are underlined.)
1. "Do you like the new song?" asked the teacher
2. "How are they increased that trouble me!" said the psalmist David.
3. "We have run into a storm," announced the pilot.
4. Father said, "You may start the chores early tonight."
5. "Look at the big snowflakes!" exclaimed Betty
6. Jesus said, "Let not your heart be troubled."

C. 1. Howard's horse
2. Carol's pen
3. David's letter
4. Wilbur's truck
5. doesn't
6. he's
7. you've
8. shouldn't

Review Two

Aim: To review and strengthen concepts taught previously in preparation for a test.

Class: Proceed as in the previous Oral Drill.

1. Jesus was preaching to the multitude the people did not want to leave Him the disciples asked Him to send the crowd away

2. They had only five loaves and two fishes to eat Jesus asked the disciples to bring the food to Him He commanded the people to sit down

3. Jesus blessed the food the disciples gave it to the people everyone ate and was full

B. Copy the correct spelling from the ones in parentheses. Use a dictionary if you are not sure.

1. The (animels, animals, anamels) splashed through the creek in the pasture.

2. The (bare, bear, bair) branch of the tree scratched the window.

3. The (sheperds, shepards, shepherds) watched their sheep all night.

4. We watched the (oreole, oriole, oriale) building its nest.

Written Practice

A. 1. Jesus was preaching to the multitude. The people did not want to leave Him. The disciples asked Him to send the crowd away.

2. They had only five loaves and two fishes to eat. Jesus asked the disciples to bring the food to Him. He commanded the people to sit down.

3. Jesus blessed the food. The disciples gave it to the people. Everyone ate and was full.

B. 1. animals
2. bare
3. shepherds
4. oriole

Extra Activity

Make a poster like the one at the bottom of this page to show your parents some things about language.

Cut the engine, the cars, and the caboose from colored construction paper. Also cut the wheels from colored paper, and paste them on the cars in their proper places. With a crayon make lines to fasten the cars together. Write the words carefully on the poster. You may draw straight lines very lightly before writing the letters to help you print the letters in a straight line.

Be ready to tell your parents about the things you have already learned in this English book.

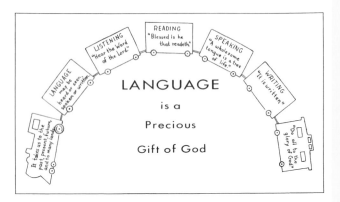

Extra Activity

Aim: To provide a creative way for pupils to show some truths about language.

Class: This project can be completed by the entire class or by each child individually. Tell pupils that you expect them to put into practice what they have learned about neatness.

A Poem to Enjoy

Little by Little

Little by little, and straight and high,
　A bush to a tall tree grows.
Little by little the days go by,
　And a bud becomes a rose.

Little by little the children grow
　Taller and taller, and then
Little by little they change, and lo,
　They turn into women and men!

Discussing the Poem

1. In what way does this poem teach us patience?
2. What were tall trees at one time?
3. If we open a rosebud, does it turn into a rose any sooner?
4. In what way did your parents become big people?
5. In what ways are all growing things alike?

Answers to Discussion Questions

1. It teaches us to be patient with things that happen little by little, such as growing up.
2. Tall trees were bushes at one time.
3. No. (Rather, we would spoil the bud by opening it.)
4. They grew little by little from children to men and women.
5. They are all becoming bigger. They all need food and water. They all have life, which God created. They all will die someday.

A Poem to Enjoy

Aim: To give practice in reading and enjoying poetry.

Class: Discuss the meaning of the poem. Read it in a singsong voice and afterward read it properly. Ask the children which way they enjoy it better. Then have several pupils practice reading it with proper expression.

Use the questions to discuss the meaning of the poem. Talk about other big things that have small beginnings, such as a large fire or a great river like the Mississippi.

Unit 2

NOUNS

NOUNS NAME — things, places, people

Kentucky

NOUNS ARE — common, proper, girl, Janet

NOUNS ARE — geese, plural, goose, singular

Building With
Nouns and Pronouns

26. Learning About Words That Name

Look around your classroom. How many things can you name? Now many people can you name? Can you name your school and the town where you live?

The words you use when you name a person, place, or thing are called **nouns.** Look at the nouns below. Which of the nouns name people? Which name places? Which name things?

mother	Canada	book	carrot
town	Susan	city	Mr. Lee
table	farmer	teacher	water
hat	tree	rabbit	New York

Nouns that name people answer the question **who.**

Who went to town? **Father** went.

Nouns that name places answer the question **what place.**

To **what place** did Father go? He went to **town.**

Nouns that name things answer the question **what.**

What did Father buy? He bought a **hammer.**

Remember: Words that name are called nouns. Nouns name people, places, and things.

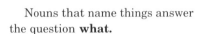

Look at the picture on the next page. Then use nouns to name what you see.

Lesson 26

Aim: To introduce nouns as words that name people, places, and things.

Oral Review:

1. What is a sentence? (a group of words with a complete thought)
2. Why is it important to use the correct punctuation marks? (Punctuation makes reading easier.)
3. Give three ways that capital letters are used. (for the first word in a sentence, for the names and initials of people, for the first word in a quotation)
4. How do we make the possessive form of a word? (by adding an apostrophe and *s*)
5. What tool should we use for learning how to spell and pronounce new words? (the dictionary)

Class: Begin by writing this sentence on the board:

—— went to —— and bought a ——.

Does the sentence tell us *who* went? to *what place* the person went? *what* the person bought? There are no nouns in the sentence—no words that name people, places, or things. Ask the class to suggest some nouns to complete the sentence. Use their suggestions to complete the sentence in several different ways.

Examples:

Mother went to town and bought a broom. Carl went to school and bought a pencil.

Point out that different nouns will make sentences mean very different things.

You may want to discuss the written work with the students before they start on it, to help them form some ideas.

★ **EXTRA PRACTICE**
Worksheet 16 (*Nouns*)

1. Write two or more nouns to name **persons** in the picture.
2. Write a noun to name the **place** where they are going.
3. Write five nouns to name **things** you see in the picture.

> Using Nouns in Sentences >

A. Use a noun to complete each sentence. Write the sentences correctly.

1. the —— ran quickly
2. a little —— played
3. three —— worked
4. the bright ——shone
5. —— is happy
6. we went to ——
7. I live in a ——
8. he saw a ——
9. God is in ——
10. where is ——

B. Write four sentences using the nouns below.

1. raccoon   2. Kevin   3. river   4. corn

> Review and Practice >

Write each list of words in alphabetical order.

1. table	2. potatoes	3. monkey	4. Arad
chair	peas	moose	Ararat
bed	pie	mole	Aram
desk	pumpkin	mouse	Arabah

●━●━●━●━●━●━●━●━●━●

Lesson 26 Answers
Using Nouns to Name
(Possible answers.)
1. boys, girls, children (Also accept proper names.)
2. school
3. books, trees, birds, clouds, lunch boxes

Using Nouns in Sentences
A. (Individual answers. Be sure they are sensible.)

B. (Individual answers.)

Review and Practice

1. bed	3. mole
chair	monkey
desk	moose
table	mouse
2. peas	4. Arabah
pie	Arad
potatoes	Aram
pumpkin	Ararat

27. Names of People and Places

Jacob asked, "**Who** went to town?"
Mae said, "A **girl** and a **boy** went to town."
Glen said, "**Carol** and **Timothy** went to town."

Jacob asked a **who** question. Mae used the nouns **girl** and **boy** to answer his question. But Jacob still did not know exactly who went to town. Glen used the names **Carol** and **Timothy.** He named two specific people. He told exactly who went to town.

Some nouns name specific places.

To **what town** did Carol and Timothy go?
Carol and Timothy went to **Lancaster.**

Lancaster names a specific place. It tells exactly which town.

Nouns that name specific people or places are called **proper nouns.** Nouns that are not specific names are called **common nouns.**

When you write a proper noun, always begin it with a capital letter. If the noun has two words, begin each one with a capital letter.

Common	Proper	Common	Proper
state	New Mexico	teacher	Sister Weber
city	Ottawa	apostle	Simon Peter
river	Red River	doctor	Dr. Williams

Remember: A common noun is not a specific name. It does not begin with a capital letter.

A proper noun is a specific name, and it begins with a capital letter. If a proper noun has two words, both words begin with a capital letter.

Lesson 27

Aim: (1) To introduce the terms *common noun* and *proper noun,* and to teach the capitalization of proper nouns. (2) To teach that if a proper noun has two words, both words must be capitalized.

Oral Review:
1. Name the two parts of a sentence. (subject and predicate)
2. What do we call the exact words of a speaker? (a quotation)
3. How should each of these items be written: the first word of a sentence, the names and initials of people, and the first word of a quotation? (with a capital letter)
4. What replaces missing letters in a contraction? (an apostrophe)
5. What is a noun? (the name of a person, place, or thing)

Class: Begin by asking, "If I say that I want a girl to go to the board, will you know which girl should go? No, I must be more specific. So I will say exactly which girl should go. ——, please go to the board and write your name. Now I want a boy to go to the board. ——, please go to the board and write your name under the other one."

Have the class look at the two names on the board. The words are nouns because they name people. But they are called proper nouns because they name specific people. Point out that every proper noun begins with a capital letter.

Write *Proper* above the two names. Then write *girl* and *boy,* and write *Common* above these. Explain that a common noun does not begin with a capital letter. Ask the class to give some more common nouns that name people. Write these in the column marked *Common.* Then ask them to name a specific person for each common noun. Write these correctly

> **Writing Proper Nouns** >

Rewrite each sentence, using a proper noun to take the place of the words in bold print. Remember to begin each proper noun with a capital letter.

1. **The minister** spoke.
2. **The girl** smiled.
3. We went to **a city.**
4. **My friend** is kind.
5. Our cousins live in **that state.**
6. We crossed the **river.**
7. **The lady** waved to us.

> **Recognizing Common and Proper Nouns** >

Copy the two nouns in each sentence. The proper nouns are not capitalized. Write them correctly.

1. The girl was singing to the baby.
2. Did samuel ever see the hudson river?
3. Does uncle roy live in manitoba?
4. My cousins live near lake michigan.
5. Did brother seth drive to the city?

> **Review and Practice** >

Write whether each of these is a **telling, asking, commanding,** or **exclaiming** sentence. Also give the correct end punctuation for each.

1. Oh, look at the large snowflakes
2. Martha washed the windows yesterday
3. Love thy neighbour as thyself
4. God in heaven is the only true God
5. Is your mother at home
6. Children, obey your parents

Lesson 27 Answers
Writing Proper Nouns
(Words in parentheses will vary.)
1. (Brother John) spoke.
2. (Martha) smiled.
3. We went to (Greenville).
4. (Kevin) is kind.
5. Our cousins live in (Virginia).
6. We crossed the (Ohio River).
7. (Mrs. Jones) waved to us.

Recognizing Common and Proper Nouns
1. girl, baby
2. Samuel, Hudson River
3. Uncle Roy, Manitoba
4. cousins, Lake Michigan
5. Brother Seth, city

Review and Practice
1. exclaiming (!)
2. telling (.)
3. commanding (.)
4. telling (.)
5. asking (?)
6. commanding (.)

★ **EXTRA PRACTICE**
Worksheet 17 (*Proper Nouns*)

n the other column. Point out the rule of capilalizing ach word when a name has more than one word (Sister Veaver, John Good).

Go on to discuss proper nouns that name specific laces. Write *town* and ask the children to name a specific town. Do the same with *country, river,* and *state.*

When assigning the written work, ask the class to ive some proper nouns that they might use in the first xercise. In the second exercise, remind them that some f the proper nouns will have two words. You may wish o use the following sentences for practice with finding ouns.

1. Uncle John enjoys watching birds.
2. All birds have keen eyes.
3. Many Indians live in the mountains of South America.
4. Grandmother gave my sister a parakeet for a pet.

> Can You Do This?

Unscramble each set of letters to spell a noun. If it is a proper noun, remember to begin it with a capital letter.

1. hojn   4. alup   7. rmya   9. souhe
2. rocn   5. kobo   8. rigl   10. pyteg
3. reet   6. naan

●━●━●━●━●━●━●━●━●

Can You Do This?

1. John   6. Anna
2. corn   7. Mary
3. tree   8. girl
4. Paul   9. house
5. book   10. Egypt

28. More About Proper Nouns

The words **Janet** and **Mrs. White** are proper nouns because they name specific people. The words **India** and **Atlanta** are proper nouns because they name specific places. Some words are proper nouns because they name specific things.

On which **day** did you stay home?
I stayed home on **Tuesday.**

The word **Tuesday** is a proper noun because it names a specific day. The names of the days of the week are all proper nouns. Each of the names begins with a capital letter.

Sunday   Tuesday   Thursday   Saturday
Monday   Wednesday   Friday

Names of holidays are proper nouns also.

Thanksgiving Day   Good Friday
Ascension Day

The names of the months are proper nouns. Each name must begin with a capital letter.

Lesson 28

Aim: To introduce the names of months, holidays, and days of the week as proper nouns; and to teach that the names of the seasons are common nouns.

Oral Review:

1. What is used to show the exact words of a speaker? (quotation marks)
2. Why is it important to use the correct punctuation marks? (Reading is made easier if the correct punctuation marks are used.)
3. What tool should we use for learning how to spell and pronounce new words? (the dictionary)
4. What is a noun? a proper noun? (the name of a person, place, or thing; the name of a specific person, place, or thing)
5. How do we write proper nouns? (Begin them with capital letters.)

Class: Review what was learned in Lesson 27 about proper nouns. Tell the class that some proper nouns are used on the calendar. The names of the months are proper nouns because they name definite periods of time. The names for the days of the week are proper nouns because each names a certain day.

Ask the class whether they can think of any other days that have special names. Give them a clue, such as "What is the name of the day set aside to remind people to be thankful?" Write *Thanksgiving Day* on the board. Also write the names of some other holidays, such as *New Year's Day, Easter, Father's Day,* and *Christmas.*

Then write *seasons* and list the names of the four seasons. Emphasize that these four nouns are not proper nouns, and they are not capitalized.

If the written assignment seems too long, you may have the class name only two days of the week and three months of the year.

January	May	September
February	June	October
March	July	November
April	August	December

But be careful! The names of the seasons are common nouns. So the names of the seasons do **not** begin with a capital letter.

spring   summer   autumn   winter

The names of roads, cities, and countries are proper nouns and should begin with a capital letter.

Lincoln Road   Bombay, India

> Writing Proper Nouns >

A. Write the following proper nouns correctly.
  1. The seven days of the week
  2. The twelve months of the year
  3. The name of your teacher
  4. The name of the country you live in
  5. The day set aside to remember that Jesus went up to heaven

B. Each sentence has three proper nouns. Find them, and write them correctly.
  1. On monday mr. carter went to trenton.
  2. Did keith visit mexico during april?
  3. We have autumn in september, october, and november.
  4. Why did sarah go to kentucky in july?
  5. One saturday last summer the webers came from alberta.
  6. Was brother david asked to preach in vineland on good friday?

Lesson 28 Answers
Writing Proper Nouns
A. 1. Sunday, Monday, Tuesday, Wednesday, Thursday, Friday, Saturday
  2. January, February, March, April, May, June, July, August, September, October, November, December
  3. (Teacher's name written correctly.)
  4. (Name of country in which you live.)
  5. Ascension Day

B. 1. Monday, Mr. Carter, Trenton
  2. Keith, Mexico, April
  3. September, October, November
  4. Sarah, Kentucky, July
  5. Saturday, Webers, Alberta
  6. Brother David, Vineland, Good Friday

◄ **EXTRA PRACTICE**
Worksheet 18 (*More Proper Nouns*)

29. Other Proper Nouns

Do you have a pet dog? Does your dog have a name? Did you ever name any of your cows or other animals? When an animal has a specific name, that name is a proper noun.

The rabbit with a lame foot is **Hopper.**
The white horse is named **Starlight.**

The name of a specific book or magazine is a proper noun.

Our teacher is reading **Sunshine Country** to us.
We enjoy the magazine called **Nature Friend.**

The name of a school, church, or building is also a proper noun.

Susan goes to **Valley Chris-tian School.**
Mark goes to **Silver Creek Mennonite Church.**
The dentist's office is in the **Lincoln Building.**

> Writing Proper Nouns >

Write the following correctly.
1. The names of two books
2. The name of a specific dog or other animal
3. The name of your school
4. The name of your church building

Lesson 29 Answers
Writing Proper Nouns
(Individual answers.)

Lesson 29

Aim: To present the names of pets, books, schools, churches, and buildings as proper nouns.

Oral Review:
1. What punctuation mark is used after a commanding sentence? (a period)
2. What is the subject of every commanding sentence? (you)
3. Explain what a proper noun is, and how it should be written. (A proper noun is the name of a specific person, place, or thing. It should be capitalized.)
4. Say *yes* or *no* to tell whether each of these should be capitalized.
   a. names of weekdays (yes)
   b. names of months (yes)
   c. names of seasons (no)
   d. names of holidays (yes)

Class: Review the kinds of proper nouns that have already been taught: specific names of people, places, holidays, the days of the week, and the months of the year. Tell the children that today they will learn about some other words that are proper nouns.

Ask the pupils to name some pets or other animals they have, and write the names on the board. Then ask for the names of some books and magazines they enjoy, and write the titles on the board. The examples in the book do not include any uncapitalized words. If the children give titles that have such words, explain simply that a little word like *the* or *of* is not capitalized unless it is the first word in the title.

Finally, ask the class to name their school and some church buildings. Write these correctly on the board.

★ **EXTRA PRACTICE**
Worksheet 19 (*Other Proper Nouns*)

> Using Nouns to Answer Questions >

Read this paragraph. Answer the questions about it by copying nouns from the paragraph. You should write nine nouns in all.

Three men went to Calgary to visit their father. They saw mountains, trees, and farms. A farmer talked to the men. The men told him about God and the Bible.

1. **Who** went on a trip?
2. To **what place** did they go?
3. **Whom** did they want to visit?
4. **What** did they see?
5. **Who** talked to them?
6. **Whom** did the men tell him about?
7. **What** did the men tell him about?

> Review and Practice >

Diagram the simple subjects and simple predicates of these sentences.

1. Jesus healed the blind man.
2. Can Alvin read?
3. Sweep the floor.
4. Joseph and Mary traveled.
5. The Israelites murmured and complained.

●━●━●━●━●━●━●━●━●

Using Nouns to Answer Questions

1. men
2. Calgary
3. father
4. mountains, trees, farms
5. farmer
6. God
7. Bible

Review and Practice

1. Jesus | healed

2. Alvin | can read

3. (you) | Sweep

4. Joseph and Mary | traveled

5. Israelites | murmured and complained

30. Reviewing What You Have Learned

> Oral Drill >

1. What kind of words have we been studying?
2. What is the work of these words?
3. What are two kinds of nouns? Give an example of each kind.
4. How should we begin each kind of noun when we write it?

> Written Practice >

A. Write the missing words for these sentences.
   1. Nouns name ——, ——, and ——.
   2. The three questions that nouns answer are ——, —— ——, and ——.
   3. A —— noun names a specific person, place, or thing. A —— noun is not a specific name.
   4. A —— noun must begin with a capital letter.
   5. The names for the days of the week and the months of the year are —— nouns.
   6. The names for the seasons of the year are —— nouns.
   7. The names of pets, books, and buildings are —— nouns.

B. Copy the fourteen common nouns in these sentences. Beside each one write a proper noun that could take its place.
   1. The man smiled at the child.
   2. My uncle went to that country.
   3. The road goes past the school and into the city.
   4. A friend lived near the ocean during one month.
   5. One day the boy went to the building and visited the doctor.

Lesson 30 Answers
Oral Drill
   1. nouns
   2. Nouns name people, places, and things.
   3. common nouns and proper nouns (Individua answers.)
   4. Begin a common noun with a small lette (unless, of course, it comes at the beginnin of a sentence). Begin a proper noun with capital letter.

Written Practice
A. 1. people, places, things
   2. who, what place, what
   3. proper, common
   4. proper
   5. proper
   6. common
   7. proper

B. (Proper nouns will vary.)
   1. man, child
   2. uncle, country
   3. road, school, city
   4. friend, ocean, month
   5. day, boy, building, doctor

Lesson 30

Aim: To review the past four lessons.

Class: Use Oral Drill for a brief review before assigning the Written Practice.

C. Use the following pairs of nouns in sentences. You may use the pictures to help you.

1. Noah, ark

2. animals, ark

3. God, rain

4. sky, rainbow

C. (Individual answers.)

> Can You Do This?

Write this paragraph correctly, using nouns to complete each sentence. Use a common noun for each blank marked **C,** and a proper noun where there is a **P.** Then read your paragraph to be sure it makes sense.

On _P_ , _P_ helped his _C_ work. He cleaned the _C_ . He hoed the _C_ . After the family ate _C_ , _P_ went to _P_ with his _C_ . They stopped at a _C_ and bought _C_ for _C_ .

Can You Do This?

(Individual paragraphs. Read some of them aloud in class to demonstrate the variety possible by a choice of different nouns.)

31. Singular and Plural Nouns

Nouns name people, places, and things. When a noun names only one person, place, or thing, it is a **singular** noun. When it names more than one person, place, or thing, it is a **plural** noun.

Most plural nouns are formed by adding **s** to the singular noun.

kitten—kittens   tree—trees

Some plural nouns are formed by adding **es** to the singular noun. This is usually done if the singular noun ends with **ch, sh, s,** or **x.**

patch—patches   glass—glasses
dish—dishes

When a noun ends with **y** after a vowel, the plural is formed by simply adding **s.**

day—days   key—keys   boy—boys

If there is a consonant before the **y,** the plural is formed by changing the **y** to **i** and adding **es.**

penny—pennies   sky—skies
fly—flies

> **Remember:** A singular noun names only one person, place, or thing. A plural noun names more than one person, place, or thing.

penny   +   penny   =   pennies

Lesson 31

Aim: To present the concept of singular and plural nouns, and to teach how most plural forms are made.

Oral Review:
1. What kind of sentence is this? *What a lovely day it is!* (an exclaiming sentence)
2. What punctuation do we use after an exclaiming sentence? (an exclamation mark)
3. Nouns name ———. (people, places, things)
4. How do we write proper nouns? (with a capital letter)
5. Tell whether the last word in each phrase should be capitalized.
   a. a dog named Sparky (yes)
   b. the season called autumn (no)
   c. a book named *Flowers* (yes)
   d. the month of April (yes)

Class: On the board write a column of singular nouns such as the following, which need only the suffix *s* to form the plural.

road   door   window   cat

Ask the class to tell how many each noun names. Then ask how to change the nouns so that they name more than one. Beside each noun, write its plural form. Explain that one noun is singular and the other is plural, and write *Singular* and *Plural* above the correct columns.

Explain the reason for adding -*es* to nouns ending with *ch, sh, s,* or *x:* it makes pronunciation easier. (Plurals such as *heroes* are not taught here.) Write several other examples and form their plurals.

church—churches   wish—wishes
class—classes   ax—axes

Call attention to the extra syllable that is formed

> Writing Plural Nouns >

A. Write the plural form of each word.

1. toy	4. lash	7. desk	10. watch
2. spy	5. coat	8. loss	11. story
3. tax	6. tray	9. pony	12. lunch

B. Write the correct plural form of each noun in parentheses.
1. The (lady) were selling ripe (berry).
2. Their (hand) were covered with (scratch).
3. The wooden (bench) are nine (inch) wide.
4. The (dress) were hanging on two (hook).
5. The (baby) were eating oatmeal (cookie).

> Using Singular and Plural Nouns >

Write three sentences to tell what you did before you came to school this morning or when you got home from school last night. Use singular and plural nouns in your sentences, and underline the nouns.

> Review and Practice >

Copy each sentence. Add quotation marks and capital letters where they are needed, and use the correct end marks.
1. Jesus asked Peter, lovest thou me
2. Pharaoh exclaimed, rise up, and get you forth from among my people
3. Jesus said, go ye therefore, and teach all nations
4. make thee an ark of gopher wood, God said to Noah

Lesson 31 Answers
Writing Plural Nouns

A. 1. toys	5. coats	9. ponies
2. spies	6. trays	10. watches
3. taxes	7. desks	11. stories
4. lashes	8. losses	12. lunches

B. 1. ladies, berries
2. hands, scratches
3. benches, inches
4. dresses, hooks
5. babies, cookies

Using Singular and Plural Nouns
(Individual answers.)

Review and Practice
(Corrected items are underlined.)
1. Jesus asked Peter, "Lovest thou me?"
2. Pharaoh exclaimed, "Rise up, and get you forth from among my people!"
3. Jesus said, "Go ye therefore, and teach all nations."
4. "Make thee an ark of gopher wood," God said to Noah.

when -es is added to the words.

Write *sky* on the board. Tell the class that when a noun ends with *y* preceded by a consonant, the *y* is changed to *i* and then -es is added. Give several more example.

city—cities   puppy—puppies
cherry—cherries

Caution the class that not all nouns ending in *y* take this change. Those that have a vowel before the *y* just take an -s. Give some examples, such as *boy, day,* and *ey.*

★ **EXTRA PRACTICE**
Worksheet 20 (*Singular and Plural Nouns*)

32. Plural Nouns and Possessive Nouns

You learned in Unit 1 that possessive forms are made by adding **'s** to words like **boy** and **dog. Boy** and **dog** are nouns. These nouns and many others have both a plural form and a possessive form.

Plural forms:

boys   girls   dogs   birds

Possessive forms:

boy's   girl's   dog's   bird's

Possessive forms tell **whose.** They show that someone owns (possesses) something. Look at the following sentences.

Whose bat is this?
    It is the **boy's** bat.
Whose dish is on the porch?
    That is the **dog's** dish.

Plural forms mean more than one. They do not need an apostrophe. In each of the following sentences, look at the two words in bold print. Do you know why one word has an apostrophe and the other does not?

The **boys** asked what the new **boy's** name was.
The **bird's** nest held four baby **birds.**

Remember: Plural forms end with **s.** Possessive forms end with **'s.** Plural forms are not made by adding **'s.**

▷ Using Plural and Possessive Forms ▷

A. Copy the correct word for each sentence.
  1. The (tulips, tulip's) are blooming.

Lesson 32

Aim: To teach the difference between plural nouns ending with -*s,* and possessive nouns ending with -*'s.*

Oral Review:

1. What do we mean by a sentence with a compound subject? (a sentence with two nouns that tell *who* or *what* the sentence is about)
2. How do we write the first word in a quotation? (with a capital letter)
3. Give a proper noun for each common noun: dog, weekday, month, holiday, school. (Individual answers.)
4. Do the names of the seasons begin with a capital letter? (no—unless, of course, the name of a season is the first word in a sentence)
5. What is a plural noun? (a noun that names more than one person, place, or thing)

Lesson 32 Answers
Using Plural and Possessive Forms
A.   1. tulips

Class: Write the following nouns on the board an ask pupils how to spell their plural forms. When the respond, add -*s* to each word.

girl   boy   friend
teacher   kitten   horse

Now write the possessive form of each word, an discuss the difference between the two forms. Mak it clear that -*s* is used to make the plural form, an -*'s* is used to make the possessive form. When w want to make a noun mean more than one, we ad -*s.* When we want to make it tell *whose,* we add -*'s.*

Have the pupils use the plural and possessiv forms in sentences of their own. Write some of th sentences on the board to show when to use -*s* an when to use -*'s.*

Note that this lesson deals only with singular pos sessive forms. Plural possessive forms (*boys', dogs'* are not taught at this level.

2. Many bright (stars, star's) glittered in the sky.

3. The (boys, boy's) coat was too small.

4. Slowly the (trucks, truck's) climbed the steep hill.

5. A (squirrels, squirrel's) tail is bushy.

6. Walk carefully on the slippery (rocks, rock's).

7. Our (teachers, teacher's) car is blue.

8. Two (cardinals, card- inal's) came to the feeder.

9. Many (nuts, nut's) fell to the ground.

10. My (brothers, brother's) shirt was torn.

B. Use each word in a sentence of your own.

1. friends   3. minister's

2. cat's   4. angels

> **Review and Practice**

Write the correct spelling to be used in each sentence. Use a dictionary if you need help.

1. We water the plants on (Wenesday, Wednesday, Wensday).

2. It seemed that a (million, milion, milloin) stars were twinkling in the sky.

3. Mother put on a clean (apron, aporn, appron).

4. Abraham built an (alter, altar, altir) to worship God.

5. My cousins have (measles, meesles, measels).

6. We stayed at home because of the (slipry, slipery, slip- pery) roads.

7. The (disiples, disciples, discipels) followed Jesus.

8. The new (calves, calfs, calfes) played in the meadow.

2. stars

3. boy's

4. trucks

5. squirrel's

6. rocks

7. teacher's

8. cardinals

9. nuts

10. brother's

B. (Individual answers.)

Review and Practice

1. Wednesday

2. million

3. apron

4. altar

5. measles

6. slippery

7. disciples

8. calves

★ **EXTRA PRACTICE**

Worksheet 21 (*Plural Nouns and Possessive Nouns*)

33. Plural Nouns Not Ending With *s*

You have learned that most singular nouns are made plural by adding **s** or **es.** But the plural form of some nouns is made in other ways.

There are seven nouns whose plural forms are made by changing the vowel.

foot—feet   man—men   louse—lice
goose—geese   woman—women   mouse—mice
tooth—teeth

The singular nouns **ox** and **child** are made plural by adding **en** and **ren.**

ox—oxen   child—children

A few nouns do not change form at all. Other words in the sentence are needed to show whether the noun is singular or plural.

One **sheep** was black.   *singular*
Many **sheep** were white.   *plural*

We saw *a* **deer.**   *singular*
They saw *some* **deer.**   *plural*

> Recognizing Singular and Plural Nouns

A. Write the two nouns in each sentence. After each noun write **S** or **P** to tell whether the noun is singular or plural.
1. The children visited a ranch.
2. Some men were plowing with oxen.
3. Many sheep were in the valley.
4. A deer was eating the strawberries.
5. A woman was plucking a goose.

Lesson 33 Answers
Recognizing Singular and Plural Nouns
A. 1. children—P, ranch—S
2. men—P, oxen—P
3. sheep—P, valley—S
4. deer—S, strawberries—P
5. woman—S, goose—S

Lesson 33

Aim: To review the concept of singular and plural nouns, and to introduce nouns which are not made plural by adding *-s* or *-es.*

Oral Review:
1. What punctuation should come after initials? (a period)
2. How are common nouns written differently from proper nouns? (Common nouns are not capitalized; proper nouns are capitalized.)
3. A noun naming only one person, place, or thing is ——. A noun naming more than one person, place, or thing is ——. (singular; plural)
4. How do we make the plural form of most nouns? (by adding *-s* or *-es*)
5. What is the difference between the possessive form and the plural form of a noun? (The possessive form ends with *-'s.*)

Class: Ask the class to explain the meaning of *singular* and *plural* and to give several examples of each. Ask them to say what letter we usually use to form the plural of a noun. Review the rules for writing plural forms as presented previously.

Tell the class that for some nouns we do not add *-s* to make the plural form. Can they think of any? Give clues:

What do you have at the end of your legs? (feet)
What are the white things you use for chewing? (teeth)

Ask them to give the singular form of these nouns. Write the two forms on the board and then write the word *goose.* Ask for and then write the plural form. Point out the change from *oo* to *ee* in these words. But remind the class that we do not do this for every word with *oo.* The plural of *boot* is *boots!*

Discuss the other irregular plurals presented in

B. Do the following.

1. Write the plural form of these singular nouns.

    boot, ox, goose, ditch, boy, deer, woman, tooth

2. Write the singular form of these plural nouns.

    children, sheep, flies, mice, feet, men, dishes

> Review and Practice >

Use a proper noun to answer each of these questions. Be sure to write it correctly.

1. Who went to the city?
2. What did the lady see?
3. To what place do you go on Sunday morning?
4. What are you reading?
5. Who is your teacher?
6. To what place do you go on Monday?

> Can You Do This? >

Write the plural nouns formed by adding the letters and the names of the pictures.

1. ad   +   = ——

2. wo   +   = ——

3. m   +   = ——

4. s   +   = ——

B. 1. boots, oxen, geese, ditches, boys, deer, wom-
en, teeth

2. child, sheep, fly, mouse, foot, man, dish

Review and Practice
(Individual answers.)

Can You Do This?
1. addresses
2. women
3. mice
4. spies

the lesson. You may wish to say that long ago many English words were made plural by changing the vowel or by adding -en. Now we have only seven words with vowel changes, and three that end with -en. (The third one is brethren.) Our language is always changing in little ways.

To teach the plural of *sheep* and *deer*, you could write both words on the board and ask whether they are singular or plural. Stress the fact that there is no way of knowing unless some other word is used with them. For now, mention only words which directly show number, such as *a, one, some, several, two,* and *many.* Verb agreement should not be taught at this point.

★ **EXTRA PRACTICE**
Worksheet 22 (*Plural Nouns Not Ending With s*)

34. Writing Nouns in a Series

James sang. Robert sang.

In the sentences above, the words **James** and **Robert** are nouns. They tell us **who** sang. We can make the two sentences become one sentence by joining the two nouns with the word **and.**

James **and** Robert sang.

We can add another sentence too.

James and Robert sang. + Kevin sang.

= **James, Robert,** and **Kevin** sang.

Now there are three nouns in a row that tell us who sang. Such a row or list is called a **series.**

When you write more than two nouns in a series, put a comma after each noun except the last one. Use **and** before the last noun.

Sue likes peaches. + Sue likes plums. + Sue likes pears.
  = Sue likes peaches, plums, and pears.
The men sang. + The women sang. + The children sang.
  = The men, women, and children sang.

Lesson 34

Aim: To teach the use of *and* and the comma when writing a series of nouns.

Oral Review:

1. What is a singular noun? a plural noun? (a noun naming only one person, place, or thing; a noun naming more than one person, place, or thing)
2. Say whether each of these is a *common* or a *proper* noun.
   a. Thanksgiving Day (proper)
   b. Tuesday (proper)
   c. summer (common)
   d. Bible (proper)
3. Give four ways that nouns can be made plural. (by adding *-s* or *-es,* by changing the vowel sound, by adding *-en* or *-ren,* by not changing the form at all)

4. Say *yes* or *no* to tell whether each noun needs an apostrophe, as used in the sentence.
   a. birds: Many birds fly south. (no)
   b. teachers: The teachers car is blue. (yes)
   c. girls: I found a girls sweater outside. (yes)

Class: Call attention to the two sentences at the beginning of the lesson. Discuss how the two nouns are joined with *and* to say who sang, and how three nouns (or four, five, and even more) can be joined in the same way. See Daniel 3:10 for an example of six nouns written in a series.

  And is usually written only before the last noun because it would be tiresome to repeat it before every one of them. A comma is used after each noun except the last one so that it is clear exactly how many different things are named. Illustrate by writing the following sentence without commas.

> Writing Nouns Together >

A. Write one sentence for each set of sentences.
  1. The boys worked. The girls worked.
  2. Luke saw a rabbit. He saw a chipmunk.
  3. Mary waved. Joy waved. Ruth waved.
  4. The flowers grew. The grass grew. The weeds grew.
  5. We found a bat. We found a ball. We found a glove.

B. Each sentence has three nouns in a series. Write that part
   of the sentence correctly.

   Example: Raccoons crows and blackbirds ate the
              corn.
   Answer: Raccoons, crows, and blackbirds

  1. I saw Melvin James and Wesley in church.
  2. We planted peas beans and potatoes.
  3. Ruth Marie and Janet went home early.
  4. The storm brought snow sleet and rain.

> Review and Practice >

In each sentence you wrote for Part A, draw a line to
divide between the complete subject and predicate. Draw one
line under each simple subject, and two lines under each
simple predicate.

●━●━●━●━●━●━●━●━●━●

Squirrels, ground hogs, rats, guinea pigs, and bea-
    vers are called rodents.

  Give further practice by asking for a number of
short sentences and having the pupils tell how they
can be written as one. They should also say where to
use commas.

  Point out that a noun series may be used in the
predicate as well as in the subject. Give an example
such as the following.

  He weeded the peas. He weeded the corn. He
    weeded the squash.
  He weeded the peas, corn, and squash.

★ **EXTRA PRACTICE**
Worksheet 23 (*Words in a Series*)

Lesson 34 Answers
Writing Nouns Together
A. (Answers for Review and Practice are also
   included.)
  1. The <u>boys</u> and <u>girls</u> | <u>worked</u>.
  2. <u>Luke</u> | <u>saw</u> a rabbit and (a) chipmunk.
  3. <u>Mary</u>, <u>Joy</u>, and <u>Ruth</u> | <u>waved</u>.
  4. The <u>flowers</u>, <u>grass</u>, and <u>weeds</u> | <u>grew</u>.
  5. <u>We</u> | <u>found</u> a bat, (a) ball, and (a) glove.

B. 1. Melvin, James, and Wesley
   2. peas, beans, and potatoes
   3. Ruth, Marie, and Janet
   4. snow, sleet, and rain

Review and Practice
(Answers are included in Part A.)

35. Reviewing What You Have Learned

> Written Practice >

A. Write the plural form of each noun.

1. city	5. man	9. sheep	13. dish
2. church	6. key	10. mouse	14. deer
3. child	7. sky	11. foot	15. inch
4. book	8. ox	12. goose	16. lily

B. Write a proper noun for each noun in numbers 1–4 above.

C. Write the following correctly.
1. the name of your school
2. the last month of the year
3. the season when leaves fall

D. Write the plural form of each noun in these sentences.
1. The baby slept.
2. The watch ticked.
3. The bird sang.
4. Who read the story?
5. Who found the toy?
6. Who drew the cross?
7. Who used the brush?
8. Who lost a tooth?

E. Write the correct word for each sentence.
1. The (wasps, wasp's) were building a nest.
2. I could feel the (suns, sun's) warm rays.
3. The (doctors, doctor's) office was neat and clean.
4. We bought two new (books, book's).
5. Neat (papers, paper's) are easy to read.

Lesson 35 Answers
Written Practice

A.			
1. cities	7. skies	12. geese	
2. churches	8. oxen	13. dishes	
3. children	9. sheep	14. deer	
4. books	10. mice	15. inches	
5. men	11. feet	16. lilies	
6. keys			

B. (Individual answers.)

C. 1. (The name of your school.)
   2. December
   3. autumn (fall)

D. 1. babies
   2. watches
   3. birds
   4. stories
   5. toys
   6. crosses
   7. brushes
   8. teeth

E. 1. wasps
   2. sun's
   3. doctor's
   4. books
   5. papers

Lesson 35

Aim: To review the concepts presented in the last nine lessons on nouns.

Oral Review:
Teacher: Write the following nouns on the board.

hands	Ann	book
foot	papers	June

1. Which words are
   a. common nouns? (hands, foot, papers, book)
   b. proper nouns? (Ann, June)
   c. singular nouns? (foot, Ann, book, June)
   d. plural nouns? (hands, papers)
2. Find the singular common nouns and give their plural forms. How is each plural form made? (feet—by changing the vowels; books—by adding -s)

3. How is a possessive form different from most plural forms? (A possessive form ends with -'s. Most plural forms end with just -s.)
4. Give the plural form of *child* and *ox*; of *deer* and *sheep*. (children, oxen; deer, sheep)
5. Tell what punctuation is needed in this phrase: *cups bowls and plates*. (a comma after *cups* and after *bowls*)

Class: Use Oral Review for class discussion before assigning the written work.

F. Write a sentence about what you see in each picture. If the picture shows two things, use two nouns together. If the picture shows three things, use three nouns together.

1.

4.

2.

5.

3.

6.

F. (Individual answers. Read some of them aloud in class to illustrate variety.)

> Can You Do This?

Complete the paragraph by using a singular noun where there is an **S** and a plural noun where there is a **P.** You may use proper nouns.

      _S_ , _S_ , and _S_ went to the _S_ last _S_ .
They saw many _P_ , _P_ , and _P_ . The _P_ were
much bigger than the _P_ that they see at home.

Can You Do This?
   (Individual paragraphs. Read some of them in class.)

36. Words That Stand for Nouns

Some words in our language take the place of nouns. When you talk about yourself, you use **I** and **me** to take the place of your own name. When you speak of someone else, you use the word **you** to take the place of the person's name.

> James called, "**I** am hiding; come find **me**."
> Keith shouted, "**You** are by the apple tree."

James used the words **I** and **me** instead of his own name. Keith was talking to James, so he used the word **you** instead of the name **James.**

The words **I, me,** and **you** are **pronouns.** Pronouns are words that stand for nouns. In the sentences below, the words in bold print are pronouns. The arrow points to the noun each pronoun is standing for.

The boys said, "**We** will help Father."

Susan asked if **she** could help too.

Father said that Susan could help **him.**

The children smiled. **They** liked to help Father.

Remember: Pronouns are words that take the place of nouns. A pronoun does the same work as a noun in a sentence.

Lesson 36

Aim: To introduce pronouns as words that take the place of nouns.

Oral Review:

1. Which sentence part tells who or what does or is something? (the subject)
2. A noun naming only one person, place, or thing is ———. A noun naming more than one person, place, or thing is ———. (singular; plural)
3. Name four ways nouns can be made plural. (by adding -s or -es, by changing the vowel sound, by adding -en or -ren, by not changing the form at all)
4. Spell the plural form of *cat*. Spell the possessive form. (cats; cat's)
5. When we write more than two nouns together, we use a ——— after each noun except the ——— one. (comma, last)

Class: Write these three sentences on the board:

> I found it.
> You saw me.
> She heard them.

Ask one child to circle the words that tell *wh found, who saw,* and *who heard.* Ask another chil to circle the words that tell *what was found, who we seen,* and *who was heard.*

Tell the class that these words are not noun They are pronouns—words that take the place nouns. If we say *Sarah,* we know who Sarah is. we say *a boy,* we understand what a boy is. But wh does *I* name? (*I* always refers to the person who speaking.) Ask the children if they can find the oth pronoun circled on the board, which stands for th name of the person who is talking. (It is the pronou *me.*) Stress the fact that whenever we use a pronou there must be a certain noun that it stands for.

> Sentences With Pronouns >

A. Copy the pronouns in bold print. Beside each one, write the noun that the pronoun stands for.

1. Mother called, "**I** will read you a story now."
2. The girls heard Mother. **They** came quickly.
3. The boys asked, "Did you call **us**?"
4. "Do **you** want to hear a Bible story?" Mother asked the boys.
5. Little Lena cried, "Read to **me** too! Please!"
6. The children said, "**We** are all ready."
7. Mother chose a story. **It** was about Abraham.
8. Abraham loved God. **He** believed God's Word.
9. Three men came to Abraham's tent. Abraham gave **them** food to eat.
10. The men told Abraham that God would give **him** a son.
11. Sarah was listening. **She** heard what the men said.
12. Later, Sarah was very happy when God gave **her** a son.

B. Write four sentences to describe yourself. Use **I** in two sentences and **me** in two sentences. The teacher will read what you wrote. Then the others can guess who wrote the sentences.

    Sample: **I** have brown hair and brown eyes.
        A girl with blond hair sits in front of **me.**

> Review and Practice >

Write whether each of these is a **telling, asking, commanding,** or **exclaiming** sentence. Also give the correct end punctuation for each.

1. What did God create on the fourth day

Lesson 36 Answers
Sentences With Pronouns

A. 1. I—Mother
    2. they—girls
    3. us—boys
    4. you—boys
    5. me—Lena
    6. We—children
    7. It—story
    8. He—Abraham
    9. them—men
  10. him—Abraham
  11. She—Sarah
  12. her—Sarah

B. (Individual answers. Check for correct pronoun usage.)

Review and Practice

1. asking (?)

Ask them to tell what noun the pronoun *you* stands for (the name of the person or people spoken to). Introduce briefly the other personal pronouns. You might want to give some quick oral drill by saying simple sentences and having them restate each sentence using pronouns. Use the names of children in the class.

Examples:
    Paul can see John. (He can **see** him.)
    Sister Alice can **see** the children. (I can see you. *or* You can see us.)

Read together the sample sentences in the text. Explain the written assignment, doing two or three sentences together orally.

★ **EXTRA PRACTICE**
Worksheet 24 (*The Work of Pronouns*)

2. He made the sun, moon, and stars
3. What a great God He is
4. He made you and me too
5. Obey Him
6. Did you know He loves you

2. telling (.)
3. exclaiming (!)
4. telling (.)
5. commanding (.)
6. asking (?)

---

37. Pronouns That Tell *Who*

Nouns that name people answer the question **who.** Pronouns can also be used to tell **who.** The pronouns **I, you, he, she, we,** and **they** can tell **who.** When you write **I,** always use a capital letter.

Nouns that name things answer the question **what.** The pronoun **it** can also answer the question **what.** But we will think of it as one of the **who** pronouns.

> "**Who** likes ice cream?" asked Father.
>
> "**You** do!" laughed Mother.
>
> "**I** do!" shouted Martha.
>
> "**We** all do!" said James. "I have a friend named Dennis. **He** likes ice cream."
>
> "I have a friend Susan," said Martha. "**She** likes ice cream."
>
> "**What** tastes good with ice cream?" Mother asked.
>
> "Cake! **It** tastes good with ice cream!" James said.
>
> "Or cookies," Martha suggested. "**They** taste good too."

Lesson 37

Aim: To present the personal pronouns in the nominative case.

Oral Review:

1. Should *winter* be capitalized in this sentence? *Soon winter will be here.* (no)
2. Spell the plural form of each noun: *berry, toy, sheep, tooth, ox.* (berries, toys, sheep, teeth, oxen)
3. What does a possessive form have that a plural form does not have? (an apostrophe)
4. Say where commas are needed in this phrase: *men women boys and girls.* (after *men, women,* and *boys*)
5. What do pronouns do? (They take the place of nouns.)

Class: Review the definition and use of pronouns. Tell the class that many pronouns are like sets of twins:

I—me, he—him, she—her, we—us, they—them. Tell them that two pronouns are identical twins: *you—you* and *it—it.* Write all these sets on the board.

God gave language to man, and language has an orderly pattern. This means that certain rules must be followed in using language. Many of these rules we learn when we first learn to talk. We learn them by hearing other people talk correctly. For example, we know that we should say *I wrote a story,* not *Me wrote a story.*

Ask the pupils which of the other pronouns on the board could be used to start the sentence "—— wrote a story." Circle the pronouns they give. Tell them that we use these pronouns to tell *who* did or is doing something. The pronoun *it* tells *what* did or is doing something. But it is included with the *who* pronouns for the sake of convenience.

Read together the short story in the lesson. Ask the class to name each pronoun and the noun that

> Pronouns That Tell *Who* >

A. Write the pronoun you would use to complete each sentence. It should stand for the noun in bold print.

1. **Steven** said, "—— see some ripe berries."
2. **Steven** tasted the berries. —— liked the juicy sweetness.
3. **Susan** picked some too. —— took them to Mother.
4. Mother told **Susan,** "—— and Steven may pick some more berries."
5. **Mother** said, "—— will make shortcake."
6. The **twins** heard Mother. —— wanted to help.
7. "Yes," Mother told the **twins.** "—— may help me."
8. "What can —— do?" the **twins** asked.
9. Mother gave the **twins** each a pan. —— greased the pans.
10. Steven and Susan brought the **berries.** —— were very red.
11. "Father does not know about the **cake,**" said Mother. "—— will be a surprise."
12. At supper, **Father** was surprised! —— ate a big piece.

B. The pronouns that tell **who** are used for the **subject** of a sentence. Memorize them: **I, you, he, she, it, we, they.**

> Singular and Plural >

Look at the pronouns you wrote for Part A. Write **S** after each pronoun that stands for a singular noun. Write **P** after each pronoun that stands for a plural noun.

Lesson 37 Answers
Pronouns That Tell *Who*

A. (Answers are included for Singular and Plural.)
1. I; S
2. He; S
3. She; S
4. You; S
5. I; S
6. They; P
7. You; P
8. we; P
9. They; P
10. They; P
11. It; S
12. He; S

B. (Oral work.)

Singular and Plural
(Answers are included in Part A.)

ach pronoun stands for. Then ask them these questions.

Which pronoun refers to the person talking? (I)
Which pronoun is used for men and boys? (he)
Which pronoun is used for girls and women? (she)
Which pronoun is not used for people? (it)
Which pronoun can be used for either people or things? (they)
Which pronoun can refer to either one person or more than one person? (you)
Which pronouns are used only for one person or thing? (I, he, she, it)
Which pronouns are used only for more than one person or thing? (we, they)

In the written work, note that in some of the senences the pronoun stands for the noun as well as the rticle before it.

38. Pronouns That Tell *Whom*

1. Amy saw the girls.　　3. The girls saw Amy.
2. Amy waved to the girls.　4. The girls waved to Amy.

In sentences 1 and 2 above, the noun **Amy** tells **who** saw and **who** waved. In sentences 3 and 4, the noun **Amy** tells **whom** the girls saw and to **whom** they waved. We can use the nouns **Amy** and **girls** to say either **who** or **whom.**

Pronouns are different. Most pronouns that say **who** cannot say **whom.** We must use other pronouns to say **whom.**

> She saw them. They saw her.
> **I** heard **him. He** heard **me.**
> **He** knew **us. We** knew **him.**

The pronouns **you** and **it** can be used both ways.

> You saw it. It saw you.
> **You** called to **it. It** came to **you.**

> Using Pronouns Correctly

A. Write the correct pronoun to complete each sentence. The pronoun should stand for the noun in bold print.
1. **Father** asked, "Is that letter for ——?"
2. The **boys** heard Mother call ——.
3. "May I go with ——?" Ken asked **Father.**
4. "Is this pie for ——?" the **men** asked.
5. Mother mended the **dress** and ironed ——.
6. **Karen** sat down. Lisa sat next to ——.
7. **Robert** likes the book his uncle gave ——.
8. "I made this card for ——," Karen told **Grand-mother.**

Lesson 38

Aim: To present the personal pronouns in the objective case.

Written Quiz:

Write the correct word for each sentence.

> singular　　plural　　verbs
> pronouns　　periods　　commas
> series　　　nouns

1. Words that name people, places, and things are ——.
2. Several nouns written in a row are called a ——.
3. When several nouns are written in a row, we put —— after all the nouns except the last one.
4. Words that take the place of nouns are ——.
5. A —— noun names only one.
6. A —— noun names more than one.

Lesson 38 Answers
Using Pronouns Correctly
A. 1. me
　2. them
　3. you
　4. us
　5. it
　6. her
　7. him
　8. you

Quiz Answers:
1. nouns　　4. pronouns
2. series　　5. singular
3. commas　6. plural

Class: Review the (nominative) pronouns from the previous lesson. Write them in a column on the board: *I, you, he, she, it, we, they.* Ask the class to say the twin for each. Write these next to the other, forming a second column.

　Now write: The girls saw ——.

　Ask the class which pronouns can be used to complete this sentence. Circle the ones they use. Explain that these pronouns are used to tell *whom:* whom somebody saw, to whom something was given, and so forth. They are not the same as the pronouns that tell *who,* and they cannot be used as subjects. (Use the analogy of identical twins to explain about *you* and *it.*)

B. The pronouns that tell **whom** are **not** used for the subject of a sentence. Memorize these pronouns: **me, you, him, her, it, us, them.**

> **Writing Sentences With Pronouns** >

Look at the pictures carefully. Then write sentences about the pictures, using the pronouns given.

1. her

3. them

2. him

4. us

> **Can You Do This?** >

Write another sentence for each picture above. Use these pronouns.

1. they   2. it   3. he   4. she

B. (Oral work.)

Writing Sentences With Pronouns
(Individual answers.)

Can You Do This?
(Individual answers.)

Read together the sample sentences in the lesson. n the exercises, ask the class to give some examples of entences to use for Writing Sentences With Pronouns. The sentences should include the noun antecedent. For xample:

Mother liked the flowers that Sharon and Ruth gave her.

The children may write two sentences for one picture f they wish. Sentences for number 3 could be:

Father wanted the boys to help him. He called for them.

EXTRA PRACTICE
Worksheet 25 (*Pronouns That Tell Whom*)

39. Choosing the Correct Pronoun

This lesson will give you practice in choosing the correct pronoun when you speak or write. The following rules will help you.

1. Use **I, you, he, she, it, we,** or **they** to say **who** did or is doing something.

    We visited Uncle Ben.
    He had a surprise in a box.

2. Use **me, you, him, her, it, us,** or **them** to say **whom** someone else saw, heard, asked, helped, and so on. Also use these pronouns after little words like **to, for, with, by, at,** and **in.**

    Aunt Mary welcomed **us.**
    The surprise was for **her.**

3. The pronoun **it** tells **what,** but we include it with the **who** and **whom** pronouns. **They** and **them** may also tell **what.**

    Fruit tastes good.   **It** tastes good.
    Father bought apples.   Father bought **them.**

> Using Pronouns Correctly >

A. In these sentences, change the nouns in bold print to pronouns, and write each sentence correctly.
   1. **Father** works at Miller's Garage.
   2. Kevin works with **Father.**
   3. My sisters help **Mother.**
   4. **Mother** asked my sisters to bake cookies.

Lesson 39 Answers
Using Pronouns Correctly
A. 1. He works at Miller's Garage.
   2. Kevin works with him.
   3. My sisters help her.
   4. She asked my sisters to bake cookies.

Lesson 39

Aim: To review and give practice in the correct use of personal pronouns.

Oral Review:
1. What is the subject in a commanding sentence? (you)
2. When we write more than two nouns together, we use a —— after each noun except the —— one. (comma, last)
3. Words that take the place of nouns are ——. (pronouns)
4. Give the twin of each pronoun: *I, he, she, we, they.* (me, him, her, us, them)
5. How are *it* and *you* different form the other pronouns? (They can tell both *who* and *whom.*)

Class: Discuss the three rules presented in the lesson; then give oral practice in establishing the correct

pattern. One method is by making a sentence chai Start by saying, "I saw him." The next person is begin his sentence with the twin of the pronoun yo used last, and end his sentence with another pr noun: "He saw her." Continue until every studer has had one or two turns.

The following sentences can be used to give pra tice like that in the written exercises.

1. *God* spoke to Moses. (*He* spoke to Moses
2. The people came to *Aaron.* (The peopl came to *him.*)
3. *The people* wanted an idol. (*They* wante an idol.)
4. Aaron made *a golden calf.* (Aaron made *it*
5. God punished *the people.* (God punishe *them.*)

B. The second sentence in each pair means the opposite of the first sentence. Write the correct pronouns to fill in the blanks.

Example: I talked to them. They talked to ———.
Answer: me

1. We listened to you. You listened to ———.
2. It looked at him. He looked at ———.
3. She sat beside me. I sat beside ———.
4. He waited for her. She waited for ———.
5. They played with it. It played with ———.

B. 1. us
   2. it
   3. her
   4. him
   5. them

> Review and Practice

A. Find each word that needs a capital letter, and write it correctly.
   1. The boys were named samuel and seth.
   2. Father went to canada last summer.
   3. We named the dog frisky and the cat tiger.
   4. On monday i visited valley view school.
   5. In february brother enos went to ohio.

Review and Practice

A. 1. Samuel, Seth
   2. Canada
   3. Frisky, Tiger
   4. Monday, I, Valley View School
   5. February, Brother Enos, Ohio

B. Diagram the simple subjects and simple predicates of these sentences.
   1. The young man came to Jesus.
   2. Run!
   3. Did Moses lead?
   4. Corn and peas grew.
   5. Lions hunted and roared.

B. 1. ___man___ | ___came___

   2. ___(you)___ | ___Run___

   3. ___Moses___ | ___did lead___

   4.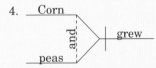

   5.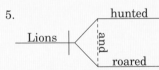

40. Reviewing What You Have Learned

> Written Practice

A. Copy all the nouns and pronouns in these sentences. The numbers in parentheses tell you how many there are in each one. Write **n.** or **pron.** after each word to tell whether it is a noun or a pronoun.

1. One Sunday, Gerald and I took a hike. (4)
2. We walked along the Yellow Beech Creek. (2)
3. Father had told us not to go into the water. (3)
4. He said, "You may watch the fish from the bank." (4)
5. Suddenly my brother spied a trout, but it was not swimming. (3)
6. It was stuck between a rock and a root. (3)
7. "Get me a stick!" Gerald shouted. (3)
8. Quickly I found a strong stick and gave it to him. (4)
9. He used it to push at the root. (3)
10. Finally the fish was free to swim away. (1)
11. It did not even wait to thank us. (2)

B. Follow these directions for playing "Guess What."

One pupil describes an animal, a food, or something else. He uses **they** in two sentences and **them** in two more sentences. The other pupils try to guess what he is describing.

1. They grow in the garden. They are red and juicy. Sometimes Mother puts them in a salad. Sometimes she uses them to make spaghetti sauce. Guess what they are.
2. Write four sentences of your own to use in playing "Guess What." Be ready to read them in class.

Lesson 40 Answers
Written Practice

A. 1. Sunday—n., Gerald—n., I—pron., hike—n
    2. We—pron., Yellow Beech Creek—n.
    3. Father—n., us—pron., water—n.
    4. He—pron., You—pron., fish—n., bank—n.
    5. brother—n., trout—n., it—pron.
    6. It—pron., rock—n., root—n.
    7. me—pron., stick—n., Gerald—n.
    8. I—pron., stick—n., it—pron., him—pron.
    9. He—pron., it—pron., root—n.
   10. fish—n.
   11. It—pron., us—pron.

B. 1. tomatoes
    2. (Individual answers. Let the pupils read the descriptions for the others to "Guess What."

Lesson 40

Aim: To review the four previous lessons.

Oral Review:

1. Find three nouns and pronouns in each sentence, and say what each one is.
   a. Susan and I wrote letters. (Susan—n., I—pron., letters—n.)
   b. She has a dog and a kitten. (She—pron., dog—n., kitten—n.)
   c. Did Carl and you find them? (Carl—n., you—pron., them—pron.)
   d. Mother went with him and me. (Mother—n., him—pron., me—pron.)
   e. They came from Ohio to visit us. (They—pron., Ohio—n., us—pron.)

2. Tell which pronoun to use in each sentence.
   a. Laura played with Carol and (I, me). (me
   b. (He, Him) and Abel offered sacrifices. (He
   c. Did (she, her) and Naomi

C. Do the following.

1. Write the seven pronouns that tell **who.** Remember that these pronouns can be used as simple subjects.

2. Write the seven pronouns that tell **whom.** Remember that these pronouns cannot be used as simple subjects.

D. Number your paper from 1 to 10. After each number write the pronoun you would use for that blank. Use each pronoun in the list only once.

he	you	them	me
it	she	they	we
I	us		

Jacob saw his friend Seth carrying a large box. "May __1__ help __2__ ?" __3__ asked.

"Yes, please. __4__ is very heavy," Seth said.

"Oh!" exclaimed Jacob. "Puppies! And __5__ are still so small!"

"Mother told __6__ to take __7__ to the barn," said Seth. "__8__ said that __9__ will keep one for a pet. The others will be given away."

"My brother and I would like one," said Jacob. "Maybe Father will let __10__ have one too!"

> Can You Do This?

After each pronoun you wrote for Part D, write the noun that the pronoun stands for.

C. 1. I, you, he, she, it, we, they
   2. me, you, him, her, it, us, them

D. (The words in parentheses are for Can You Do This?)

1. I (Jacob)
2. you (Seth)
3. he (Jacob)
4. it (box)
5. they (puppies)
6. me (Seth)
7. them (puppies)
8. she (Mother)
9. we (Seth and his family)
10. us (Jacob and his brother)

Can You Do This?

(Answers are given in Part D.)

41. When a Noun and a Pronoun Work Together

You usually know which pronoun to use to tell **who** or **what** when you use a pronoun alone. But using a noun and a pronoun together might give you trouble.

Who read the book?
> James read the book. **She** read the book.
> James and **she** read the book.

Whom did they see?
> They saw Sally. They saw **me.**
> They saw Sally and **me.**

When you are not sure which pronoun to use, think of your sentence as two sentences.

Leroy and (**I** or **me?**) ran to school.
> *Think:* Leroy ran. **I** ran.
> *Say:* Leroy and **I** ran.

Father called Kevin and (**she** or **her**?).
> *Think:* Father called Kevin. Father called **her.**
> *Say:* Father called Kevin and **her.**

God saw Moses and (**they** or **them**?).
> *Think:* God saw Moses. God saw **them.**
> *Say:* God saw Moses and **them.**

> Choosing the Correct Pronoun >

A. Write the correct word to complete each sentence.
1. Keith and (I, me) mowed the **lawn.**
2. Father helped Seth and (we, us) to hoe **weeds.**
3. Mary and (she, her) are ten **years** old.
4. Uncle Ken sent a **letter** to my **brother** and (I, me).

Lesson 41 Answers
Choosing the Correct Pronoun

A. 1. I
   2. us
   3. she
   4. me

Lesson 41

Aim: To teach the correct use of pronouns in a compound subject or object.

Oral Review:

1. How is a common noun different from a proper noun? (A common noun is the name of a person, place, or thing, and it is not capitalized. A proper noun is the name of a specific person, place, or thing, and it is capitalized.)
2. Give the nouns in this sentence, and tell whether they are common or proper: *My brother worked for Doctor Clark last summer.* (brother—common, Doctor Clark—proper, summer—common)
3. Tell whether these nouns need apostrophes as used in the sentences.
   a. boys: The little boys mother was busy. (yes)
   b. farmers: What is in the farmers field? (yes)
   c. cows: Two cows are in the field. (no)

4. Give the seven pronouns that tell *who.* (I, you, he, she, it, we, they)
5. Give the seven pronouns that tell *whom.* (me, you, him, her, it, us, them)

Class: On the board write these two sentences:

> Mark said, "—— caught a raccoon."
> Mark said, "Kevin and —— caught a raccoon."

Ask the class to say which pronoun they should use to stand for Mark's name in the first sentence. Write *I* in the blank. Then ask them to give the pronoun they would use in the second sentence. If they say "I"—good! If they say "me," explain that the pronoun is doing the same work in both sentences. So the correct pronoun for both sentences is *I.*

Use the following sentences for further practice. Ask the class to first state the sentence as two separate sentences and then correctly as one sentence.

5. May we pick some **flowers** for Susan and (she, her)?
6. The **puppy** followed Jason and (he, him).

B. In Part A, look at the words in bold print. Write whether each one is singular (**S**) or plural (**P**).

C. For each sentence, write the correct pronoun to take the place of the noun or nouns in bold print.
  1. Paul and **Silas** sang in prison.
  2. Did Mary and **Martha** listen to Jesus?
  3. Did Jesus speak to James and **John**?
  4. God helped Joseph and **Mary** to flee.
  5. Jesus spoke to **men and women.**

> Writing Sentences With Pronouns >

Write four sentences using these phrases correctly.
  1. Carol and us   3. Lois and he
  2. my teacher and I   4. A friend and me

◆━◆━◆━◆━◆━◆

42. Using Commas With Nouns and Pronouns

When you write three or more nouns together, you should use a comma after each noun except the last one. You should use the word **and** before the last noun. When you use two or more nouns together with a pronoun, treat the pronoun like a noun and use the same comma rule.

> **John** ran. **Mary** ran. **I** ran.
> **John, Mary,** and **I** ran.

Duane and (he, him) played in the snow.
Karen played with Betty and (she, her).
Jesus died for (they, them) and (we, us).

After the students seem able to do this, work in reverse; give them two sentences to be joined into one. The first kind of practice develops reasoning for correct pronoun usage. The second kind helps to improve speaking and writing skills.

Please help Ann. Please help (I, me). Please help Ann and <u>me</u>.
Carl came early. (I, Me) came early. Carl and <u>I</u> came early.
(He, Him) ate the fruit. (She, Her) ate the fruit. <u>He</u> and <u>she</u> ate the fruit.

Look at the lesson together and discuss the examples given in each section. Explain that the children should use this method of dividing a sentence into two sentences as a help in doing the written assignment.

5. her
6. him

B. 1. S
   2. P
   3. P
   4. S, S
   5. P
   6. S

C. 1. he
   2. she
   3. him
   4. her
   5. them

Writing Sentences With Pronouns
(Individual answers.)

──────────

★ **EXTRA PRACTICE**
Worksheet 26 (*Using a Noun and a Pronoun Together*)

◆━◆━◆━◆━◆━◆

Lesson 42

Aim: (1) To teach the use of commas in a series that includes nouns and pronouns. (2) To give additional practice with using the correct pronoun in a compound subject or object.

Oral Review:
  1. What punctuation mark is put after an asking sentence? (a question mark)
  2. How should we change an asking

Seth saw **John.** Seth saw **Mary.** Seth saw **me.**
Seth saw **John, Mary,** and **me.**

Remember: When you write three or more nouns or pronouns together, use a comma after each noun or pronoun except the last one.

If you use a noun and a pronoun together and are not sure which pronoun to use, think what you would say if you were using the pronoun alone.

Father, Mother, and (**I** or **me**?) visited Aunt Joy.
   Think: **I** visited Aunt Joy.
   Say: Father, Mother, and **I** visited Aunt Joy.

> Writing Sentences Correctly >

A. Write one sentence for each set of sentences.
  1. Karen waved. Joy waved. I waved.
  2. They waved to Karen. They waved to Joy. They waved to me.
  3. Please help Paul. Please help Luke. Please help me.
  4. Can you find the boys? Can you find us?
  5. Noah laughed. David laughed. He laughed.
  6. Jesus preached. Paul preached. Peter preached.

B. Pretend you are one of the children in each picture. Give names to the other two children. Then write two sentences for each picture. Use the children's names and the pronoun **I** in one sentence. Use their names and **me** in the other sentence.

Lesson 42 Answers
Writing Sentences Correctly
A. 1. Karen, Joy, and I waved.
  2. They waved to Karen, Joy, and me.
  3. Please help Paul, Luke, and me.
  4. Can you find the boys and us?
  5. Noah, David, and he laughed.
  6. Jesus, Paul, and Peter preached.

B. (Individual answers.)

---

sentence before diagraming it? (Change it to a telling sentence.)
3. Words that take the place of nouns are ——. (pronouns)
4. Give the twin of each pronoun: *I, him, she, we, them.* (me, he, her, us, they)
5. Give the correct pronouns to use in these sentences.
  a. A letter came for Rachel and (I, me). (me)
  b. (She, Her) and I were invited to go on a trip. (She)
  c. (They, Them) and Father helped Dale and (we, us). (They, us)

Class: Review the use of commas in a noun series. Explain that a series of nouns and pronouns together uses commas in the same way. Write an example on the board, such as the last sentence in the text. Ask the class to give several more sentences using two or more

nouns together with a pronoun.

Additional oral practice can be given by askin[g] each child to say one sentence about himself and tw[o] other people, using *I* in the sentence. Then each chil[d] should do the same and use the pronoun *me.* Suc[h] oral practice should be given frequently to help th[e] students become accustomed to saying and hearin[g] the correct pronoun.

Explain the written exercises, especially Part [B.] The pupils' sentences in that part should illustra[te] the correct use of commas.

  Examples:
    John, Ruth, and I played with the kitten[s.]
    The kitten climbed all over John, Rut[h]
    and me.

★ **EXTRA PRACTICE**
  Worksheet 27 (*Commas With Nouns and Pronouns*)

> **Review and Practice** >

Write correctly each word that needs an apostrophe.
1. The horses couldnt pull the heavy load.
2. Five cows were in the farmers corn.
3. The children cant find Arnolds dog.
4. The girls used Mothers dishes.
5. Davids work was to take care of his fathers sheep.

●━━━━●━━━●━━━●━━━●━━━━●

43. Another Use for Commas

When we talk to someone, we often begin by saying the person's name. Then we say the rest of the sentence. When you write a sentence like this, use a comma after the name or names of the people who are spoken to.

> Karen, you are in third grade.
> Boys and girls, I want you to write a poem.

Now you know two ways to use commas.
1. Use a comma after each word except the last one in a series of nouns and pronouns.
2. Use a comma after the name of the person or people to whom you are talking.

> James and Lois, you may plant peas, beans, and corn.

Review and Practice
1. couldn't
2. farmer's
3. can't, Arnold's
4. Mother's
5. David's, father's

Lesson 43

Aim: To teach the use of a comma with a noun of direct address.

Oral Review:
1. What is the correct way to write initials? (Capitalize initials and put a period after each one.)
2. Give the seven pronouns that tell *who*. Then give the seven that tell *whom*. (I, you, he, she, it, we, they; me, you, him, her, it, us, them)
3. Which pronouns can tell both *who* and *whom*? (*you* and *it*)
4. When a noun and a pronoun are used together, how can you decide which pronoun form is correct? (Think of the sentence as two sentences.)
5. Tell where commas should be used in these sentences.
   a. James Luke and I came early. (after *James* and *Luke*)
   b. Jesus loved him Martha and Mary. (after *him* and *Martha*)
   c. Mother said that Rita you and I should do the dusting. (after *Rita* and *you*)

Class: This lesson is included in the section on pronouns in preparation for the next lesson, which teaches that a noun and a pronoun must not be used together to name the same person or thing. Since a noun and pronoun *are* used together in direct address, the concept of direct address is presented first so that the students will not be confused in the next lesson.

On the board write several examples of sentences with direct address, some of them volunteered by the class. Explain the correct use of the comma. Point out that it is used because we pause after saying the name of the person we are talking to.

Read together the short explanation given in

> **Using Commas Correctly** >

A. Write the following sentences correctly, using commas where they are needed.

1. Uncle Roy do you grow rye corn and oats?
2. Susan you may bring flour sugar and milk.
3. Father may Mark Faith and I pick berries?
4. Boys and girls you may make cards for Kevin and Luke.
5. Mother a dog chased Joy Ruth and me.
6. Carl and Mark you may help Lee Simon and me.
7. Father tell us the story of Shadrach Meshach and Abednego.
8. Children did you know that dolphins and porpoises are whales?

B. Each sentence has one comma that is not needed. Copy the word before the incorrect comma.

Example: Samuel, please help James, with his work.
Answer: James

1. Mother, today Karen, forgot her lunch.
2. Sue, Betty, and I, shared our lunches with her.
3. Alvin, I want to thank you, for your letter.
4. Carla and Marie, brought apples, peaches, and pears.
5. Mother, will we plant peas, and beans this year?

> **Review and Practice** >

Copy each sentence. Add quotation marks and capital letters where they are needed, and use the correct end marks.

1. why are the windows open asked Mother
2. father said, I will pop some corn
3. it is snowing exclaimed Jerry
4. grandmother said, please sing a hymn

Lesson 43 Answers
Using Commas Correctly

A. 1. Uncle Roy, do you grow rye, corn, and oats?
2. Susan, you may bring flour, sugar, and milk.
3. Father, may Mark, Faith, and I pick berries?
4. Boys and girls, you may make cards for Kevin and Luke.
5. Mother, a dog chased Joy, Ruth, and me.
6. Carl and Mark, you may help Lee, Simon, and me.
7. Father, tell us the story of Shadrach, Meshach, and Abednego.
8. Children, did you know that dolphins and porpoises are whales?

B. 1. Karen
2. I
3. you
4. Marie
5. peas

Review and Practice

(Corrected items are underlined.)

1. "Why are the windows open?" asked Mother.
2. Father said, "I will pop some corn."
3. "It is snowing!" exclaimed Jerry.
4. Grandmother said, "Please sing a hymn."

the text and discuss the sample sentences. As you look at the last sentence, ask the children to say why each comma was used (series or direct address).

★ **EXTRA PRACTICE**
Worksheet 28 (*More About Commas*)

44. When to Use Pronouns

When someone uses a **pronoun** without first using a noun to name the person or thing, you cannot tell whom or what the person is talking about. You do not know what noun the pronoun is standing for.

They ran across the field.

It tasted good!

When someone uses a **noun,** you know whom or what the person is talking about.

The **boys** ran across the field.
The **grapefruit** tasted good!

If you are saying or writing just one sentence about a person or thing, use a noun. If there is more than one sentence, use a noun in the first sentence. Then you may use a pronoun in the second sentence.

Esther petted the lamb. **She** held **it** in her arms.
Carl and Lee are twins. **They** both have brown hair
and blue eyes.

Never use a noun and a pronoun together to name the same person or thing.

Lesson 44

Aim: (1) To teach that a pronoun should be used only when it is clear what noun the pronoun stands for. (2) To teach that a pronoun must not be used as a repetition of its antecedent.

Oral Review:

1. Should the names of the four seasons be capitalized? (no)
2. What is a plural noun? (a noun that names more than one person, place, or thing)
3. Give the correct pronoun for each sentence.
   a. Mary and (she, her) went early to Jesus' grave. (she)
   b. The women told Peter and (he, him) that Jesus was gone. (him)
   c. (He, Him) and John ran to Jesus' tomb. (He)
4. Three or more nouns in a row are called nouns in a ———. We put a ——— after each noun except the ——— one. (series, comma, last)
5. Tell why each comma is needed in this sentence: *Carol, please bring me a pen, an envelope, and a stamp.* (The comma after *Carol* is needed because it is the name of a person spoken to. The commas after *pen* and *envelope* are needed because they are nouns in a series.)

Class: If the pupils were to hear someone say, "They were in our garden last night," would they know what *they* means? Ask for some suggestions: some cows, rabbits, raccoons, and so forth. On the board write the nouns they suggest.

Then ask if they would know what *they* means in these sentences: "We often see two deer on our farm. They were in our garden last night." The children should recognize that *they* is referring to the deer.

Explain that when we want to say just one sentence about something, we must use a noun to name

Say: **Mother** helped Sister Ruth today.
Not: Mother *she* helped Sister Ruth today.

Say: **Paul and I** found a lizard.
Not: Paul and I *we* found a lizard.

> Sentences With Nouns and Pronouns >

A. Write the second sentence in each pair. Fill in the blanks with pronouns that stand for the nouns in bold print in the first sentence.
1. **Mark** was riding his **bicycle.**
   —— had just learned how to ride ——.
2. **Kevin** has some **rabbits.**
   —— feeds —— every day.
3. **Mother** is baking a **pie.**
   —— will serve —— for supper.
4. **Susan** helped **Amos** to bed the calves.
   Then —— helped —— feed the pigs.
5. **Carl** played with the **puppies.**
   —— was gentle with ——.
6. **Maria** found the **key.**
   —— used —— to unlock the door.
7. **Sister Barbara** read stories to the **children.**
   —— reads to —— each day after lunch.
8. The **bees** are gathering **nectar.**
   —— use —— to make honey.
9. **Father** played with the **boys.**
   —— taught —— a new game.

B. Rewrite these sentences, using a noun to tell what each pronoun stands for.
1. They found it in the barn.
2. She thanked him for it.

Lesson 44 Answers
Sentences With Nouns and Pronouns
A. 1. He had just learned how to ride it.
   2. He feeds them every day.
   3. She will serve it for supper.
   4. Then she helped him feed the pigs.
   5. He was gentle with them.
   6. She used it to unlock the door.
   7. She reads to them each day after lunch.
   8. They use it to make honey.
   9. He taught them a new game.

B. (Underlined nouns will vary.)
   1. The <u>boys</u> found a <u>calf</u> in the barn.
   2. <u>Karen</u> thanked <u>Father</u> for the <u>doll</u>.

the person or thing. When we make more than one statement about the person or thing, we can use a pronoun after we use a noun to say what or whom we are talking about. Give a few sentences following this pattern, and then ask the children to give some of their own.

Example:
   Karen and Lee are cousins. They are both in third grade.

After practice with this concept, explain that it is not correct to use a noun and a pronoun together to refer to the same person or thing. We should not say, "Paul he was sick yesterday." This is the same as saying, "Paul Paul was sick yesterday." We should just say, "Paul was sick yesterday."

★ **EXTRA PRACTICE**
Worksheet 29 (*Using Pronouns Correctly*)

> Review and Practice >

A. Write whether each of these is a **telling, asking, commanding,** or **exclaiming** sentence.
  1. You and Barbara clean the kitchen
  2. Elijah was a prophet
  3. She hoed and planted
  4. What a beautiful butterfly that is
  5. How are you feeling this morning
  6. Watch the baby

B. Copy the sentences in Part A, and add the correct end marks. In sentences 1–3, draw one line under each simple subject, and two lines under each simple predicate.

●━━●━━●━━●━━●━━●━━●━━●━━●━━◆

45. Reviewing What You Have Learned

> Written Practice >

A. Use **I** or **me** to complete each sentence. Write the correct pronoun on your paper.
  1. Laura and —— learned a poem.
  2. May John, Mark, and —— have an apple?
  3. The lamb lay down between Susan and ——.
  4. Where will Lois, Carl, and —— go?
  5. Will you help Keith and —— with the work?
  6. My friend and —— each had two cookies.

Review and Practice

A. 1. commanding
   2. telling
   3. telling
   4. exclaiming
   5. asking
   6. commanding

B. 1. <u>You</u> and <u>Barbara</u> <u>clean</u> the kitchen.
   2. <u>Elijah</u> <u>was</u> a prophet.
   3. <u>She</u> <u>hoed</u> and <u>planted</u>.
   4. What a beautiful butterfly that is!
   5. How are you feeling this morning?
   6. Watch the baby.

◆━━●━━●━━●━━●━━●━━●━━●━━●━━●

Lesson 45 Answers
Written Practice

A. 1. I
   2. I
   3. me
   4. I
   5. me
   6. I

Lesson 45

Aim: To review the previous four lessons.

Oral Review:
  1. What are two ways that commas should be used? Give an example of each. (after nouns in a series, after the name of a person spoken to; Individual answers.)
  2. When a noun and a pronoun work together, what should we do if we are not sure which pronoun to use? (Divide the sentence into two different sentences.)
  3. What are two times when pronouns should *not* be used? (when it is not clear what noun the pronoun stands for, right after a noun that names the same person or thing)

Class: Review the concepts taught by asking the questions in Oral Review. Discuss the written exercises as needed.

B. Write the correct pronouns to take the place of the nouns in bold print.
1. Father took **the boys** along to the woods.
2. Carl saw the boys and **Father** in the barn.
3. Aunt Lois and **Uncle Mark** visited us.
4. Did you ever meet Alice and **Joy**?
5. Mother took **the girls** along to town.
6. Alice and **Joy** used to live in Mexico.

C. Write the following sentences correctly. Use capital letters and commas where they are needed.
1. David you are the same age as keith paul and i.
2. Mother we will not have school during june july and august.
3. Esther i saw lois ruth and you last monday.
4. Joyce you may read new neighbors and missing popcorn.
5. Kevin went sledding with noah amos and me last winter.

D. Write two sentences to go with each picture. Do not use any pronouns in the first sentence. Use at least one pronoun in the second sentence.

1.

2.
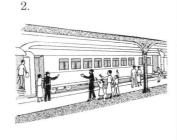

B. 1. them
   2. him
   3. he
   4. her
   5. them
   6. she

C. (Corrected items are underlined.)
1. David, you are the same age as Keith, Pau
   and I.
2. Mother, we will not have school during Jun
   July, and August.
3. Esther, I saw Lois, Ruth, and you last Monda
4. Joyce, you may read New Neighbors and Miss
   ing Popcorn.
5. Kevin went sledding with Noah, Amos, an
   me last winter.

D. (Individual answers.)

> **Can You Do This?**

The person who wrote the following paragraph made many mistakes. Can you write it correctly?

James seth and I we like to read. Father he gave us a new book last friday. It is called pedro. Pedro lives in guatemala. His parents and him learn about Jesus. My brothers and me will let you borrow the book. You may share it with sarah and martha and lois and glenn.

●━●━●━●━●━●━●━●

46. Pronouns That Tell *Whose*

Sometimes we use the possessive form of a noun to tell **whose** something is.

This book is **John's.**   That doll is **Karen's.**

In the first sentence above, **John's** means **John's book.** In the second sentence, **Karen's** means **Karen's doll.**

In the following sentences, possessive pronouns take the place of **John's book** and **Karen's doll.** These pronouns tell **whose** in the same way as the words they stand for.

This book is **his.**   That doll is **hers.**

Here are some more sentences with possessive pronouns. All these pronouns tell **whose.**

The green pencil is **mine.**
I think this pen is **yours.**
That yellow house is **ours.**
The new Bible is **his.**

Can You Do This?
(Corrected items are underlined.)

James, Seth, and I like to read. Father gave us a new book last Friday. It is called Pedro. Pedro lives in Guatemala. His parents and he learn about Jesus. My brothers and I will let you borrow the book. You may share it with Sarah, Martha, Lois, and Glenn.

────────────

Lesson 46

Aim: To introduce the personal possessive pronouns.

Oral Review:
1. What is a quotation? How should we write the first word of a quotation? (the exact words of a speaker; Capitalize the first word.)
2. Tell where commas are needed in these sentences.
   a. Dennis these books are for you Carl and Susan. (after *Dennis, you,* and *Carl*)
   b. Father school will be closed next Monday Tuesday and Wednesday. (after *Father, Monday,* and *Tuesday*)
   c. Keith was playing with Robert Samuel and me. (after *Robert* and *Samuel*)
3. Use a (noun, pronoun) if you write just one sentence about a person or thing. After that you may use a ——. (noun; pronoun)
4. What is wrong with this sentence? *Paul he was*

hurt in an accident. (We should not use a pronoun right after the noun it stands for.)

Class: Ask someone to tell what a pronoun does. (It takes the place of a noun.) So far the pupils have worked with pronouns that answer the questions *who, whom,* and *what.* Write these three question on the board. Explain that the pronouns they will work with in today's lesson answer another question: *whose.*

Use the first two example sentences in the lesson to show how possessive pronouns take the place of all the words in a possessive phrase. Illustrate as follows.

This book is John's.
= This book is John's book.
= This book is his.

Then point to your shoes and ask, "Whose shoes are these?" The class will probably respond: *yours.*

You have learned that the possessive form of a noun should end with **'s.** But **'s** is **not** used with any possessive pronouns. **Yours, hers, ours,** and **theirs** just end with **s.**

Wrong: This sweater must her's.
Right: This sweater must be hers.

Remember: Possessive pronouns tell **whose.** The words **mine, yours, his, hers, ours,** and **theirs** are possessive pronouns.

> Using Pronouns to Tell *Whose*

A. Write the correct pronoun to complete each sentence.
1. The book that belongs to me is ——.
2. The coat that belongs to him is ——.
3. The shoes that belong to her are ——.
4. The caps that belong to them are ——.
5. The paper that belongs to you is ——.
6. The pens that belong to us are ——.

B. Write a possessive pronoun for each blank. It should stand for the phrase in bold print.
1. These boots are **Jerry's boots.** They are ——.
2. That car is **the Masts' car.** It is ——.
3. Please give me **my pencil.** It is ——.
4. **Sister Martha's coat** is black. —— is black.
5. Is **your coat** blue? Is —— blue?

C. Write each sentence correctly.
1. This shoe is her's.
2. Was your's lost?
3. The blue book is our's.
4. Their's is the red one.

Lesson 46 Answers
Using Pronouns to Tell *Whose*
A. 1. mine
   2. his
   3. hers
   4. theirs
   5. yours
   6. ours

B. 1. his
   2. theirs
   3. mine
   4. Hers
   5. yours

C. 1. This shoe is hers.
   2. Was yours lost?
   3. The blue book is ours.
   4. Theirs is the red one.

★ **EXTRA PRACTICE**
Worksheet 30 (*Possessive Pronouns*)

Write this pronoun on the board. Ask one of your pupils, as you point to his shoes, "Whose shoes are those?" He should answer: *mine.* Work with the class in listing the other possessive pronouns: his, hers, ours, theirs. You might ask questions such as these: Whose room is this? Whose books are those? Whose house is out there?

Stress the fact that *-'s* is used to form possessive nouns but not possessive pronouns. Possessive pronouns end with just *-s*—never with *-'s.* (We do use *-'s* with pronouns to form contractions—*he's* for *he is, she's* for *she is,* and *it's* for *it is.* But this need not be mentioned at this point.)

There are actually two groups of pronouns that tell *whose;* the other group is *my, your, his, her, its, our,* and *their.* But these pronouns function as adjectives that modify nouns. Therefore, they are taught in Unit 4 with other adjectives. *Its* is not included in this lesson because this word seldom stands alone as a pronoun.

> Review and Practice >

Write the correct spelling to be used in each sentence. Use a dictionary if you need help.

1. Please hand me the (scissors, sissors, scisors).
2. The (soldeirs, soldiers, solders) crucified Jesus.
3. I visited my aunt in the (hospital, hospittal, hospitel).
4. There will be no school (tommorrow, tommorow, tomorrow).
5. These (banannas, bananas, bannanas) are not ripe.
6. I copied the cake (receipt, recipe, receipe) for Aunt Mary.
7. (Febrary, Febuary, February) is a short month.
8. Beth (received, recieved, reieved) an invitation to the wedding.

●━━●━━●━━●━━●━━●━━●

47. Pronouns for People and Things

You have learned that pronouns take the place of nouns. When you use a pronoun, you must choose the right one for the noun it replaces. You must also choose the right one for the way it is used in the sentence.

I, me, and **mine** are three pronouns that you can use instead of your own name when you talk about yourself. Read how Lee used these pronouns.

Lee said, "That new book is **mine. I** read it last week after Father gave it to **me.**"

We use one set of pronouns to talk about one other person or thing, and another set to talk about more than one person

Review and Practice

1. scissors
2. soldiers
3. hospital
4. tomorrow
5. bananas
6. recipe
7. February
8. received

5. How are possessive nouns and possessive pronouns spelled differently? (Possessive nouns end with *-'s.* Possessive pronouns end with *-s.*)

Class: Review the concepts presented in the first paragraph. Emphasize that pronouns must be chosen according to the nouns they replace, and according to the way they are used in a sentence. Illustrate with the following example.

Laura is my sister. <u>She</u> is in first grade.

Point out that we do not say *He* or *It,* because Laura is a girl. We do not say *They,* because we are talking about only one person. We do not say *Her,* because the pronoun is the subject of the sentence.

Read the second paragraph together, then read and discuss the paragraph about Lee.

Go on to the next paragraph and ask the question it contains. The answer is the third person pronouns: singular—*he, him, his, she, her, hers, it;* plural—*they,*

Lesson 47

Aim: (1) To give a general summary of personal pronouns before a new kind of pronoun is presented in the next lesson. (2) To introduce three of the second person singular pronouns with which the children are probably familiar through Bible reading.

Oral Review:

1. What is the subject in this sentence: *Did Sarah laugh?* (Sarah)
2. If a sentence has three or more nouns in a series, use a —— after each noun except the —— one. (comma, last)
3. What are two times that you should *not* use a pronoun? (when it is not clear what noun the pronoun stands for, and right after the noun that the pronoun stands for)
4. Give some pronouns that tell *whose.* (mine, yours, his, hers, ours, theirs)

or thing. Do you know what these pronouns are?

You and **yours** are two pronouns that stand for the name of a person to whom we are talking. We use these pronouns whether we are talking to one person or more than one person.

In the Bible, different pronouns are used when the speaker is talking to only one person. Three of them are **thou, thee,** and **thine.** Here is a verse that uses these three pronouns.

> And Samuel said unto him, The Lord hath rent the kingdom of Israel from **thee** this day, and hath given it to a neighbour of **thine,** that is better than **thou.**

1 Samuel 15:28

Using Pronouns Correctly

A. Rewrite each sentence, using pronouns to take the place of the words in parentheses.
   1. Mother said, "(Mother) think this pan is (Mother's) because it looks like the one (Mother) bought last week."
   2. The teacher told the children, "(Children) may each choose a pencil as (children's). (Teacher) will put names on the pencils so that (children) know which one is (children's)."
   3. Jane said, "This ruler is (Jane's), but (Jane) will let someone else use (ruler). Please give (ruler) back to (Jane) when you are finished with (ruler)."

Lesson 47 Answers
Using Pronouns Correctly
A. 1. Mother said, "I think this pan is mine becaus it looks like the one I bought last week."
   2. The teacher told the children, "You may eac choose a pencil as yours. I will put names o the pencils so that you know which one i yours."
   3. Jane said, "This ruler is mine, but I will le someone else use it. Please give it back to m when you are finished with it."

them, theirs. You could give drill on most of these by having one pupil read the paragraph about Lee, using different pronouns and pretending that Lee is talking about his brother. Another pupil could change the pronouns a second time, pretending that Lee is talking about his sister; and then a third pupil could change the pronouns again, pretending that Lee is talking about his cousins.

Discuss briefly the second person pronouns, and then the archaic pronouns introduced in the paragraph following. Do not spend much time with the latter; they are mentioned primarily to teach the children that these words are pronouns. The pronoun *thy* is not included because it functions as an adjective.

4. Charles said, "The neighbors helped (my family) pick our strawberries. Then (my family) helped (neighbors) pick (neighbors' strawberries)."

B. Write **thou, thee,** or **thine** for each blank.
   1. Jesus said, "Neither do I condemn ———."
   2. The father said, "Son, ——— art ever with me, and all that I have is ———."

Review and Practice

Diagram the simple subjects and simple predicates of these sentences.
   1. The angel shut the lions' mouth.
   2. Is William sick?
   3. Pull weeds.
   4. Pots and pans clattered.
   5. Ministers preached and taught.

48. Pronouns That Tell *Which One*

This, that, these, and **those** are four more pronouns. They are used to tell **which one** or **which ones.** In these sentences, the arrows point to the nouns that these pronouns stand for.

This is a good cookie.   **These** are good cookies.

Use **this** or **these** when talking about something nearby.

---

4. Charles said, "The neighbors helped us pick our strawberries. Then we helped them pick theirs."

B. 1. thee
   2. thou, thine

Review and Practice

1. angel | shut

2. William | is

3. (you) | Pull

4. Pots
   and
   pans | clattered

5. Ministers | and
   preached
   taught

Lesson 48

Aim: To introduce the four demonstrative pronouns.

Oral Review:
   1. What replaces the missing letter or letters in a contraction? (an apostrophe)
   2. If a sentence begins with the name of a person spoken to, what punctuation should come after the name? (a comma)
   3. Give the three pronouns that you can use instead of your own name. Give the two that stand for the name of a person spoken to. (I, me, mine; you, yours)
   4. Give possessive pronouns to replace these: *Andrew's, people's, my family's, Sharon's.* (his, theirs, ours, hers)
   5. Give the pronouns that we use instead of these: *thou, thee, thine.* (you, you, yours)

Class: Write the word *which* on the board. Tell the class that this is another question answered by some pronouns. We ask questions such as: Which book is yours? Which cookies did Sharon bake?

Write *this, that, these,* and *those* on the board. Tell the class that these pronouns tell *which one* or *which ones.* Illustrate with the first two example sentences in the lesson.

Point out that these pronouns take the place of two words, the same as possessive pronouns do. *This* means *this cookie* (first sentence) in the same way that *mine* may mean *my shoes.* (The four demonstrative pronouns are adjectives when they come before the noun they refer to. This usage is taught in Unit 4.)

Ask the class which two of these pronouns we use when talking about something close by, and which two we use when talking about something farther away. Ask which two pronouns we use when talking about only one thing, and which two we use when

This is an old tree.

These are old trees.

Use **that** or **those** when talking about something farther away.

That is an old book.

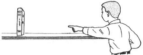

Those are old books.

Use **this** or **that** when talking about only one person or thing. Use **these** or **those** when talking about more than one person or thing.

These are the older kittens.
Those are my brothers.

Remember: This, that, these, and **those** are pronouns that tell which one or which ones.

---

talking about more than one thing. You can then give a short oral exercise, having the class tell which pronoun to use when talking about

    a. one boy nearby.
    b. two cows out in the field.
    c. several cookies on a plate you are holding.
    d. one apple tree in the distance.

Think of other examples and give as much practice as necessary.

To expand the written assignment for those children who finish quickly, ask them to try writing all the pronouns they have learned about so far this year. Remind them not to forget the three that are used in the Bible.

> Using *This, That, These, and Those*

A. Use **this, that, these,** or **those** to complete each sentence. The word in parentheses tells whether the noun names something nearby or farther away.

1. (nearby) —— is our church building.
2. (farther) —— is our deacon.
3. (farther) —— are my friends.
4. Is (nearby) —— the book you use?
5. (nearby) —— are the verses we learned.
6. (nearby) —— are our songbooks.
7. (farther) —— is today's verse.
8. Are (farther) —— the stairs to the basement?

B. The children in the picture are talking. Complete their sentences by using **this, that, these,** or **those** in the first blank, and a noun from the picture in the second blank.

1. —— are high ——.
2. —— is a friendly ——.
3. —— are sweet-smelling ——.

> Review and Practice

Copy the three nouns in each sentence. After each noun write **C** or **P** to tell whether the noun is common or proper.

1. School is closed during June and July.
2. Martha planted tomatoes and peppers.
3. Susan helped her aunt and uncle.
4. Brian and Edward used the tiller.
5. My sister likes spring and summer best.

●━━━━━━━━━●

Lesson 48 Answers
Using *This, That, These,* and *Those*

A. 1. This
   2. That
   3. Those
   4. this
   5. These
   6. These
   7. That
   8. those

B. (Possible answers.)
   1. Those are high mountains.
   2. This is a friendly dog.
   3. These are sweet-smelling flowers.

Review and Practice
   1. school—C, June—P, July—P
   2. Martha—P, tomatoes—C, peppers—C
   3. Susan—P, aunt—C, uncle—C
   4. Brian—P, Edward—P, tiller—C
   5. sister—C, spring—C, summer—C

49. Using *This, That, These,* and *Those*

Do you know what a habit is? It is something we do over and over again without really thinking about it. Some habits are good and some are poor. Perhaps we have some poor language habits. Then we must work hard to break the poor habits and put good habits in their place.

Here are some rules for using **this, that, these,** and **those.** The rules can help you break some poor habits you might have in using these words.

1. Do not say **this here, these here, that there,** or **those there. This** means "the one right here." **That** means "the one over there."

This is an interesting book.

That is a gentle horse.

2. Do not use **them** as a subject. Use **those, these,** or **they.**

   Wrong: **Them** are my friends.
   Right: **Those** are my friends.
   Right: **They** are my friends.

> Using Pronouns Correctly

A. Find the mistakes in the sentences below. Rewrite each sentence correctly.
   1. Them are good apples.
   2. That there is Uncle Carl's truck.

Lesson 49 Answers
Using Pronouns Correctly

A. 1. Those (They, These) are good apples.
   2. That is Uncle Carl's truck.

Lesson 49

Aim: To teach the incorrectness of some common misuses of demonstrative pronouns.

Oral Review:
1. Words that stand for nouns are ———. (pronouns)
2. Find the mistakes in these sentences.
   a. They lived for hundreds of years. (There is no noun to tell what *They* stands for.)
   b. Adam he lived 930 years. (It is not correct to use a pronoun right after the noun it stands for.)
   c. This is your's and that is her's. (Possessive pronouns do not need apostrophes.)
3. Give the pronouns that tell *whose.* (mine, yours, his, hers, ours, theirs)
4. The words *this, that, these,* and *those* are pronouns that tell ———. (which one or ones)

Class: Tell the class that years ago there were n● rules to say how words should be spelled. The sam● word was spelled in several different ways. This wa● confusing. Finally certain spellings became known a● the correct ones, and it was expected that everyon● learn these correct spellings.

We would think it strange to have a languag● where words do not have to be spelled a certain way● But some people seem to forget that words shoul● also be used a certain way. When God made th● world, He caused everything to work together in a● orderly way. The words in a language should wor● together in an orderly way too. We must try to follo● the rules that help our language to be as tidy an● orderly as we like our clothes and homes to be.

Discuss the rules in today's lesson. Your respon● sibility in teaching this lesson does not end with● correcting the written assignment. For many o● your pupils, it is likely that poor speech habits hav●

3. This here is my coat.
4. Are them the chickens you bought?
5. That there is the shelf for the jars.
6. Is this here a book you have read?
7. Redwood trees get much taller than any of these here.
8. Our fields were brown, but those there were green.

B. Write the pronouns you would use in each blank. Use **this, that, these,** and **those.**
   1. John was holding a rabbit. "——— is my pet," he said.
   2. "——— is his home," he said as he pointed to a cage across the lawn.
   3. "Would he like to eat ———?" Mary asked, holding out some lettuce leaves.
   4. "Yes, he likes to eat ———," John said.

C. Write six sentences. Follow these directions.
   1–4. Use **this, that, these,** and **those** correctly.
   5, 6. Use **they** and **them** correctly.

> Can You Do This?

Write the pronouns **thou, thee,** and **thine.** Find each pronoun in your Bible. When you find a verse that has one of the pronouns in it, write the reference beside the pronoun on your paper.

●-●-●-●-●-●-●-●-●-●

3. This is my coat.
4. Are those (they, these) the chickens you bought?
5. That is the shelf for the jars.
6. Is this a book you have read?
7. Redwood trees get much taller than any of these.
8. Our fields were brown, but those were green.

B. 1. This
   2. That
   3. these
   4. those

C. (Individual answers. Accept sentences in which the demonstrative pronouns are used as adjectives, as in "This apple is good.")

Can You Do This?
(Individual answers. Encourage children with extra time to do this exercise.)

lready been formed. Enlist means of trying to correct hese habits throughout the year. Talking with experinced teachers should provide you with several workble methods.

EXTRA PRACTICE
Worksheet 31 (*Correcting Poor Speech Habits*)

50. Reviewing What You Have Learned

A. Write all the pronouns you find in the sentences below. Each sentence is a line from a song. Do you know the songs the sentences are taken from?

1. Jesus loves me, this I know.
2. This is my Father's world.
3. Abide with me, I need Thee every day, to lead me safe through all the weary way.
4. Break Thou the bread of life, dear Lord, to me.
5. Were the whole realm of nature mine, that were a present far too small.
6. These, great God, to Thee we owe, source whence all our blessings flow.
7. Christ our God, to Thee we raise this our hymn of grateful praise.
8. My Jesus, I love Thee, I know Thou art mine.
9. This is the day the Lord hath made, He calls the hours His own.
10. We are Thine, do Thou befriend us.

You should have found thirty pronouns. Did you?

B. Write a pronoun that tells **whose** to complete each sentence. The pronoun should stand for the noun or nouns in bold print.

1. "We finished the job that was ———," said **Kathy and Susan.**
2. "Which job is ———?" asked **Robert.**
3. "——— is cleaning the boots," Mother told **Robert.**
4. **Robert** cleaned the boots that were ———.
5. Little **Lena** brought ——— for Robert to clean.
6. "Where are ———?" Robert asked the **girls.**
7. "——— are already clean," the **girls** told Robert.
8. The **girls** had cleaned ——— earlier.

Lesson 50

Aim: To review the previous four lessons.

Written Quiz:

1. When we begin a sentence with the name of the person being talked to, we put a ——— after the person's name.
2. What three pronouns can you use instead of your own name?
3. What two pronouns can take the place of the person's name to whom you are talking?
4. **This, that, these,** and **those** are pronouns that tell what?
5. Write this sentence, correcting the four mistakes: **This here is your's and that there is her's.**

Quiz Answers

1. comma
2. I, me, mine (Also accept *my.*)

Lesson 50 Answers

A. (Possessive pronouns used as adjectives a[re] acceptable for some answers. Song titles are giv[en] in parentheses.)

1. me, this, I (*Jesus Loves Me*)
2. This (*This Is My Father's World*)
3. me, I, Thee, me (*Abide With Me*)
4. Thou, me (*Break Thou the Bread of Life*)
5. mine, that (*When I Survey the Wondro[us] Cross*)
6. These, Thee, we (*Praise to God, Immort[al] Praise*)
7. Thee, we, this (*For the Beauty of the Earth*)
8. I, Thee, I, Thou, mine (*My Jesus, I Love The[e]*)
9. This, He, His (*This Is the Day the Lord Ha[th] Made*)
10. We, Thine, Thou, us (*Saviour, Like a She[p]herd Lead Us*)

B. 1. ours
2. mine
3. Yours
4. his
5. hers
6. yours
7. Ours
8. theirs

3. you, yours (Also accept *your.*)
4. which one (or ones)
5. This is yours and that is hers.

Class: Ask the class to name some pronouns tha[t] have been studied. Remind them of the three use[s] in the Bible. List the pronouns on the board as the[y] are given.

C. Write each sentence correctly.
   1. Those there were picked this morning.
   2. Them are the tools he brought.
   3. Is this here the book you wanted?
   4. The car is their's and the truck is our's.

D. Write a sentence for each pronoun below. You may want to write about something in the picture.
   1. these   2. those   3. this   4. that

C. 1. Those were picked this morning.
   2. Those (They, These) are the tools he brought.
   3. Is this the book you wanted?
   4. The car is theirs and the truck is ours.

D. (Individual answers. Accept sentences with pronouns used as adjectives.)

Review One

> Oral Drill

A. Answer these questions.
   1. What is a noun?
   2. What is the difference between a proper and a common noun?
   3. What work does a pronoun do in a sentence?
   4. How can you know which pronoun to use when you use both a noun and a pronoun in a sentence?

Review One Answers
Oral Drill

A. 1. A noun is the name of a person, place, or thing.
   2. A proper noun is the name of a specific person, place, or thing, and it begins with a capital letter. A common noun is not a specific name, and it does not begin with a capital letter.
   3. A pronoun takes the place of a noun.
   4. Divide the sentence into two sentences, and think which pronoun you would use then.

Review One

Aim: To review and strengthen concepts taught in previous lessons in preparation for a test.

Class: Do the Oral Drill in class. Watch for areas in which extra practice may be needed. Scan the written assignment to give opportunity for pupils' questions.

B. Tell whether each of these pronouns is singular or plural.

it	they	his	me
mine	hers	she	them
you	ours	him	us

C. Read these sentences, putting in pronouns where they belong.
1. John said, "The blue lunch box is John's."
2. "Those books belong to the twins," said the twins.
3. Jesus healed the sick people when the sick people came to Jesus.
4. Mary told Mother, "Mary brought these for Mother."

D. Give answers to the following.
1. What are two rules for using commas that you have learned?
2. Say where the commas belong in these sentences.
   a. Roy you may pass out the songbooks.
   b. Isaiah Jeremiah and Ezekiel were prophets.
   c. Jesus healed the lepers the crippled and the blind.
   d. Joanna please pick up the toys.
   e. Yesterday Lee Samuel and I went fishing.
   f. The farmer raises oats corn rye and hay.
   g. She Mother and Katie went to town.

> Written Practice >

A. Copy the three nouns in each sentence.
1. Jesus spoke about the lilies and the birds.
2. The Bible tells us that God created the world.
3. Beans and corn were growing in the garden.

B. it—singular, his—singular
   mine—singular, she—singular
   you—singular *or* plural, him—singular
   they—plural, me—singular
   hers—singular, them—plural
   ours—plural, us—plural

C. 1. John said, "The blue lunch box is mine."
2. "Those books belong to us," said the twins.
3. Jesus healed the sick people when they came to Him.
4. Mary told Mother, "I brought these for you."

D. 1. Use a comma after the name of a person you are speaking to.
   Use a comma after each noun or pronoun in series, except the last one.
2. a. Roy, you may pass out the songbooks.
   b. Isaiah, Jeremiah, and Ezekiel were prophets.
   c. Jesus healed the lepers, the crippled, and the blind.
   d. Joanna, please pick up the toys.
   e. Yesterday Lee, Samuel, and I went fishing.
   f. The farmer raises oats, corn, rye, and hay.
   g. She, Mother, and Katie went to town.

Written Practice

A. 1. Jesus, lilies, birds
   2. Bible, God, world
   3. Beans, corn, garden

B. Find the proper nouns in these sentences, and write them correctly.
   1. I got a letter from aunt sarah who lives in lancaster, pennsylvania.
   2. We will try to paint the fence on tuesday, before we get busy with our summer work.
   3. Mother forgot that vera's and joyce's birthdays are both in july.
   4. We got a horse named star from uncle albert.
   5. The people in the car asked the way to maple view church last sunday morning.
   6. We could not find doctor brown's office right away because he had moved to the riverside building.
   7. Last winter our family read trouble at windy acres.

C. Write the plural form of each word.
   1. toy   4. deer   7. fork   10. dish
   2. mouse   5. pear   8. sheep   11. tooth
   3. chair   6. fly   9. pony   12. church

D. Write **a** or **b** to tell which phrase is written correctly.
   1. a. the dogs collar
      b. the dog's collar
   2. a. the dolls on the shelf
      b. the doll's on the shelf
   3. a. two red apples
      b. two red apple's
   4. a. the carpenters hammer
      b. the carpenter's hammer
   5. a. his sharp pencils
      b. his sharp pencil's

B. 1. Aunt Sarah, Lancaster, Pennsylvania
   2. Tuesday
   3. Vera's, Joyce's, July
   4. Star, Uncle Albert
   5. Maple View Church, Sunday
   6. Doctor Brown's, Riverside Building
   7. Trouble at Windy Acres

C. 1. toys   7. forks
   2. mice   8. sheep
   3. chairs   9. ponies
   4. deer   10. dishes
   5. pears   11. teeth
   6. flies   12. churches

D. 1. b
   2. a
   3. a
   4. b
   5. a

Review Two

>Oral Drill>

A. Choose the correct pronoun for each sentence, and say why you made that choice.
1. Uncle Levi gave the puppy to (he, him).
2. (This, These) are sweet cherries.
3. (She, Her) was on a ladder cleaning windows.
4. Since Carl was sick, we sang some songs for (him, he).
5. Baby Rhoda walked across the floor to (I, me).
6. When our neighbors helped us, we thanked (they, them).
7. Fannie's handwriting looks like (yours, your's).
8. Is (this, that) a star or a planet?
9. When Aunt Rachel was sick, Mother wrote a letter to (she, her).
10. The dish with flowers on it is (their's, theirs).

B. Say what is wrong with each sentence.
1. They made a noise like owls.
2. That there is a maple tree.
3. It made a bright flash.
4. This here is good water.
5. The boys they worked hard.
6. Them are big snowflakes.
7. Mother she said we may each have an apple.
8. I didn't find Jason and he.
9. They make nice gifts.
10. Them are sweet, juicy peaches.
11. Have you and her finished the dishes?
12. This here is a store that sells hats.

Review Two Answers
Oral Drill
A. (Reasons are given in parentheses.)
1. him (follows *to;* tells *whom*)
2. These (*cherries* is plural)
3. She (tells *who*)
4. him (follows *for;* tells *whom*)
5. me (follows *to;* tells *whom*)
6. them (tells *whom*)
7. yours (no apostrophe in possessive pronoun)
8. that (refers to something distant)
9. her (follows *to;* tells *whom*)
10. theirs (no apostrophe in possessive pronoun)

B. 1. It is not clear what made a noise like owls.
2. *There* should be omitted.
3. It is not clear what made a bright flash.
4. *Here* should be omitted.
5. *They* should be omitted.
6. *Them* should be replaced by *these, those,* or *they.*
7. *She* should be omitted.
8. *He* should be replaced by *him.*
9. It is not clear what things make nice gifts.
10. *Them* should be replaced by *these, those,* or *they.*
11. *Her* should be replaced by *she.*
12. *Here* should be omitted.

Review Two

Aim: To review and strengthen concepts taught in previous lessons in preparation for a test.

Class: Proceed as in the previous review.

> Written Practice >

A. For each blank write a pronoun that tells **whose.**
1. My book is ———.
2. Their furniture is ———.
3. Our playground is ———.
4. The toys that belong to them are ———.
5. The Bible that belongs to you is ———.
6. The lunch box that belongs to her is ———.
7. The songbook that belongs to him is ———.
8. The cap that belongs to me is ———.

B. Write a pronoun that tells **which** for each blank.
1. (nearby) ——— is a collie.
2. (farther) ——— are the Rocky Mountains.
3. (farther) ——— looks like a pileated woodpecker.
4. (nearby) ——— are blackberry bushes.
5. (nearby) ——— is a hummingbird's nest.
6. (farther) ——— is the Ohio River.
7. (nearby) ——— are feathers from a goldfinch.
8. (farther) ——— are geese.

Written Practice
A. 1. mine
   2. theirs
   3. ours
   4. theirs
   5. yours
   6. hers
   7. his
   8. mine

B. 1. This
   2. Those
   3. That
   4. These
   5. This
   6. That
   7. These
   8. Those

Extra Activity

Your teacher will help you make a little booklet of fifteen pages. Call your booklet **Building Blocks of English.** Collect pictures for the first pages to illustrate nouns.

You may put pictures of people on the first three pages. Write a name under each picture, such as **Arthur, Mother, baby, girl,** or **man.**

Collect pictures of places for the next three pages, and label the names of the places, such as **city, farm, school,** and **home.**

For the last three pages in the noun section, find pictures of things and label them.

Under the names of people, places, and things, write pronouns that could stand for the names.

The last part of the booklet will be completed at the end of Unit 3.

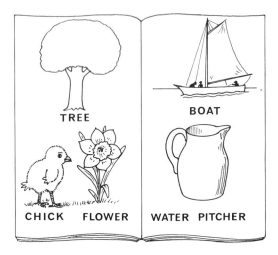

Extra Activity

Aim: To provide a creative way for additional practice in recognizing nouns.

Class: This activity is optional, but it provides faster pupils with a worthwhile spare-time project. You may wish to make a sample booklet to show to the class. Be sure that those pupils who start the project also complete it. Screen the books from which the children will cut their pictures.

The last half of the booklet will be completed at the end of Unit 3.

A Poem to Enjoy

A Child's Prayer

God, make my life a little light,
　　Within the world to glow;
A little flame that burneth bright
　　Wherever I may go.

God, make my life a little flower
　　That giveth joy to all;
Content to bloom in native bower
　　Although its place be small.

God, make my life a little song
　　That comforteth the sad;
That helpeth others to be strong,
　　And makes the singer glad.
　　　　　—*M. Betham-Edwards*

Discussing the Poem

1. The first line of each stanza in the poem follows an English rule that you learned in this unit. What is it?
2. How can your life be a little light?
3. Discuss with your teacher the meaning of **native bower** in the second stanza.
4. How can a little song help others to be strong?
5. Who is the singer in the last line of the last stanza?

Answers to Discussion Questions

1. A comma is used after the name of the person spoken to. *or* Capitalize proper nouns.
2. If you live right, your life will show other people how to live. It will also cheer and encourage others.
3. A bower is a shelter of leafy branches, often with flowers among them. "Content to bloom in native bower" means "content to be my best wherever I find myself."
4. A little song can encourage others to keep on when they may be tempted to give up.
5. The singer is the child of the title (*A Child's Prayer*).

Poem to Enjoy

Aim: To teach inspirational poetry, to teach rhyme, and to teach proper reading of poetry.

Class: Discuss the meaning of the poem, using the questions in the textbook as well as any other thoughts you or the pupils might have. Discuss little ways in which it is possible to brighten someone's day.

Read the poem with proper expression. Ask several pupils to do the same. Memorization is optional. This can be used as another spare-time project for faster pupils. It may also be used for penmanship practice.

Unit 3

Building Blocks or Blocking Blocks

With blocks before the wagon's wheels,
  It's hard to make it go.
And blocks within a person's mind
  Make learning very slow.

The words "I can't" are like a block
  Inside your little head.
They will not let you understand
  The things that you have read.

Use building blocks, "I think I can,
  For God is helping me."
Then work with eagerness and joy,
  And wonders you will see.

Building With Verbs

51. Action Verbs

My kitten **follows** me everywhere.
The children **sang** a new song.

The first sentence above tells about the kitten. Which word in the sentence tells what the kitten **does**? Which word in the second sentence tells what the children **did**?

The words **follows** and **sang** are **action verbs.** Action verbs tell what action someone or something **does** or **did.**

Mice **nibble.** Turnips **grow.**
Puppies **wiggle.** Rivers **flow.**
Babies **sleep.** Parents **pray.**
Children laugh, work, learn, and play!

Remember: Action verbs are words that tell what action a person or thing **does** or **did.**

> Finding Action Verbs >

Write the action verbs you find in the following sentences.
1. Jesus spoke.
2. The people listened.
3. The children came to Jesus.
4. Jesus healed many sick people.
5. One leper thanked Jesus.
6. Zacchaeus climbed a tree.
7. The Lord called to Zacchaeus.
8. The man gave money to the poor.
9. Jesus walked through the town.
10. His disciples followed.
11. James and John mended their nets.

Lesson 51 Answers
Finding Action Verbs
1. spoke
2. listened
3. came
4. healed
5. thanked
6. climbed
7. called
8. gave
9. walked
10. followed
11. mended

Lesson 51

Aim: To introduce action verbs.

Oral Review:
1. The sentence part that tells *who* or *what* is the ———. (subject)
2. Give three pronouns that you can use instead of your own name. (I, me, mine)
3. Give two pronouns that tell *whose.* (any two: mine, yours, his, hers, ours, theirs)
4. Give the pronouns that tell *which one* or *which ones.* (this, that, these, those)
5. What is wrong with each sentence?
   a. That there is my brother. (*There* should be left out.)
   b. Them are roses. (*Them* should not be used as a subject. Use *they, these,* or *those.*)

Class: Write a noun such as *kittens* on the board. Ask

the class to say some things that kittens do—fo example, purr, play, climb, scratch. Write the word they say on the board. Tell them that all these actio words are verbs.

Write the word *children* on the board, and ask fo some verbs that tell what children do. Write thes verbs on the board.

Read together the little rhyme in today's lessor Ask the pupils to give the nouns in it. Then ask ther to say what verb goes with each noun.

Explain the written assignment. You might war to do two or three sentences together in class.

★ **EXTRA PRACTICE**
Worksheet 32 (*Action Verbs*)

12. Jesus wept.
13. Today people read the Bible.
14. Our ministers preach the truth.
15. We sing songs about God.
16. We thank God for His many gifts.

> Using Verbs >

The pictures below show what the children did on Saturday. Give each child in the pictures a name. Then write a sentence to tell what each child did. Underline the verbs you use. You should have five sentences.

12. wept
13. read
14. preach
15. sing
16. thank

Using Verbs
(Sentences should follow this pattern. If helping verbs are used, it is acceptable to underline only the main verb.)

Thomas <u>mowed</u> the lawn.
Sarah <u>was sweeping</u> the porch.

> Review and Practice

Copy each sentence. Add quotation marks and capital letters where they are needed, and use the correct end marks.

1. the purple flowers are violets, said Mother
2. ralph exclaimed, look at the large arrowhead I found
3. would you like to play outside today asked Brother John
4. the zookeeper said, please do not feed the animals

●━●━●━●━●━●━●

52. More About Action Verbs

Verbs are important words. Every complete sentence has a verb. Sometimes the verb is the last word in the sentence. Sometimes the verb is in the middle of the sentence. In a request or command, the verb might be the first word in the sentence. Sometimes the verb might be the only word in the sentence!

> Ruth **sings.**   The dog **ran** outside.
> **Sing** softly, children.   **Run!**

Many action verbs show actions we can easily see or hear.

> Carl **feeds** the lamb.
>
> The thunder **rumbled.**

Some action verbs tell about actions we cannot easily see or hear.

> We **believe** in God.   Jay **likes** the puppy.

Review and Practice
(Corrected items are underlined.)

1. "The purple flowers are violets," said Mother
2. Ralph exclaimed, "Look at the large arrow head I found!"
3. "Would you like to play outside today?" asked Brother John.
4. The zookeeper said, "Please do not feed the animals."

Lesson 52

Aim: To review action verbs, and to present action verbs that do not show physical action.

Oral Review:

1. A telling sentence ends with a ———. Give an example. (period; Individual examples.)
2. Say two pronouns that stand for the name of the person to whom you are talking. (you, yours)
3. Give the pronouns that we use instead of *thou,* *thee,* and *thine.* (you, you, yours)
4. What is wrong with these sentences?
   a. This here is the pen I brought. (*Here* should be left out.)
   b. That there is a good cake. (*There* should be left out.)
   c. Them are the men I saw. (*Them* should not be used as a subject.)
5. Words that show action are called ———. (verbs)

Class: Explain that every complete sentence has a verb. Then read the first paragraph of the lesson in class, and write on the board the four sentences after it. As you write each sentence, have the class say which word is the verb.

When all four sentences are written, ask the children *where* the verb is found in each sentence. Emphasize that the verb can be almost anywhere in a sentence. It might even be the only word. This explanation should help to prevent the mistake of choosing the second or the last word in a sentence and calling it a verb.

To teach verbs that express mental action, tell the children that some verbs show action we cannot see or hear. Discuss the sample sentences in the lesson and give several more examples.

> Job trusted in God.
> God knows all things.

Believe and **like** are action verbs. They tell about actions that our hearts and minds do. Here are some more heart-and-mind action verbs.

trust   love   think

Can you think of any more?

> Recognizing Action Verbs >

Copy the verb in each sentence.
1. Abraham trusted God.
2. Lot wanted the best land.
3. Paul worshiped God.
4. We respect our ministers and teachers.
5. Children honor their parents.
6. The people enjoyed the special meetings.
7. Kathy likes her Sunday school lessons.
8. Father believes the promises in the Bible.
9. Praise God for all things.
10. Remember the truths of God's Word.

> Using Verbs >

Use verbs to complete the poem below. Copy the poem neatly.

God made the sun that __1__ up high.
He __2__ the birds that __3__ and __4__ ,
The bees that __5__ , the wind that __6__ ,
And every little plant that __7__ .

Then God __8__ us and __9__ us eyes
That we might __10__ the earth and skies.
So let us __11__ the God above,
Who fashioned all the world in love.

Lesson 52 Answers
Recognizing Action Verbs
1. trusted
2. wanted
3. worshiped
4. respect
5. honor
6. enjoyed
7. likes
8. believes
9. Praise
10. Remember

Using Verbs
(Possible answers.)

1. shines	7. grows
2. made	8. made
3. sing	9. gave
4. fly	10. see
5. buzz (hum)	11. praise (thank, trust)
6. blows	

Ask the class for suggestions as you list more verbs that refer to feelings and thoughts.

want	enjoy	respect
honor	love	think
hope	praise	remember

When assigning the written work, remind the class that a verb can be found at different places in a sentence. Tell them that two of the sentences are commands that tell what *you* should do. In these sentences the verb is the first word. To find the verb in a command, think: You should do what?

For the poem, encourage the children to use words that rhyme; but accept any word that is suitable for a given blank. The blanks are numbered to make checking convenient in case you do not require copying the poem.

> **Review and Practice**

Write the plural form of each noun.

1. baby   3. sheep   5. box
2. dress   4. donkey   6. bush

━●━●━●━●━●━●━●━●━

53. Verbs That Tell About the Past

The boys **worked.**
The boys **work.**
The boy **works.**

The words **worked, work,** and **works** are verbs in the sentences above. How are these three verbs different?

Work and **works** tell about an action that happens in the present. It might happen one time today, or it might happen every day.

The boys **work** hard. (now)
That boy **works** hard. (every day)

Worked tells about an action that happened sometime in the past.

The boys **worked** with Father yesterday.
The boy **worked** for Mr. Smith last summer.

Most verb forms that tell about the past end with **ed.** When the present form ends with **e,** the e is dropped before **ed** is added. When the present form ends with a consonant and then **y,** the **y** is changed to **i** before **ed** is added.

Lesson 53

Aim: To explain that some verbs are used to tell about the past, and that most of these verbs end with *-ed.*

Oral Review:

1. Name the two parts of a sentence. (subject and predicate)
2. Give four pronouns that tell *which one* or *which ones.* (this, that, these, those)
3. Correct this sentence: *Them are maple trees.* (Those *or* these *or* They are maple trees.)
4. Most verbs are words that show ———. (action)
5. Give two verbs that tell about actions we cannot easily see or hear. (Possible answers: think, feel, like)

Class: Read the first paragraph in class, and ask for answers to the question at the end. Explain that *work, works,* and *worked* are three different forms of the same

verb. Just as nouns have different forms to show whether they are singular or plural, so verbs have different forms to tell about different times.

Tell the class that the past form of a verb can be called its *ed* form. Tell them that you will say a sentence, and also say part of a second sentence. They should finish the second sentence by saying the *ed* form of the verb you used.

Sometimes we play tag.
Yesterday we ——— tag. (played)

We brush our teeth.
This morning we ——— them. (brushed)

When assigning the written work, you may want to do a few examples from each exercise together. Especially make sure the directions for Part B are understood.

> Using the Past Form >

A. Rewrite each sentence below. Begin each new sentence with the word **Yesterday.** Then change the verb to its past form.

> **Example:** The boys play.
> **Answer:**   Yesterday the boys played.

1. The men work.
2. The boys help.
3. The women cook.
4. The girls bake.
5. The babies cry.
6. The dogs bark.
7. The people pray.
8. We study the Bible.

B. Write a sentence for each picture on the next page. Follow these directions.
   a. Use proper nouns to name the people.
   b. Use the past form of a verb.
   c. Underline the verb you use.

Lesson 53 Answers
Using the Past Form
A. 1. Yesterday the men worked.
   2. Yesterday the boys helped.
   3. Yesterday the women cooked.
   4. Yesterday the girls baked.
   5. Yesterday the babies cried.
   6. Yesterday the dogs barked.
   7. Yesterday the people prayed.
   8. Yesterday we studied the Bible.

1.

2.

3.

4.

5.

6.

> Review and Practice >

1. Write **I** and the six other pronouns that tell **who.**
2. Write **me** and the six other pronouns that tell **whom.**

B. (Possible answers.)
1. Susan <u>jumped</u> rope.
2. Janet <u>peeled</u> potatoes.
3. Baby Leon <u>waved</u>.
4. Karen and Ruth <u>picked</u> flowers.
5. Brother Martin <u>preached</u>.
6. Mark <u>climbed</u> the ladder.

Review and Practice

1. I, you, he, she, it, we, they
2. me, you, him, her, it, us, them

54. Past Forms Without *ed*

The past forms of many verbs do not end in **ed.** Some past forms are made by changing the vowel sound.

see—saw	grow—grew
eat—ate	come—came
run—ran	begin—began
sing—sang	throw—threw

Some past forms are **very** different from the present form.

bring—brought	buy—bought
catch—caught	leave—left
think—thought	go—went

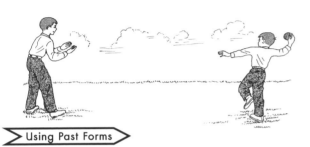

> Using Past Forms >

A. Copy the verb in the first sentence of each set. Then use the past form of that verb to complete the second sentence. Write the sentences you make.

   Example: Sometimes the Yoders come to our house.
              They ——— yesterday.
   Answer: come; They came yesterday.

   1. Usually we all sing. Last night we ———.
   2. On Sunday we go to church. We ——— last Sunday.

Lesson 54 Answers
Using Past Forms
A. 1. sing; Last night we sang.
   2. go; We went last Sunday.

Lesson 54

Aim: To introduce past forms that do not end with *-ed.*

Oral Review:

1. What kind of subject does this sentence have? *James and John were fishermen.* (a compound subject)
2. Words like *John's* and *ours* are called ——— forms. (possessive)
3. Action words are called ———. (verbs)
4. What kind of words tell about actions we cannot easily see or hear? (verbs)
5. What ending is used to make most verbs tell about the past? (-ed)

Class: Ask the class to say what letters we usually add to a verb to make the past form. Tell them that the past forms of many verbs do not have *-ed.* Use the following as an example.

We sing every day. This morning we ———.

Write *sing* and *sang* on the board. Then discuss the first group of irregular verbs in the lesson, having the children tell how the vowel sounds change.

Ask the class to give more verbs whose past forms are made by changing the vowel sound. Here are some of them.

blow—blew	rise—rose
break—broke	draw—drew
ride—rode	give—gave
know—knew	take—took

Discuss the verbs in the second group also. Point out especially the verb *bring* with its past form. Here are more verbs whose past forms are quite different from the present forms.

teach—taught	sell—sold
do—did	tell—told

3. Our school begins at eight-thirty. One day it —— at nine o'clock.
4. We bring our Bibles. Carl —— a new one this morning.
5. We leave school at three o'clock. Yesterday James —— early.

B. Copy each verb in these sentences. After each verb write its past form.

1. Think carefully.
2. Catch the ball.
3. Throw it to me.
4. Eat your apple.
5. Please buy this.
6. Run inside.
7. The trees grow.
8. I see the books.

> Review and Practice >

Copy each sentence, and add commas where they are needed.

1. We had apples sandwiches punch and cookies at the picnic.
2. Betty will you please water the flowers?
3. Jesus spoke about sheep flowers birds and fruit.
4. Mother we picked all the peas.

> Can You Do This? >

Write the correct past form of each verb below. None of them use **ed.**

1. meet
2. drive
3. tell
4. sweep
5. know
6. read
7. hide
8. cut
9. sell
10. cost
11. find
12. put

What is unusual about the past forms for the verbs **cut, cost,** and **put**? What about the verb **read**?

---

3. begins; One day it began at nine o'clock.
4. bring; Carl brought a new one this morning
5. leave; Yesterday James left early.

B. 1. think, thought
2. catch, caught
3. throw, threw
4. eat, ate
5. buy, bought
6. run, ran
7. grow, grew
8. see, saw

Review and Practice

1. We had apples, sandwiches, punch, and coo ies at the picnic.
2. Betty, will you please water the flowers?
3. Jesus spoke about sheep, flowers, birds, ar fruit.
4. Mother, we picked all the peas.

Can You Do This?

1. met
2. drove
3. told
4. swept
5. knew
6. read
7. hid
8. cut
9. sold
10. cost
11. found
12. put

The past forms of *cut, cost,* and *put* are the sam as the present forms. The verb *read* looks the sam but has a different vowel sound.

Have the pupils practice using all these past forms in oral sentences.

Explain the written work. Encourage all the pupils who can to do Can You Do This? Give them the hint of using the verb in a sentence and then changing it to past time. They can use a dictionary if they need more help.

★ **EXTRA PRACTICE**
Worksheet 33 (*Past Forms of Verbs Without -ed*)

55. Reviewing What You Have Learned

A. Make three columns on your paper. Label them **Nouns,**
Pronouns, and **Verbs.** Write the words from each
sentence below in the correct columns.

1. James tagged me.
2. You saw Lois.
3. We thank God.
4. I like carrots.
5. Rabbits eat them.
6. God made me.
7. They respect Father.
8. Moses led them.
9. Catch it, Ruth!
10. Read this, Paul.

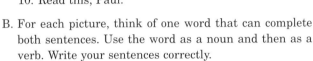

Lesson 55 Answers

A.	Nouns	Pronouns	Verbs
1.	James	me	tagged
2.	Lois	You	saw
3.	God	We	thank
4.	carrots	I	like
5.	Rabbits	them	eat
6.	God	me	made
7.	Father	They	respect
8.	Moses	them	led
9.	Ruth	it	Catch
10.	Paul	this	Read

B. For each picture, think of one word that can complete
both sentences. Use the word as a noun and then as a
verb. Write your sentences correctly.

1. a. Carl has two ——.   2. a. The girls spilled ——.
   b. He —— the nails.   b. They —— the flowers.

B. 1. a. Carl has two hammers.
      b. He hammers the nails.
   2. a. The girls spilled water.
      b. They water the flowers.

Lesson 55

Aim: To review the past four lessons on verbs.

Oral Review:

1. Most verbs are words that express ——. (action)
2. Some actions cannot be seen or heard. They take
   place in our ——. (minds *or* hearts)
3. Give the past form of each verb: *play, help, walk,*
   try, obey. (played, helped, walked, tried, obeyed)
4. Also give the past forms of these: *sing, eat, run,*
   catch, blow. (sang, ate, ran, caught, blew)

Class: Use Oral Review to refresh the concepts taught
in the last several lessons. Discuss and explain the written work as needed.

3. a. Each boy has a ———.   4. a. The ——— is hot.
   b. They ——— the lawn.   b. We ——— the shirts.

C. Write the past form of each verb.

1. sing	6. go	11. close
2. bring	7. come	12. throw
3. eat	8. buy	13. leave
4. try	9. say	14. think
5. catch	10. open	15. grow

D. Complete this paragraph by writing the past form of each verb in parentheses. Use a dictionary if you need help.

   Yesterday Father (1. go) to town and (2. buy) a new lawn mower. He (3. bring) it home in the truck. Father (4. tell) us that he had an accident. The truck (5. slide) on the wet road. The mower (6. fall) off the truck. Neither the truck nor the mower was (7. damage). Father (8. thank) God. He (9. say) that God (10. take) care of him.

●━━●━━●━━●━━●━━●━━●

3. a. Each boy has a rake.
   b. They rake the lawn.
4. a. The iron is hot.
   b. We iron the shirts.

C.
1. sang	6. went	11. closed
2. brought	7. came	12. threw
3. ate	8. bought	13. left
4. tried	9. said	14. thought
5. caught	10. opened	15. grew

D.
1. went
2. bought
3. brought
4. told
5. slid
6. fell
7. damaged
8. thanked
9. said
10. took

56. Singular and Plural With Verbs

You have learned that different forms of a verb are used to tell about different times. One form is used for telling about the present. A different form is used for telling about the past.

Different verb forms are also used to tell about singular or plural subjects. Look at the two sentences below.

The boys like ice cream.

That boy likes ice cream.

The first sentence tells about more than one boy. The verb **like** does not end with **s.**

The second sentence tells about only one boy. The verb **likes** does end with **s.** This **s** form is used to tell about only one person or thing.

Carl **writes** well.   Carl and Ben **write** well.
The dog **barks.**   The dogs **bark.**

The **s** form is also used with the pronouns **he, she,** and **it.**

He sees me.   She sees us.   It sees them.

Do you remember the rules for adding **s** to nouns that end with **s, ch, sh, x,** or a consonant followed by **y**? Follow the same rules to write the **s** form of verbs with these endings.

catch—catches   pass—passes
wash—washes   try—tries

Lesson 56

Aim: To introduce the third person singular form (the *s* form) of verbs.

Oral Review:

1. An asking sentence ends with a ———. Give an example. (question mark; Individual examples.)
2. Action words are called ———. (verbs)
3. Give the past form of *work.* (worked)
4. When adding *-ed* to words ending in *y,* when should the *y* be changed to *i*? Give an example. (when a consonant comes before the *y;* Possible example: try—tried)
5. Give a verb that is a past form not ending with *-ed.* (Possible answers: went, said, gave)

Class: Discuss the two example sentences after the second paragraph. Ask: "What are the two verbs used? Which sentence tells about only one boy? With what letter does that verb end?" Explain that we call this form of the verb the *s* form. We use it when talking about only one person or thing.

Ask: "Would we say *like* or *likes* with the word *I*? Even though *I* names only one person, we do not use the *s* form with it. We do not use the *s* form with the pronoun *you* either."

Discuss the adding of *-es* to verbs with certain endings. When assigning the written work, do several examples in Part A together to make sure the pupils understand that they are to change the noun to its singular form.

★ **EXTRA PRACTICE**
Worksheet 34 (*Singular and Plural With Verbs*)

> **Using Singular and Plural With Verbs** >

A. Rewrite each sentence, changing the noun in bold print to its singular form. Use the **s** form of the verb.

Example: The **stars** twinkle.
Answer: The star twinkles.

1. The **cars** pass us.
2. The **birds** fly away.
3. The **ministers** preach.
4. The **men** teach the truth.
5. The **bears** run into the woods.
6. The **babies** cry loudly.
7. The **teachers** tell Bible stories.
8. The **ducks** walk across the floor.
9. The **boys** sing for our neighbor.
10. The **girls** bake cookies.
11. The **women** patch clothes.
12. The **families** read the Bible.

B. Write **go** or **goes** for each sentence.

1. I —— home.
2. You —— home.
3. He —— home.
4. She —— home.
5. It —— home.
6. We —— home.
7. They —— home.
8. Each boy —— home.

> **Review and Practice** >

Write whether each of these is a **telling, asking, commanding,** or **exclaiming** sentence. Also give the correct end punctuation for each.

1. Did you know that God calls all the stars by name
2. What a great God He is

Lesson 56 Answers
Using Singular and Plural With Verbs

A. 1. The car passes us.
    2. The bird flies away.
    3. The minister preaches.
    4. The man teaches the truth.
    5. The bear runs into the woods.
    6. The baby cries loudly.
    7. The teacher tells Bible stories.
    8. The duck walks across the floor.
    9. The boy sings for our neighbor.
    10. The girl bakes cookies.
    11. The woman patches clothes.
    12. The family reads the Bible.

B. 1. go   5. goes
   2. go   6. go
   3. goes   7. go
   4. goes   8. goes

Review and Practice
   1. asking (?)
   2. exclaiming (!)

3. The earth is about 93 million miles away from the sun

4. If it were much closer or farther away, we would burn up or freeze

5. Think about this

6. How wise and wonderful our God is

> Can You Do This? >

1. Use a dictionary to help you find and write the **s** form of each verb.
   a. mix   b. buzz   c. do   d. say

2. In two of the verbs above, the vowel sound changes when the **s** form is made. Which two are they?

━━●━●━●━●━●━●━●━━

57. The Verb *Be*

You have already met the action verbs, such as **work** and **think**. Some action verbs tell about action you can see, and some tell about action you cannot see.

But sometimes you are told to **be** something rather than to **do** something. Then the verb **be** is used. Here are two **be** commands from the Bible.

Be ye kind.   **Be** not deceived.

The verb **be** has these eight different forms.

I **am** happy.   Carl **is** my brother.
We **are** children.   Jonah **was** a prophet.
The men **were** there.   **Be** a good sport.
Ann had **been** sick.   Are you **being** helpful?

3. telling (.)
4. telling (.)
5. commanding (.)
6. exclaiming (!)

Can You Do This?

1. a. mixes   c. does
   b. buzzes   d. says

2. do (does) and say (says)
   (*Does* is pronounced /duz/, and *says* is pronounced /sez/.)

Lesson 57

Aim: To introduce the verb *be* in its eight forms.

Oral Review:

1. A commanding sentence ends with a ———. Give an example. (period; Individual examples.)

2. Words that tell about actions we cannot easily see or hear are ———. (verbs)

3. Give an example of a past form that ends with *-ed.* (Individual answers.)

4. Give the past forms of these: *dig, ring, sit, write.* (dug, rang, sat, wrote)

5. When do we use the *s* form of a verb? (when we talk about just one person or thing)

Class: Remind the class that every complete sentence must have a verb. Then write the following sentence on the chalkboard.

    We are people.

Point out that the verb is *are,* but it is not an action verb. It is a verb that shows *being.* Almost every verb shows action, but the verb *be* is a special exception.

Tell them that you will say some more sentences. They should listen closely and see if they can name the form of *be* in each sentence. Write the forms of *be* on the board as the pupils say them.

    I am the teacher.
    Keith is a boy.
    You are the pupils.
    David was a king.
    Moses and Aaron were brothers.
    Be thankful.
    The weather has been cool.
    The Samaritan was being kind.

Read together the two sentences that the pupils are to remember. Have them memorize the definition

---

Remember: A verb is a word that shows action or being. The eight forms of **be** are **am, is, are, was, were, be, been,** and **being.**

> Discussing the Verb *Be* >

1. What are the eight forms of **be**?
2. Which form is used only with **I**?
3. Which form is used to give a command?
   Choose from these for numbers 4 to 6.

   is   are   was   were

4. Which two forms are used to talk about just one other person or thing?
5. Which two forms are used with **you** or when talking about more than one person or thing?
6. Which two forms are used to talk about the present? Which two are used to talk about the past?

> Using the Verb *Be* >

A. Write the form of **be** that you would use to complete each sentence. Use each form only once.
1. I —— in school right now.
2. Jesus —— born in Bethlehem.
3. —— you at home last evening?
4. Brother Wayne —— our deacon.
5. —— kind to one another.
6. Ants and bees —— insects.
7. Where have you ——?
8. The boys were —— too noisy.

Lesson 57 Answers
Discussing the Verb *Be*

1. am, is, are, was, were, be, been, being
2. am
3. be
4. is, was
5. are, were
6. is, are; was, were

Using the Verb *Be*
A. 1. am
   2. was
   3. Were
   4. is
   5. Be
   6. are
   7. been
   8. being

of a verb. It would be good if they also memorized the eight forms of *be*. The forms should always be repeated in the same order when they are recited.

Include Discussing the Verb *Be* in the class discussion. You may also wish to assign it as part of the written work.

B. Now use the forms of **be** in sentences of your own. Write eight sentences, one for each form you learned. Be ready to read your sentences aloud without the verb. See if your classmates can guess which form you used.

> **Verbs of Action and Being**

Copy the verb in each sentence, and write whether it shows **action** or **being.**

1. Nathan is at home.
2. Ann brings the book.
3. I see you.
4. We are at school.
5. The girls sang.
6. Father bought oil.
7. Where were you?
8. Trix runs away.

> **Review and Practice**

Diagram the simple subjects and simple predicates of these sentences.

1. Camels travel steadily.
2. Will Jesus come back?
3. Lilacs and daffodils bloomed.
4. Come here.
5. Jesus preached and prayed.
6. Did Leon ride carefully?

B. (Individual answers. Give opportunity for the children to read their sentences in class.)

Verbs of Action and Being

1. is, being
2. brings, action
3. see, action
4. are, being
5. sang, action
6. bought, action
7. were, being
8. runs, action

Review and Practice

1. Camels | travel

2. Jesus | will come

3. Lilacs
    daffodils and bloomed

4. (you) | Come

5. Jesus and preached
                    prayed

6. Leon | did ride

58. Using Verbs With *There*

Look at the sentences below. What is the simple subject of each one?

    a. A bluebird is in the tree.
    b. A cardinal was in the tree earlier.
    c. Two robins are in the tree.
    d. Some sparrows were in the tree too.

Sentences **a** and **b** are each telling about only one bird. We use **is** and **was** when telling about only one person or thing.

Sentences **c** and **d** each tell about more than one bird. We use **are** and **were** when telling about more than one person or thing.

You can rewrite the four sentences above, using the word **there.** When you do this, be careful to use the correct verb.

    a. There is a bluebird in the tree.
    b. There was a cardinal in the tree earlier.
    c. There are two robins in the tree.
    d. There were some sparrows in the tree too.

Remember: When beginning a sentence with the word **there,** use **is** or **was** if you are talking about only one person or thing. Use **are** or **were** if you are talking about more than one person or thing.

> **Writing Sentences With *There***

Write a sentence to tell what you see in each picture. Begin each sentence with **There is** or **There are.**

Lesson 58

Aim: To drill correct usage of *is, are, was,* and *were* in sentences that begin with *there.*

Oral Review:

1. An exclaiming sentence ends with ——. Give an example. (an exclamation mark; Individual examples.)
2. Give the past form and *s* form of each verb: *like, run, fly, stay, cry.* (liked, likes; ran, runs; flew, flies; stayed, stays; cried, cries)
3. Say what is wrong with this sentence: *The baby like milk.* (The *s* form of the verb should be used.)
4. Give the eight forms of *be.* (am, is, are, was, were, be, been, being)

Class: Review the forms of *be* taught in the preceding lesson. Ask the class which ones we use when talking about only one person or thing, and which ones we use when talking about more than one person or thing

Read together the first set of four sentences about birds. Compare each sentence with its equivalent in the second set. Discuss why we use *is* and *was* in the first two sentences of each set, and *are* and *were* in the other two sentences.

Tell the class that when we want to begin a sentence with the word *there,* we must stop and think Will we be telling about more than one person o thing? If so, we must use *are* or *were,* not *is* or *was*

Give some sample sentences and ask the clas which verb should be used.

There —— some visitors here yesterda (were)

There —— two balls in the closet. (are a were)

There —— water on the floor. (is *or* was)

Note: In a sentence beginning with *There,* th

1.

4.

2.

5.

3.

6.

> Using *Was* and *Were* >

Write **was** or **were** to tell how to complete each sentence correctly.

1. There —— a special meeting at church.
2. There —— some men from Africa at the service.
3. There —— two brethren from India attending also.
4. There —— a family from the Philippines.
5. There —— three boys who spoke Spanish.
6. There —— many people in the meeting.

words are rearranged from the normal subject—predicate order to *There*—predicate—subject. *There* temporarily replaces the subject and is called an expletive.

★ **EXTRA PRACTICE**
Worksheet 35 (*Using Verbs With There*)

Lesson 58 Answers
Writing Sentences With *There*
(Possible answers.)
1. There are three birds in the tree.
2. There are two books on the shelf.
3. There is a cat on the chair.
4. There are some sheep in the field.
5. There is a cake on the table.
6. There are some girls on the porch.

Using *Was* and *Were*
1. was
2. were
3. were
4. was
5. were
6. were

> **Review and Practice**

A. Write the plural form of each noun.
1. child
3. brush
5. army
2. valley
4. fox
6. church

B. Write correctly each noun that needs a capital letter.
1. The man was moved to the riverview hospital.
2. We crossed the mississippi river with uncle ben and aunt martha.
3. The children went to the airport in greenville to meet jonathan and lee.

Review and Practice

A. 1. children
2. valleys
3. brushes
4. foxes
5. armies
6. churches

B. 1. Riverview Hospital
2. Mississippi River, Uncle Ben, Aunt Martha
3. Greenville, Jonathan, Lee

59. Meeting More Action Verbs

The eight forms of **be** show being, but all other verbs show action. In this lesson you will meet some more action verbs.

The words **do, does,** and **did** are action verbs. **Do** and **does** tell about the present. **Did** tells about the past.

I **do** the chores.
John **does** the milking.
Karen **did** the ironing.

Sometimes we use **do, does,** or **did** with another verb to ask a question. Then these words are helping verbs. **Do, does,** or **did** comes first in the question, and the other verb comes later.

Do the pupils **have** their books?
Does Brother David **preach** every week?

Lesson 59

Aim: To present the verb *do* in its various forms, and to teach that this verb is used in questions. (2) To present *have* in its various forms.

Oral Review:
1. What is a proper noun? (The name of a particular person, place, or thing)
2. Give the past form of
   a. help, try, play. (helped, tried, played)
   b. sing, stand, teach. (sang, stood, taught)
3. Give the correct verb in each sentence.
   a. The sun (shine, shines) all the time. (shines)
   b. The stars always (shine, shines) too. (shine)
4. Give the eight forms of *be*. (am, is, are, was, were, be, been, being)
5. When you begin a sentence with *There is* or *There are,* how can you tell which verb to use? (Use *is* if you are talking about only one person or thing.

Use *are* if you are talking about more than on person or thing.)

Class: Write *do, does,* and *did* on the board. Poir out that these are all forms of the same verb. *Doe* is the *s* form. *Did* is the past form.

Use the example sentences after the first para graph to show how these forms are used as mai verbs. Tell the children that this lesson teache another way that these verbs are used.

Have the children read the three questions in th lesson text. Ask them to say the verb that begin each question. Then call attention to the other ver in each sentence. Explain that when we use one ver to help another verb, we call the first one a helpin verb.

Present the verbs *have, has,* and *had*. At thi point, these words are introduced only to have th children recognize them as verbs.

Did everyone **learn** a Bible verse?

The words **have, has,** and **had** are action verbs too. **Have** and **has** tell about the present. **Had** tells about the past.

> We **have** some baby chicks.
> Keith **has** the ball!
> Jason **had** his turn last.

Like **do, does,** and **did,** the forms of **have** are sometimes used as helping verbs. You will learn more about helping verbs in a later lesson.

> ▷ Using *Do, Does,* and *Did* ▷

A. Write **do** or **does** to complete each sentence.
  1. Father —— the planting.
  2. The boys —— the picking.
  3. The girls —— the husking.
  4. Who —— the eating?
  5. We all ——!

B. For each sentence write **Do, Does,** or **Did** and the other verb that is used. The words in parentheses tell whether the sentence is about the present or the past.

  Example: —— Uncle Abner catch a fish? (past)
  Answer: Did catch

  1. —— Sister Anna read the story of Job? (past)
  2. —— Job suffer much pain? (past)
  3. —— you know the names of his three friends? (present)
  4. —— the story teach us a lesson? (present)
  5. —— it help us to be patient? (present)

Lesson 59 Answers
Using *Do, Does,* and *Did*
A. 1. does
   2. do
   3. do
   4. does
   5. do

B. 1. Did read
   2. Did suffer
   3. Do know
   4. Does teach
   5. Does help

Using *Have, Has,* and *Had*

A. Write a sentence for each picture. Use **has** or **have** to tell what the person or people are holding.

1.   2.

B. Write a sentence about your breakfast. Use **had** in your sentence.

Review and Practice

A. Rewrite each phrase as a possessive phrase with an apostrophe.
1. the bicycle of Timothy
2. the toys of Brenda
3. the dish of Mother
4. the letter of Paul

B. One word in each sentence has a mistake. Write that word correctly.
1. Is this Fred's book or is it your's?
2. Uncle John's farm is next to our's.
3. Her's is blue, and Barbara's is yellow.
4. Grandpa's birdhouse is larger than their's.

Using *Have, Has,* and *Had*

A. (Possible answers.)
1. Leon has an ice cream cone.
2. The girls have kittens in a basket.

B. (Possible answer.)
I had cereal for breakfast.

Review and Practice

A. 1. Timothy's bicycle
2. Brenda's toys
3. Mother's dish
4. Paul's letter

B. 1. yours
2. ours
3. Hers
4. theirs

60. Reviewing What You Have Learned

A. Write a form of **be** for each sentence. Use each form only once.

1. I —— ready now.
2. Job —— patient.
3. These trees —— tall.
4. Mae —— busy today.
5. We have —— there.
6. You —— there too.
7. Please —— quiet.
8. Are you —— kind?

B. The verb in each sentence is a past form. Write the form that would be used if the sentence were telling about the present.

1. Joseph threw the ball.
2. Kevin caught it.
3. Mark was inside.
4. He had chicken pox.
5. Ginger ran outside.
6. Mother did the mending.
7. The girls were with her.
8. They had some embroidery.

C. After each verb you wrote in Part B, write **A** if it shows action or **B** if it shows being.

D. Rewrite each sentence, beginning it with **There.**

1. Some money is in the missionary offering.
2. Some songs about heaven are in the hymnbook.
3. Four lepers were outside the city.
4. A crippled man was by the gate.
5. Three crosses were on a hill.

E. Copy the two verbs in each question.

1. Does James have a Bible?
2. Did his father give it to him?

Lesson 60 Answers

A. 1. am
   2. was
   3. are
   4. is
   5. been
   6. were
   7. be
   8. being

B. (Answers for Part C are included.)
   1. throws, A
   2. catches, A
   3. is, B
   4. has, A
   5. runs, A
   6. does, A
   7. are, B
   8. have, A

C. (Answers are included in Part B.)

D. 1. There is some money in the missionary offering.
   2. There are some songs about heaven in the hymnbook.
   3. There were four lepers outside the city.
   4. There was a crippled man by the gate.
   5. There were three crosses on a hill.

E. 1. Does have
   2. Did give

Lesson 60

Aim: To review the last four lessons.

Oral Review:

1. A verb form like *walks* is used to tell about just one person or thing. What do we call such a verb form? (the *s* form)
2. Give the eight forms of *be*. (am, is, are, was, were, be, been, being)
3. Tell whether to use *is* or *are*.
   a. There —— many stars in the sky. (are)
   b. There —— a bird flying over the field. (is)
   c. There —— five books on the table. (are)
4. Tell whether to use *was* or *were*.
   a. There —— a man named Job. (was)
   b. There —— twelve disciples who followed Jesus. (were)
   c. There —— many people at the wedding. (were)

5. Give two groups of action verbs that may also be helping verbs. (do, does, did; have, has, had)

Class: Use Oral Review to refresh the concepts learned in the last several lessons. Emphasize the proper use of *is, are, was,* and *were* in sentences beginning with *There.* Discuss and explain the written work as needed.

3. Does he know Psalm 23?
4. Did you ever read about Elijah?
5. Does your sister go to school?
6. Do bobwhites build nests on the ground?

F. Find these words in the sentences above. Write them on your paper.
1. four proper nouns
2. six common nouns
3. four pronouns

G. Each sentence tells about the picture above it. Copy the sentences, and use **do** or **does** in each blank.

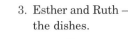

1. Father ——— the milking.

3. Esther and Ruth ——— the dishes.

2. James and John ——— the chores.

4. Mother ——— the baking.

3. Does know
4. Did read
5. Does go
6. Do build

F. 1. James, Bible, Psalm, Elijah
2. father, sister, school, bobwhites, nests, ground
3. it, him, he, you (Also accept *his* and *your.*)

G. 1. Father does the milking.
2. James and John do the chores.
3. Esther and Ruth do the dishes.
4. Mother does the baking.

61. Helping Verbs

You have learned that **do, does,** and **did** can be used with another verb to ask a question. When **do, does,** and **did** are used in this way, they are **helping verbs.**

Forms of **be** can also be used as helping verbs.

> The birds <u>**are**</u> **singing** cheerily.
> Jesus <u>**was**</u> **sent** into the world.

Some other helping verbs are forms of **have. Has** is the **s** form of **have. Had** is the past form.

> We <u>**have**</u> **studied** the lesson.
> English class <u>**has**</u> **begun.**
> Doris <u>**had**</u> **finished** her other work.

Many past forms of verbs may be used with or without a helping verb.

> Mother **baked** some cookies.
> Mother <u>**has**</u> **baked** some cookies.
>
> The boys **brought** a new bat.
> The boys <u>**have**</u> **brought** a new bat.

Sometimes a verb has two forms that tell about the past. One form is called a **past form** and must not be used with a helping verb. The other form is called the **helper form** and must always be used with a helping verb. **Have, has,** and **had** are the helping verbs used with helper forms.

> I **saw** the ocean.   I <u>**have**</u> **seen** the ocean.
> Carl **went** there.   Carl <u>**has**</u> **gone** there.
> The man **was** here.   The man <u>**had**</u> **been** here.

Remember: Three sets of helping verbs are forms of **do,** forms of **be,** and forms of **have.** Forms of **have** are used with the helper forms of verbs.

Lesson 61

Aim: (1) To introduce three sets of helping verbs: forms of *do,* forms of *be,* and forms of *have.* (2) To teach that some past forms of verbs (past participles) must be used with helping verbs, and that forms of *have* are used with these forms.

Oral Review:

1. Name the two parts of a sentence. Which part tells what the person or thing does or did? (subject and predicate; predicate)
2. When do we use the *s* form of a verb in a sentence? (when the subject is singular)
3. Give the eight forms of *be.* (am, is, are, was, were, be, been, being)
4. Give a sentence that begins with *there,* telling about more than one person or thing. (Individual answers.)
5. The words *do, does, did* and *have, has, had* are (nouns, verbs). (verbs)

Class: Remind the children that some sentences have a verb phrase instead of just one verb. In the lesson text, point out the difference between the example sentences that use helping verbs and those that do not.

Ask the class to say which verbs are being helped in the example sentences. Write the verb and its helper on the board. Beside each phrase, write the simple past form of the same verb.

Write some other past forms on the board. Ask the pupils to try to think of the helper form that goes

> Using the Helping Verbs >

A. For each sentence write **was, were, have,** or **has** and the verb that is being helped.
1. Jesus —— crucified on Calvary.
2. We —— sung four songs.
3. Jesus —— gone to heaven.
4. Mark —— eating his lunch.
5. Karen and Jane —— visiting school.
6. God —— given us many good things.
7. Where —— your shoes last seen?

B. Rewrite each sentence. Use **have** or **has** and a form of the verb in bold print.

Examples: He **smiled.**   School **began.**
Answers: He **has smiled.**   School **has begun.**

1. I gave it.   5. Father prayed.
2. She baked it.   6. The bell rang.
3. He caught it.   7. We were there.
4. They made it.   8. You did it.

> Review and Practice >

Write the simple subject and simple predicate of each sentence. Be careful! Each simple predicate is a verb phrase.
1. Have you seen my new book?
2. Did the letter come?
3. Is your arm healing?
4. Does Mother want us to help?
5. Are the yellow kittens playing?

●–●–●–●–●–●–●–●–●

Lesson 61 Answers
Using the Helping Verbs
A. 1. was crucified
   2. have sung
   3. has gone
   4. was eating
   5. were visiting
   6. has given
   7. were seen

B. 1. I have given it.
   2. She has baked it.
   3. He has caught it.
   4. They have made it.
   5. Father has prayed.
   6. The bell has rung.
   7. We have been there.
   8. You have done it.

Review and Practice
1. you have seen
2. letter did come
3. arm is healing
4. Mother does want
5. kittens are playing

with each past form. This will be easier if you begin sentences for them.

   rang—The bell rang.
   The bell has ——. (rung)

   ate—The children ate lunch.
   They have ——. (eaten)

   began—School began.
   School had ——. (begun)

Point out that helper forms *must* be used with helping verbs. It is not correct to say "I seen the ocean" or "We been there." On the other hand, it is just as incorrect to say "Carl has went there" and "The children have ate lunch." This point is drilled further in later lessons.

★ **EXTRA PRACTICE**
Worksheet 36 (*Helping Verbs*)

62. *Did—Done* and *Saw—Seen*

When we use a helping verb together with another verb, we have a verb phrase. Read the sentences below, pointing to the verb phrase in each.

Uncle Paul has done the chores.
The sparrows have seen the crumbs.

Done and **seen** are helper forms. When you use **done** or **seen,** always use a helping verb too. When you do not want to use a helping verb, use the past forms **did** and **saw.**

Ray **did** the chores today.
John **had done** them yesterday.

Ruth **saw** a woodpecker today.
Mary **had seen** it before.

The verb forms that end with an **n** or **un** sound are usually the helper forms (the forms that need a helping verb).

Past Form	Helper Form	Past Form	Helper Form
saw	seen	ran	run
grew	grown	began	begun
tore	torn	sang	sung
went	gone	gave	given

> Using Different Verb Forms >

Write a different form of the verb in bold print to complete each set of sentences. Use the past form for sentence **a.** Use the helper form for sentence **b.**

1. I **see** it!
   a. I ——— it!
   b. I have ——— it!

Lesson 62 Answers
Using Different Verb Forms

1. a. saw   b. seen

Lesson 62

Aim: To teach the correct use of *did, done, saw,* and *seen.*

Oral Review:

1. What are two kinds of words that need an apostrophe? (possessive nouns and contractions)
2. Give the eight forms of *be.* Which one do we use when giving a command? (am, is, are, was, were, be, been, being; be)
3. A sentence beginning with *There is* should tell about (one, more than one) person or thing. (one)
4. Give three verb forms beginning with *d* that can be main verbs or helping verbs. (do, does, did)
5. Give three verb forms beginning with *h* that can be main verbs or helping verbs. (have, has, had)

Class: Write *did* and *done* on the board. Ask the class which form needs a helping verb. Tell them that we should not use *done* unless we use a helping verb with it. We should not say, "He *done* it." We should never say, "I *done did* it." What should we say?

Tell them that there are two other verbs that are sometimes used incorrectly. Write *saw* and *seen* on the board. Discuss the correct use of each of these.

Ask the class to say what sound comes at the end of *done* and *seen.* Point out that when the past form and the helper form are different, the form that ends with the *n* sound is usually the one that needs a helping verb. Read together the first set of past forms in the chart in the pupil's lesson. Ask the class if they can think of two more verbs whose past forms rhyme with *grew* and *grown.* Write *knew—known* and *threw—thrown* on the board.

2. We **do** the work.
   a. We —— the work.
   b. We have —— the work.
3. The cows **run.**
   a. The cows ——.
   b. The cows have ——.
4. Mother **sings.**
   a. Mother ——.
   b. Mother has ——.
5. The grass **grows.**
   a. The grass ——.
   b. The grass has ——.

2. a. did   b. done
3. a. ran   b. run
4. a. sang   b. sung
5. a. grew   b. grown

> Writing Sentences With Different Verb Forms >

A. Think about some place you have gone with your family. Was it to the zoo? Was it to the store? Write three sentences telling what you saw. Use the verb **saw** in your sentences.

B. Think about three interesting things you have seen. Write three sentences using the verb phrase **have seen.**

> Review and Practice >

Copy each sentence. Add quotation marks and capital letters where they are needed, and use the correct end marks.
1. do you have strawberries for sale Mother asked the lady
2. yes, I do, answered the lady
3. she said, i will get some for you
4. Ruth exclaimed, what large strawberries

Writing Sentences With Different Verb Forms
A. (Individual answers.)

B. (Individual answers.)

Review and Practice
(Corrected items are underlined.)
1. "Do you have strawberries for sale?" Mother asked the lady.
2. "Yes, I do," answered the lady.
3. She said, "I will get some for you."
4. Ruth exclaimed, "What large strawberries!"

Tell the class that sometimes the past form and the helper form have only a vowel difference. The form with the short *u* sound is usually the helper form. Read together the second set of examples given in the chart.

63. *Came—Come* and *Went—Gone*

Use forms of **come** to tell about a person or thing that moves toward you. The past form of **come** is **came.** The helper form is **come.** If you use **come** to tell about the past, be sure to use a helping verb.

> Lester **came** last night.
> Grandfather **has come** for a visit.

Use forms of **go** to tell about a person or thing that moves away from you. The past form of **go** is **went.** The helper form is **gone.** Never use a helping verb with **went.** Always use a helping verb with **gone.**

> Lester **went** to Mexico last week.
> Grandfather **has gone** back home.

▷ Reviewing Verbs ▷

1. What is a verb?
2. What are the eight forms of **be**?
3. How is the past form of most verbs made?
4. Give three sets of helping verbs that you have learned.

▷ Using the Correct Verb ▷

A. Write **came, come, went,** or **gone** to complete each sentence correctly.
   1. Father has —— to Manitoba.
   2. He —— there last week.
   3. Aunt Ruth has —— to stay with us.
   4. Uncle Paul —— with Father.
   5. Mother had —— to the airport with Father.
   6. Aunt Ruth —— home with her.

Lesson 63

Aim: To teach the correct usage of *came—come* and *went—gone.*

Written Quiz:
1. Words that show action are called ——.
2. Past forms are usually made by adding ——.
3. Write the past forms of these: **eat, catch, go, pray, smile.**
4. Write the eight forms of **be.** Underline the form that we use only with **I.**
5. Underline the correct words.
   a. Verbs like **helps** and **comes** are used to tell about (one thing, more than one thing).
   b. When a sentence begins with **There are,** it should tell about (one thing, more than one thing).
   c. The boys (did, done) all the chores for Father.
   d. We (saw, seen) five deer in our field.

Lesson 63 Answers
Reviewing Verbs
1. A verb is a word that show action or being.
2. am, is, are, was, were, be, been, being
3. The past form of most verbs is made by adding *-ed.*
4. forms of *do* (do, does, did); forms of *be* (am, is, are, was, were, be, been, being); forms of *have* (have, has, had)

Using the Correct Verb
A. 1. gone
   2. went
   3. come
   4. went
   5. gone
   6. came

Quiz Answers:
1. verbs
2. ed
3. ate, caught, went, prayed, smiled
4. am, is, are, was, were, be, been, being
5. a. one thing
   b. more than one thing
   c. did
   d. saw

Class: People in different areas of the country have their own grammatical difficulties. Try to address the particular difficulty or misuse that you know your pupils face. The most common problems with the verbs of this lesson are to use *went* with a helping verb and *come* (past participle) without a helping verb. If your pupils have trouble with this, drill correct usage in presenting this lesson.

Give the class oral practice in correct verb usage

B. Answer each question with a complete sentence. Use **came** or **went** in your answers.

1. When did you come to school?
2. When did you go home?
3. Did your teacher come to school?
4. Where did you go last Sunday?

C. Copy the rhyme, using **gone** and **come** correctly.

1. Bright autumn has ——
    With gold-colored trees,
   While summer has ——
    With the birds and the bees.

2. Now autumn has ——,
    And here in its place
   Cold winter has ——
    With a clean, snowy face.

3. Have all the gay birds
    —— far, far away?
   No, little snowbirds
    Have —— here to stay.

> Can You Do This? >

Try writing your own rhyme about something that **has come** and something that **has gone.** Maybe you will want to write a rhyme about winter going and springtime coming.

●━●━●━●━●━●━●━●━●

B. (Possible answers.)
1. I came at eight-thirty.
2. I went home yesterday.
3. Yes, she came to school.
4. I went to church last Sunday.

C. 1. Bright autumn has <u>come</u>
        With gold-colored trees,
       While summer has <u>gone</u>
        With the birds and the bees.

2. Now autumn has <u>gone</u>,
        And here in its place
       Cold winter has <u>come</u>
        With a clean, snowy face.

3. Have all the gay birds
        <u>Gone</u> far, far away?
       No, little snowbirds
        Have <u>come</u> here to stay.

Can You Do This?
    (Encourage children to try writing a rhyme a directed.)

by having each say a sentence with a particular verb. Correct improper usage now and in future instances. For most students it will be more difficult to break poor speech habits than to follow the rules when writing.

Reviewing Verbs may be included in the oral drill, or it may be assigned as written work.

64. The Little Word *Not*

We use **do, does,** or **did** with another verb when we want to ask a question. We also use **do, does,** or **did** with another verb when we want to use the word **not.**

The little word **not** is not a verb. The word **not** stands between the helping verb and the main verb in a verb phrase.

> John <u>does</u> **not** <u>go</u> to school.
> The men <u>do</u> **not** <u>have</u> a Bible.
> Father <u>did</u> **not** <u>meet</u> the visitor.

Not can also be used with the helping verbs **has, have,** and **had.**

> Paul <u>has</u> **not** <u>forgotten</u> Psalm 1.
> We <u>have</u> **not** <u>read</u> that book.
> Grandfather <u>had</u> **not** <u>seen</u> it before.

We do not need a helping verb to use **not** with a form of **be.**

> I <u>am</u> **not** tired.   It <u>is</u> **not** cold.
> You <u>are</u> **not** sick.   We <u>were</u> **not** sad.

Sometimes the word **not** is joined to a verb to make a contraction. To do this, take the **o** out of **not** and put in an **apostrophe** (').

> did n<del>o</del>t—didn't   is n<del>o</del>t—isn't
> has n<del>o</del>t—hasn't   are n<del>o</del>t—aren't

Lesson 64

Aim: (1) To teach that *not* appears in many verb phrases, yet it is not a verb. (2) To teach the formation of simple contractions with *not*.

Oral Review:

1. An asking sentence ends with ———. Give an example. (a question mark; Individual examples.)
2. Forms of *be* may be ——— verbs or ——— verbs. (main, helping)
3. Give the two other sets of verbs that may be main verbs or helping verbs. (do, does, did; have, has, had)
4. Which verb forms are usually the ones that need a helping verb? (the forms ending with an *n* or *un* sound)
5. What is wrong with each sentence?
   a. We done the dishes for Mother. (*Done* should be *did,* or the helping verb *have* should be used with *done.*)
   b. The boys seen that they would be late. (*Seen* should be *saw.*)
   c. A robin come into the yard. (*Come* should be *came.*)
   d. The children have went to school. (*Went* should be *gone,* or the helping word *have* should be left out.)

Class: Ask the class some questions for which the obvious answer is *no.* Write the questions as you ask them. Tell the class to answer with complete sentences. Write their answers also.

Examples:

> <u>Does</u> a bird <u>have</u> four legs?
> No, a bird <u>does</u> not <u>have</u> four legs.

> <u>Do</u> rivers <u>flow</u> uphill?
> No, rivers <u>do</u> not <u>flow</u> uphill.

Writing Contractions

A. Write the contractions of these words.
1. does not
2. do not
3. have not
4. had not
5. was not
6. were not

B. Which of the verbs above changes its vowel sound from /o͞o/ to /ō/ when used in a contraction?

Using *Not* in Sentences

A. Answer each question in a complete sentence that starts with **No.** Put a comma after **No,** and use **not** in your sentences.
1. Are you in fifth grade?
2. Does a baby know many words?
3. Did Adam obey God?
4. Was Ahab a good king?
5. Have you seen God?
6. Has God forgotten His promises?

B. Circle the word **not** in each sentence you wrote for Part A. Underline each verb twice.

Can You Do This?

Some contractions with the word **not** need other changes. Can you write the contractions for these words?
1. will not
2. can not

Point out the similarity of the verbs in the questions and answers.

Explain that we use *do, does,* and *did* to make sentences with the word *not.* When the word *not* is used in a sentence, there are usually two verbs. Sometimes the two verbs will be a form of *do* and a main verb. Sometimes the helping verb will be a form of *have.*

Example:
Have you finished third grade?
No, we have not finished third grade.

Discuss the fact that no helping verb is needed when *not* is used with a form of *be.* Use the lesson examples to illustrate.

Explain what is meant by contractions and how they are formed with the word *not* and various verbs. This aspect of the lesson probably does not need much drill because contractions are also taught in spelling class.

Lesson 64 Answers
Writing Contractions
A. 1. doesn't
2. don't
3. haven't
4. hadn't
5. wasn't
6. weren't

B. The verb *do* changes its vowel sound.

Using *Not* in Sentences
A. (Underlining and circles are for Part B.)
1. No, I am not in fifth grade.
   (*Or:* No, we are not in fifth grade.)
2. No, a baby does not know many words.
3. No, Adam did not obey God.
4. No, Ahab was not a good king.
5. No, I have not seen God.
   (*Or:* No, we have not seen God.)
6. No, God has not forgotten His promises.

B. (Answers are included in Part A.)

Can You Do This?
1. won't
2. can't

★ **EXTRA PRACTICE**
Worksheet 37 (*Contractions*)

65. Reviewing What You Have Learned

A. Write the verb phrases that are used in these sentences. Be careful! Sometimes other words come between a verb and its helper.

1. Jason has gone to Mexico.
2. Did he go with his family?
3. His father and he had flown on a jet.
4. His mother and sister are staying home.
5. Does Sarah miss her brother?
6. She has not seen him for ten days.
7. Do Jason and his father write letters?
8. They have written two letters.
9. Sarah was reading one letter.
10. The second letter has not come yet.

B. Copy these verbs. Beside each one, write whether it can complete sentence **a** or sentence **b.** If the verb can be used both ways, write **both.**

a. Thomas ———.	b. Thomas has ———.

1. went	3. tried	5. ran
2. run	4. gone	6. came

Also copy these verbs. Write whether they would fit in sentence **c, d,** or **both.**

c. Thomas ——— it.	d. Thomas has ——— it.

7. given	10. brought	13. sung
8. saw	11. seen	14. done
9. ate	12. did	15. lost

C. Write three sentences. In each sentence use a verb from the columns in Part B.

Lesson 65 Answers

A.
1. has gone
2. Did go
3. had flown
4. are staying
5. Does miss
6. has seen
7. Do write
8. have written
9. was reading
10. has come

B.
1. went—a		9. ate—c
2. run—b		10. brought—both
3. tried—both		11. seen—d
4. gone—b		12. did—c
5. ran—a		13. sung—d
6. came—a		14. done—d
7. given—d		15. lost—both
8. saw—c		

C. (Individual answers.)

Lesson 65

Aim: To review the previous four lessons.

Oral Review:
1. What kind of word must every sentence have? (a verb)
2. What two things do verbs show? (action and being)
3. Where can the verb be found in a sentence? (anywhere)
4. How is the past form of most verbs made? (by adding -ed)
5. Is the s form used with a singular subject or a plural subject? (a singular subject)
6. What are the eight forms of be? (am, is, are, was, were, be, been, being)
7. What are three sets of helping verbs? (do, does, did; have, has, had; forms of be)
8. Which helping verbs work together with past forms that need a helper? (have, has, had)
9. What little word is often used with verbs, but it is not a verb? (not)
10. In a contraction, the apostrophe takes the place of what? (the letter or letters that are left out)

Class: The Oral Review is longer than usual because this is the last lesson on verbs. You may use it for class discussion, or have the pupils give written answers to the questions.

D. Write the contractions of these words.

1. is not   4. were not   7. do not
2. are not   5. did not   8. has not
3. was not   6. does not   9. have not

E. Using the verb that is given, write a sentence about each picture.

1. thrown

3. seen

2. eaten

4. sung

F. Copy the wrong word in each sentence. Beside it write the correct word that should be used.

1. One evening Samuel done the chores.
2. Lois and me fed the sheep.
3. Father had went to town earlier.
4. He brung home a surprise for Mother.
5. Lois and her went out to the car.
6. They seen a box in the trunk.
7. There was twenty baby chicks in the box!

D. 1. isn't   4. weren't   7. don't
   2. aren't   5. didn't   8. hasn't
   3. wasn't   6. doesn't   9. haven't

E. (Possible answers.)
   1. Kevin has thrown the ball.
   2. The Millers have eaten.
   3. The children have seen the camels.
   4. The people have sung.

F. 1. done—did
   2. me—I
   3. went—gone
   4. brung—brought
   5. her—she
   6. seen—saw
   7. was—were

66. Subjects and Predicates

The subject is the sentence part that tells who or what the sentence is about. The noun or pronoun that tells who or what is called the **simple subject.**

The predicate tells what the subject does or is. The verb is called the **simple predicate.**

Most sentences have more words than just the simple subject and the simple predicate. The other words make the meaning of the sentence clearer. The simple subject and all the words that make its meaning clearer are called the **complete subject.** The simple predicate and all the words that make its meaning clearer are called the **complete predicate.**

COMPLETE SUBJECT   COMPLETE PREDICATE
The rich young **ruler** | **walked** away sadly.
                      ↑   ↑
             simple subject   simple predicate

To find the simple subject, first find the simple predicate (the verb). Then ask **who** or **what** with it. The noun or pronoun that tells who or what is the simple subject. Remember that there may be more than one simple subject or simple predicate.

Steven and **Charles** came. Who came?
Frogs swim and hop. What swim and hop?

To find the subject and predicate in an asking sentence, first change it into a telling sentence.

Can Carol sing?   Carol | can sing.
May John and I read?   John and I | may read.

Lesson 66

Aim: (1) To review that a sentence is composed of a subject and a predicate. (2) To teach the difference between the *simple* subject and predicate, and the *complete* subject and predicate.

Oral Review:
1. What is a sentence? (a group of words with a complete thought)
2. Use *do, does,* and *did* as helping verbs in questions. (Individual questions.)
3. Tell which verb form in each pair needs a helper.
   a. flown, flew (flown)
   b. began, begun (begun)
   c. gave, given (given)
   d. taken, took (taken)
4. What is wrong with this sentence? *I seen a fox this morning.* (*Seen* should be *saw.*)
5. The word *not* (is, is not) a verb. (is not)

Class: Review the concept of subjects and predicates as taught in Unit 1. Remind the class that the simple subject is the noun or pronoun that tells what the sentence is about. Often the simple subject is one word, but sometimes it is two or more. Give an example of each.

Crows cawed.   Boys and girls played.

Give the same review of simple predicates.

Plants grow.   Mark slipped and fell.

Clarify the difference between simple subjects and complete subjects, and between simple predicates and complete predicates. The former are usually individual words, but the latter are whole sentence parts. The simple subject and predicate may be compared to the seeds from which the rest of the sentence grows.

Review finding the subject and predicate in a

Remember: The two main parts of a sentence are the subject and the predicate. The simple subject is the noun or pronoun that tells who or what. The simple predicate is the verb or verb phrase that tells what the subject does or is.

Recognizing Sentence Parts

A. Copy these sentences. Draw a line to divide each one between the complete subject and the complete predicate.
 1. Beautiful white snow clung to the trees.
 2. The two balls rolled down the steps.
 3. My blue sweater tore yesterday.
 4. Three men sheared the sheep swiftly and skillfully.

B. In each sentence you wrote for Part A, underline the simple subject once and the simple predicate twice.

C. Rewrite these as telling sentences. Then underline each simple subject once and each simple predicate twice.
 1. Did you listen?
 2. Will Father and Mother come soon?
 3. Can seals and otters swim well?

Writing Sentences

Use each group of words as the subject of a telling sentence.
 1. robins and wrens   3. my family and I
 2. lions and tigers   4. Peter and John

Lesson 66 Answers
Recognizing Sentence Parts
A. (Underlining is for Part B.)
 1. Beautiful white <u>snow</u> | <u>clung</u> to the trees.
 2. The two <u>balls</u> | <u>rolled</u> down the steps.
 3. My blue <u>sweater</u> | <u>tore</u> yesterday.
 4. Three <u>men</u> | <u>sheared</u> the sheep swiftly and skillfully.

B. (Answers are included in Part A.)

C. 1. <u>You</u> <u>did listen</u>.
 2. <u>Father</u> and <u>Mother</u> <u>will come</u> soon.
 3. <u>Seals</u> and <u>otters</u> <u>can swim</u> well.

Writing Sentences
(Individual answers.)

question by changing the question into a statement. You could point out that the simple subject in a question often splits a verb phrase in half.

★ **EXTRA PRACTICE**
Worksheet 38 (*Subjects and Predicates*)

> Review and Practice >

Write the correct words for these sentences.
1. (They, Them) brought us a new pony.
2. The letter was for Thomas and (I, me).
3. Roger and (he, him) washed the car.
4. We picked some flowers for Grandmother and (she, her).
5. (We, Us) and (they, them) attended church last night.

> Can You Do This? >

Use each group of words in Writing Sentences as the subject of an asking sentence.

━━━━━━━━━━━━

67. Nouns After Action Verbs

The verb is the main word in the predicate of a sentence. The verb is called the simple predicate. There are other important words in the predicate too. These words help to make the meaning of the verb clearer.

Sometimes a noun after an action verb helps to make its meaning clearer. It does this by receiving the action of the verb. The noun that receives the action is called the **direct object.** Pronouns may also be direct objects.

Charles picked **berries.**   The boys found **us.**

What did Charles pick? Whom did the boys find? The words in bold print give the answers. They receive the action of **picked** and **found.**

Review and Practice
1. They
2. me
3. he
4. her
5. We, they

Can You Do This?
(Individual answers.)

Lesson 67

Aim: To introduce direct objects as nouns in the predicate that receive the action of the verb.

Oral Review:
1. Words that name are called ———. (nouns)
2. A verb phrase has one ——— verb and one or more ——— verbs. (main, helping)
3. Choose the correct words in these sentences.
   a. He (did, done) his work. (did)
   b. We (saw, seen) many interesting things. (saw)
   c. Have you (came, come) here before? (come)
   d. Ann had (went, gone) home before I (came, come). (gone, came)
4. Spell the contractions for *is not, were not, does not,* and *have not.* (isn't, weren't, doesn't, haven't)
5. What is the *complete subject* of a sentence? How can you find the *simple subject*? (The complete subject is the sentence part that tells who or what the sentence is about. To find the simple subject, first find the verb and then ask *who* or *what* with it.)

Class: Review the two main sentence parts. Ask: "What is the main word in the predicate?" (The verb, or simple predicate.) Write several examples that have only a verb in the predicate.

The three men <u>worked</u>.   <u>Can</u> dogs <u>swim</u>?

Then write sentences like the following on the board.

Jesus raised.   Mother makes.
Adam named.   Father bought.

These sentences do not seem complete because they do not tell *whom* Jesus raised, *what* Adam named, and so forth. This is because the idea of some action verbs is not complete unless there is a receiver of the action. The receiver is called the *direct object.*

To find the direct object in a sentence, say the simple subject and the simple predicate together, and then say "Whom?" or "What?" The noun or pronoun that tells whom or what is the direct object. Can you find the direct objects in these sentences?

> James kicked the ball.
> The hammer hit the nail.
> Carol called her.
> Anna welcomed them.
> Noah built a huge ark for all the animals.

Remember: A noun or pronoun that receives the action of a verb is called a direct object. The direct object is part of the complete predicate.

> Using Direct Objects >

A. Complete each sentence with a direct object. You may use nouns or pronouns.
  1. Timothy helped ——.
  2. The men built ——.
  3. Do you wash the ——.
  4. John baptized ——.
  5. Children sang ——.
  6. My teacher helps ——.
  7. Grandmother brought ——.
  8. David tended ——.
  9. We made ——.
  10. Father chased ——.

B. Write five sentences, using a direct object in each sentence. Underline the direct objects.

Lesson 67 Answers
Using Direct Objects
A. (Possible answers.)
  1. Paul
  2. houses
  3. dishes
  4. Jesus
  5. songs
  6. me
  7. berries
  8. sheep
  9. pictures
  10. calves

B. (Individual answers.)

Point out the difference between the subject and the direct object. The subject is the *doer* of the action, and the direct object is the *receiver* of the action.

Add *Lazarus, the animals, bread,* and *a book* to the four sentences above. The thought of each sentence is now complete because we know who or what received the action.

★ **EXTRA PRACTICE**
Worksheet 39 (*Direct Objects*)

A. Write the correct form of each verb in parentheses to complete these sentences.
   1. Lee has (catch) the ball.
   2. Elam had (throw) it.
   3. Have you (do) the chores?
   4. The cows have (eat) the hay.
   5. Has Father (bring) any feed?
   6. Abraham (begin) his journey early.

B. Copy each direct object in Part A.

Review and Practice

A. 1. caught
   2. thrown
   3. done
   4. eaten
   5. brought
   6. began

B. 1. ball
   2. it
   3. chores
   4. hay
   5. feed
   6. journey

68. Diagraming Nouns After Action Verbs

A diagram is a drawing that shows how something is made. A diagram gives a clearer understanding of how an object is put together.

Do you see how the diagram below gives a clearer picture of how a bicycle is made?

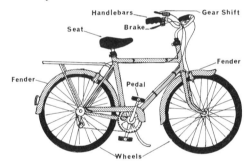

A **sentence diagram** should help you understand the different parts of a sentence and how the different parts work together.

Here is a sentence diagram of a simple subject and a simple predicate.

When you diagram a sentence, start with a base line like the one above. Draw a line through the base line. Then find the simple predicate (the verb or verb phrase), and put it to the right of the dividing line. Find the simple subject by asking **who** or **what** with the simple predicate, and put it to the left of the dividing line.

A sentence with a direct object is placed on a diagram like this.

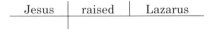

The line between the simple subject and the simple predicate goes all the way through the base line. But the line between the simple predicate and the direct object goes only to the base line.

> Reviewing Direct Objects >

Number your paper from 1 to 10. After each number write the direct object that is used in that sentence.
1. Mary wrote a letter.
2. David killed Goliath.

Lesson 68 Answers
Reviewing Direct Objects
1. letter
2. Goliath

Have them diagram only the simple subject, simple predicate, and direct object in each of these sentences.

Two hungry deer ate our corn.
Our little dog can play many tricks.

★ **EXTRA PRACTICE**
Worksheet 40 (*Diagraming Sentences With Direct Objects*)

3. Barbara made popcorn for us.
4. Birds build snug nests.
5. Men print many books.
6. We visited them.
7. Peter caught fish.
8. Jesus told parables.
9. The boys made snowmen.
10. Julia fried pancakes yesterday.

> **Diagraming Sentences**

Diagram the simple subject, simple predicate, and direct object in each sentence. If a sentence is a command with **you** understood, put **you** in parentheses.

1. Farmers milk cows.
2. Chickens lay eggs.
3. Wash the dishes.
4. Cardinals eat seeds.
5. God made stars.
6. Rake the leaves.

> **Review and Practice**

Write the plural form of each noun.
1. dish   3. ox   5. peach
2. class   4. turkey   6. enemy

3. popcorn
4. nests
5. books
6. them
7. fish
8. parables
9. snowmen
10. pancakes

Diagraming Sentences

1. Farmers | milk | cows

2. Chickens | lay | eggs

3. (you) | Wash | dishes

4. Cardinals | eat | seeds

5. God | made | stars

6. (you) | Rake | Leaves

Review and Practice

1. dishes   4. turkeys
2. classes   5. peaches
3. oxen   6. enemies

69. More About Action Verbs

You have learned about direct objects and how to find them in sentences. But you should not expect to find a direct object after every action verb, because not every sentence has a direct object. The following sentences do not have direct objects, but they are still complete.

>   Many parents worked busily.
>   The children helped cheerfully.

How can you tell if a sentence has a direct object? Say the simple subject and the simple predicate together, and then ask **whom** or **what.** The noun or pronoun that answers the question is the direct object. If there is no noun or pronoun to answer the question, the sentence does not have a direct object.

Study the examples below. The sentences on the left are complete, even though they have no direct objects. The sentences on the right have direct objects.

We wrote.	We wrote **letters.**
Eve ate.	Eve ate **fruit.**
Martha washed.	Martha washed **clothes.**
Mother sang cheerily.	Mother sang **songs.**
The boys played happily.	The boys played **games.**

Be especially careful with sentences like the last two in the left column. Think: Does **cheerily** tell what Mother sang? Does **happily** tell what the boys played? Both answers are **no.** So these sentences do not have direct objects.

Lesson 69

Aim: To teach that not every action verb is followed by a direct object.

Oral Review:

1. What must we remember when we write proper nouns? Give three examples. (Proper nouns must be capitalized. Individual examples.)
2. In words like *isn't* and *haven't,* what letter is replaced by the apostrophe? What word does this letter belong to? (o; not)
3. How can you find the simple subject of a sentence? (Find the verb and ask *who* or *what* with it.)
4. Give the complete predicate in this sentence: Mother writes letters. What is the direct object? (writes letters; letters)

5. Diagram this sentence: Mother writes letters

Mother	writes	letters

Class: Illustrate sentences without direct objects by reading the two example sentences after the first paragraph and asking "What?" and "Whom?" (The parents worked what? The children helped whom?) It does not seem sensible to ask these questions after some action verbs. (See first sentence.) Even if it is sensible, there is not always a word to answer the question. (See second sentence.)

Use the second set of example sentences for further drill. Emphasize that a direct object *must* be a noun or pronoun that answers the question *whom* or *what.* If there is no such noun or pronoun, the sentence has no direct object—even though it may

> Finding Direct Objects >

A. Decide whether each sentence has a direct object. If it does, copy the direct object on your paper. If it does not, write **no**.

1. Sarah laughed.
2. Abel offered a sacrifice.
3. Jesus loves children.
4. Daniel prayed daily.
5. Aaron made an idol.
6. Peter wept bitterly.
7. The ravens brought food.
8. Jesus healed many people.
9. David wrote many psalms.
10. Read this book carefully.
11. Lot chose the best land.
12. Paul made tents.
13. Stephen preached earnestly.
14. God gave commandments.

B. Diagram the simple subject and simple predicate of sentences 1–10 in Part A. Also diagram the direct object if there is one.

> Review and Practice >

1. Using three nouns in a series, write a sentence saying what you see in your classroom.
2. Using four proper nouns in a series, write a sentence about four people in the Bible.
3. Using three nouns in a series, write a sentence about three foods that you like.

A. 1. no
2. sacrifice
3. children
4. no
5. idol
6. no
7. food
8. people
9. psalms
10. book
11. land
12. tents
13. no
14. commandments

B. 1. Sarah | laughed
2. Abel | offered | sacrifice
3. Jesus | loves | children
4. Daniel | prayed
5. Aaron | made | idol
6. Peter | wept
7. ravens | brought | food
8. Jesus | healed | people
9. David | wrote | psalms
10. (you) | Read | book

Review and Practice
(Individual answers. Check for correct use of commas with nouns in series.)

...ave words that tell *how, when,* or *where.* You may ...vish to mention that words like *cheerily* and *happily* ...re adverbs, which the pupils will study later.

In Part B of the exercises, the pupils are instructed ...o diagram only simple subjects, simple predicates, and ...irect objects. Remind them that simple subjects and ...irect objects are always nouns or pronouns, and that ...imple predicates are always verbs. In later lessons they ...vill learn about the other words in sentences and how ...o diagram them.

★ **EXTRA PRACTICE**
Worksheet 41 (*More About Direct Objects*)

70. Reviewing What You Have Learned

> Oral Drill >

Use these sentences to do Parts A, B, C, and D.
1. The quetzal is a beautiful bird.
2. Pittsburgh and Philadelphia are cities in Pennsylvania.
3. Gorillas and chimpanzees are apes.
4. Owls catch many mice.
5. Do rocks contain minerals?
6. Pennies and dimes are money.
7. Jesus arose on the third day.
8. God created the whole world in six days.
9. Moose have huge antlers.
10. Feed your rabbits.
11. Sinai and Ararat are mountains.
12. Trains haul much freight.
13. Turtles lay eggs in the sand.
14. Firs and cedars are tall trees.
15. Beavers cut down trees with their teeth.

Lesson 70

Aim: To review and strengthen concepts taught earlier, and to evaluate how well students have mastered these concepts.

Class: Do the Oral Drill in class. For further drill, have students go to the chalkboard and diagram the main parts of some sentences in the Oral Drill. (Use only sentences 4, 5, 7, 8, 9, 10, 12, 13, and 15; the other sentences do not have action verbs.)

For Part D of Oral Drill, point out that if a sentence has a form of *be* as the main verb, it cannot have a direct object. Only action verbs can have receivers of the action.

Lesson 70 Answers
Oral Drill
A–B.
1. quetzal | is
2. Pittsburgh, Philadelphia | are
3. Gorillas, chimpanzees | are
4. Owls | catch
5. rocks | Do contain
6. Pennies, dimes | are
7. Jesus | arose
8. God | created
9. Moose | have
10. (You) | Feed
11. Sinai, Ararat | are
12. Trains | haul
13. Turtles | lay
14. Firs, cedars | are
15. Beavers | cut

C.
1. is a beautiful bird
2. are cities in Pennsylvania
3. are apes
4. catch many mice
5. Do contain minerals
6. are money
7. arose on the third day
8. created the whole world in six days
9. have huge antlers
10. Feed your rabbits
11. are mountains
12. haul much freight
13. lay eggs in the sand
14. are tall trees
15. cut down trees with their teeth

D.
1. no
2. no
3. no
4. yes; mice
5. yes; minerals
6. no
7. no
8. yes; world
9. yes; antlers
10. yes; rabbits
11. no
12. yes; freight
13. yes; eggs
14. no
15. yes; trees

A. Tell what the simple subject is in each sentence.

B. Tell what the simple predicate is in each sentence.

C. Tell what the complete predicate is in each sentence.

D. Say **yes** or **no** to tell whether each sentence has a direct object. If it does, say what it is.

> Written Practice

A. Write **true** or **false** for each sentence.
1. Every sentence has a subject and a predicate.
2. The complete subject is the noun that tells who or what the sentence is about.
3. The noun that receives the action of the verb is called the direct object.
4. The direct object is diagramed on a slanted line under the verb.
5. Every action verb is followed by a direct object.

B. Diagram only the simple subjects, simple predicates, and direct objects of these sentences.
1. Mother baked good cookies.
2. We ate them.
3. Jesus did many miracles.
4. The chickens ate greedily.
5. The busy bees are making honey.
6. Many farmers raise wheat.
7. Father nailed the boards tightly.
8. The carpenters were working hard.
9. John baptized Jesus.
10. The mailman delivered the mail early.

Written Practice

A. 1. true
2. false
3. true
4. false
5. false

B. 1. Mother | baked | cookies

2. We | ate | them

3. Jesus | did | miracles

4. chickens | ate

5. bees | are making | honey

6. farmers | raise | wheat

7. Father | nailed | boards

8. carpenters | were working

9. John | baptized | Jesus

10. mailman | delivered | mail

Building Paragraphs

A paragraph, I think you'll find,
    Is built much like a train.
The sentences are like the cars,
    Each is complete and plain.
But when they're linked in order clear
    With topic in the lead,
They're off in one direction to
    Perform a noble deed.

The words are like the passengers,
    There's great variety,
To show our minds the things we hear,
    And smell, and taste, and see.
We gather information through
    Our senses, which is good.
But we need other helpers too,
    To get the facts we should.

Since we are just one person and
    Our knowledge is so small,
To other people and to books
    For further help we call.
The dictionary neighbor friend
    Right in our classroom lives;
We should consult him often for
    The knowledge that he gives.

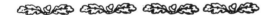

71. Meeting the Paragraph

Do you know how to write a paragraph? First write several sentences about one topic. Be careful to write your sentences in the order the things happened.

1. Moses was taking care of the sheep.
2. Suddenly he saw a burning bush.
3. God spoke to Moses from the bush.

To write your sentences as a paragraph, **indent** the first sentence about half an inch from the left margin. Write the sentences one after another. Keep the left margin very straight, except for the first line. Keep the right margin as straight as you can.

> Moses was taking care of the sheep. Suddenly he saw a burning bush. God spoke to Moses from the bush.

Remember: The sentences in a paragraph should tell about one subject. They should be in correct order. The paragraph should be written in correct form, with the first line indented.

Lesson 71

Aim: To introduce the correct form of a paragraph, and to teach that the sentences in a paragraph should all tell about one topic.

Oral Review:

1. Is 's used to spell the plural form or the possessive form of a noun? (possessive form)
2. Say the complete predicate in this sentence: *Jesus healed people.* (healed people)
3. What is the simple subject of *Jesus healed people*? (Jesus)
4. What is a direct object? How do we diagram it? (a noun or pronoun that receives the action of a verb; We put a straight line between the verb and the noun.)
5. Use *played* in a sentence with a direct object. Then use *played* without a direct object. (Individual answers.)

Class: Ask the class to help you write a paragraph about one topic. You could suggest writing about Samuel, and list the following sentences on the board.

(1) Hannah prayed for a boy.
(3) Samuel worked for Eli, the priest.
(4) His mother visited him every year.
Once Saul tore Samuel's robe.
(2) God gave Hannah a boy named Samuel.

Cross out the sentence that does not belong (the fourth one). Number the remaining sentences in the order they happened. Finally, show the class how to write the sentences in correct form as a paragraph. You can further illustrate paragraph indentation by pointing out the form of each paragraph in the lesson.

> Working With Paragraphs >

A. Which group of sentences below can be used to write a paragraph? Find the group and write the sentences correctly in paragraph form.
  1. a. God told Noah to build an ark.
     b. Noah was the father of Shem.
     c. Jesse was David's father.
  2. a. God told Noah to build an ark.
     b. He told Noah what size to make it.
     c. Noah did exactly what God said.

B. Write a sentence about each picture. Then write your sentences in paragraph form.

1.

2.

3.

> Review and Practice >

Copy each verb. Then write a verb phrase, using **have** and the helper form of the verb.
  1. begin   5. cry   9. take
  2. bring   6. come   10. catch
  3. sing   7. see   11. throw
  4. talk   8. find   12. pray

Lesson 71 Answers
Working With Paragraphs
A. (Group 2 can be used.)

  God told Noah to build an ark. He told Noah what size to make it. Noah did exactly what God said.

B. (Possible paragraph.)

  One day a sheep was eating the peas. Karen and Carl ran after the sheep. They shut him back in his pen.

Review and Practice
  1. begin, have begun
  2. bring, have brought
  3. sing, have sung
  4. talk, have talked
  5. cry, have cried
  6. come, have come
  7. see, have seen
  8. find, have found
  9. take, have taken
  10. catch, have caught
  11. throw, have thrown
  12. pray, have prayed

72. Writing Sentences in Correct Order

Read the sentences below. Which sentence tells what happened first? second? third?

    a. Father and Uncle Ray said they would do Mr. White's chores.

    b. One day Mr. White fell and hurt his leg.

    c. The doctor told him to stay in bed for a week.

When you write a paragraph, always write the sentences in correct order. Here is how the three sentences from above should be written.

> One day Mr. White fell and hurt his leg. The doctor told him to stay in bed for a week. Father and Uncle Ray said they would do Mr. White's chores.

> Writing in Correct Order >

A. Read the paragraph below. Can you tell what happened? Rewrite the paragraph, putting the sentences in correct order.

> Finally the snowman was finished. One day we had a deep snow. Then we made two smaller balls. Jason and I decided to make a snowman. Next we stacked the little balls on the big ball. First we made one big ball.

Lesson 72 Answers
Writing in Correct Order

A.   One day we had a deep snow. Jason and I decided to make a snowman. First we made one big bell. Then we made two smaller balls. Next we stacked the little balls on the big ball. Finally the snowman was finished.

Lesson 72

Aim: To teach the concept of writing sentences in correct order in a paragraph.

Oral Review:

1. When is *-es* used to make the plural form of a noun? (when the noun ends with *s, x, ch,* or *sh*)
2. Tell whether an apostrophe should be used in each sentence.
   a. The boys wore their coats. (no)
   b. One boys coat was torn. (yes)
   c. Two boys had blue coats. (no)
3. What do we call a noun that receives the action of a verb? (a direct object)
4. How should we write the first line of a paragraph? (Indent it.)
5. All the sentences in a paragraph should tell about ———. (one topic)

Class: Read the first paragraph of the lesson and the three sentences after it. Then copy the sentences on the board in paragraph form, and ask why the paragraph is confusing. (The sentences are not in the right order. The first one gives the result, and the second one gives the cause.) The correctly written paragraph is better because it says things in the right order.

Then read together the sentences in Part A. Discuss which sentence should come first, second, and so forth. Have the students write the paragraph correctly as part of their assignment.

Note: Chronological order is not the only way to arrange sentences in a good paragraph. Order in many paragraphs is based on a progression of thought rather than a sequence of events. This concept is too advanced for most third graders. But they do need to learn that a paragraph cannot be made from just any group of sentences. Sentences must

B. Write the numbers of the pictures in the order they probably happened. Write a sentence for each picture. Use your sentences to write a paragraph.

1.

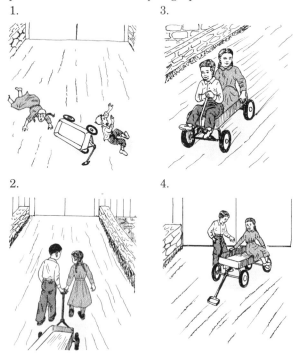

3.

2.

4.

> Review and Practice >

Use the paragraph about the snowman to do these things. Do not write any word more than once.

1. Copy five singular nouns.
2. Copy one plural noun.
3. Copy two pronouns.

B. (Correct order is 2, 4, 3, 1. Individual paragraphs.)

Review and Practice

1. day, snow, Jason, snowman, ball
2. balls
3. we, I

be about the same topic and they must be arranged by an orderly plan if the result is to be an acceptable paragraph.

★ **EXTRA PRACTICE**
Worksheet 42 (*Writing Sentences in Correct Order*)

73. The Topic of a Paragraph

A paragraph should tell about only one thing. That one thing is called the **topic** of the paragraph. Often the first sentence tells what the topic of a paragraph is. This sentence is called the **topic sentence.**

> Jeremiah was a faithful prophet. He spoke the words that God told him to speak. Even after he was in prison, Jeremiah continued speaking God's Word.

What is the first sentence in the paragraph above? Do the other sentences tell about Jeremiah? Do they tell how he was a faithful prophet?

Now read the paragraph below. Which sentence is the topic sentence of the paragraph? Also find the one sentence that does not belong.

> Jonah was a prophet of God. One day God told Jonah to go to Nineveh. He told Jonah to tell the people that they were wicked. Amos was a prophet too. Jonah went to Nineveh and told the people everything God had said.

> **Writing About One Topic**

A. Read the paragraph below. Then answer the questions that follow.

> Corn is an important crop. Farmers raise corn to feed to their animals. They also feed oats to their animals. Some corn is used to make cooking oil, cornmeal, and margarine.

1. What is the topic of the paragraph?
2. Which sentence does not belong?
3. Why do farmers raise corn?
4. What are some things made from corn?

Lesson 73 Answers
Writing About One Topic
A. 1. corn
   2. They also feed oats to their animals.
   3. Farmers raise corn as feed for animals and food for people.
   4. Cooking oil, cornmeal, and margarine are some things made from corn.

Lesson 73

Aim: To rivet the fact that a paragraph should have one main topic.

Oral Review:
1. Words that name are called ———. What do they name? (nouns; people, places, things)
2. True or false: Every action verb is followed by a direct object. (false)
3. Diagram this sentence: *Help me.*

   (you) | Help | me

4. What kind of margins should we have when we write a paragraph? (We should keep the left margin very straight, except for the first line, and the right margin as straight as we can.)
5. Sentences in a paragraph should be written in what order? (in the order that the things happened)

Class: Call attention to the lesson title. Remind the class that every sentence has a subject that tells what the whole sentence is about. In the same way, every good paragraph has a topic—one main idea—that the whole paragraph is about.

Read together the paragraphs about Jeremiah and Jonah, and answer the questions about them. Then write another topic sentence on the board. Ask the class to give some sentences that would belong in the same paragraph.

Examples:
> On Sunday we enjoy going to church. (What things do we enjoy there?)
> Spring is my favorite season. (For what reasons?)

B. Choose one of the topics pictured. Write a paragraph about the topic.

Our Garden　　　My Family　　　Sunday School

> Review and Practice

Diagram the simple subject and simple predicate of each sentence. Also diagram the direct object if there is one.

1. Run quickly!
2. Children play games.
3. Call Mary.
4. Did you run?
5. Catch the ball!
6. Winter has come.

74. Choosing a Good Title

A good title tells you what a paragraph is about before you read it. Which of these do you think would be a good title for the paragraph on the next page?

    a. Ostrich Eggs
    b. The Size of a Bird
    c. Eggs Large and Small
    d. A Trip to the Farm

B. (Individual paragraphs.)

Review and Practice

1. ___(you) | Run___

2. ___Children | play | games___

3. ___(you) | Call | Mary___

4. ___you | Did run___

5. ___(you) | Catch | ball___

6. ___Winter | has come___

Mothers do many things. (What are some of them?)

Any one of the sentences above may be used to build sample paragraphs in class. The questions should help the pupils to think of suitable details to add.

★ **EXTRA PRACTICE**
Worksheet 43 (*The Topic of a Paragraph*)

Lesson 74

Aim: To guide the students in choosing a good title for a paragraph.

Written Quiz:
  1. Underline the correct words.
    a. Yesterday a new boy (came, come) to school.

    b. Have you ever (went, gone) to a museum
  2. Underline the verb phrase in this sentence.
    Samuel did not come for seven days.

  3. Diagram these sentences.
    a. Roses are blooming.
    b. Mother picked peas.
  4. Give the letters of these sentences in the orde
    that they should be written.
      (a) When the Flood came, Noah and his fam
    ily were safe in the ark. (b) God told Noah t
    build an ark. (c) Noah did as God said.
  5. Give the letter of the sentence that does no
    belong.
      (a) Daniel prayed three times a day
    (b) Wicked men were watching and listening
    (c) Ezra also prayed earnestly. (d) The me
    told the king that Daniel was praying to Go
    (e) Daniel was thrown into the lions' den.

Eggs come in many sizes. An ostrich egg is as big as two dozen chicken eggs. The egg of a robin is much smaller. But the smallest bird egg is the hummingbird's. It is only as big as a bean!

If you chose **c,** you are right. Only the title "Eggs Large and Small" tells what the whole paragraph is about.

Look at the way titles are written. The first word and every important word is capitalized. A little word like **of, and, a, to, on,** or **the** is not capitalized unless it is the first word of the title.

> **Writing Titles** >

A. Write each title correctly.
1. nests on the ground
2. baskets and mud
3. different kinds of nests
4. a hanging nest
5. four kinds of birds

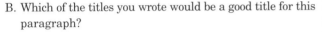

B. Which of the titles you wrote would be a good title for this paragraph?

> Birds build many kinds of nests. The oriole builds a hanging nest that swings like a basket. The robin builds a nest of mud and grass. Some birds, like the meadowlark, build their nests right on the ground.

> **Review and Practice** >

A. Copy any ten nouns from the paragraph in Part B above. Write **S** after each singular noun and **P** after each plural noun.

Lesson 74 Answers
Writing Titles
A. 1. Nests on the Ground
   2. Baskets and Mud
   3. Different Kinds of Nests
   4. A Hanging Nest
   5. Four Kinds of Birds

B. Different Kinds of Nests

Review and Practice
A. (Any ten of these.)

birds—P	nest—S
kinds—P	mud—S
nests—P	grass—S
oriole—S	birds—P
nest—S	meadowlark—S
basket—S	nests—P
robin—S	ground—S

Quiz Answers:
1. a. came
   b. gone
2. did come

3. a. <u>Roses</u> | <u>are blooming</u>

   b. <u>Mother</u> | <u>picked</u> | <u>peas</u>

4. b, c, a
5. c

Class: Discuss the text of today's lesson, then look at the paragraphs in the previous lesson. Write three possible titles on the board for the paragraph about Jeremiah. Ask the class which title they think best tells what the paragraph is about. (The star indicates the best choice.)

   A Man in Prison

   God's Word
   *A Faithful Prophet

Do the same with the other two paragraphs from Lesson 73.

   A Man and a Whale
   *How God Used Jonah
   Amos and Jonah

   *Why Corn Is Important
   What Farmers Feed Their Animals
   How Margarine Is Made

As each correct title is chosen, discuss why the other titles do not fit. Point out that each of the other titles does fit some of the details in the paragraph, but it does not really tell what the whole paragraph is about.

Discuss and drill the capitalizing of words in a title; book titles could be used for more practice. The

B. Write a title of your own for this paragraph.

> Some birds are not able to fly. A penguin will swim, but it will never fly. The big ostrich has wings too small for flying. The emu, rhea, kiwi, and cassowary are four other birds whose wings cannot take them into the air.

C. Are there any words in the paragraph above that you cannot pronounce? Find them in the dictionary and be ready to pronounce them in class.

B. (Possible answers.)
   Birds That Never Fly
   Birds That Cannot Fly
   Not All Birds Fly

C. (Pronunciations for the more unfamiliar bird names.)
   emu   (EE myoo)
   rhea   (REE uh)
   kiwi   (KEE wee)
   cassowary   (KASS uh wair' ee)

75. Reviewing What You Have Learned

> Oral Drill >

1. When you write a paragraph, in what order should you write the sentences in the paragraph?
2. The sentences in a paragraph must all tell about ———— .
3. In what form should a paragraph be written?
4. How might you be able to tell what the topic of a paragraph is?
5. What does a good title do for us?
6. How should titles be written?
7. What words in titles are often not capitalized?
8. When should these words be capitalized?

Lesson 75 Answers:
Oral Drill

1. Write the sentences in the order the things happened.
2. one topic
3. The first line should be indented, the left margin should be straight, and the right margin should be as straight as possible.
4. You might be able to tell by reading the first sentence, which is often the topic sentence.
5. A good title tells us what the paragraph is about before we read it.
6. The first word and all the important words should be capitalized.
7. Little words like *of, and, a, to,* and *the* are often not capitalized.
8. These words should be capitalized when they are the first word of a title.

"little words" include articles, prepositions, and conjunctions of three letters or less. They are not capitalized because they are not as important as the other words.

★ **EXTRA PRACTICE**
Worksheet 44 (*Working With Titles*)

Lesson 75

Aim: To review and strengthen concepts taught in the last four lessons.

Class: Do the Oral Drill in class. In the Written Practice (Part A), you could write one of the paragraphs together in class. Discuss the pupils' suggestions and point out why they are or are not logical.

> Written Practice

A. Make a good paragraph from each group of sentences. Remember the rules you learned about writing paragraphs.

Group 1

God confounded their language.

The people decided to build a tower that would reach to heaven.

Solomon built a temple.

God came down to see the tower that they had made.

The people were scattered because they could not understand each other anymore.

Group 2

They uncovered the roof and let him down in front of Jesus.

A sick man had four friends.

The man got up and carried his bed.

They brought the man to Jesus.

Jesus healed him.

Peter's wife's mother was sick.

B. Write a good title for each paragraph you wrote in Part A.

C. Write the title of a book or a story you have read.

D. Write these titles correctly.
1. rachel changes her mind
2. stephen's shopping trip
3. the cost of a lie
4. the two full dishes
5. learning to trust
6. the sick calf.

Written Practice

A.   Group 1

 The people decided to build a tower that would reach to heaven. God came down to see the tower that they had made. God confounded their language. The people were scattered because they could not understand each other anymore.

Group 2

 A sick man had four friends. They brought the man to Jesus. They uncovered the roof and let him down in front of Jesus. Jesus healed him. The man got up and carried his bed.

B. (Possible answers.)
First paragraph: The Unfinished Tower
Second paragraph: Jesus Heals a Sick Man

C. (Individual answers.)

D. 1. Rachel Changes Her Mind
 2. Stephen's Shopping Trip
 3. The Cost of a Lie
 4. The Two Full Dishes
 5. Learning to Trust
 6. The Sick Calf

7. grandmother remembers
8. arlene finds the answer

E. What is the topic of this paragraph? Write it on your paper.

> The baby grouse, a speckled ball of softness, was two weeks old. He had been the last of the chicks to hatch. He was more eager than his brothers and sisters to be up and going this mountain morning in June. As dawn began flushing the slope with daylight, he grew restless.

7. Grandmother Remembers
8. Arlene Finds the Answer

E. a baby grouse

Review One

A. Answer these questions.
1. What is an action verb?
2. Give some examples of action verbs.
3. Give the eight forms of **be.**
4. How is the verb **be** different from other verbs?
5. What are some verbs which show action that cannot easily be seen or heard?
6. What is meant by the past form of a verb?
7. Which verbs do we use when we talk about someone owning or possessing something?
8. Which verb forms usually need a helping verb?

B. All these sentences are about the present time. Tell how each one should be changed, and why.
1. Aunt Mary make quilts.
2. My brothers cuts down that tree.

Review One Answers
Oral Drill

A. 1. An action verb is a word that expresses actio⦀
   2. (Possible answers.) run, smile, work, sin⦀ pray
   3. am, is, are was, were, be, been, being
   4. The verb *be* just says that something *is* or *wa⦀* (It shows existence.) All other verbs expre⦀ action. (They show occurrence.)
   5. (Possible answers.) think, feel, hope, lik⦀ believe
   6. The past form of a verb is the form that sho⦀ past action.
   7. have, has, had
   8. the forms ending with an *n* or *un* sound

B. 1. *Make* should have the *s* form because t⦀ subject is singular.
   2. *Cuts* should not have the *s* form because t⦀ subject is plural.

Review One

Aim: To reinforce and evaluate concepts taught earlier.

Class: Do the Oral Drill in class. It would also be good to discuss each part of the Written Practice.

3. The pony pull the cart.
4. The cat meow when it is hungry.
5. Brother William study the Bible.

C. Say the two verbs used in each sentence below.
1. Have the boys done the chores?
2. Did you pick many blackberries?
3. Will you walk with me to the creek?
4. Has the flight to Chicago left?
5. Did you give the note to Mother?
6. Were you driving through the rain?
7. I am going on a trip.

> Written Practice >

A. Copy the verb or verb phrase in each sentence.
1. You are in the third grade.
2. You are doing your English lesson.
3. Was your other lesson done neatly?
4. Your teacher has helped you.
5. This is a review lesson.
6. Begin right away.
7. You have a pencil and some paper.
8. Did you read each sentence carefully?

B. Write the past form of each verb.
1. jump   4. try
2. paint   5. gather
3. like   6. carry

C. Write the past form of each verb. Also write a verb phrase using **has** and the helper form.
1. see   3. come
2. throw   4. do

3. *Pull* should have the s form because the subject is singular.
4. *Meow* should have the s form because the subject is singular.
5. *Study* should have the s form because the subject is singular.

C. 1. Have done   5. Did give
2. Did pick   6. Were driving
3. Will walk   7. am going
4. Has left

Written Practice
A. 1. are
2. are doing
3. Was done
4. has helped
5. is
6. Begin
7. have
8. Did read

B. 1. jumped   4. tried
2. painted   5. gathered
3. liked   6. carried

C. 1. saw, has seen
2. threw, has thrown
3. came, has come
4. did, has done

D. Write four sentences of your own, using verbs you wrote for Parts B and C.

E. Write the correct word for each sentence.
1. There (is, are) two robins' nests in that tree.
2. There (is, are) a spider web on the rosebush.
3. There (was, were) two big crows on the fence.
4. There (is, are) some tadpoles darting through the water.
5. There (was, were) many bees buzzing around the clover blossoms.

D. (Individual answers.)

E. 1. are
   2. is
   3. were
   4. are
   5. were

Review Two

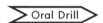

Answer these questions.
1. What is a contraction?
2. The word **not** is not a ——.
3. The verb in a sentence is called the —— ——.
4. What is a complete predicate?
5. What is a direct object?
6. On a sentence diagram, how is the line between the simple subject and the simple predicate different from the line between the simple predicate and the direct object?
7. Which group of sentences makes a good paragraph? What is wrong with the other group?

Review Two Answers
Oral Drill
1. A contraction is a word like *didn't* for *di* *not*. The apostrophe takes the place of the in *not*.
2. verb
3. simple predicate
4. A complete predicate is a simple predicat and all the words that make its meaning clearer.
5. A direct object is a noun or pronoun tha receives the action of a verb.
6. The line between the simple subject and the simple predicate goes all the way through the base line. The line between the simpl predicate and the direct object goes only t the base line.
7. The first group. In the second group, the sen tences do not talk about the same topic.

Review Two

Aim: To strengthen and evaluate concepts taught previously in preparation for a test.

Class: Do Oral Drill in class. Discuss Written Practice as needed.

Africa is a large continent with many forests. More than eight hundred languages are spoken in Africa. Many Africans cannot read and write. Their main food is grain.

Job was a righteous man who had seven sons and three daughters. Jacob had twelve sons. Baby Moses was put into a basket in the river. John the Baptist preached along the Jordan.

8. In the group you chose, how can you tell what the topic is without reading every sentence?
9. Think of a good title for the paragraph.
10. How should titles be written?

> Written Practice >

A. Copy one wrong word from each sentence, and write the correct word beside it.
1. Jonah had ran away instead of preaching.
2. We sung the new hymn over and over.
3. "Your shirt is tore," said Robert.
4. The airplane pilot has flew to Europe many times.
5. The potato plants have grew since the rain.
6. The Pilgrims begun thinking about coming to America.

B. Use **came, come, went,** or **gone** to finish these sentences.
1. Elijah —— up by a whirlwind into heaven.
2. Jesus said, "I will —— again."
3. Jesus had —— to the garden before.
4. He had —— out of the tomb before Mary came.
5. The disciples —— fishing.

8. You can read the first sentence. (It is the topic sentence.)
9. (Possible answer.) The Land of Africa
10. The first word and all important words should be capitalized.

Written Practice

A. 1. ran—run
2. sung—sang
3. tore—torn
4. flew—flown
5. grew—grown
6. begun—began

B. 1. went
2. come
3. gone
4. come *or* gone
5. went

C. Copy each word that is used wrong, and beside it write the correct word.
1. Mother had went to the neighbors.
2. While she was gone, I done all the dishes.
3. I seen an unusual bird outside the window.
4. I had never saw such a bird before.

D. Write contractions for these words.

1. have not	4. should not
2. do not	5. would not
3. can not	6. could not

E. Diagram the simple subjects, simple predicates, and any direct objects in these sentences.
1. Abraham trusted God.
2. Elijah prayed earnestly.
3. David killed the giant.
4. Paul and Silas were in prison.

● ● ● ● ● ● ● ● ●

C. 1. went—gone
2. done—did
3. seen—saw
4. saw—seen

D. 1. haven't
2. don't
3. can't
4. shouldn't
5. wouldn't
6. couldn't

E. 1. Abraham | trusted | God

2. Elijah | prayed

3. David | killed | giant

4. Paul and Silas | were

Extra Activity

You may continue working on your booklet **Building Blocks of English.** For the first three pages in the verb section, collect pictures that show action. Below each picture, write a verb that tells what action is being done.

On the next three pages, put pictures for the phrases **have gone, have seen, have run, have come, have given,** and **have done.** Write sentences with these phrases under the pictures.

For the phrase **have gone,** you could use a picture of a place where you have gone. Then you could write a sentence like this one: I have gone to the store.

Here are a few more examples.

a. I have seen a goldfinch. (Write this sentence under a picture of a goldfinch.)

b. I have run to the house. (Write this sentence under a picture of a house.)

c. The robins have come. (Write this sentence under a picture of some robins.)

Remember to do your work neatly. Check the dictionary if you do not know how to spell a word.

Extra Activity

Aim: To give added drill with verbs, and to provide fast workers with a profitable project.

Class: This project is optional, but be sure the pupils who start it also finish it. Check their work from time to time.

(All answers are individual work.)

A Poem to Enjoy

The Swing

How do you like to go up in a swing,
  Up in the air so blue?
Oh, I do think it the pleasantest thing
  Ever a child can do!

Up in the air and over the wall,
  Till I can see so wide,
Rivers and trees and cattle and all
  Over the countryside.

Till I look down on the garden green,
  Down on the roof so brown—
Up in the air I go flying again,
  Up in the air and down!
                    —*Robert Louis Stevenson*

A Poem to Enjoy

Aim: (1) To help pupils appreciate good poetry. (2) To help pupils read and recite poetry with proper expression.

Class: Discuss the poem, using the questions in the textbook or any questions you or the pupils may have. Point out that this is a poem which can be read with much feeling, and give practice reading it that way. Each pupil could choose one of the stanzas and read it, using proper expression.

This poem is a good one for pupils to memorize. It may also be used for an art project. Each pupil could draw a swing and neatly copy the poem underneath or beside it.

Discussing the Poem

1. How many verbs and verb phrases can you find in this poem?
2. Find and read the question in the poem.
3. Read each sentence that ends with an exclamation mark.
4. Why do you think these sentences end with an exclamation mark?
5. Which two of these feelings are expressed in the poem? excitement, fear, sadness, delight, worry
6. What does the poet see when he is going high in the air on a swing?
7. What does the poet see when he is coming down again?

Answers to Discussion Questions

1. eight—do like, go, do think, can do, can see, look, go, flying (Verbals are also counted as verbs.)
2. How do you like to go up in a swing, / Up in the air so blue?
3. Oh, I do think it the pleasantest thing / Ever a child can do!

   Up in the air I go flying again, / Up in the air and down!
4. Both sentences are said with strong feeling (the excitement of going up high in a swing).
5. excitement, delight
6. rivers, trees, cattle, countryside
7. garden, roof

Unit 4

Building With
Adjectives and Adverbs

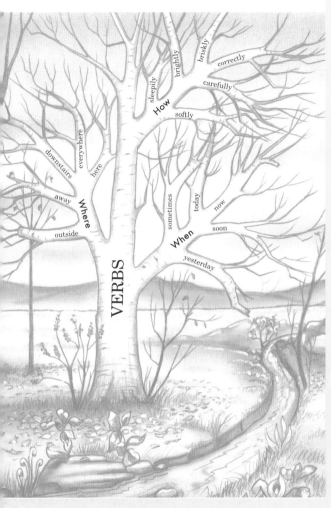

76. Words That Tell *What Kind Of*

An **adjective** is a word that describes a noun. Many adjectives answer the question **what kind of.** This question may have many different answers.

What kind of banana? (yellow, ripe, delicious)
What kind of rose? (red, fragrant, wild)
What kind of kitten? (little, furry, playful)

What adjectives can you use to describe the things in these pictures?

Tell what nouns these adjectives might describe.

young   sad   heavy   crooked

Adjectives are often used just before the nouns they describe. On a sentence diagram, adjectives are placed on slanted lines under the nouns they describe.

Lesson 76

Aim: To introduce adjectives, and to show that many adjectives tell *what kind of* about nouns.

Oral Review:

1. Words that stand for nouns are ———. (pronouns)
2. How do we write the first line in a paragraph? (Indent it.)
3. In what order should we write the sentences in a paragraph? (in the order that things happened)
4. All the sentences in a paragraph must tell about ———. (one topic)
5. In a title, should a word like *of, and, to,* or *the* ever be capitalized? (It should not be capitalized unless it is the first word in the title.)

Class: Read the first paragraph of the lesson in class. Explain that a noun names a person, place, or thing, but an adjective helps us to give a better picture of what the noun names. Then have the students use adjective in phrases to describe the various items pictured i the lesson. Examples: a yellow banana, a red ros a little kitten, a cold ice cube, hot water, a cuddl teddy bear.

Go on to the next part and ask the class wha nouns each of the four adjectives might describ Examples: a young man, a sad story, a heavy loa a crooked path.

Discuss the diagraming of sentences with adje tives. You could give diagraming practice at th board by using sentences like the following, whic contain phrases from the lesson.

I like ripe bananas.
Fragrant roses are blooming.
Use hot water.

★ **EXTRA PRACTICE**
Worksheet 45 (*Working With Adjectives*)

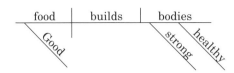

Good food builds **strong, healthy** bodies.

food	builds	bodies

Good ╱   *strong* ╱ *healthy* ╱

> **Remember:** Adjectives are words that describe nouns. Many adjectives tell **what kind of.**

▷ Working With Adjectives ▷

A. Copy all the adjectives used in this poem to tell **what kind of.** There are eleven all together.

A Great Gray Elephant

A great gray elephant,
   A little yellow bee,
A tiny purple violet,
   A tall green tree,
A red and white sailboat
   On a blue sea—
All these things
   You gave to me
   When You made my eyes to see—
Thank You, God.

       —*Reprinted with permission of
       National Society to Prevent Blindness*

**Lesson 76 Answers
Working With Adjectives**

A. great, gray, little, yellow, tiny, purple, tall, green, red, white, blue

B. Write two sentences about things you can see, two about things you can hear, and two about things you can feel. Use one or two adjectives in each sentence.

> **Examples:** I can see **feathery white** clouds.
> I can hear **quiet** whispers.
> I can feel **icy wet** slush.

C. Diagram these sentences.
1. Happy little children were playing.
2. Red hens lay brown eggs.
3. We planted tiny black seeds.

> **Can You Do This?**

Think of a noun to go with each adjective. Write the adjective and the noun together in a phrase.

> **Example:** rocky
> **Answer:** rocky fields

1. salty	3. silent	5. faithful
2. fluffy	4. damp	6. fresh

●—●—●—●—●—●—●—●

77. Words That Tell *How Many* and *How Much*

You have learned that adjectives can tell **what kind of.** Adjectives can also tell **how many.** Number words are adjectives that tell exactly **how many.**

> **Five** little lambs were in the meadow.
> Uncle Lewis has **forty-two** cows.

B. (Individual answers.)

C. 1.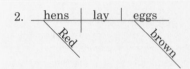
   children | were playing
   Happy little

2.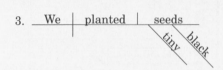
   hens | lay | eggs
   Red   brown

3. We | planted | seeds
                  tiny black

Can You Do This?
   (Possible answers.)
   1. salty popcorn (peanuts)
   2. fluffy cotton (clouds)
   3. silent night (room)
   4. damp towel (clothes)
   5. faithful brethren (God)
   6. fresh water (lettuce)

Lesson 77

Aim: To introduce adjectives that express amount or quantity, and to teach the difference in the use of *many* and *much.*

Oral Review:
1. Words that show action are ———. Give three examples. (verbs; Individual examples.)
2. Why must the sentences in a paragraph be written in the right order? (so that the reader can understand what happened)
3. What is meant by the topic of a paragraph? (the one main thing or idea that the paragraph tells about)
4. Explain how titles should be capitalized. (Capitalize all the important words. Do not capitalize a little word like *of, and, to,* or *the* unless it is the first word in the title.)
5. The words *big, cold,* and *red* are ———. What

question do they answer? (adjectives; what kind of)

Class: It would be good to put up a chart labeled *Adjectives,* with four columns to show the different questions that adjectives answer. Label the first column *What kind of?* and the second column *How many?* and *How much?* (Make *Which?* and *Whose?* columns as you come to those lessons.) Fill in the first column with adjectives from the previous lesson and the second column with adjectives from today's lesson. Such a chart will be especially useful when the pupils must learn to distinguish adjectives from adverbs.

The children should easily recognize most number words as such. The other words that tell *how many* or *how much* should also be familiar to most third graders. Point out that these words are adjectives because they describe nouns.

Words like **some, many,** and **several** are also adjectives. They tell **how many** without giving an exact number.

>**Some** boys played ball.
>**Many** people live near us.
>**Several** girls helped Aunt Mary.

The word **no** can also tell **how many. No** means **not any** when it is used this way.

>**How many** apples are on the tree?
>There are **no** apples on the tree.

Some nouns name things we cannot count. We can use adjectives that tell **how much** with these nouns. The adjectives **some, much, all,** and **no** tell **how much.**

>The people ate **some** food.
>Did **much** snow fall last night?
>God made **all** the water in the seas.
>**No** rain fell last month.

Adjectives that tell **how many** or **how much** are diagramed like other adjectives.

>One tall tree had no leaves.

>⟩ Telling *How Many* and *How Much* ⟩

A. Write a sentence about each picture on the next page. Use an exact number word in each sentence to tell **how many.**

Discuss the difference between things that are counted as individual items (such as eggs, boxes, houses, and people) and things that cannot be counted (as flour, sugar, water, and sand). We use *many* for words in the first group, and *much* for words in the second group. If your pupils have trouble using these words correctly, give some oral drill.

★ **EXTRA PRACTICE**
Worksheet 46 (*Adjectives That Tell How Many and How Much*)

1.

3.

2.

4.

B. Write **many** or **much** for each sentence.
   1. Is there —— sand by the ocean?
   2. Can you find —— seashells?
   3. Do you eat —— carrots?
   4. Does that goat give —— milk?
   5. Did Jesus heal —— sick people?

C. Complete each sentence with one adjective that tells
   how many and one adjective that tells **what kind of.**
   Write the sentence you make.

   Example: We found —— —— seashells.
   Answer: We found nine pretty seashells.

Lesson 77 Answers
Telling *How Many* and *How Much*
A. (Possible answers.)
   1. Three squirrels were chattering in the tree.
   2. Four girls were jumping rope.
   3. The house had one broken window.
   4. I have four coins in my hand.

B. 1. much
   2. many
   3. many
   4. much
   5. many

1. Father found —— —— rabbits.
2. They were hiding in —— —— weeds.
3. Each rabbit had —— —— ears.
4. We gave them —— —— lettuce to eat.

> **Review and Practice** >

Write the correct word for each sentence.
1. There (is, are) three baby robins in the nest.
2. There (were, was) a leak in the roof.
3. There (are, is) not much salad left.
4. There (were, was) two thieves crucified with Jesus.
5. There (was, were) much excitement as the fire spread.

●━●━●━●━●━●━●━●━●

78. Words That Tell *Which*

Some adjectives describe nouns by telling **which.** Four of these adjectives are **this, that, these,** and **those.** These words point out exactly which person, place, or thing is being talked about.

> Suppose someone says, "A house was sold."
> Then you may ask, "Which house was sold?"
> The person might answer, "That house was sold."

This and **that** are used with singular nouns. **These** and **those** are used with plural nouns. **This** and **these** are used to talk about something close by. **That** and **those** are used to talk about something farther away.

> <u>This</u> **pencil** is not mine.
> <u>That</u> **star** was a little farther east last night.

C. (Possible answers.)
1. Father found three young rabbits.
2. They were hiding in some tall weeds.
3. Each rabbit had two little ears.
4. We gave them some crisp lettuce to eat.

Review and Practice
1. are
2. was
3. is
4. were
5. was

Lesson 78

Aim: To teach the adjectives that describe nouns by telling *which* (demonstrative adjectives and ordinal numbers).

Oral Review:
1. When should we use the *s* form of a verb? (when the subject is singular)
2. When we write a paragraph, what should we do with a sentence that does not tell about the same topic as the others? (Take it out.)
3. Which words in this title should be capitalized? *on the way home* (on, way, home)
4. What words do adjectives describe? (nouns)
5. What questions do adjectives answer? (what kind of, how many, how much)

Class: Review *this, that, these,* and *those* as pronouns that tell *which one.* (See Unit 2, Lesson 48.) These words

are pronouns when they stand alone. But when they are used with nouns, they are adjectives that tell *which.* Illustrate with these sentences.

> <u>These</u> books are mine. (adjective)
> <u>Those</u> are mine too. (pronoun—stands for *those books*)

Point out that if it were not for words that tell *which,* we would often be confused when people try to tell us something. To demonstrate, give a command such as "Bring the book to me" (without saying which one).

Introduce ordinal numbers (you need not use the term). These adjectives tell *which* by showing the position of a person or thing. Show that all these adjectives except *first* and *second* are formed from adjectives that tell *how many* (number words).

> three—third   five—fifth   eight—eighth

<u>These</u> **pencils** are dull.
<u>Those</u> **stars** form the Big Dipper.

Words like **first, second,** and **tenth** also tell **which.** Many of these adjectives are formed from adjectives that tell **how many.**

four—fourth   fifteen—fifteenth
seven—seventh

In **which** grade are you?
I am in **third** grade.

Adjectives that tell **which** are diagramed in the same way as other kinds of adjectives.

That man teaches sixth grade.

> **Remember:** This, that, these, and **those** are adjectives that tell **which.** Words like **first, second,** and **tenth** also tell **which.**

> Using Words That Tell *Which* >

A. Use **This, That, These,** or **Those** to complete each sentence. The word in parentheses tells whether the noun names something nearby or farther away.
  1. (nearby) —— ducks are mallard ducks.
  2. (farther) —— book has good stories.
  3. (farther) —— birds are flying south.
  4. (nearby) —— shirt needs a button.

Lesson 78 Answers
Using Words That Tell *Which*
A. 1. These
   2. That
   3. Those
   4. This

These sentences may be used for additional practice. Conclude by adding a *Which?* column to your chart of adjectives.

David was the second king of Israel.
On the third day Jesus rose from the dead.
The believers gathered together on the first day of the week.
Pentecost came on the fiftieth day after Passover.

5. (farther) —— silos are really tall.
6. (nearby) —— sharp stones hurt my feet.
7. (nearby) —— baby is feeding himself.
8. (farther) —— train is loaded with coal.

B. Diagram sentences 2, 4, and 7 in Part A. Include **This, That, These,** or **Those** on your diagrams.

C. In each sentence, copy the adjective that tells **which.**
   1. God created light on the first day.
   2. He made the firmament on the second day.
   3. On the third day, God divided the earth and seas.
   4. He made the sun, moon, and stars on the fourth day.
   5. On the fifth day, God created fish and fowls.
   6. He made the animals and man on the sixth day.
   7. On the seventh day, God rested.

> Can You Do This? >

Change these to adjectives that tell **which.** You may use a dictionary for help with correct spelling.
   1. eight   3. twelve   5. eighteen
   2. nine   4. fifteen   6. twenty

●━━●━━●━━●━━●━━●━━●

79. Reviewing What You Have Learned

> Oral Drill >

Use these sentences to do the exercises that follow.
   a. God made many different birds.
   b. One large, lovely bird is the swan.

5. Those
6. These
7. This
8. That

B. 2.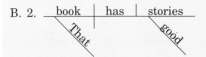

4.

7.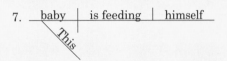

C. 1. first   5. fifth
   2. second   6. sixth
   3. third   7. seventh
   4. fourth

Can You Do This?
   1. eighth   4. fifteenth
   2. ninth   5. eighteenth
   3. twelfth   6. twentieth

Lesson 79

Aim: To review the previous three lessons.

Class: Use Oral Drill to review the three kinds of adjectives that have been studied. Remind the pupils that all these are adjectives because they describe nouns.

    c. Swans have beautiful white feathers.

    d. This long gray feather comes from a heron.

    e. Uncle David saw two storks on his first trip to Florida.

    f. You can see some pink flamingos at the Philadelphia Zoo.

1. Find eight adjectives that tell **what kind of.**
2. Find four adjectives that tell **how many.**
3. Find two adjectives that tell **which.**
4. Find seven common nouns.
5. Find four proper nouns. (Some have more than one word.)

> Written Practice

Use the six sentences in Oral Drill to do A and B.

A. Answer with the correct words or sentence letters.
1. Which sentence has a form of the verb **be**?
2. a. Which two sentences have verbs that are past forms?
   b. What are the nouns that receive the action of these verbs?

B. Diagram sentence **a.** Diagram the simple subject, simple predicate, and direct object of sentence **e.**

C. For each sentence, choose and write the correct word to tell **which.**
1. (This, These) cookies are delicious.
2. Grandmother sent (this, these) pie over for us.
3. We should wash (that, those) jars first.
4. Mother said, "Pick up (this, these) toys."
5. (That, Those) Bible was a birthday gift.

Lesson 79 Answers
Oral Drill
1. different, large, lovely, beautiful, white, long, gray, pink
2. many, one, two, some
3. This, first
4. bird(s), swan(s), feather(s), heron, storks, trip, flamingos
5. God, Uncle David, Florida, Philadelphia Zoo

Written Practice
A. 1. b
  2. a. a and e
     b. birds, storks

B. a.

  e.   Uncle David | saw | storks

C. 1. These
  2. this
  3. those
  4. these
  5. That

D. Change each word in parentheses to an adjective that tells **which.**
1. Seth was the (three) son of Adam.
2. Thursday is the (five) day of the week.
3. The (four) plague on Egypt was the plague of flies.
4. In the (ten) plague, the oldest sons died.

D. 1. third
   2. fifth
   3. fourth
   4. tenth

E. Help each sentence to tell more about the picture by adding at least one adjective that tells **what kind of** and one adjective that tells **how many.** You may also add **a, an,** or **the.** Write the sentences you make.

1. Puppies chewed on boot.   3. Boys picked apples.

2. Snow covered trees.   4. Girls sang for lady.

E. (Possible answers.)
1. The two little puppies chewed on a big ragged boot.
2. The white snow covered some small bare trees.
3. Three boys picked some ripe apples.
4. Several girls sang for the old lady.

80. *A, An,* and *The*

A, an, and **the** are adjectives that are used before nouns. These little words can be called **noun markers.** Whenever we see **a, an,** or **the,** we know that a noun will soon follow.

> We saw **a** black bear and **an** enormous elephant at **the** new zoo.

A and **an** are used only with singular nouns. Use **a** before a consonant sound. Use **an** before a vowel sound.

> We saw **a b**ig walrus.
> Did you ever see **an a**lligator?

The can be used with both singular and plural nouns.

> **The** one building had many snakes in it.
> **The** snakes were all in glass cages.

Noun markers and other adjectives that come before nouns are diagramed on slanted lines below the noun.

> The tall yellow giraffes ate green leaves.

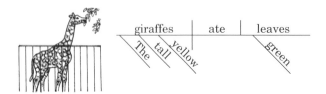

> Working With Noun Markers

A. Write a correct noun marker for each sentence.
1. Genesis is ——— first book in the Bible.
2. Father read us ——— story from Genesis.
3. ——— elderly man was visiting us.

Lesson 80 Answers
Working With Noun Markers
A. 1. the
    2. a *or* the
    3. An *or* The

Lesson 80

Aim: To teach about the adjectives *a, an,* and *the,* which are called noun markers. (They are also called the articles.)

Oral Review:
1. The words *it* and *they* are ———. (pronouns)
2. Give some little words that are usually not capitalized in titles. Which word in a title is always capitalized? (Possible answers: of, and, to, the; the first word)
3. Give two adjectives that tell *what kind of.* (Individual answers.)
4. Words that tell *how many* describe things that (can, cannot) be counted. Words that tell *how much* describe things that (can, cannot) be counted. (can; cannot)
5. Give an adjective that tells *which* about one thing close by. Give an adjective that tells *which* about

more than one thing farther away. (this; those

Class: Explain that *a, an,* and *the* are special adjec tives. They always mark the coming of a noun, an they can never be used except before the noun the tell about. Sometimes other adjectives separate thes words from the nouns they are marking.

The can be used with singular or plural noun but *a* and *an* are used only with singular noun *A* is used before consonant sounds, and *an* befor vowel sounds.

You could also point out that *a* and *an* (the indef nite articles) are used when a speaker is not refer ring to any particular person, place, or thing. *Th* (the definite article) is used in referring to one par ticular item or group of items. The sentence *Bring m a chair* can be used to illustrate; *a chair* means "an chair." By contrast, *Bring me the chair* would refer t a particular chair that has been identified previously

4. He listened to —— story Father read.
5. —— man who visited us was named Joshua.
6. Joshua is —— name from the Bible.
7. —— name means "Jehovah is salvation."
8. It is —— easy name to remember.

B. Rewrite each sentence, changing the noun in bold print to its singular form. Use **a** or **an** as a noun marker.
   1. **Ostriches** may grow to be 8 feet tall.
   2. **Giraffes** may become 18 feet tall.
   3. **Anacondas** may be more than 30 feet long.
   4. Blue **whales** may grow to 100 feet long.
   5. Redwood **trees** may be 365 feet high.

> **Diagraming Sentences**

Diagram theses sentences.
1. An owl was seeking food.
2. The owl caught a mouse.
3. Some owls catch fish.
4. Father saw a large gray owl.

> **Review and Practice**

Copy each sentence. Add quotation marks and capital letters where they are needed, and use the correct end marks.
   1. would you like to hear a story Grandfather asked the children
   2. yes, yes shouted the children
   3. grandfather said, everyone must sit down
   4. the children said, we like Grandfather's stories

Show that noun markers are diagramed in the same way as other adjectives. The following sentences can be used for diagraming practice at the board.

   A kind girl helped the woman.
   The brown puppy is playing.
   A yellow daisy bloomed.
   An anteater has a long, sticky tongue.

You may wish to add a small column labeled *Noun Markers* to your chart of adjectives.

★ **EXTRA PRACTICE**
Worksheet 47 (*Noun Markers*)

---

4. the
5. The
6. a
7. The
8. an

B. 1. An ostrich may grow to be 8 feet tall.
   2. A giraffe may become 18 feet tall.
   3. An anaconda may be more than 30 feet long.
   4. A blue whale may grow to 100 feet long.
   5. A redwood tree may be 365 feet high.

Diagraming Sentences

1.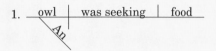

2.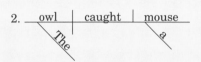

3.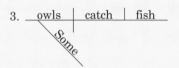

4.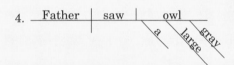

Review and Practice
(Corrected items are underlined.)
   1. "Would you like to hear a story?" Grandfather asked the children.
   2. "Yes, yes!" shouted the children.
   3. Grandfather said, "Everyone must sit down."
   4. The children said, "We like Grandfather's stories."

81. Words That Tell *Whose*

A word that tells **which** about a noun is an adjective. A word that tells **whose** about a noun is also an adjective.

> **Carl's** brother is in fourth grade.
> The **rabbit's** fur feels silky.

Carl is a noun because it names a person. But **Carl's** is an adjective because it tells **whose.** In the same way, **rabbit** is a noun because it names a thing. But **rabbit's** is an adjective because it tells **whose.**

To use a noun as an adjective that tells **whose,** put **'s** after it. This is called the **possessive form** of the noun.

> girl—girl's   dog—dog's   Eve—Eve's

Now look at these sentences.

> His brother is in fourth grade.
> Its fur feels silky.

His and **its** take the place of words like **Carl's** and **rabbit's.** Other words like these are **my, your, her, our,** and **their.** All these words are adjectives because they tell **whose.**

Adjectives that tell **whose** are diagramed like other adjectives.

> Naaman's maid helped her master.

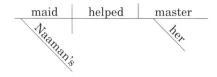

Lesson 81

Aim: To introduce the use of possessives as adjectives.

Oral Review:

1. Give two pronouns that tell *whose.* (any two: mine, yours, his, hers, ours, theirs)
2. What questions do adjectives answer? (what kind of, how many, how much, which)
3. Adjectives like *second* and *fifth* answer the question ———. (which)
4. Give an adjective telling *which* about one thing farther away. Give an adjective telling *which* about more than one thing nearby. (that; these)
5. Which three adjectives are called noun markers? (a, an, the)

Class: Read the first paragraph together; then call attention to the example sentences after it. Ask, "Whose brother? Whose fur?" Then write the following sentences on the board. Have the class tell which words answer the question *whose,* and which noun they are describing.

1. I have Tom's book.
2. Is Sarah's coat in the closet?
3. Please bring Father's keys.
4. Mr. Meyer's house is gray.

Discuss the correct formation of possessive nouns. (This was also taught in Unit 1.) Give different pupils these nouns and have them write the possessive forms on the board.

> Paul   John   tree
> Lydia   man   cow

Go on to discuss possessive pronouns. Do not refer to them as pronouns, however, because this may be confusing to the students. (The grammatical term for these words is *pronominal adjectives;* they are

> Working With Words That Tell *Whose*

A. Copy the adjectives that tell **whose.** After each adjective, write the noun that it describes.
   1. Jacob was Isaac's son.
   2. Rebekah was his mother.
   3. Jacob wanted Esau's birthright.
   4. Rebekah helped her son to get the blessing.
   5. Laban's daughters were Rachel and Leah.
   6. Rebekah was their aunt.

B. Diagram sentence 3 in Part A.

C. Write the possessive form of each noun.
   1. Kevin   4. baby   7. fish
   2. man   5. goose   8. fox
   3. Linda   6. brother   9. women

D. Change each group of words to a phrase that contains a possessive form.

   Example: a coat for a boy
   Answer: a boy's coat

   1. the book belonging to my sister
   2. the joy of a father
   3. the toys belonging to him
   4. the tail of it

> Review and Practice

   1. Write **I** and the six other pronouns that tell **who.**
   2. Write **me** and the six other pronouns that tell **whom.**

Lesson 81 Answers
Working With Words That Tell *Whose*
A. 1. Isaac's—son
   2. his—mother
   3. Esau's—birthright
   4. her—son
   5. Laban's—daughters
   6. their—aunt

B.

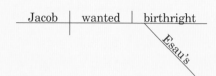

C. 1. Kevin's   4. baby's   7. fish's
   2. man's   5. goose's   8. fox's
   3. Linda's   6. brother's 9. women's

D. 1. my sister's book
   2. a father's joy
   3. his toys
   4. its tail

Review and Practice
   1. I, you, he, she, it, we, they
   2. me, you, him, her, it, us, them

ronouns in essence but adjectives in function.) Use
he following sentences in the same manner as those
sted above.

   5. His book is torn.
   6. Did you see my paper?
   7. These are her shoes.
   8. Can you find your car?

   Ask the class for an adjective to take the place of
ach possessive noun on the board: Paul—his, Lydia—
er, and so forth.

   Discuss the diagraming of adjectives that tell *whose;*
his should help to rivet the fact that possessive forms
re adjectives. Sentences 1, 6, and 8 from above can
e used for further illustration. Conclude by adding a
Whose? column to your chart of adjectives.

EXTRA PRACTICE
Worksheet 48 (*Adjectives That Tell* Whose)

> Can You Do This?

Write an adjective that tells **whose** for each sentence. The adjective should refer to the noun in bold print.

1. "Are these —— boots, **Lee**?" Paul asked.
2. "No, those are —— boots," Lee said, looking at **Mark.**
3. "I must help **Joy** find —— boots," said Judy.
4. "Here are —— boots!" exclaimed **Joy.**
5. "Now we can do —— chores," the **children** said.

Can You Do This?

1. your
2. his
3. her
4. my
5. our

●━●━●━●━●━●

82. Using Adjectives Correctly

In Lesson 78, you learned about adjectives that tell **which.** Four of these adjectives are **this, that, these,** and **those.**

These four adjectives are sometimes used incorrectly. It is not correct to say "this here" or "that there." **Here** and **there** are not needed for telling **which.** We know that the thing being talked about is here or there.

Read these sentences correctly.

This here pen writes well.
Those there birds are sea gulls.
Ann baked these here cookies.
That there dish belonged to Grandmother.

Them is a pronoun, and you must not use it as an adjective. You should never say "them apples." Say "those apples" instead.

Read these sentences correctly.

Lesson 82

Aim: To teach the incorrectness of using *here* or *there* with *this, that, these,* and *those;* and of using *them* in place of *those.*

Oral Review:

1. Words that tell about actions we cannot easily see or hear are ——. (verbs)
2. What questions do adjectives answer? (what kind of, how many, how much, which, whose)
3. Where are adjectives placed on a sentence diagram? (on slanted lines below the nouns they describe)
4. Why are some adjectives called noun markers? (They show that a noun will soon follow.)
5. The form of a noun that tells *whose* is called a —— form. (possessive)

Class: Call attention to two similar objects in the room, one nearby and one farther away. Refer to each object in a sentence with *this* or *that.* Ask the pupil how they know which item you are talking about. Point out that *this* and *that* are sufficient; you do not need to use *here* or *there* with these words. Show that the same is true of *these* and *those.*

Review the pronoun *them.* Emphasize that it is always a pronoun and never an adjective. So it must never be used just before a noun. You may wish to let the students remind each other if they hear incorrect usage of *them* or the demonstrative adjectives.

The incorrectness of "this here" and "that there" is also taught in Unit 2, Lesson 49.

We picked them raspberries yesterday.
Kevin was playing with them blocks.
Them towels are clean.
Edna helped Mother plant them flowers.

> **Remember:** Do not use **here** or **there** with **this, that, these,** or **those.** Do not use **them** as an adjective. Use **those** instead.

> Practice With Adjectives >

A. Read each sentence. If it is correct, write **correct.** If it is not correct, rewrite it correctly.

1. Jesus fed all those people.
2. All them icicles melted yesterday.
3. That there rainbow is brighter than the other one we saw.
4. We found this here arrowhead in our field.
5. John gathered these eggs last night.
6. That there cat followed us home.
7. Father bought them chairs at an auction.
8. This baby robin fell out of its nest.
9. That there creek is rising.
10. Them people are Chinese.
11. That hymnbook was a birthday gift.
12. Stand on this here stool to change the bulb.

Lesson 82 Answers
Practice With Adjectives

A. 1. correct
2. All those icicles melted yesterday.
3. That rainbow is brighter than the other one we saw.
4. We found this arrowhead in our field.
5. correct
6. That cat followed us home.
7. Father bought those chairs at an auction.
8. correct
9. That creek is rising.
10. Those people are Chinese.
11. correct
12. Stand on this stool to change the bulb.

B. Write four sentences of your own, using **this, that, these,** and **those** correctly.

B. (Individual answers.)

> Review and Practice

A. Write correctly each noun that needs a capital letter.
1. Jesus visited the home of mary, martha, and lazarus.
2. The twins were named larry and harry.
3. john adams and james polk were presidents.

B. Write each title correctly.
1. butterfly brown
2. chippy the chipmunk
3. boats and trains

Review and Practice

A. 1. Mary, Martha, Lazarus
2. Larry, Harry
3. John Adams, James Polk

B. 1. Butterfly Brown
2. Chippy the Chipmunk
3. Boats and Trains

•••••••••••

83. Reviewing What You Have Learned

You have learned that many different adjectives are used to describe people, places, and things. Adjectives can answer different questions.

Which? What kind of?

> **That large** book has **pretty** pictures.
> **Those** books belong on **this** shelf.

How many? How much?

> These **three** cows give **no** milk.

Whose?

> **Paul's** old coat is too small.
> **His** new jacket fits well.

Lesson 83

Aim: To review the use of various adjectives, and to give practice in recognizing them.

Written Quiz:

Choose two adjectives that belong in each group below.

our	five	that	happy
the	warm	some	third
Mary's	an		

1. What kind of?
2. How many or how much?
3. Which?
4. Whose?
5. Now markers

Quiz Answers:
1. happy, warm
2. five, some
3. that, third
4. our, Mary's
5. the, an

Class: Discuss the review as given in the text. Hav the students offer other examples for each questio Recall the correct use of *this, that, these,* and *thos* before a noun, and the fact that we should never sa "them boys" or "them coats." Review the adding of - to nouns to form adjectives that tell *whose.*

For Part C, tell the pupils to first think of five more adjectives to describe what they are thinkir of. (See the words in bold print in Part B.) The they can write sentences in which they use thes adjectives.

Noun markers are also adjectives. They show that a noun will soon follow.

The boy ate **a** cookie and **an** apple.

When you write, use adjectives to make your sentences more interesting. Your adjectives will answer questions that people might have about the nouns you use.

> Helping Your Sentences Grow >

A. Write adjectives to answer the questions below each sentence. Then rewrite each sentence, adding the words you wrote.

   Example: Girls played with dolls.
              How many girls? What size girls? Whose dolls?
   Answer: four, little, Karen's
              Four little girls played with Karen's dolls.

1. Boys found a puppy.
   How many boys? What size boys?
2. Men caught the bull.
   How many men? What kind of men? What size bull? What kind of bull?
3. Kittens were playing with a ball.
   Whose kittens? How many kittens? What size kittens? What color kittens? Which ball? What size ball?

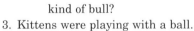

B. Guess what these are.
1. This drink is **sweet** and **sour.** Mother makes it **cold** by putting ice into it. Usually it is **yellow,** but sometimes it is **pink.**

Lesson 83 Answers
Helping Your Sentences Grow
A. (Individual answers. Let the students share their sentences in class to show how adjectives change the picture of nouns.)

B. 1. lemonade

2. This food tastes best when it is **hot.** Part of it is **red** and part is **white.** The white part is **long** and **thin,** like strings. The red part is **thick** and **runny,** like gravy.

C. Think of something you like to eat or drink. Write several sentences to describe it, like the ones in Part B. Use at least five adjectives. Then see if your classmates can guess what it is.

2. spaghetti

C. (Individual answers. Give opportunity for the students to read their descriptions in class.)

●━●━●━●━●━●━●━●

84. Words That Tell *How*

Some words are used with verbs to tell **how** something is done. These words are called **adverbs.** Read the sentences below. Can you find the word in each sentence that tells **how** Carl worked?

Carl worked slowly.   Carl worked cheerfully.
Carl worked quickly.   Carl worked carefully.

Slowly, quickly, cheerfully, and **carefully** are adverbs that tell **how.** Which of the adverbs tells how Carl worked

a. when he was happy?
b. when he was very tired?
c. when he was using a sharp knife?
d. when he was in a hurry?

Can you think of other times when Carl might work slowly, quickly, cheerfully, and carefully?

Remember: An adverb is a word that describes a verb. Many adverbs tell **how** something is done.

Lesson 84

Aim: To introduce adverbs, and to teach that many adverbs tell *how.*

Oral Review:

1. How do we diagram a sentence that has a direct object? (We put a straight line between the verb and the direct object.)
2. Where do we place adjectives on a sentence diagram? (on slanted lines below the nouns they describe)
3. Give an adjective telling *which* about more than one thing farther away. Give an adjective telling *which* about one thing close by. (those; this)
4. Change each noun to an adjective that tells *whose: boy, dog, girl, doll.* (boy's, dog's, girl's, doll's)
5. Correct each sentence.
   a. Grandfather lives in that there house. (Grandfather lives in that house.)

b. Please bring them boxes inside. (Please bring those boxes inside.)

Class: Introduce adverbs as words that describe the actions of verbs. In the lesson text, ask the class for answers to the questions about how Carl worked when he was happy, very tired, and so forth. Their answers should be given in sentences like the following.

Carl worked cheerfully when he was happy.
Carl worked slowly when he was very tired.

Then ask for sentence endings to tell about other times that Carl might have worked slowly, quickly, cheerfully, and carefully.

Carl worked slowly when his cousin was visiting.
Carl worked cheerfully when Grandfather helped him.

Using Adverbs

A. The following sentences tell about people talking. From this list, choose an adverb to tell **how** the people talked. Use each adverb only once.

loudly	sadly	slowly
cheerfully	quietly	eagerly

1. "The baby is sleeping," Mother said ——.
2. The boys had some exciting news. They all talked ——.
3. The children were happy in spite of the rain. They talked ——.
4. Uncle Ben was hard of hearing, so Aunt Anna always talked ——.
5. Marian is learning Spanish, but she still speaks it very ——.
6. Grandmother spoke —— about a neighbor who did not love Jesus.

B. Copy each sentence beginning, and underline the adverb in it. Then write an ending for the sentence which tells why that adverb is used.

Example: The sheep bleated loudly because ——.
Answer: The sheep bleated <u>loudly</u> because a dog frightened them.

1. Lois smiled happily when ——.
2. Grandfather dressed warmly because ——.
3. Mother drove carefully on ——.
4. The children worked quietly because ——.
5. Our dog barks loudly if ——.

C. Draw two lines under each verb in the sentences you wrote for Part B.

Lesson 84 Answers
Using Adverbs
A. (Some answers may be interchanged.)
1. quietly
2. eagerly
3. cheerfully
4. loudly
5. slowly
6. sadly

B. (Answers for Part C are included here. Sentence endings will vary.)
1. Lois <u>smiled</u> <u>happily</u> when ——
2. Grandfather <u>dressed</u> <u>warmly</u> because ——
3. Mother <u>drove</u> <u>carefully</u> on ——
4. The children <u>worked</u> <u>quietly</u> because ——
5. Our dog <u>barks</u> <u>loudly</u> if ——

C. (Answers are included in Part B.)

For Part B of the exercises, it would be good to explain that adverbs may be found almost anywhere in a sentence. This point is taught in the next lesson.

★ **EXTRA PRACTICE**
Worksheet 49 (*Adverbs That Tell How*)

> Review and Practice

A. Write the eight forms of **be.**

B. Copy each sentence, adding commas where they are needed.
 1. Peter please bring me a drink.
 2. On our walk we saw squirrels flowers cattails and butterflies.
 3. Marie please dust the chairs the dresser and the table.

●━━●━━●━━●━━●━━●━━●

85. More About Adverbs

Words that tell **how** something was or is done are **adverbs.** We can make many adverbs by adding **ly** to adjectives.

quiet—quiet**ly**	faithful—faithfu**ly**
swift—swift**ly**	usual—usual**ly**

Not all adverbs end in **ly.**

> The boys sang **well.**
> Karen tried **hard** to finish her work.

Nor are all words ending in **ly** adverbs.

> **July** is usually very warm. (noun)
> God will **supply** our needs. (verb)
> Saturday was a **lovely** day. (adjective)

Adverbs can be found at different places in sentences.

> **Quietly,** Father left the room.

Review and Practice

A. am, is, are, was, were, be, been, being

B. 1. Peter, please bring me a drink.
 2. On our walk we saw squirrels, flowers, cattails, and butterflies.
 3. Marie, please dust the chairs, the dresser, and the table.

Lesson 85

Aim: (1) To teach the formation of adverbs from adjectives by adding -ly. (2) To teach the diagraming of adverbs.

Oral Review:

 1. What is a quotation? (the exact words of a speaker)
 2. Where do we put noun markers and other adjectives when we diagram a sentence? (on slanted lines below the nouns)
 3. Words that tell *whose* are ——. (adjectives)
 4. We do not need to use the words —— and —— after *this, that, these,* and *those.* (here, there)
 5. Words that tell *how* something was or is done are ——. (adverbs)

Class: Review the use of adverbs as introduced in the previous lesson. Ask the class to give the four adverbs from the first page of that lesson; write them on the board as they are given. Have someone tell what is the same about the ending of each adverb.

Make it clear that many adverbs, *but not all,* end in -*ly.* Tell the class that if we take off the -*ly* from these adverbs, we will have an adjective. Ask the class what adjective goes with each adverb written on the board.

Discuss other adjective-adverb pairs. Begin by using the adverbs from Part A of the previous lesson, then ask the pupils to give other examples.

Call attention to the adverbs that do not end in -*ly;* two more examples are *still* and *fast.* Also use the examples in the text to show that not all words ending in -*ly* are adverbs.

Discuss the fact that adverbs may be found at different places within a sentence. Read the three examples given in the lesson. You need not explain at this point the subtle differences of meaning that

Father **quietly** left the room.
Father left the room **quietly.**

Each of the sentences above would be diagramed with the adverb under the verb.

> Working With Adverbs >

A. In each sentence, copy the adjective that tells **what kind of.** Then change the adjective to an adverb.
   1. The minister spoke in a serious voice.
   2. Jehu was a furious driver of his chariot.
   3. The sad prophet wept over Jerusalem.
   4. We should speak kind words.

B. For each blank, write one of the adverbs you made in Part A.
   1. Jeremiah looked ——— at the ruins of the city.
   2. If we speak ———, it will help us to make friends.
   3. Brother Hoover ——— warned against doing wrong.
   4. The watchman knew whose chariot it was because it was driven ———.

C. Diagram the following sentences.
   1. Can Michael run fast?
   2. The four men worked diligently.
   3. Sally reads well.
   4. Sit still.
   5. Sister Lena patiently explained the lesson.

often result from changes in adverb position. Make it clear, however, that the adverb is telling *how* about the verb and is therefore part of the predicate.

   Point out that adverbs are diagramed in much the same way as adjectives: on slanted lines below the words they describe. Stress the point that no matter where the adverb is found, it is always diagramed below the verb it describes.

EXTRA PRACTICE
Worksheet 50 (*Adverbs Ending in* ly)

Lesson 85 Answers
Working With Adverbs
A. 1. serious, seriously
   2. furious, furiously
   3. sad, sadly
   4. kind, kindly

B. 1. sadly
   2. kindly
   3. seriously
   4. furiously

C. 1. Michael | can run \ *fast*

   2. men | worked \ *The* \ *four* \ *diligently*

   3. Sally | reads \ *well*

   4. (you) | Sit \ *still*

   5. Sister Lena | explained | lesson \ *patiently* \ *the*

> Review and Practice >

Copy the correct pronoun for each sentence.
1. Lester and (he, him) went for a walk.
2. Our cousins and (they, them) went along.
3. Father asked Sarah and (I, me) to help him.
4. The surprise was for Rebecca and (she, her).
5. The mailman had packages for the neighbors and (we, us).

Review and Practice
1. he
2. they
3. me
4. her
5. us

●━━●━━●━━●━━●━━●━━●━

86. Words That Tell *When*

Adverbs are used to answer the question **how.** Adverbs can also answer the question **when.**

In the sentences below, which words answer the question **when**?

Sometimes Elisha went to Shunem.
He usually stayed in the same house.
The man and woman always welcomed him.

The words **sometimes, usually,** and **always** are adverbs that tell **when.**

When did Elisha go to Shunem? **sometimes**
When did he stay in the same house? **usually**
When did the man and woman welcome him? **always**

Here are some other adverbs that answer the question **when.**

never	often	seldom	once
ever	already	finally	twice
soon	now	later	frequently

Lesson 86

Aim: To teach that many adverbs tell *when.*

Oral Review:
1. Give an example of a past form that does not end with *-ed.* (Individual answers.)
2. What punctuation is needed when a noun is changed to an adjective that tells *whose*? (an apostrophe)
3. Correct these sentences.
   a. How did this here window get broken? (How did this window get broken?)
   b. Them birds are starlings. (Those birds are starlings.)
4. Some adjectives can be changed to adverbs by ———. (adding *-ly*)
5. Words like *hard* and *fast* may be —— or ——. (adjectives, adverbs)

Class: Begin by writing this sentence on the board

   Larry runs swiftly.

Ask the class to give the verb and adverb in the sentence. Now add the word *usually* to the beginning of the sentence. Tell the class that this word is also an adverb. It does not answer the question *how,* but *when.*

In the lesson text, ask the class to use the list of adverbs in sentences. Then review the two questions which they have learned that adverbs can be used to answer.

You might want to explain the pictures in the lesson text. Some children are deaf and use a special sign language for speaking. But even in sign language, adverbs are used to answer the questions *when* and *how.* The one boy is signing *when.* The other is signing *now.*

They always welcomed him gladly.

Remember: Many adverbs tell **how** or **when** something is done.

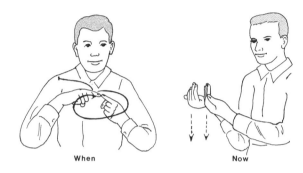

When   Now

▷ Using Adverbs ▷

A. Write the adverb you find in the first sentence of each pair. Then choose one of the following adverbs to complete the second sentence: **now, seldom, once, often.**

1. a. Aunt Eva is usually happy.
   b. She is —— sad.
2. a. Susan seldom dries the dishes.
   b. She —— washes them.
3. a. We already learned about nouns and verbs.
   b. —— we are learning about adverbs.
4. a. Sometimes birds come to our window.
   b. —— we saw a pair of cardinals.

Lesson 86 Answers
Using Adverbs

A. 1. a. usually
      b. seldom
   2. a. seldom
      b. often
   3. a. already
      b. Now
   4. a. Sometimes
      b. Once

★ **EXTRA PRACTICE**
Worksheet 51 (*Adverbs That Tell When*)

B. Write adverbs to complete each sentence. Use an adverb from the lesson that tells **when** if there is a **W.** Use an adverb that tells **how** if there is an **H.**
   1. Grandfather __W__ works H̲.
   2. Does your mother __W__ talk __H__ ?
   3. Paul's brother __W__ walks __H__ .
   4. Do you __W__ write your lessons __H__ ?
   5. Those girls __W__ read a book __H__ .

C. Diagram the sentences in Part B, including the adverbs you wrote. Check your work. Did you put each adverb under the verb it describes? Did you put each adjective under the noun it describes?

Review and Practice

Write whether each of these is a **telling, asking, commanding,** or **exclaiming** sentence. Also give the correct end punctuation for each.
   1. Try to play quietly
   2. Mother will clean the house today
   3. What a loud noise the tractor makes
   4. Were you out in the rain
   5. Read the Bible
   6. God made everything out of nothing

B. (Individual answers.)

C. (Adverbs on slanted lines will vary.)

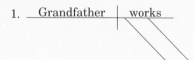

1.   Grandfather | works

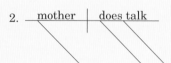

2.   mother | does talk

3.   brother | walks
      Paul's

4.   you | do write | lessons
                           your

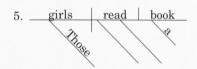

5.   girls | read | book
      Those   a

Review and Practice
   1. commanding (.)
   2. telling (.)
   3. exclaiming (!)
   4. asking (?)
   5. commanding (.)
   6. telling (.)

87. Words That Tell *Where*

You know that adverbs may tell **how** and **when.** Adverbs may also tell **where.**

Where did Keith go?
Keith went **outside.**
Where does Esther sleep?
Esther sleeps **upstairs.**

The words **outside** and **upstairs** are adverbs that answer the question **where.** Here are some other words that can be used as adverbs to answer the question **where.**

away	everywhere	nowhere
here	somewhere	inside
there	anywhere	downstairs

You have now learned three questions that adverbs can answer. Can you say what these questions are? Can you give an adverb to answer each question?

Remember: Adverbs may tell **how, when,** or **where.**

Lesson 87

Aim: To teach that adverbs can answer the question *where.*

Oral Review:

1. Give the pronouns that tell *which one* or *which ones.* (this, that, these, those)
2. Correct these sentences.
   a. Them trees were uprooted in the storm. (Those trees were uprooted in the storm.)
   b. That there is a good story. (That is a good story.)
3. Words that tell *how* or *when* something is done are ——. (adverbs)
4. Where may adverbs be found in sentences? (almost anywhere)
5. Where are adverbs placed on a sentence diagram? (on slanted lines under the verbs they describe)

Class: Begin by reviewing the use of adverbs to answer the questions *how* and *when.* Then write a sentence using an adverb to tell *where.* Tell the class that the sentence contains an adverb that answers another question. Can they find it?

James and Mary live there.

Tell the class that you will say some sentences. They should try to think of an adverb that tells *where* to complete each.

Betty carried the jars ——.
In the summer, flies are ——.
Carl was sick, so he had to stay ——.

Go over the list of *where* adverbs given in the lesson. Ask the students to use these words in sentences of their own.

★ EXTRA PRACTICE
Worksheet 52 (*Adverbs That Tell Where*)

> Using Adverbs in Sentences >

A. Each sentence has one or two adverbs that tell **where.**
Find each adverb and write it on your paper.
1. Keith was sure his new mittens had to be somewhere.
2. He thought he had looked everywhere, but he could not find them anywhere.
3. He put on his blue coat and went outside.
4. He thought about the big barn and decided to look there.
5. He could find them nowhere.
6. "Did you put them away?" Mother asked when he came back inside.
7. Suddenly Keith stopped looking downstairs in the dark basement.
8. He ran upstairs to his clothes closet.
9. "I found them!" he called. "I had put them right here."

B. Write four adjectives that are used in the sentences above.

C. Write a sentence for each picture. Use the adverbs given.

1. away   2. downstairs

Lesson 87 Answers
Using Adverbs in Sentences
A. 1. somewhere
   2. everywhere, anywhere
   3. outside
   4. there
   5. nowhere
   6. away, inside
   7. downstairs
   8. upstairs
   9. here

B. new, blue, big, dark
(Also accept *sure, his, the, right,* and *clothes.*)

C. (Individual answers.)

> Review and Practice >

Choose the correct verb form for each sentence.
1. I (did, done) my work.
2. We (saw, seen) a crane flying over the lake.
3. He has (grew, grown) six inches since his last birthday.
4. The baby had (tore, torn) the book before I saw what was happening.
5. Jesus has (went, gone) to heaven.
6. After He left, the disciples (began, begun) to preach.
7. Lynn has (ran, run) to the store many times.
8. An oriole (come, came) to the feeder yesterday.

●━●━●━●━●━●━●━●━●

88. *How*, *When*, and *Where*

You have learned that words which tell **how, when,** or **where** are adverbs.

The children played.
> How? **happily**   When? **often**   Where? **outside**
> The children often played happily outside.

The question words **how, when,** and **where** are also adverbs. Diagram these questions words the same as other adverbs. Remember to capitalize the first word of the sentence.

How does it work?

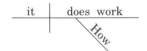

Review and Practice
1. did
2. saw
3. grown
4. torn
5. gone
6. began
7. run
8. came

Lesson 88

Aim: To review the use of adverbs, and to teach that the question words *how, when,* and *where* are also adverbs.

Written Quiz:
1. Underline the word that is an adverb: **house, old, softly, jump.**
2. Underline the best answer: Adverbs in sentences are found (at the beginning, in the middle, in different places, at the end).
3. Write the adverb in each sentence, and tell what question it answers.
   a. Benny and I slept upstairs.
   b. Yesterday it rained.
   c. Mother gently rocked the baby.

Quiz Answers:
1. softly
2. in different places
3. a. upstairs—where
   b. Yesterday—when
   c. gently—how

Class: Review the use of adverbs. Tell the class that the words *how, when,* and *where* are adverb also. Ask for some questions using these words. Write the questions on the board.

Give practice diagraming sentences with adverbs by giving each child a different sentence to diagram at the board. Discuss the sentences and their diagrams together. Mention that adverbs "add to the verb" and are therefore placed under the verb on a diagram.

★ **EXTRA PRACTICE**
Worksheet 53 (How, When, *and* Where)

Where do you keep your dog?

```
   you   |  do keep  |   dog
_____|_____|_____
         \           \
       Where         your
```

> **Remember:** The question words **how**, **when**, and **where** are adverbs.

> **Working With Adverbs**

A. Find and write the adverbs used in these sentences. Numbers 4 and 5 have two adverbs each.
   1. When will Father leave?
   2. How did the boys work?
   3. Where did Jay find the book?
   4. Where will the girls go now?
   5. When do birds fly away?

Lesson 88 Answers
Working With Adverbs
A. 1. When
   2. How
   3. Where
   4. Where, now
   5. When, away

B. Diagram the questions in Part A.

C. Write adverbs to answer the questions below each sentence. Then rewrite each sentence, using the same adverbs.

> **Example:** The children played tag.
> Where? When?
> **Answer:** downstairs, seldom
> The children seldom played tag downstairs.

1. James ran.
   Where? How?
2. He walked.
   Where? When?
3. We raked leaves.
   Where? When?
4. The men worked.
   When? How?

> **Can You Do This?**

Write sentences using adverbs to answer the questions in Part A.

89. Reviewing What You Have Learned

A. Copy the verbs and verb phrases in these sentences. Beside each write the adverb that tells **how** the action was done. Number 8 has two adverbs.
1. Father drives carefully.
2. The children waited patiently.
3. Lois did her lessons well.
4. Do the cows stand still for you?
5. Does Mr. Martin talk quietly?
6. Cheerfully, Martha dried the dishes.

Lesson 89

im: To review the previous five lessons.

ral Review:
1. Tell how each part of speech is used.
   a. noun (It is the name of a person, place, or thing.)
   b. pronoun (It takes the place of a noun.)
   c. verb (It shows action or being.)
   d. adjective (It describes a noun.)
   e. adverb (It describes a verb.)
2. What questions do adjectives answer? (what kind of, which, how many, how much, whose)
3. Which adjectives are noun markers? (a, an, the)
4. What questions do adverbs answer? (how, when, where)
5. What part of speech is each word in this sentence? *They easily found the two white rabbits.* (They—pro.; easily—adv.; found—v.; the—adj.; two—adj.; white—adj.; rabbits—n.)

B. 1. Father | will leave — When

2. boys | did work — the / How

3. Jay | did find | book — Where / the

4. girls | will go — the / Where / now

5. birds | do fly — When / away

C. (Individual answers.)

Can You Do This?
(Individual answers.)

Lesson 89 Answers
A. 1. drives—carefully
2. waited—patiently
3. did—well
4. Do stand—still
5. Does talk—quietly
6. dried—Cheerfully

7. Grandfather prayed earnestly for us.

8. Slowly and cautiously, Lee crossed the ice.

B. Write the two adverbs used in each sentence. After each one, write whether it tells **how, when,** or **where.**
1. The wind blew fiercely outside.
2. Suddenly an old tree crashed loudly.
3. Father dashed downstairs and ran outside.
4. The chickens were already running everywhere.
5. Soon we were all trying hard to catch them.
6. Finally no more chickens could be found anywhere.
7. We could all go inside then.
8. "Now we can sleep," Mother said thankfully.

C. Change each adjective to an adverb.
1. nice	3. glad	5. brave
2. kind	4. loud	6. swift

D. Match each sentence with its diagram shape. Then copy the shape and write the words where they belong.
1. The faithful prophet prayed.
2. Suddenly a heavy rain fell.
3. Where did the prophet go?
4. He went away.
5. Did the wicked queen ever find him?

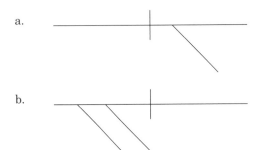

a.

b.

---

7. prayed—earnestly

8. crossed—Slowly, cautiously

B. 1. fiercely—how; outside—where
2. Suddenly—when; loudly—how
3. downstairs—where; outside—where
4. already—when; everywhere—where
5. Soon—when; hard—how
6. Finally—when; anywhere—where
7. inside—where; then—when
8. Now—when; thankfully—how

C.
1. nicely	3. gladly	5. bravely
2. kindly	4. loudly	6. swiftly

D. 1. (b.)   prophet | prayed   The faithful

2. (d.)   rain | fell   a heavy Suddenly

3. (c.)   prophet | did go   the Where

4. (a.)   He | went   away

5. (e.)   queen | did find | him   the wicked ever

Class: Use Oral Review in the class discussion. It would be good to look at the five diagram patterns in Part D before assigning the written work. Ask these questions about them.

Which diagram shows that the sentence has a direct object? (e)

Which diagram has one adjective and one adverb? (c)

Which diagram has one adverb and no adjectives? (a)

Which diagram has two adjectives and no adverbs? (b)

How many of each does diagram d have? (2 adjectives, 1 adverb)

You may also wish to discuss Part E of the written work.

c.

d.

e.
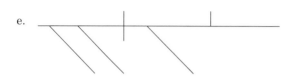

E. Name the child in each picture, and write a sentence with a quotation to tell what he might be saying. Use an adverb to tell **how** the child is speaking. Be sure to use quotation marks correctly.

1.

2.

E. (Possible answers.)
1. "Do you think it is looking for nuts?" Larry whispered softly.
2. "May we make a snowman at recess?" Carla asked excitedly.

90. Recognizing Adjectives and Adverbs

Adjectives describe nouns. They tell **what kind of, which, whose, how many,** or **how much.** They also include the noun markers **a, an,** and **the.** Each sentence below has two adjectives.

Dorcas was **a faithful** Christian.
She did **many kind** deeds.

Adverbs usually describe verbs. They can tell **how, when,** or **where** something is done. Each of these sentences has an adverb.

Dorcas lived **faithfully.**
She spoke **kindly.**

Each of the following sentences has an adjective and an adverb.

The <u>helpful</u> people worked <u>cheerfully</u>.
      adj.   adv.

<u>Tomorrow</u> the <u>cloudy</u> sky may clear.
adv.   adj.

<u>When</u> did the <u>new</u> boy come?
adv.   adj.

Adjective Family   Happily   Adverb Family

Lesson 90

Aim: To give practice with recognizing adjectives and adverbs.

Oral Review:

1. The sentence part that tells what someone *does* is the ———. (predicate)
2. Words that tell *what kind of, which,* or *how many* are ———. They describe ———. (adjectives; nouns)
3. Words that tell *how, when,* or *where* are ———. They describe ———. (adverbs; verbs)
4. How are some adjectives changed to adverbs? (by adding *-ly* to the adjectives)
5. When the words *how, when,* and *where* are used to ask questions, they are ———. (adverbs)

Class: Ask the class to tell what an adjective is. Ask them to give some examples. What kind of words do adjectives usually describe?

Ask what adverbs are, and what three questions they can answer. What kind of words do adverbs describe when they tell *how, when,* or *where?*

Write some sentences on the board, and ask the class to name the adjective and the adverb in each.

The black cow mooed loudly.
The tired people walked away.
Yesterday a strong wind was blowing.
Where did he find the blue shirt?
How did the sick calf eat?

In Part B of the exercises, you may wish to do some of the sentences in class.

★ **EXTRA PRACTICE**
Worksheet 54 (*Adjectives and Adverbs*)

> Using Adjectives and Adverbs >

A. Copy the words in bold print. Beside each write **adj.** or **adv.** to tell which it is.
1. The **tired** girls went **upstairs.**
2. **Colorful** leaves lay **everywhere.**
3. The **older** boys worked **hard.**
4. **Soon white** snow will cover the ground.
5. **Where** can you find a **wild** tiger?
6. **When** will the **red** tulips bloom?
7. **How** can a **little** bird sing?
8. Has the **cold** weather come **already?**

B. Use adjectives and adverbs to complete these sentences. Write each sentence correctly.
1. The two **adj.** boys played **adv.**
2. "I see a **adj.** animal," David said **adv.**
3. "May I wear my **adj.** shoes **adv.?**" Paul asked.
4. Joan found three **adj.** books **adv.**
5. **Adv.** the **adj.** sunshine melted the snow.

C. Use these pairs of adjectives and adverbs to write your own sentences.
1. happy, always
2. hot, carefully
3. clean, away

> Review and Practice >

Write the plural form of each noun.
1. match   3. woman   5. foot
2. chimney   4. country   6. mouse

●━━━━━━━━━━●

Lesson 90 Answers
Using Adjectives and Adverbs
A. 1. tired—adj.; upstairs—adv.
   2. Colorful—adj.; everywhere—adv.
   3. older—adj.; hard—adv.
   4. Soon—adv.; white—adj.
   5. Where—adv.; wild—adj.
   6. When—adv.; red—adj.
   7. How—adv.; little—adj.
   8. cold—adj.; already—adv.

B. (Words in parentheses will vary.)
   1. The two (little) boys played (happily).
   2. "I see a (huge) animal," David said (excitedly).
   3. "May I wear my (new) shoes (today)?" Paul asked.
   4. Joan found three (new) books (yesterday).
   5. (Swiftly) the (warm) sunshine melted the snow.

C. (Individual answers.)

Review and Practice
1. matches   4. countries
2. chimneys   5. feet
3. women   6. mice

91. *Well* and *Good*

Well is usually an adverb that tells **how** something is done.

> Please dry the dishes **well**.
> My little sister can read **well**.

Well may also mean **not sick**.

> Is Janet sick?
> No, she is **well**.

Use **good** only to answer the question **what kind of.**

> **What kind of** book is this?
> This is a **good** book.

Never use **good** to tell **how** something is done.

> **How** does Ken sing?
> *Wrong:* Ken sings **good**.
> *Right:*   Ken sings **well**.

Remember: Well is usually an adverb that tells **how** something is done. **Well** may also mean **not sick. Good** is always an adjective that tells **what kind of** about a noun.

> Using *Well* and *Good*

A. Write a complete sentence to answer each question. Use **good** or **well** in each answer.
1. How should Michael scrape the barn floor?
2. Is Lois still sick?

Lesson 91 Answers
Using *Well* and *Good*
A. (Wording may vary slightly.)
1. Michael should scrape the barn floor well.
2. Lois is well.

Lesson 91

Aim: To teach the correct use of *well* and *good.*

Oral Review:
1. In a commanding sentence, the subject is ———. The sentence ends with a ———. (you; period)
2. Adjectives describe ———. Adverbs describe ———. (nouns, verbs)
3. The words *how, when,* and *where* are ———. (adverbs)
4. Where may adverbs be found in a sentence? (in different places)
5. Words like *fast* and *high* may be ——— or ———. (adjectives, adverbs)

Class: Write the word *well* on the board. Explain that the word can be used two ways. We use *well* when we want to say *how* something is or was done. Illustrate with the sentences after the first paragraph.

Point out that we do not say *Janet is good* when we mean *Janet is not sick*. The word *well* in this sense means the same as *whole* in the Bible. See John 5:6 for one example.

When we use *well* to tell *how* something is or was done, we are using it as an adverb. Here are two more sentences that illustrate this use of *well.*

> Mark did his work well.
> Karen draws well.

The word *good* is always an adjective. It must never be used as an adverb. We should never say:

> Mark did his work good.
> Karen draws good.

The adjective *good* does come after forms of *be* in sentences like "This apple is good." Then *good* is a predicate adjective. But you need not mention this unless someone asks about it.

3. What kind of shoes are those?
4. How do the boys play?
5. How did the children work together?
6. What kind of dog is Shep?

B. Write whether you should use **good** or **well** to complete
each sentence.
1. Tim was sick, but today he is ——.
2. Did you scrub your hands ——?
3. She read a —— story to us.
4. God does all things ——.
5. God gives —— things to us.
6. The doctor thinks Aunt Ann will soon be ——.
7. That is a —— picture.
8. Susan can draw ——.
9. Uncle Paul cannot walk —— since the accident.
10. Moses was a —— leader.
11. Did the people listen ——?
12. Did the girls do —— work?
13. They worked very ——.
14. Brother Arnold cannot hear ——.

> Review and Practice >

Write each sentence correctly.
1. These here apples were picked up from the ground.
2. Those there were picked from the tree.
3. Them apples make good pies.
4. That there basket of apples has been sold.
5. We threw them wormy apples to the pigs.

3. Those are good shoes.
4. The boys play well.
5. The children worked together well.
6. Shep is a good dog.

B. 1. well
    2. well
    3. good
    4. well
    5. good
    6. well
    7. good
    8. well
    9. well
    10. good
    11. well
    12. good
    13. well
    14. well

Review and Practice
1. These apples were picked up from the ground.
2. Those were picked from the tree.
3. Those apples make good pies.
4. That basket of apples has been sold.
5. We threw those wormy apples to the pigs.

Tell the class that you will say some sentences. They
should use *good* or *well* in each blank.

Mary made —— cookies.
Leon sings ——.
Was David a —— king?
Sarah can sew ——.
Do you behave ——?
Is she sick or ——?
Jesus is the —— Shepherd.
The —— ground produced ——.

Explain that in all these sentences, *good* tells *what
kind of* about a noun. *Well* tells *how* about a verb, unless
it means *not sick*.

★ **EXTRA PRACTICE**
Worksheet 55 (Well *and* Good)

92. More About Adverbs and Adjectives

You have learned that many adverbs which tell **how** end in **ly.** Here are some of them.

bravely	gently	sadly	clearly
easily	slowly	swiftly	happily

Some adverbs that tell **how** do not end in **ly.** The words below do not end in **ly.** They can be used as adjectives or adverbs.

hard	high	right
fast	low	wrong

We saw a **fast** horse. (adjective)
The horse was running **fast.** (adverb)

Remember: Some words may be adjectives or adverbs. If the word describes a noun, it is an adjective. If it describes a verb, it is an adverb.

> To Do Together

Read each word aloud. Tell whether it can be used as an adjective, an adverb, or both.

sweetly	happily	right	nicely
gentle	careful	pleasant	kind
sweet	loudly	pleasantly	happy
good	carefully	nice	high
hard	loud	kindly	fast

> Using Adverbs and Adjectives

A. Which of the words from To Do Together could you use to complete the sentence below? List all of them.

Lesson 92 Answers
To Do Together

sweetly—adv.	right—both
gentle—adj.	pleasant—adj.
sweet—adj.	pleasantly—adv.
good—adj.	nice—adj.
hard—both	kindly—adv.
happily—adv.	nicely—adv.
careful—adj.	kind—adj.
loudly—adv.	happy—adj.
carefully—adv.	high—both
loud—both	fast—both

Lesson 92

Aim: To teach the correct use of words that may be either adjectives or adverbs.

Oral Review:
1. Give the eight forms of *be.* (am, is, are, was, were, be, been, being)
2. Which adjectives are called noun markers? (a, an, the)
3. Adjectives describe ———. Adverbs describe ———. (nouns; verbs)
4. What three questions do adverbs answer? (how, when, where)
5. When *well* tells how something is done, it is ———. *Well* may also mean ———. (an adverb; "not sick")

Class: Ask the class how they can tell whether a word is being used as an adjective or an adverb. They should be

able to say what questions each answers, and what part of speech it describes.

Write two sentences on the board. Tell them that the underlined word is sometimes an adjective and sometimes an adverb. Ask them to tell which way it is used in each sentence.

The boy learned a <u>hard</u> lesson.
The children all worked <u>hard</u>.

Emphasize: When a word describes a noun, it is an adjective. When a word describes a verb, it is an adverb.

Call attention to the six words which may be adjectives or adverbs, and use some of them in sentences. Ask the class to tell how you used each word.

The boy waded through <u>high</u> water.
The birds fly <u>high</u>.

Do your work <u>right</u>.
You gave the <u>right</u> answer.

How did the people sing?
The people sang ———.

B. Which of the words could you use to complete this sentence? List all of them.

In what kind of voice did Mary talk?
Mary spoke in a ——— voice.

> **Recognizing Words**

A. Tell whether each word in bold print is an **adjective** or an **adverb.**
1. James watched a **swift** worker.
2. The man was working **swiftly.**
3. The rope has a **tight** knot.
4. Hold **tight** to the rope.
5. Boaz was a **near** kinsman.
6. Jesus came **near** and healed the man.
7. John writes **well.**
8. John is a **good** writer.

B. Diagram sentences 1, 2, 3, and 7.

> **Practice With *Good* and *Well***

Write the correct word for each sentence.
1. God blessed us with a (good, well) rain last night.
2. Some old people do not hear (good, well).
3. He does not feel (good, well).
4. Everything went (good, well).
5. He is a (good, well) carpenter.
6. This is (good, well) material.

That was a <u>fast</u> trip.
He ran <u>fast</u>.

To Do Together is a class exercise. Emphasize the correct usage of *nice* and *nicely.* You could also point out that if a word has two forms—one with *–ly* and one without—usually the *-ly* form is an adverb and the other is an adjective.

For Using Adverbs and Adjectives, you may wish to tell students how many possibilities there are for each exercise.

Using Adverbs and Adjectives
A. sweetly   pleasantly
   happily   kindly
   loudly   nicely
   carefully   high
   right   fast

B. gentle   pleasant
   sweet   nice
   good   kind
   careful   happy
   loud   high
   (Also accept *right* and *fast.*)

Recognizing Words
A. 1. adjective
   2. adverb
   3. adjective
   4. adverb
   5. adjective
   6. adverb
   7. adverb
   8. adjective

B. 1.

2.

3.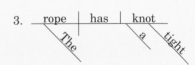

4.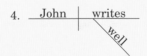

Practice With *Good* and *Well*
   1. good   4. well
   2. well   5. good
   3. well   6. good

93. The *No* Words

Some words have the idea of "not." These words may be called **no** words.

The little word **not** is a **no** word. This word is not a verb. It is an adverb. The **no** words **never** and **nowhere** are also adverbs.

I did not run.   Penguins never fly.

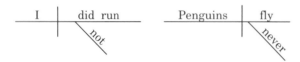

Betty went nowhere.

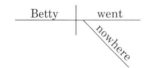

Nothing, nobody, and **none** are some other **no** words. All the **no** words have the idea of "not."

Never means **not ever.**
Nowhere means **not anywhere.**
Nothing means **not anything.**
Nobody means **not anybody.**
None means **not any.**

How many of the **no** words can you use to tell about this picture?

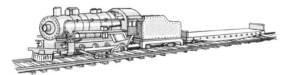

Lesson 93

Aim: (1) To introduce the *no* words. (2) To teach that *not* and some other *no* words are adverbs.

Oral Review:
1. Which verb forms usually need a helping verb? (those ending with an *n* or *un* sound)
2. The words *how, when,* and *where* are ———. (adverbs)
3. Words like *fast* and *high* may be ——— or ———. (adjectives, adverbs)
4. When *fast* or *high* is used in a sentence, how can you tell whether it is an adjective or an adverb? (If the word describes a noun, it is an adjective. If it describes a verb, it is an adverb.)
5. Use *well* or *good* in each sentence.
   a. This is a ——— tool. (good)
   b. This tool works ———. (well)
   c. Grandmother cannot hear ———. (well)

Class: On the board write the words *not, never,* and *nowhere.* Ask the class if they remember what kind of words *never* and *nowhere* are. (They are adverbs that tell *when* and *where.*)

Explain that the word *not* is an adverb too. We cannot really say that *not* tells *how, when,* or *where,* but it is still an adverb because it describes the verb. (Actually, it reverses the meaning of the verb.) Emphasize: *Not* is *not* a verb.

Not, never, and *nowhere* are adverbs; but *nothing, nobody,* and *none* are pronouns. (They are indefinite pronouns, the same as *something* and *someone.*) This distinction need not be mentioned to the pupils, for the main purpose of this lesson is to have them recognize *no* words and understand that they are not verbs. In the sentences to be diagramed, all *no* words are adverbs.

> Working With the *No* Words >

A. Use a **no** word to complete each sentence.
1. The birds had —— to eat.
2. Jason —— saw a deer before.
3. When Uncle Carl opened the door, —— was there.
4. —— of the boys could catch the ball.
5. Ray does —— have any boots.
6. "You will go —— tomorrow," Father said.

B. Write a **no** word to replace each phrase in bold print.
1. **Not anybody** had seen Elijah for many days.
2. He was **not anywhere** to be found.
3. The widow had **not anything** but some meal and oil.
4. Baal's prophets prayed for fire, but **not any** came.

C. Diagram these sentences.
1. Jesus never changes.
2. The car could go nowhere.
3. The people had not eaten.

> Review and Practice >

A. Write the two words that each contraction stands for.

1. didn't	4. don't	7. doesn't
2. isn't	5. aren't	8. weren't
3. hasn't	6. wasn't	9. won't

B. Use four of the above contractions in sentences.

●━━●━━●━━●━━●━━●━━●

Take time to talk about the picture in the lesson text. Have the class use *no* words in sentences like the following.

The train does not have any wheels.
It will go nowhere.

Nobody is on the train.
Nothing is on the cars.

★ **EXTRA PRACTICE**
Worksheet 56 (*The No Words*)

Lesson 93 Answers
Working With the *No* Words

A. 1. nothing
2. never
3. nobody
4. None
5. not
6. nowhere

B. 1. Nobody
2. nowhere
3. nothing
4. none

C. 1.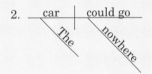

2.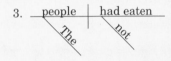

3.

Review and Practice

A.
1. did not		6. was not
2. is not		7. does not
3. has not		8. were not
4. do not		9. will not
5. are not		

B. (Individual answers.)

94. Using the *No* Words Correctly

Do the following sentences sound correct?

> I have not not ever gone.
> Mark does not have not anything to do.

The sentences do not sound right because the word **not** is used twice in them. That is why these sentences are also not correct.

> *Wrong:* I have**n't** **never** gone.
> *Wrong:* Mark does**n't** have **nothing** to do.

The contractions **haven't** and **doesn't** each have **not** in them. So we must not use another **no** word with them. Here are the correct ways.

> *Right:* I haven't ever gone.
>   I have never gone.

> *Right:* Mark doesn't have anything to do.
>   Mark has nothing to do.

The phrase **am not** has no contraction. Some people say **ain't,** but that is not a proper word to use.

DON'T   EVER   NEVER

Lesson 94

Aim: To teach the correct use of negative words, especially the avoidance of double negatives.

Oral Review:

1. An exclaiming sentence ends with ——. Give an example. (an exclamation mark; Individual examples.)
2. Tell whether these words are used as adjectives or adverbs.
   a. *high:* The sick child had a high temperature. (adjective)
   b. *still:* Please sit still. (adverb)
   c. *fast:* An eagle is a fast flier. (adjective)
3. Finish these sentences with *well* or *good.*
   a. Martha reads ——. (well)
   b. She is a —— reader. (good)
   c. Jesus made sick people ——. (well)
4. The words *never, nowhere,* and *not* are (adjectives, adverbs). (adverbs)

Class: Ask the class to give the *no* words discussed in Lesson 93, and write them on the board. Include the word *not* and the contractions containing *not.*

Explain that sometimes we hear these words misused. Then read the first paragraph in the lesson and discuss the example sentences. Here is another one to write on the board.

> I did not not ever see a whale.

After someone has pointed out the error, write:

> I did not never see a whale.

Do they see that the *not* meaning is also repeated in this sentence? Now write:

> I didn't never see a whale.

Can they see where the *not* meaning is repeated now?

> **Remember:** When you use one **no** word, STOP! Do not use another **no** word with it. Do not use **ain't** in any sentence.

Using the *No* Words

A. In each sentence, copy the correct word so that the sentence has just one **no** word.
   1. Janice isn't going (anywhere, nowhere).
   2. Have you (never, ever) seen the ocean?
   3. Carol doesn't want (nothing, anything) to eat.
   4. We didn't (ever, never) read that book.
   5. (Somebody, Nobody) was at school yesterday.
   6. Claire wants (nothing, something) hot to eat.
   7. We could find it (anywhere, nowhere).
   8. Couldn't (anybody, nobody) help the blind girl?
   9. Don't you have (no, any) money?
   10. (Any, None) of them are finished yet.

B. Read each sentence. If it has a mistake, write the sentence correctly. If it is correct, write **correct.**
   1. Suppose nobody ever did his share of the work.
   2. Then nothing would never get done.
   3. Everybody has something to do.
   4. There isn't nobody who can excuse himself.
   5. There isn't nowhere that work can be avoided.
   6. None of the shirkers will be a winner.

Review and Practice

Copy each sentence, adding commas where they are needed.
   1. Levi Joseph Dan and Asher were sons of Jacob.

Lesson 94 Answers
Using the *No* Words
A. 1. anywhere
    2. never
    3. anything
    4. ever
    5. Nobody
    6. nothing
    7. nowhere
    8. anybody
    9. any
    10. None

B. 1. correct
   2. Then nothing would ever get done.
   3. correct
   4. There isn't anybody (*or* is nobody) who can excuse himself.
   5. There isn't anywhere (*or* is nowhere) that work can be avoided.
   6. correct

Review and Practice
   1. Levi, Joseph, Dan, and Asher were sons of Jacob.

Point out that we would probably never say the first sentence, and maybe not the second. But when we use contractions, it is easy to forget and use another *no* word. To say the third sentence is really the same as saying the first or second.

The use of *ain't* can be a strong habit among children who hear older people use it regularly. You could point out that this is really a form of laziness; besides meaning *am not*, the word is also used as a catchall term for *is not, are not, have not,* and *has not.* Put forth special effort to break this habit in any children affected by it.

Emphasize the rule at the end of the lesson by having the class read it in unison.

★ **EXTRA PRACTICE**
Worksheet 57 (*Using the No Words Correctly*)

2. Children can you name some mountains in the Bible?

3. Some mountains in the Bible are Mount Carmel Mount Ararat and Mount Sinai.

4. Wayne and Donald can you name some foods in the Bible?

5. Some foods in the Bible are bread honey meat and fruit.

> Can You Do This? >

Write three sentences about this picture. Use a different **no** word in each sentence.

95. Reviewing What You Have Learned

A. Write whether each word or phrase makes you think of an **adjective** or an **adverb**.

1. Describes nouns	7. Which?
2. Describes verbs	8. When?
3. How?	9. How much?
4. What kind of?	10. Not
5. How many?	11. Good
6. Where?	12. A, an, the

Lesson 95

Aim: To review the previous five lessons.

Oral Review:

1. Adjectives are not hard to recognize because they answer the questions ——. (what kind of, how many or how much, which, whose)

2. We can also recognize adjectives because they describe ——. (nouns)

3. Adverbs are not hard to recognize because they answer the questions ——. (how, when, where)

4. We can also recognize adverbs because they describe ——. (verbs)

5. Use *good* or *well* in each sentence.
   a. The children played —— today. (well)
   b. They had a —— time. (good)
   c. Sleep —— tonight. (well)

---

2. Children, can you name some mountains i the Bible?

3. Some mountains in the Bible are Mount Car mel, Mount Ararat, and Mount Sinai.

4. Wayne and Donald, can you name some food in the Bible?

5. Some foods in the Bible are bread, hone meat, and fruit.

Can You Do This?
(Individual answers.)

Lesson 95 Answers

A. 1.	adjective	7.	adjective
2.	adverb	8.	adverb
3.	adverb	9.	adjective
4.	adjective	10.	adverb
5.	adjective	11.	adjective
6.	adverb	12.	adjective

6. Give the rule for using *no* words. (When you use one *no* word, stop! Do not use another *n* word with it.)

Class: Use Oral Review in the class discussion. G over the written exercises to make sure the pupil understand them.

B. Write **well** or **good** for each sentence.
1. The children listened ——.
2. This is a —— cake.
3. Are those your —— shoes?
4. That horse can run ——.
5. Eva was sick but will soon be ——.
6. Can Larry write ——?
7. Uncle Bert cannot see very ——.
8. Is that a —— book?
9. Do your lessons ——.
10. Scrub the pans ——, please.

C. Write a **no** word for each meaning.
1. not ever   4. not any
2. not anything   5. not anywhere
3. not anybody

D. Write the correct words to make each pair of sentences mean the same.
1. a. We have ——.
   b. We don't have (any, none).
2. a. I —— saw it.
   b. I didn't (ever, never) see it.
3. a. He hasn't ——.
   b. He has (anything, nothing).
4. a. It isn't ——.
   b. It is (anywhere, nowhere).
5. a. I saw ——.
   b. I didn't see (anybody, nobody).

E. Pretend you are the teacher. Correct what each child said.
1. "I didn't never read that book."
2. "He doesn't have none."

B. 1. well
    2. good
    3. good
    4. well
    5. well
    6. well
    7. well
    8. good
    9. well
    10. well

C. 1. never
    2. nothing
    3. nobody
    4. none
    5. nowhere

D. 1. a. none   b. any
   2. a. never   b. ever
   3. a. anything   b. nothing
   4. a. anywhere   b. nowhere
   5. a. nobody   b. anybody

E. 1. I didn't ever read that book.
      or I never read that book.
   2. He doesn't have any.
      or He has none.

3. "We don't see nothing."
4. "She's not going nowhere."
5. "He ain't never had nothing."

F. Write a sentence using a **no** word for each picture.
1.   2.

●━━●━━●━━●━━●━━●━━●

96. Writing a Story From Pictures

Look at the picture and answer these questions. What do you see? What is the weather like? What are the people doing?

Now read this paragraph. Does it answer all the questions?

3. We don't see anything.
   or We see nothing.
4. She's not going anywhere.
   or She's going nowhere.
5. He never had anything.
   or He hasn't ever had anything.

F. (Possible answers.)
1. Nobody is in school.
2. There is nothing in the basket.

Lesson 96

Aim: To give the students guidance and practice in writing paragraphs from pictures.

Oral Review:
1. An (adverb, adjective) tells *how* something is done. (adverb)
2. Use *fast* in two sentences, first as an adjective and then as an adverb. (Individual answers.)
3. Finish these sentences with *well* or *good*.
   a. Mary is not feeling ———. (well)
   b. We had a ——— rain yesterday. (good)
   c. This pen writes ———. (well)
4. *Never, nowhere,* and *not* are ——— words. They are used as ———. (no; adverbs)
5. Tell what is wrong with this sentence: *He hasn't never been at the zoo.* Say the sentence correctly in two ways. (It has two *no* words. He has never been at the zoo. He hasn't ever been at the zoo.)

Class: This lesson will be taught the most effectively if you show a large picture in which something is happening. Using the picture, encourage the students to help write a paragraph about what they see. Write the sentences they suggest on the board.

Discuss the picture and paragraphs given in today's lesson. Explain that when we see a picture we can write only what we *think* is happening. Different people will have different ideas. Discuss the differences in the two paragraphs. Ask the class to give some other ideas about what might have been happening in the hay field.

★ **EXTRA PRACTICE**
Worksheet 58 (*Writing a Story From Pictures*)

One warm, sunny day, Jason and Paul helped Father in the hayfield. When they were finished, Father climbed onto the tractor seat. The boys climbed onto the big pile of hay. Then away they went as the tractor pulled the loaded wagon to the big hay barn.

When you write about pictures, you can write what you **think** happened. Here is another paragraph about the picture.

Jason and Paul had helped Father all afternoon in the dusty hayfield. Now Father had a treat for them. He said he was going to take the hay to a neighbor. Quickly Jason and Paul climbed onto the pile of hay. Then they rode *bump, bump, bump* as Father drove out the lane.

> ## Looking at Pictures >

1.   2.   3.

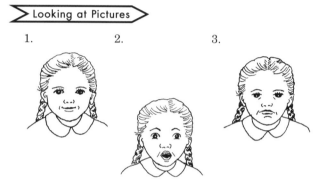

What do you think happened to make Karen feel the way these pictures show? Answer by writing this sentence in three different ways, once for each picture.

Karen was —— when ——.

Lesson 96 Answers
Looking at Pictures

(Possible answers.)

1. Karen was happy when she surprised Mother by doing the dishes.
2. Karen was surprised when Father gave her a new book.
3. Karen was sad when her baby brother was sick.

> Writing What You Think Happened >

A. Answer these questions about the picture.

1. Is it morning or evening?
2. Who do you see?
3. What are they doing?
4. Why are they doing it?

B. Write a paragraph about the picture. Use your answers to the questions to help you. Then write a title to tell what your paragraph is about.

> Review and Practice >

Write the correct word for each sentence.
1. Mother ironed the (girls, girl's) dress.
2. The (boy's, boys) went fishing.
3. The (birds, bird's) feet were frozen.
4. The (teachers, teacher's) had a meeting today.
5. We found a (dogs, dog's) collar in the woods.

Writing What You Think Happened

A. (Possible answers.)
1. evening
2. two children
3. They are putting away toys and setting the table.
4. They want to surprise Mother. Father will soon be home. Company is coming.

B. (Individual paragraphs. Check for proper capitalization in the title.)

Review and Practice
1. girl's
2. boys
3. bird's
4. teachers
5. dog's

97. Using Words to Make Pictures

What picture does the following sentence put into your mind?

Michael came down the stairs.

What pictures do these sentences put into your mind?

Michael dashed down the stairs.
Michael tiptoed down the stairs.
Michael slid down the stairs.
Michael stumbled down the stairs.

Do you see how the verbs in these four sentences give a better picture of what happened?

Clearer word pictures can also be made by the use of better nouns.

Lucy gave the sick girl a gift.
Lucy gave the sick girl a book.
Lucy gave the sick girl a game.
Lucy gave the sick girl a puzzle.

What nouns are used in the last three sentences to make a clearer word picture? Can you think of some other nouns that could be used?

Remember: When you write, use nouns and verbs that give a clear picture of what happened.

> Choosing Better Words >

A. Write a different verb instead of **went** for each sentence to give a clearer picture of what happened. You may choose from these: crawled, hurried, tiptoed, sailed, skipped, toddled, bicycled.

Lesson 97

Aim: To teach the use of words that give a clear picture of what is happening.

Oral Review:

1. Tell whether each word is an adjective or an adverb.
   a. *high:* The water rose high. (adverb)
   b. *still:* I could see my face in the still water. (adjective)
   c. *fast:* The train was coming fast. (adverb)
2. *Good* is always an (adjective, adverb). *Well* is an (adjective, adverb) when it tells how something is done. (adjective; adverb)
3. The word *not* is not a verb, but ———. (an adverb)
4. Finish this rule: When you have used one *no* word in a sentence, ——— (stop! Do not use another *no* word in the same sentence.)

5. When you write a story about a picture, how do you know what to write? (Write what you think happened.)

Class: Write the word *came* on the board. Read the first part of the lesson and discuss how the other verbs give a clearer picture than *came*. Then ask for other words instead of *came* that would tell better how Michael came.

ran, walked, skipped, hurried, trudged, marched

Explain that our word pictures will be clearer if we use more specific verbs. Then ask for some verbs that could be used instead of *ate*.

nibbled, gulped, gobbled, pecked, devoured

Discuss the different nouns used in the second part of the lesson. Give other nouns that can be

1. Mother went to the kitchen.
2. Kevin went to the barn.
3. Susan went downstairs.
4. Baby Lena went to Grandfather.

B. Rewrite each sentence, using a different noun for **animal.**
You may need to change **an** to **a.**
1. An animal got into our garage.
2. Paul found an animal under the porch.
3. Father thinks an animal is eating our sweet corn.
4. Martha saw an animal in the attic.

C. Remember that adjectives help make word pictures too.
Write a different adjective to complete each sentence.
You may choose from these: hot, warm, cold, sweet, dry,
fresh, stale.
1. Slowly Cathy sipped the
—— lemonade.
2. Peter quickly gulped the
—— water.
3. Mary drank the ——
broth carefully.
4. The calf noisily sucked
the —— milk.

D. Copy the verb and adverb used in each sentence in Part C.

> Review and Practice >

Choose the correct verb form for each sentence.
1. We (did, done) all the garden work yesterday.
2. I have (saw, seen) that car a number of times.
3. This tomato plant has really (grew, grown).
4. Grandfather and Grandmother have (went, gone) home.
5. Yesterday we (come, came) to school earlier than usual.

Lesson 97 Answers
Choosing Better Words
A. (Probable answers.)
1. hurried
2. skipped *or* bicycled
3. tiptoed *or* skipped
4. crawled *or* toddled

B. (Possible answers are in parentheses.)
1. (A raccoon, A dog, A rabbit) got into our garage
2. Paul found (a skunk, a rabbit, a snake) under
the porch.
3. Father thinks (a ground hog, a raccoon) is eating our sweet corn.
4. Martha saw (a bat, a mouse, a squirrel) in the
attic.

C. (Probable answers.)
1. cold *or* sweet
2. cold *or* stale
3. hot
4. warm *or* fresh

D. 1. sipped, slowly
2. gulped, quickly
3. drank, carefully
4. sucked, noisily

Review and Practice
1. did
2. seen
3. grown
4. gone
5. came

replaced to make clearer word pictures.

building—house, hotel, store, mansion, skyscraper
fruit—apples, pears, grapes, oranges, bananas

★ **EXTRA PRACTICE**
Worksheet 59 (*Clear Word Pictures*)

98. Writing Smoothly

What is wrong with this picture? It is broken into pieces. Each part should be joined to the next.

When we write, we need to join ideas together. We should try to make one clear word picture.

> A cow stood in the lane. It was big. It was black and white.
> It had two sharp horns.

The ideas in the four sentences above do not fit together smoothly. Read the sentence below. Does it have the same ideas?

> A big black and white cow with two sharp horns stood in the lane.

Read the sentences below. Can you think of a way to say all the ideas in one clear sentence?

> A boy chased the cow. He was tall. He had a blue jacket. He had a brown cap.

Maybe this will help you.

> A —— boy with —— and —— chased the cow.

> Writing Ideas More Smoothly >

A. Write each set of ideas in one sentence. Use the sentence form to help you. You may use more than one word in each blank.

Lesson 98

Aim: To give the students guidance in writing longer sentences.

Oral Review:

1. Diagram this sentence: Two boys were doing their lessons.

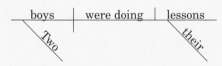

2. We can recognize adjectives because they describe ——. We can recognize adverbs because they describe ——. (nouns; verbs)

3. The words *never, nowhere,* and *no* are ——. (adverbs)

4. Say each sentence correctly in two ways.
   a. The children didn't have nothing to eat. (The children didn't have anything to eat. The children had nothing to eat.)
   b. I couldn't find no pencil. (I couldn't find any pencil. I could find no pencil.)

5. What kind of nouns and verbs should you use when you write? (Use nouns and verbs that give a clear picture of what happened.)

Class: Individual reading ability will greatly influence how well each child is able to handle this lesson. Those who are still able to read only short, choppy sentences will have more difficulty writing several thoughts as one sentence. Encourage each student to do his best.

Write several short sentences on the board. Guide the class into combining these sentences into one.

> Paul ate an apple. Paul is my brother. The apple was green.
> My brother Paul ate a green apple.

1. A dog barked playfully. It was little. It was brown and white.

  A —— —— dog barked playfully.

2. Last summer we saw a walrus. It was at the zoo. It was big and brown. It had long tusks.

  Last summer at —— we saw a —— —— walrus with ——.

B. Use the questions beside the pictures to help you write one sentence about each picture.

1.

What happened?
What size is the puppy?
What kind of ears does it have?

2. What time of day is it?
What is the bird doing?
What size is the bird?
Where is the bird sitting?

> Review and Practice >

A. Write **I** and the six other pronouns that tell **who.** Then write **me** and the six other pronouns that tell **whom.**

B. Write the correct word for each sentence.
  1. There (was, were) eight people saved in the ark.
  2. There (is, are) a Bible storybook on the shelf, which has that story.
  3. There (is, are) other stories in it too.
  4. There (was, were) a man named Job.
  5. There (was, were) three men cast into a fiery furnace.

Lesson 98 Answers
Writing Ideas More Smoothly
A. 1. A little brown and white dog barked playfull
   2. Last summer at the zoo we saw a big brow
       walrus with long tusks.

B. (Possible answers.)
   1. A little puppy with floppy ears slid on the ic
   2. One morning a little bird was singing in a tre

Review and Practice
A. I, you, he, she, it, we, they
   me, you, him, her, it, us, them

B. 1. were
   2. is
   3. are
   4. was
   5. were

    In the last part of the lesson, make it clear that each blank in the longer sentence can stand for more than one word.

★ **EXTRA PRACTICE**
Worksheet 60 (*Writing Smoothly*)

99. Sharing an Experience

"Were you ever surprised?" Sister Faye asked the class.

"I was surprised when Grandfather rode our bicycle," Keith answered.

"I was surprised when our mothers brought a hot lunch to school," Lois added.

Were **you** ever surprised? What happened to surprise you? Read about the surprise one girl had.

I was surprised when Grandmother gave me a teddy bear for my birthday. I was so happy I couldn't say a word. Later I wrote a letter to Grandmother. I told her I really liked the cuddly brown bear.

Look at this picture. How do you think the boy feels? Why do you think he feels that way? What do you think is going to happen? Where do you think he might be going?

> Writing About Your Own Experiences >

A. Think about times that you have had special feelings. Then write an ending for each sentence.
1. I was happy when ————.
2. I was surprised when ————.
3. I was excited when ————.
4. I was sorry when ————.
5. I was tired after ————.

Lesson 99 Answers
Writing About Your Own Experiences
A. (Individual answers.)

Lesson 99

Aim: To guide the students in writing about personal experiences.

Oral Review:
1. Say three pronouns that you can use instead of using your own name. (I, me, mine)
2. The word *not* is not a verb but an ————. (adverb)
3. Finish this rule: When you have used one *no* word in a sentence, ———— (stop! Do not use another *no* word in the same sentence.)
4. For each word, say a word that gives a clearer picture: traveled, good, fast. (Possible answers: sailed, flew; delicious, enjoyable; swift, speedy)
5. Combine these short sentences into one smooth, clear sentence. A jet roared by. It was huge and shiny. It was overhead. (A huge shiny jet roared by overhead.)

Class: Read the first three paragraphs of the lesson together, then ask the children if they were ever surprised. What surprised them? Share an experience of your own to encourage them in sharing theirs.

Discuss possible answers for the questions about the boy in the picture. Explain that there is no one correct answer.

Tell the class that we often have different feelings. We can write about what makes us feel different ways. Ask, "Do you remember a time when you were very hungry? Why did you feel that way? Let's suppose that a boy named John was hungry. We'll write a paragraph about him." With the students suggesting sentences, write a paragraph such as the following on the board.

One evening John was very hungry. He had worked in the garden all afternoon. He had

B. Write a paragraph about an experience you have had. Follow these steps.

1. Choose one of the sentences you wrote for Part A. Use it to begin your paragraph.
2. Write other sentences to tell more about your experience. Remember to tell things in the order that they happened.
3. Write a title for your paragraph.

> **Extra Practice** >

1. Write a paragraph about a time when you helped someone.
2. Write a paragraph about a day at school that was different from other days.

> **Review and Practice** >

Copy the correct pronoun for each sentence.
1. James and (he, him) ran a race.
2. Mother gave Ruth and (she, her) some apples.
3. Father called Mary and (I, me).
4. Should Beth and (she, her) wash the dishes?
5. My brother and (I, me) saw a snake.
6. Did you help Luke and (they, them)?

●━●━●━●━●━●━●━●━●

B. (Individual paragraphs. Check for correct form.

Extra Practice
(Individual paragraphs.)

Review and Practice
1. he
2. her
3. me
4. she
5. I
6. them

hoed and hoed. Now he could hardly wait for supper.

Encourage the students to write about real experiences as they do the exercises. At this age most children are still open enough to share their thoughts willingly.

100. Reviewing What You Have Learned

> Written Practice

A. Replace each word in bold print with a word or group of words that gives a clearer picture.
1. Little Allen was playing with his **toys.**
2. Mother gave the sick woman some **food.**
3. Jay's **clothing** was torn.
4. Paul **took** the heavy box to the shed.
5. When we came near, the ducks **went** away.
6. Dennis **looked** out the window.

B. Use the ideas in each group of sentences to write one sentence. A pattern is given to help you with the first two.
1. It happened last evening. Paul saw a fawn. It was little and spotted. It was near the woods.

—— Paul saw a —— —— fawn near ——.

2. Levi finished the book. He did it quickly. It was new. It was about birds.

Levi —— finished the —— book ——.

3. The kitten is tiny. It is gray. Sarah named it Puffball.

C. Finish each sentence so that it tells about the picture at the right. Write your sentences in paragraph form.
1. Rhoda laughed when ——.
2. The puppy looked funny with ——.
3. Finally ——.

D. Write a different ending for each sentence.
1. I laughed when ——.
2. I had fun the day we ——.

Lesson 100 Answers
Written Practice
A. (*Possible answers.*)
1. tractors, blocks
2. soup, warm sandwiches
3. shirt, trousers, jacket
4. dragged, carried
5. swam, waddled, flew
6. peeked, stared

B. (Wording of sentence 3 may vary.)
1. Last evening Paul saw a little spotted fawn near the woods.
2. Levi quickly finished the new book about birds.
3. Sarah named the tiny gray kitten Puffball.

C. (Possible paragraph.)

Rhoda laughed when Spot tried to squeeze through the fence. The puppy looked funny with its head poked through the hole. Finally the puppy squeezed through.

D. (Individual answers.)

Lesson 100

Aim: To review the previous four lessons.

Written Quiz:
1. Words that tell **what kind of** are ——.
2. Words that tell **how** something is done are ——.
3. Write whether the words in bold print are **adjectives** or **adverbs.**
   a. Those shoes fit **well.**
   b. We had a **hard** rain today.
   c. The eagle flew **high** into the air.
4. How many **no** words should be used in one sentence?
5. Ideas do not run together smoothly if a paragraph has too many —— sentences.

Quiz Answers:
1. adjectives
2. adverbs
3. a. adverb
   b. adjective
   c. adverb
4. one
5. short

Class: Go over all the exercises in class. Be sure the children understand how each part is to be done.

In the second half of the lesson, give opportunity for the pupils to read their sentences and paragraphs in class.

3. I was hungry after ——.
4. I got cold when ——.

E. Use one of the sentences you wrote for Part D to begin a paragraph. Finish your paragraph by writing more sentences about your experience.

> **Can You Do This?**

Try finishing this paragraph by using your own words and phrases in the blanks.

> One —— Mark and his —— were ——. Their —— had told them they could ——. When they started to ——, they found that the —— was ——. Then they were really ——!

Review One

> **Oral Drill**

1. What words do adjectives describe? Where do adjectives belong on a sentence diagram?
2. What are four questions that adjectives can answer?
3. Tell how to use **a** and **an** correctly in a sentence. Why are they called noun markers?
4. What words do adverbs describe? What three questions do adverbs answer?
5. Tell how you would change each of these adjectives to an adverb.

swift	quiet	pleasant
wise	sweet	prayerful

Review One

Aim: To review and strengthen concepts taught in previous lessons in preparation for a test.

Class: Proceed as in previous review lessons, using the method you find most successful.

E. (Check each paragraph for correctness.)

Can You Do This?
(Possible paragraph.)
One evening Mark and his brother were glad. Their father had told them they could play. When they started to slide, they found that the sliding board was freshly painted. Then they were really surprised!

Review One Answers
Oral Drill

1. Adjectives describe nouns. Adjectives are diagramed on slanted lines under the nouns they describe.
2. Adjectives can answer the questions *what kind of, how many* (*how much*), *whose,* and *which.*
3. Use *a* before a consonant sound. Use *an* before a vowel sound.
    A and *an* (also *the*) are called noun markers because they always mark the coming of a noun.
4. Adverbs describe verbs. Adverbs answer the questions *how, when,* and *where.*
5. Add *-ly* to each word.

swiftly	quietly	pleasantly
wisely	sweetly	prayerfully

6. On a sentence diagram, where does an adverb belong?
7. Say what adverbs are used in these sentences.
   a. Yesterday a strong wind was blowing.
   b. The news traveled swiftly.
   c. Spring had finally come.
   d. The book could not be found anywhere.
   e. The snow fell silently.
   f. I should write a letter now.
   g. When will the birds return?
   h. Everyone is here today.

▷ Written Practice ▷

A. Diagram these sentences.
   1. The tulips are blooming.
   2. The swan glided gracefully.
   3. Lions roar fiercely.
   4. Snow and sleet were falling swiftly.
   5. The light shone brightly.

B. Write **many** or **much** to complete each sentence.
   1. Abraham saw —— stars in the sky.
   2. Jesus healed —— people.
   3. The prophets spoke —— about sin.
   4. —— animals went into the ark with Noah.
   5. When God sent the flood, there was —— water on the earth.

C. Write the possessive form of each word.
   1. Henry   4. you   7. man   10. bird
   2. Mark   5. Aaron   8. child   11. woman
   3. me   6. Edna   9. fox   12. Peter

D. Copy all the adjectives in these sentences. The numbers in parentheses tell how many there are.

6. An adverb belongs on a slanted line under the verb it describes.
7. a. Yesterday   e. silently
   b. swiftly   f. now
   c. finally   g. When
   d. not, anywhere   h. here, today

Written Practice

A. 1.

2.

3.

4.

5.

B. 1. many
   2. many
   3. much
   4. Many
   5. much

C. 1. Henry's   7. man's
   2. Mark's   8. child's
   3. my   9. fox's
   4. your   10. bird's
   5. Aaron's   11. woman's
   6. Edna's   12. Peter's

1. God created the lovely earth in six days. (3)
2. God made green grass and beautiful flowers. (2)
3. He made two great lights. (2)
4. He made tiny insects and huge whales. (2)
5. Then God made the man in His image. (2)
6. God rested on the seventh day. (2)
7. Adam's wife was named Eve. (1)

D. 1. the, lovely, six
2. green, beautiful
3. two, great
4. tiny, huge
5. the, His
6. the, seventh
7. Adam's

Review Two

> Oral Drill >

1. What question does **well** answer?
2. What other meaning does **well** have?
3. Is **not** a verb or an adverb?
4. On a sentence diagram, where does **not** belong?
5. Correct each sentence and read it aloud.
   a. I don't have nothing to do.
   b. There wasn't nobody there.
   c. He doesn't have no pencil.
   d. They weren't going nowhere.
   e. Charles doesn't never walk to school.
   f. We do not have no time to play.
6. Read each set of sentences. Then say all the ideas together in one clear sentence.
   a. Our rabbit is white. It got out on the road. It was killed by a car. This happened yesterday.
   b. Jesus had twelve disciples. He told them to get into a boat. He told them to go across the sea. It was the Sea of Galilee.
7. Change each verb in bold print to a verb that gives a

Review Two Answers
Oral Drill

1. *Well* usually answers the question *how.*
2. *Well* also means "not sick."
3. *Not* is an adverb.
4. The word *not* belongs on a slanted line unde the verb.
5. a. I don't have anything to do. *or* I have noth ing to do.
   b. There wasn't anybody there. *or* There wa nobody there.
   c. He doesn't have any pencil. *or* He has n pencil.
   d. They weren't going anywhere. *or* They wer going nowhere.
   e. Charles doesn't ever walk to school. *o* Charles never walks to school.
   f. We do not have time to play. *or* We have n time to play.
6. a. Yesterday our white rabbit got out on th road and was killed by a car.
   b. Jesus told His twelve disciples to get int a boat and go across the Sea of Galilee.

Review Two

Aim: To review and strengthen concepts taught in previous lessons in preparation for a test.

Class: Proceed as in previous review lessons.

clearer word picture.
  a. Mother Robin **went** home to her babies.
  b. "Lord, save me," **said** Peter.
  c. The family **liked** the trip to the zoo.
  d. John **took** the picnic basket to the pond.
  e. Father **looked** quickly at the clock.

> Written Practice

A. Copy the one (1) or two (2) adverbs used in each sentence. After each adverb, write whether it tells **how, when,** or **where.**
  1. We played quietly because Joy was sleeping. (1)
  2. Now it is raining hard. (2)
  3. Moses bowed humbly before God. (1)
  4. Everyone was here yesterday. (2)
  5. The train carried the passengers swiftly. (1)
  6. The cruel soldiers spoke roughly to Jesus. (1)
  7. Baby Keturah played happily today. (2)

B. Diagram these sentences.
  1. The new books are here.
  2. The waves roared loudly.
  3. Mother baked a delicious pie yesterday.
  4. That dog is not sleeping.
  5. Levi and Leon did their work right.

C. Write **well** or **good** for each blank.
  1. Grandfather is in bed because he is not ———.
  2. The picture turned out ———.
  3. You need a ——— light in order to read ———.
  4. Roy cannot hear ——— since he was sick.
  5. Grandmother brought some ——— homemade bread.
  6. The carpenters did a ——— job.

7. (Possible answers.)
  a. flew
  b. cried
  c. enjoyed
  d. carried
  e. glanced

Written Practice
A. 1. quietly—how
  2. Now—when; hard—how
  3. humbly—how
  4. here—where; yesterday—when
  5. swiftly—how
  6. roughly—how
  7. happily—how; today—when

B. 1.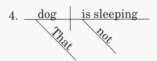

  2.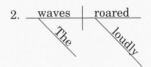

  3.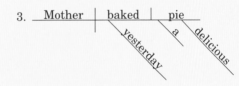

  4.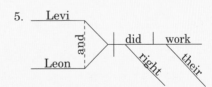

  5.

C. 1. well
  2. well
  3. good, well
  4. well
  5. good
  6. good

Extra Activity

1. Find pictures of scenery, pictures from a coloring book, or other pretty pictures. Try to think of at least six adjectives to describe each picture. Paste six little strips of paper on your picture, and write the first letter of each adjective on them. Be sure the papers are big enough. Exchange papers with someone in your class, and see if he can write the right adjectives on the papers.

2. Make a list of all the adverbs you see when you are reading and all the adverbs you hear when people talk. See how many adverbs you can write on your list in one week.

Extra Activity

Aim: To exercise the practical use of adjectives and adverbs.

Class: The teacher should prepare a picture like the one described in the textbook. Fill in the adjectives in class. Try to think of several different adjectives that could be used, but point out that we should always try to use the most exact ones.

The finished papers should make an attractive wall display. If the teacher thinks it desirable, pupils could stick adjective labels on objects in the classroom. Examples: *brown* on the teacher's desk, *round* on the globe, and *clear* on a window.

The teacher should make it a point to use adverbs freely. Tell pupils that any adverbs they use correctly may also be added to their lists.

A Poem to Enjoy

Obedience

If you're told to do a thing,
And mean to do it really,
   Never let it be by halves—
Do it fully, freely!
   Do not make a poor excuse,
Waiting, weak, unsteady:
   All obedience, worth the name,
Must be prompt and ready.
                —Phoebe Cary

Discussing the Poem

1. Why does it not pay to do things by halves?
2. What does it mean to do something fully and freely?
3. Find the word **waiting** in the last stanza. How is it disobedient to wait?
4. What is true obedience?
5. In the first stanza, why does the last line end with an exclamation mark?
6. Practice reading this poem with good expression.

Answers to Discussion Questions

1. If we do things by halves, we usually have to go back and do them right.
2. It means doing the whole job well and doing it willingly.
3. When we are told to do something, we should do it right away. As long as we are still waiting (unnecessarily), we are disobedient.
4. It is "prompt and ready" obedience—doing things right away and doing them gladly.
5. This line expresses strong feeling.
6. (Oral work.)

A Poem to Enjoy

Aim: To give practice in reading and enjoying good poetry.

Class: Practice reading the poem with proper expression. Use the questions at the bottom of the page to discuss the poem.

Unit 5

Descriptions

Directions

Building With
Our Language

Letters

Poetry

101. Looking at the Dictionary Again

It is easy to become careless with chores at home when we are in a hurry. It is also easy to become careless in reading and writing when we are in a hurry. That is why we must be reminded to use the dictionary. Even if we are in a hurry, it is still quicker and easier to use the right words and spell them correctly the first time. Otherwise, we may have to do a lesson over because it has so many mistakes.

One help in finding words quickly is to think where the word is found in the dictionary. If the word starts with the letters **a** to **g,** open in the front part of the dictionary. If the word starts with **h** to **p,** open in the middle, and if it starts with **q** to **z,** open near the back. Then you will not be as far from the right place as if you just opened the dictionary anywhere.

You learned in Unit 1 that the dictionary gives the meanings and pronunciations of words. The dictionary also tells what part of speech a word is. Sometimes an abbreviation is used to show this. Do you know what these abbreviations stand for?

n.	v.	adj.
pron.	adv.	

> **Using the Dictionary**

A. On the next page are two lists of words found in the Bible. Copy each list in alphabetical order. Then after each word, write **front, middle,** or **back** to tell where you would open the dictionary to find the word.

Lesson 101

Aim: To review and reinforce the importance of using the dictionary.

Oral Review:

1. Give the simple subject in this sentence: *Has Anna read?* (Anna)
2. Words that tell *what kind of* or *which* are ———. (adjectives)
3. Words that tell *how, where,* or *when* are ———. (adverbs)
4. Give words that have clearer pictures than these: *bird, cleaning.* (Possible answers: robin, sparrow, owl; washing, scrubbing, sweeping)
5. Combine these short sentences into one clear, smooth sentence. *We had an accident. We were on the way to town. This happened yesterday.* (Yesterday we had an accident on the way to town.)

Class: Review Unit 1, Lessons 2 and 3, on using the dictionary. Point out that our minds grow with every new word we learn, and the dictionary is one of our greatest helpers in learning new words.

Give each pupil a dictionary, and have them practice opening to the front, middle, and back parts of the dictionary. Have each one say which letter he opened to. You could also have them try opening to specific letters of the alphabet.

Call attention to the way parts of speech are shown in the classroom dictionaries (abbreviated or spelled out). Give practice with finding parts of speech by writing words on the board for the pupils to look up in the dictionary. Here are some suggestions:

mirth (noun)	dormant (adjective)
hereby (adverb)	persist (verb)
cancel (verb)	winsome (adjective)
token (noun)	ordeal (noun)

1. warrior
   earthly
   zealous
   altogether
   lament

2. ointment
   violent
   captivity
   manifest
   excellent

B. After each answer in Part A, write whether the word is a **noun,** a **verb,** an **adjective,** or an **adverb.** Use the dictionary if you are not sure.

C. Under each picture are two words. With the help of the dictionary, choose and copy the word that would probably be used in writing about the picture.

1. talon—talent

3. pedestrian—passenger

2. antler—antenna

4. transit—transom

Lesson 101 Answers
Using the Dictionary

A. (Answers for Part B are included.)
   1. altogether, front, adverb
      earthly, front, adjective
      lament, middle, verb
      warrior, back, noun
      zealous, back, adjective
   2. captivity, front, noun
      excellent, front, adjective
      manifest, middle, verb *or* adjective
      ointment, middle, noun
      violent, back, adjective

B. (Answers are included in Part A.)

C. 1. talon
   2. antler
   3. passenger
   4. transom

5. plume—plum

6. petal—pedal

5. plume
6. petal

> **Review and Practice**

A. Write the eight forms of **be.**

B. Write the past form of each verb.
   1. jump   3. do   5. catch
   2. like   4. point   6. make

Review and Practice

A. am, is, are, was, were, be, been, being

B. 1. jumped   3. did   5. caught
   2. liked   4. pointed   6. made

102. Homophones

Some words are pronounced the same, but they have different spellings and meanings. Such words are called **homophones.** The words in each of these sets are homophones.

not—knot   to—too—two
die—dye   dear—deer

Do you know which homophones to use in these sentences?

I had a (not, knot) in my shoestring.
There was (too, two) much salt in the soup.

Lesson 102

Aim: To give practice in correct usage and spelling of homophones (formerly called homonyms).

Oral Review:
1. What is the simple predicate in this sentence: *Can dogs swim?* (Can swim)
2. Give words that have clearer pictures than these: *food, happy.* (Possible answers: bread, meat, cake; joyful, glad, merry)
3. What happens when a paragraph or story has too many short sentences? (The ideas do not run together smoothly.)
4. What are some things that a dictionary tells you? (spelling, pronunciation, meaning, part of speech)
5. Where should you open the dictionary so that you can find a word quickly? (Open to the front, middle, or back—whichever part has the word you want to find.)

Class: Write the following sentence on the board and have the children find what is wrong with it.

How much do you way?

If they say that *way* is not spelled right, ask w-a-y does not spell a word. Call attention to th lesson title, and explain what homophones are.

In the sentence you wrote on the board, see if the can find two other words that could be one of a se of homophones (do—due—dew; you—ewe—yew) As pupils what they should do if they are not sure whic homophone to use in a sentence they are writing. T give practice, provide each pupil with a dictionar Write the following sentences on the board.

My uncle had a public (sail, sale) when he qu farming.

One (pane, pain) of glass was broken out o the window.

Mother will (dye, die) the cloth.
My baby sister is very (deer, dear).

> **Remember: Homophones** are words that are pronounced alike, but their spellings and meanings are different.

> Using Homophones >

A. Number your paper from 1 to 12, and copy the correct homophone from each pair in bold print. Use the dictionary when you are not sure.

> We (1) **no, know** it is not (2) **right, write** to (3) **steel, steal**, and we (4) **would, wood** not want to (5) **due, do** such a thing. But sometimes we (6) **might, mite** steal and (7) **knot, not** realize what we are doing. If we carelessly make others (8) **weight, wait** for us, we are stealing time away from them. (9) **Their, There** time is valuable (10) **to, too**, and we should (11) **be, bee** careful not to (12) **waste, waist** it.

B. Write sentences to show that you know how to use all the following homophones correctly.
   1. a. whole   3. a. piece
      b. hole   b. peace
   2. a. some   4. a. him
      b. sum   b. hymn

> Review and Practice >

Write whether each of these is a **telling, asking, commanding,** or **exclaiming** sentence. Also give the correct end punctuation for each.

Have the children find all four words in the dictionary and decide which is the correct one to use in each sentence.

★ **EXTRA PRACTICE**
Worksheet 61 (*Homophones*)

Lesson 102 Answers
Using Homophones
A. 1. know
    2. right
    3. steal
    4. would
    5. do
    6. might
    7. not
    8. wait
    9. Their
    10. too
    11. be
    12. waste

B. (Individual answers.)

1. Do not touch the wet paint
2. What a beautiful morning
3. Are you invited for dinner
4. God called Paul
5. Put the tools away after you are finished
6. How fast the firemen worked

> Can You Do This?

How many pairs of homophones can you write? See if you can write at least five pairs that are not used in this lesson.

●━━●━━●━━●━━●━━●

103. Words With More Than One Meaning

There are many words that have more than one meaning. Notice the different meanings of the words in bold print in each sentence below.

1. Mother will **dress** the chicken.
   Sandra put on her best **dress.**
2. That **letter** is a vowel.
   I wrote a **letter** to a friend.
3. An eagle can **fly** very high.
   Please swat that **fly.**

E

If a word has more than one meaning, the dictionary gives the different meanings under different numbers. When you are reading and need to find the meaning of a word in the dictionary, you must think which meaning

Review and Practice
1. commanding (.)
2. exclaiming (!)
3. asking (?)
4. telling (.)
5. commanding (.)
6. exclaiming (!)

Can You Do This?
(Possible answers. Give extra credit for each pair of homonyms.)

ate—eight	pair—pear
been—bin	pray—prey
nay—neigh	rain—rein
pail—pale	ring—wring

Lesson 103

Aim: (1) To teach that many words have more than one meaning, and that the different meanings are found in the dictionary. (2) To help the children choose the correct meaning for a word in a given sentence.

Oral Review:
1. Spell the plural form of *foot, woman, glass,* and *mouse.* (feet, women, glasses, mice)
2. Say the correct part of speech for each clue.
   a. Words that name people, places, and things. (nouns)
   b. Words that show action or being. (verbs)
   c. Words that take the place of nouns. (pronouns)
   d. Words that tell *how.* (adverbs)
   e. Words that tell *what kind of.* (adjectives)
3. Combine these short sentences into one clear, smooth sentence. *Joseph's brothers pulled off his coat. It was a beautiful coat. They threw him into*

a pit. (Joseph's brothers pulled off his beautiful coat and threw him into a pit.)
4. Tell where you would open the dictionary to find each word: *toboggan, blizzard, moccasin* (back, front, middle)
5. What are homophones? Give an example. (words that are pronounced alike but spelled differently; Individual answers.)

Class: Write the word *lie* on the board, and then write these two sentences.

Mother told us to lie down and sleep.
It is wrong to tell a lie.

Point out the difference in the meanings of *lie.* Have pupils find *lie* in the dictionary and check for more than one meaning. Point out that in this case *lie* is found as two separate entries. Many other words with different meanings have both meanings in the same entry.

would fit in the sentence you have read. For example, if you look up **dress** in a dictionary, you might find these meanings.

> **dress** 1. A piece of clothing worn by women. 2. To put clothes on. 3. To get ready for use. 4. To put medicine or a bandage on a wound.

Look at the first pair of example sentences at the beginning of this lesson. Which meaning would fit in the first sentence? Which meaning would fit in the second sentence? This is easy to decide by the way the word is used in the sentences.

▷ Finding Words in the Dictionary ▷

Number your paper from 1 to 8, and copy each word in bold print. Then find the word in a dictionary, and write the correct meaning for that sentence.

1. The builders lifted the heavy **beam**.
2. Mother's words made Susan **beam** with happiness.
3. A **beam** of sunlight shone through the clouds.
4. You may **pick** the book you like best.
5. Please do not **pick** the flowers.
6. We must scald and **pick** the chicken.
7. Please **wait** until I come back again.
8. I will **wait** on the table.

▷ Showing Different Meanings ▷

Each of these words has more than one meaning. Use each word in two sentences, showing two different meanings.

1. well   2. seal   3. pen

Lesson 103 Answers
Finding Words in the Dictionary
(Wording of definitions may vary.)

1. beam—large, long piece of wood or metal
2. beam—smile or look happy
3. beam—ray of light
4. pick—choose
5. pick—pull away or gather
6. pick—prepare by removing feather
7. wait—stay
8. wait—act as a servant

Showing Different Meanings
(Individual answers. Be sure that the pupils understand both meanings of each word, and that their sentences are not copied from the dictionary.)

In the lesson text, discuss the sentences in which words are used with different meanings. Ask the pupils to give other examples. As answers are given, find the different meanings in the dictionary. Make sentences with the different meanings as time allows.

Note: Words with more than one meaning are in two classes. One class includes words like *dress,* whose meanings are related yet distinctly different. These words have the same roots, and they are found in the dictionary as single entries with different definitions. The other class includes words like *lie* (recline) and *lie* (an untruth)—essentially different words that happen to have the same spelling. These latter are homographs, and they come from different roots. They are therefore found as two separate entries in the dictionary. The difference between these classes need not be explained to the pupils at this point.

★ **EXTRA PRACTICE**
Worksheet 62 (*Words With More Than One Meaning*)

104. Synonyms and Antonyms

Did you ever get tired of doing a job in the same way over and over again? Sometimes it helps to do it in a different way. You are still doing the same work, but it is more interesting and you enjoy it more.

This is also true with words. Instead of using the same word over and over, you can use **synonyms** to make your sentences more interesting. Synonyms are words whose meanings are the same or nearly the same.

Read the following sentences, and see if you can think of synonyms for the words in bold print. Use a dictionary to find more synonyms.

> A **good** smell came from the kitchen.
> I heard **happy** sounds from the children outside.
> For a long time I watched the **pretty** sunset.
> The horses **ran** across the field.

Antonyms are words that have opposite meanings. Try to think of an antonym for each word below.

noisy	crooked	cloudy
sharp	empty	cheerful

Remember: Words that mean the same or nearly the same are **synonyms.** Words with opposite meanings are **antonyms.**

> **Using Words of Similar Meaning**

Number your paper from 1 to 7, and write a synonym for each word in bold print. You may get help from a dictionary or look at the lists in the following part.

Lesson 104

Aim: (1) To teach the use of synonyms for changing ordinary sentences to more colorful ones. (2) To teach the definition and use of antonyms.

Oral Review:

1. A simple subject may be a ——— or a ———. (noun, pronoun)
2. A ——— receives the action of a verb. (direct object)
3. It is not hard to find words in a dictionary, because they are in ———. Where should you open the dictionary to find a word quickly? (alphabetical order; Open the dictionary near the place where the word is found.)
4. Give a homophone for each word: *beat, hair, reed, wood.* (beet, hare, read, would)
5. If a word has more than one meaning, how can you know which meaning in the dictionary is the one you want? (Think which meaning would fit in the sentence you have read.)

Class: Before teaching the lesson, check classroom dictionaries to see if synonyms are given for the boldface words in the sentences listed. If so, explain what synonyms are and have pupils find synonyms in the dictionary for the boldface words. Otherwise, ask them for suggestions or list the following.

> good—delicious, sweet
> happy—joyful, merry
> pretty—lovely, beautiful, colorful
> ran—galloped, raced, trotted

Point out that sentences are clearer and more expressive when a variety of words is used.

The hummingbird family is the (1) **smallest,** most (2) **lively,** and most (3) **brightly** colored of all our feathered friends. Their (4) **strong** wings move so (5) **fast** when they are flying that one can hardly see them. Their rapidly moving wings make a buzzing sound, and that is why they are called hummingbirds. Except for a (6) **weak** twitter, they have no voice or song. Their bill is usually long and (7) **thin** and is sometimes curved.

> Matching Words of Opposite Meaning

Write the words in the first column in alphabetical order. Beside each word you wrote, write an antonym from the second column.

powerful	slowly
active	weak
swiftly	largest
slender	dully
tiniest	strong
feeble	broad
brilliantly	sluggish

> Review and Practice

Copy each sentence. Add quotation marks and capital letters where they are needed, and use the correct end marks.

1. what a bright, sunny day exclaimed Mother
2. may we have a picnic the children asked
3. mother said, that would be a good idea
4. the children said, we will help you get ready

Lesson 104 Answers
Using Words of Similar Meaning
(Probable answers.)

1. tiniest   5. swiftly
2. active   6. feeble
3. brilliantly   7. slender
4. powerful

Matching Words of Opposite Meaning
(Check for alphabetical order.)
    active—sluggish
    brilliantly—dully
    feeble—strong
    powerful—weak
    slender—broad
    swiftly—slowly
    tiniest—largest

Review and Practice
(Corrected items are underlined.)

1. "What a bright, sunny day!" exclaimed Mother.
2. "May we have a picnic?" the children asked.
3. Mother said, "That would be a good idea."
4. The children said, "We will help you get ready."

Here are antonyms for the six words after the last paragraph.

noisy—quiet	empty—full
sharp—dull	cloudy—clear
crooked—straight	cheerful—sad

Use this memory aid to help the pupils remember the meaning of *synonym* and *antonym: Synonym* and *same* both begin with the letter *s,* and *antonym* and *against* both begin with the letter *a.*

★ **EXTRA PRACTICE**
Worksheet 63 (*Synonyms and Antonyms*)

105. Reviewing What You Have Learned

> Oral Drill

1. We can think of the dictionary as being divided into —— parts.
2. In which part of the dictionary would you find the following words?

    celebrate   tumult   melon   village

3. What are synonyms?
4. Give some examples of synonyms.
5. What are antonyms?
6. Give some examples of antonyms.
7. What are homophones?
8. Tell whether these pairs are **synonyms, antonyms, or homophones.**
    a. little—tiny   e. sea—see
    b. sum—some   f. cold—hot
    c. tired—weary   g. hair—hare
    d. whole—hole   h. early—late
9. These are words with more than one meaning. Use each one in two different ways.
    a. bark   b. match   c. swallow
10. When you write sentences, how can you make them more interesting?

> Written Practice

A. Copy each word; and write **front, middle,** or **back** to show where you would find it in the dictionary.
    1. leader   3. comma   5. tiger
    2. volume   4. eclipse   6. mother

Lesson 105 Answers
Oral Drill

1. three
2. celebrate—front
   tumult—back
   melon—middle
   village—back
3. Synonyms are words that mean the same or nearly the same.
4. (Have the class give synonyms for *big, nice, loud,* and *clean.*)
5. Antonyms are words that are opposite in meaning.
6. (Have the class give antonyms for the words in number 4.)
7. Homophones are words that are pronounced alike, but their spellings and meanings are different.
8. a. synonyms   e. homophones
   b. homophones   f. antonyms
   c. synonyms   g. homophones
   d. homophones   h. antonyms
9. (Dual meanings are listed.)
   a. bark—the outer covering of a tree; make sound like a dog
   b. match—be alike; something used to start fires
   c. swallow—pass food from the mouth to the stomach; a bird
10. Use words that are colorful and expressive. Do not use the same words over and over.

Written Practice
A. 1. leader—middle   4. eclipse—front
   2. volume—back   5. tiger—back
   3. comma—front   6. mother—middle

Lesson 105

Aim: To review the last four lessons.

Class: Before the pupils open their books for class, ask the following questions.
1. Where can we find the spellings and meanings of words? (in the dictionary)
2. What do we call words that sound the same but are spelled differently? (homophones)
3. What do we call words that mean the same or nearly the same? (synonyms)
4. What do we call words with opposite meanings? (antonyms)

Go over Oral Drill in class.

B. Choose and copy the correct spelling of each word. Use a dictionary for help.
1. balloon, baloon
2. gelaten, gelatin
3. diarie, diary
4. jungle, jungel

C. If a sentence has a mistake, copy the wrong word and write the correct one beside it. If it has no mistake, write **correct.**
1. In the wintertime the trees are bear.
2. The young man was the widow's only son.
3. We did not by many groceries last week.
4. The weight of the baby makes Mother tired.
5. It was raining, sew we did not have the picnic.
6. The farmer kept his tools in a steal building.

D. Write sentences showing two meanings for each word.
1. tie   2. mine   3. train   4. trip

E. Write two synonyms for each word in bold print. Choose them from the lists.
1. **take**   lovely   march
2. **walk**   swift   haul
3. **nice**   stroll   speedy
4. **fast**   carry   enjoyable

F. Write an antonym for each of these words.
1. right   4. clean   7. soft
2. day   5. high   8. over
3. wet   6. rough   9. Neat

B. 1. balloon   3. diary
   2. gelatin   4. jungle

C. 1. bear—bare
   2. correct
   3. by—buy
   4. correct
   5. sew—so
   6. steal—steel

D. (Individual answers.)

E. 1. carry, haul
   2. stroll, march
   3. lovely, enjoyable
   4. swift, speedy

F. 1. right—wrong *or* left
   2. day—night
   3. wet—dry
   4. clean—dirty
   5. high—low
   6. rough—smooth *or* gentle
   7. soft—hard *or* loud
   8. over—under
   9. neat—sloppy (careless)

106. Describing a Thing

When you describe a thing, you should tell about that thing and its different parts. Your description should answer questions like the following.

What color is it?   How big is it?
How does it feel?   What shape does it have?

If you describe a book, you might tell about the cover, the story, and the pictures. If you describe a flower, you might talk about the stem, the roots, the leaves, and the blossom. You would probably tell about the fragrance of the flower too.

If you write a description about something, you should carefully observe the thing you will describe. You may also get information from other people or from a **reference book.** A reference book is a book used to find information, such as a dictionary or an encyclopedia.

When you use a reference book, write short notes of things you want to remember. Never copy information word for word. For example, here is a paragraph about kangaroos that you might find in a reference book.

> Kangaroos are furry animals that **hop** on their hind legs. A baby kangaroo stays in its mother's **pouch** until it is about eight months old. Kangaroos can hop as fast as **forty miles per hour.** They use their long **tails for balance** when they are hopping.

In this paragraph, the **key words** are in bold print. The key words give main ideas that you may want to write in notes. Your notes might look like this.

Kangaroos hop on their hind legs.
A mother kangaroo has a pouch for her baby.

Lesson 106

Aim: To give the children help and practice in writing a good description of a thing.

Oral Review:

1. Finish this rule: When you use one *no* word, ——— (stop! Do not use another *no* word in the same sentence.)

2. What are some things that a dictionary shows you? (spelling, pronunciation, meaning, part of speech)

3. Words that sound alike but are spelled differently are ———. Give an example. (homophones; Individual answers.)

4. Words that mean the same or nearly the same are ———. Give an example. (synonyms; Individual answers.)

5. Words with opposite meanings are ———. Give an example. (antonyms; Individual answers.)

Class: Begin by asking the pupils, "Did you ever hear this little rhyme? 'The world is so full of such wonderful things, / I'm sure we should all be as happy as kings.' Let us name some of those wonderful things."

As various pupils name things, write them on the board, leaving a generous space between the words. Then ask what is interesting about each thing. As pupils respond, write the information in sentence form under the item you are discussing. When you feel that enough has been written, say, "It would really be good to write about all these interesting things." Be very enthusiastic, but express sadness that you cannot write everything, thus whetting their appetites.

Point out that in describing a thing, we sometimes need to use a reference book. Explain that reference books are books in which we look up information; we do not usually read them from beginning to end.

Kangaroos can go forty miles per hour.
Kangaroos use their tails for balance.

When you write your description, you would use notes like these to help you write sentences in your own words.

> **Taking Notes** >

Passenger pigeons were pinkish gray doves that once lived in America. They flew in great flocks containing millions of birds. Greedy hunters kept killing the birds by thousands and thousands. The last passenger pigeon died in a zoo in 1914.

A. Copy three key words or phrases from the paragraph above that would be helpful in taking notes.

B. Use your key words or phrases to write a set of notes on the paragraph above.

> **Writing a Description** >

Choose one of these pictures. Then get a reference book and take notes about the thing you have chosen.

Write a paragraph to describe that thing. Use some of the questions in the lesson to help you. Proofread your description when it is finished.

Lesson 106 Answers
Taking Notes

A. (Possible answers.)
　　pinkish gray doves, America, great flocks, greedy hunters, last passenger pigeon

B. (Possible answers.)
　Passenger pigeons were pinkish gray doves.
　Long ago these birds lived in America.
　They flew in great flocks.
　Greedy hunters killed thousands of the birds.
　The last passenger pigeon died in 1914.

Writing a Description
(Individual descriptions. They should follow the points taught in the lesson. Also check for correct spelling and general neatness.)

Besides dictionaries and encyclopedias, reference books include concordances, atlases, and handbooks such as bird guides.

Discuss note-taking and explain what is meant by key words. For practice in class, you could have the students pick out key words in some of the sentences you wrote on the board. Then they could write notes in their own words.

The descriptions they write in these lessons are to be saved for a booklet. See the Extra Activity at the end of this unit.

107. Describing a Place

Have you ever taken a trip to the mountains, the ocean, or a park? When you got home, did you like to describe to your friends the things you saw? You are describing a place when you do this.

You cannot visit some places, but you can learn many things from others who describe places to you. You should learn to describe in the same way so that others can also enjoy places they cannot visit. In order to give a good description, observe the place closely while you are there. In your mind keep a good picture of the things you have seen.

When you describe a place, think of good picture words to use. Following are some examples.

> The river was like a silver ribbon.
> The wind whispered softly through the trees.

If you tell about people or animals, think of verbs that describe their actions well. Use words such as **scampered, strolled, grazed,** and **wandered.** Also use words that tell **how, when,** and **where.**

Do not think that only the mountains, the ocean, or the park are good places to describe. Close your eyes for a moment, and imagine that you are at home in your kitchen. Use the following questions to help you think of a good way to describe it.

> How large is the place?   What do you hear?
> What things do you see?   What do you smell?
>
> What feelings do you have when you are there?

Lesson 107

Aim: (1) To give the children practice in writing a good description about a place. (2) To help them see that it is not only faraway places that are interesting.

Oral Review:
1. What questions are answered by adjectives? By adverbs? (what kind of, how many or how much, which, whose; how, when, where)
2. Finish this sentence: Homophones are words that are pronounced alike, but ———. (their meanings and spellings are different)
3. If a word has more than one meaning, how can you know which meaning in the dictionary is the one you want? (Think which meaning would fit in the sentence you have read.)
4. Why should you use synonyms instead of using the same words over and over? (It is tiresome to read or hear the same words again and again.)

5. What is a reference book? What are key words (a book used to find information; words that give main ideas that you may write in notes

Class: If possible, bring to class pictures of place of interest. Have the class choose one they like, an together write a description of the board. Make i as colorful as possible. After it has been written, g over it again and improve it where necessary, with pupils' help.

Then show pictures of places around home i possible, or of other ordinary places. Also write description of one of these pictures. After the descrip tion has been written, compare the two and poin out that both descriptions are vivid and colorful. I we keep our eyes open, we will see many interestin things around us.

In discussing the exercises, ask the children t tell about an interesting place they have visited

The same questions can help you describe your father's shop, the pasture field, or the grocery store. Perhaps your teacher can suggest other good places to describe.

> **Studying a Description** >

Read this description, and answer the questions about it.

Niagara Falls is an awesome sight. The foamy water of the Niagara River plunges swiftly over the falls with a steady roar that can almost be felt. You can hear the roar long before you get to the falls. A great cloud of mist rises constantly overhead and makes the air feel damp and chilly. After dark, powerful lights shine on the falls in colors of white, red, yellow, blue, and green.

1. What adjective describes the water? What verb and adverb together help you to "see" the water going over the falls?
2. What are some ways that the sound at Niagara Falls is described?
3. How does the air feel near the falls?
4. Which adjective tells what kind of lights shine on the falls? What colors are the lights?

> **Describing a Place** >

Write a description about a place. It may be a room in your home, or a place that you have visited. The questions in the lesson will help you.

Use good picture words so that others can "see" the place you describe. Proofread your description when it is finished.

Lesson 107 Answers
Studying a Description
1. foamy; plunges swiftly
2. steady roar, roar that can almost be felt, you can her the roar long before you get to the falls
3. damp and chilly
4. powerful; white, red, yellow, blue, and green

Describing a Place
(Individual descriptions. Make sure they are not copied word for word from the encyclopedia. Also check for the other points mentioned in the lesson: nouns and adjectives that make good word pictures, verbs and adverbs that describe actions well, and sentence variety.)

This discussion should help them to think of a place to write about.

★ **EXTRA PRACTICE**
Worksheet 64 (*Describing a Place*)

108. Describing a Person

Sometimes we get to know a person whom others of our family or friends have not met. Then we may want to describe that person to those who do not know him.

God made people according to a certain pattern. Almost everyone has two eyes, two ears, a nose, a mouth, two arms, and two legs. So when we describe a person, we need to tell about things that not every person has. The following rules and questions will help to describe a person well.

1. **Think of how the person looks.** Is he tall, short, or of medium height? About how old is he? What color are his eyes? Does he wear glasses? What color is his hair? Is it straight or wavy?

2. **Think of how the person talks and acts.** What kind of voice does he have? Is he talkative, or is he usually quiet? What things does he enjoy doing?

3. **Think of how the person is like another person.** Does he look or talk like someone else you know? Who is about his size?

4. **Think kind thoughts.** When you write about someone, describe him just as kindly as you would want him to describe you. Do not write anything about others that you would not want others to write about you.

We need to remember that the way people look is not the most important thing. Kindness, honesty, and thoughtfulness are much more important than how we look.

Lesson 108

Aim: To give the children help and practice in writing a good description of a person.

Oral Review:

1. How can you find the simple subject of a sentence? (Find the verb and ask *who* or *what* with it.)

2. Give one synonym and one antonym for each word: *fast, near, bright.* (Possible answers: swift, slow; close, far; brilliant, dark)

3. If you write a description about something and use a reference book to find information, you should look for ――― to take notes. (key words)

4. What should you *not* do when you get information from a reference book? (You should not copy information word for word.)

5. Try to think of good ――― when you describe a place. (picture words)

Class: Have the children observe one another and tell how they are all alike. In what ways are they different from one another? Help them to think of how they look, how they speak and walk, and what activities they enjoy or do not enjoy.

Together write a description of a person on the board, following the directions given in the exercises. Show variations in sentence beginnings. For example, do not start every sentence with "This person has." Some suggestions are, "His size makes it easy for him to slip through tight places." "He is a little heavier than some people his age." Ask pupils for suggestions on sentence variations.

Emphasize that we must be kind in describing a

> **Observing and Describing Someone** >

A. Choose a person to describe. Use the helps in the lesson to write a good description about him.

B. Proofread your description and correct all the mistakes you can find. Then rewrite the description.

> **Review and Practice** >

Write correctly each noun that needs a capital letter.
1. During the night, cottontail and hopper got out of their cages.
2. I watched linda and rachel playing with their dolls.
3. Snow fell in illinois and iowa.
4. Many people visit niagara falls.

Lesson 108 Answers
Observing and Describing Someone
  (Individual descriptions. They should follow the points listed in the lesson. Also check for correct spelling and general neatness.)

Review and Practice
  1. Cottontail, Hopper
  2. Linda, Rachel
  3. Illinois, Iowa
  4. Niagara Falls

erson, and that kindness is much more important than ne's appearance. You could mention the boy who was ɔ be met at a train station by an uncle he had never een before. One point in his mother's description was, Your uncle will probably be helping someone get off he train."

109. Describing Orally

It is good to be able to give descriptions **orally.** To give something orally means to give it in speaking, not writing.

There are certain rules to be followed in speaking. It is courteous to speak plainly and pronounce words correctly so that others can easily understand. You should not sound as though your mouth is full of food or your jaws are stiff.

Be careful not to use too many **ands.** Stop at the end of each sentence, and then begin a new one. Do not connect a long string of sentences with many **ands.**

Look pleasant, and speak pleasantly. You do not enjoy listening to a grumbly or whiny voice. So you should not speak in such a voice either.

> Pronouncing Words Correctly and Clearly

The following words are often mispronounced. The second word in each group is misspelled to show how many people pronounce it. Practice using the words correctly in sentences.

1. slept	slep	6. get	git
2. wheel	weel	7. cold	col
3. kept	kep	8. coming	comin
4. can	kin	9. color	keller
5. catch	ketch	10. barking	barkin

> Using Fewer *Ands*

Write the following paragraph correctly, using more periods and fewer **ands.**

Lesson 109 Answers
Pronouncing Words Correctly and Clearly
(Oral work.)

Lesson 109

Aim: To help the children give good oral descriptions by pronouncing words clearly and correctly, by not using too many *ands,* and by looking pleasant and speaking pleasantly.

Oral Review:

1. Names of specific people and places are ——. (proper nouns)
2. Tell whether the words in each pair are homophones, synonyms, or antonyms: *lovely—beautiful, smooth—rough, ceiling—sealing.* (synonyms, antonyms, homophones)
3. A book used for finding information is a ——. Instead of copying information word for word, you should look for —— when you take notes. (reference book; key words)
4. True of false: Even a common place like a meadow is a good place to describe. (true)

5. How can you follow the Golden Rule when you write a description of a person? (Do not write anything about others that you would not want others to write about you.)

Class: Begin by reading or telling the following paragraph as it is written, and have the children say what is wrong with it. (Put added stress on the underlined words.)

If a baby elephant wanders away from its mother into the tall grass where there is danger, it is apt to <u>git</u> a good <u>spankin</u> from its mother <u>and</u> with a smack of her trunk she sends him rollin, <u>and</u> the baby elephant does not like this <u>and</u> he falls down on the ground and just lies still.

(Problems: Not all the words are pronounced correctly. All the sentences are connected with *ands.*)

Then read the paragraph as corrected here so

From our window one day, I saw an eagle swoop down after a pheasant and the pheasant was hiding in the grass and saw the eagle coming and before the eagle got it, the pheasant flew away and the eagle did not catch it.

> ▷ Giving a Description Orally ▷

Think of a person, place, or thing to describe. Observe it carefully, and get other information about it. Think how you are going to describe it. Practice describing it to yourself until you can do it well. Be ready to give your description in front of the class.

◆━◆━◆━◆━◆━◆━◆

Using Fewer *Ands*

(Students' paragraphs may vary somewhat.)

From our window one day, I saw an eagle swoop down after a pheasant. The pheasant was hiding in the grass and saw the eagle coming. Before the eagle got it, the pheasant flew away. The eagle did not catch it.

Giving a Description Orally

(Oral work.)

hat the children can see what a difference it makes.

If a baby elephant wanders away from its mother into the tall grass where there is danger, it is apt to get a good spanking from its mother. With a smack of her trunk, she sends him rolling. The baby elephant does not like this. He falls down on the ground and just lies still.

Point out that in giving oral descriptions, we must void two extremes. We should speak clearly and natu-ally, but not with exaggerated enunciation. We should ot use too many *ands*, but neither should we speak in hort, choppy sentences.

Note that in the exercises, the first and third parts re oral work to be done in class.

110. Reviewing What You Have Learned

> Oral Drill >

1. Give some questions that are helpful for describing
   a. a thing.   b. a place.   c. a person.
2. What is a reference book?
3. What are key words? How are they helpful for writing a description?
4. What should you **not** do when you use a reference book for help to write a description?
5. When you are visiting a place, what can you do that will help you describe the place well?
6. What is more important about a person than how he looks?
7. What does it mean to give something orally?
8. Why is it courteous to speak clearly and plainly?
9. You should not use too many —— when you talk or write.

> Written Practice >

A. Below are two descriptions. Write the number of the one that is better. Write at least three things that are wrong with the other description.
   1.   The albatross is a large sea bird that is found over most of the oceans. In hopes of getting food, these birds sometimes follow a ship for days. Sailors can catch the albatross with a line and a hook baited with meat. Only one egg is laid by the female albatross. She lays it on the bare ground, and it hatches in about eighty-one days.

Lesson 110 Answers
Oral Drill
1. a. What color is it? How big is it? How does i feel? What shape does it have?
   b. How large is it? What do you hear? What d you see? What do you smell? What feeling do you have when you are there?
   c. How does the person look (height, age eyes, hair)? How does he talk and act What does he like to do? How is he lik another person?
2. A reference book is a book used to fin information.
3. Key words give main ideas that can be writte in notes. The notes can be used to write th description.
4. You should not copy the information word fo word.
5. You can observe the place carefully.
6. kindness (or the way he acts)
7. To give something orally means to say i (instead of writing it).
8. Speaking clearly and plainly is courteou because that makes it easier for other peopl to understand.
9. ands

Written Practice
A. Number 1 is the better description.

Lesson 110

Aim: To review and strengthen concepts taught earlier.

Class: Use Oral Drill in the usual manner for reviews. Observe which pupils do not respond readily, and give them extra practice.

2. The albatross is a large sea bird, and it is found over most of the oceans. The albatross will follow a ship for days, and that is because it wants something to eat. The albatross can be caught with a line and a hook by sailors, and sailors are men who sail in ships on the ocean. The albatross lays one egg and she lays it on the bare ground and it hatches in about eighty-one days. Many birds fly south.

B. There is one mistake in each sentence below. Write the sentences correctly.
1. I'm gonna surprise Mother and wash the dishes.
2. You may wear my mittens so that your hands don't git cold.
3. God took the weels off the Egyptians' chariots.
4. The old lady fell down as she was comin up the street.
5. God kin see the whole earth at once.

●━●━●━●━●━●━●━●━●

111. Making Introductions

You have probably been in a group where most of the people were strangers to you. You may have wanted to talk with someone, but you did not know how to start. Would you have been glad if someone had helped you?

Sometime you might take a friend to a place where most of the people are strangers to him. Your friend will feel the same way you felt when you were the stranger. Would you be able to help him feel more comfortable?

(Things that are wrong with the other description.)
It uses too many *ands*.
Margins are not straight.
Sentences do not all tell about one topic.
Sentences do not have enough variety. (Most of them start with "The albatross.")

B. 1. I'm going to surprise Mother and wash the dishes.
2. You may wear my mittens so that your hands don't get cold.
3. God took the wheels off the Egyptians' chariots.
4. The old lady fell down as she was coming up the street.
5. God can see the whole earth at once.

Lesson 111

Aim: To give guidance and practice in making introductions properly.

Oral Review:
1. Give the pronouns that are used to tell *which one* or *which ones*. What words should not be used with them? (this, that, these, those; here, there)
2. Try to think of good —— when you describe a place. (picture words)
3. What is more important than the way a person looks? (kindness, courtesy, following the Golden Rule)
4. Finish these sentences about oral descriptions.
    a. Speak —— and pronounce words ——. (clearly, correctly)
    b. Be careful not to use too many ——. (ands)
    c. Look —— and speak ——. (pleasant, pleasantly)

Class: Discuss the purpose of an introduction. You may be able to mention incidents from your own experience that would have been more comfortable if proper introductions had been made.

Point out that the rules for making introductions are based on respect: respect for the older person, for one's mother, and for women and girls. Also stress that introductions should be relaxed and natural, not stiff and formal. An introduction is not a performance, but a thoughtful way of helping people to get acquainted. It is more important to help strangers feel comfortable in each other's presence than to say everything exactly right.

Also explain how to introduce oneself to a stranger if there is not one to make an introduction. The most common way is to shake hands and say, "Hello, my name is . . ."

Allow some time for making introductions in class.

You can help your friend by **introducing** him to a person you know. Here are some rules for making introductions.

1. To introduce a younger person to an older person, say the older person's name first.

    Say: Grandfather, this is my friend David Good.
    David, this is my grandfather.

2. To introduce a man to a woman or a boy to a girl, say the woman's or girl's name first.

    Say: Janet, this is my cousin Peter Wells.
    Peter, this is Janet Moyer.

3. To introduce someone to your mother, say **Mother** first.

    Say: Mother, this is Bernice Nichols.
    Bernice, this is my mother.

4. To introduce two men, two women, two boys, or two girls to one another, say either name first.

    Say: Lois, this is Mary Stewart.
    Mary, this is Lois Martin.

> Following the Rules for Introductions >

A. Read these introductions. Write the number of the rule that is followed in each one.
   1. Mother, this is Sister Yoder, my teacher.
      Sister Yoder, this is my mother.
   2. Sister Yoder, this is my father.
      Father, this is my teacher, Sister Yoder.
   3. Shirley, this is Carol Hall.
      Carol, this is Shirley Baker.
   4. Father, this is my friend Roy Lake.
      Roy, this is my father.

Lesson 111 Answers
Following the Rules for Introductions
A. 1. 3
   2. 2
   3. 4
   4. 1

B. These introductions are not made correctly. Write why each one is wrong.
1. Susan, this is my aunt Marie.
   Aunt Marie, this is my friend Susan Bond.
2. Brother Shank, this is my mother.
   Mother, this is my teacher, Brother Shank.

> Introducing Others >

A. Suppose you need to make the following introductions. Write what you would say, using real names.

1. Your teacher to your mother.
2. Your father to your teacher.
3. A friend in school to your father.
4. A classmate to your cousin (boy to boy or girl to girl).

B. Be ready to make an introduction in class.

> Review and Practice >

Write sentences as described here.
1. A sentence with an adverb telling **how.**
2. A sentence with an adverb telling **when.**
3. A sentence with an adverb telling **where.**
4. A sentence using **well** correctly.
5. A sentence using **good** correctly.

●━●━●━●━●━●━●━●

B. 1. The older person's name should be said first.
   2. *Mother* should be said first. (Also, a woman's name should be said before a man's name.)

Introducing Others
A. (Individual answers.)

B. (Oral work.)

Review and Practice
   (Individual answers.)

112. Using a Telephone

We should be kind and courteous when we speak over the telephone. Sometimes we are not courteous but do not realize it. Can you think of some things that are not courteous to do when you use the telephone?

The following rules and picture should help you to use the telephone correctly.

1. Be sure you have the right number, and dial it carefully.
2. Let the telephone ring long enough that the one you are calling has plenty of time to answer (about seven times if necessary). If the person cannot get around well, give him extra time to get to the telephone.
3. When someone answers the telephone, give him your name.
4. When you answer the telephone, say "Hello" and give your name or your family name.

      Examples: Hello, this is John Martin.
                  Hello, this is the Martins'.

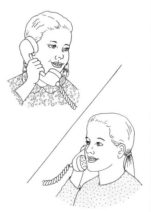

5. Hold the mouthpiece about an inch from your mouth. Speak clearly and loudly enough to be heard easily, but do not shout.
6. Hold the receiver lightly against your ear.
7. If someone calls and leaves a message, write it down right away. Read it back to the caller to make sure you wrote it correctly.

Lesson 112

Aim: To give guidance and practice in using the telephone correctly.

Oral Review:

1. Where do we put adjectives and adverbs on a sentence diagram? (on slanted lines below the words they describe)
2. True or false: Only places like a zoo, the ocean, or the mountains are worthwhile to describe. (false)
3. How can you follow the Golden Rule when you write a description of a person? (Do not write anything about others that you would not want others to write about you.)
4. When you give a description orally
   a. how should you speak? (Speak clearly.)
   b. how should you pronounce words? (Pronounce words correctly.)
   c. what should you avoid? (Avoid using too

many *ands.* Avoid speaking in a grumbly or whiny voice.)
5. Which person's name would you say first if you were introducing
   a. a younger person and an older person? (the older person's name)
   b. a man and woman? (the woman's name)
   c. your mother and your friend? (Mother)

Class: Discuss some of the reasons why we use a telephone. It may be to report a fire, to call a plumber, or to get or give information. Tell the children that if we do not know where to call, in case of danger or fire, we can call the operator.

Discuss the picture with the children. Stress the importance of dialing the correct number. Show them a telephone directory, and point out how names are listed alphabetically according to the last name.

Here are some things that are *not* courteous to do

> Using the Telephone >

Below are some correct and some incorrect ways of using the telephone. Write **correct** for the ones that are correct. For the incorrect ones, write what the person **should** have done.

1. Alice was not sure about Uncle John's telephone number, and Mother was busy. So Alice made a guess and happened to dial the wrong number.
2. Timothy called Grandfather, who walked with a cane. He let the telephone ring a long time to give Grandfather plenty of time to get to the telephone.
3. Ruth answered the telephone and said, "Hello, this is Ruth Yoder."
4. Sister Mary called while Mother was gone. When Mother came home, Eunice had forgotten what Sister Mary said.
5. Mother called Dr. Brown's office. She said who was calling and asked to make an appointment for David.
6. Gerald was trying to read a book while he answered the telephone. The person who was calling had a hard time understanding him.

> Making Telephone Calls >

Practice having a telephone conversation with one of your classmates. Be sure you are courteous.

> Review and Practice >

Diagram these sentences.
1. My uncle built a new house.
2. Come here.

Lesson 112 Answers
Using the Telephone

1. Alice should have made sure she had the right number or waited until Mother had time to help her.
2. correct
3. correct
4. Eunice should have written down what Sister Mary said.
5. correct
6. Gerald should have laid down his book until he was finished talking on the telephone.

Making Telephone Calls
(Oral work.)

Review and Practice

1.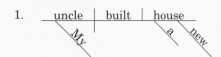

2.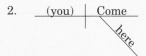

hen using the telephone.

1. Talk so softly that the other person can hardly hear, or so loudly that he has to hold the receiver away from his ear.
2. Call someone late at night, or at any time when we know it is inconvenient for him. (We need to be careful if we call someone in a different time zone.)

Note that the exercise, Making Telephone Calls, is ral work. To give realistic practice, have the pupils use oy telephones and "call" each other for specific reasons. Examples: to ask for (or give) an assignment missed ecause of absence, to ask a sick classmate how he is etting along, to ask for (or offer) a ride when transporation is needed, to give an invitation.

3. Dwight and Daniel found a dollar.
4. Albert has not read this book.
5. The black puppy came yesterday.

●━━●━━●━━●━━●━━●━━●

113. How to Do Something

Mother's guests wanted the directions for making her cake. She carefully wrote how much of each thing to use. What else do you think she wrote?

Remember these rules when you give directions on how to do something.

1. Give the directions in the right order. Say what to do first, second, and so on.
2. Say everything that needs to be done. Say how much of each thing is needed.
3. Make the directions clear and short. Do not give unnecessary details.

> Working With Directions >

Read each set of directions, and answer the questions.

Planting Tomatoes

Dig holes at least 1 yard apart. For tomato plants that are 9–12 inches tall, make each hole about 4 inches deep. Remove the plants from their pots, being careful to leave some soil on the roots. Set them in the holes, and fill the holes with water. Then fill the holes gently with soil, and pack it firmly around the plants. Water your plants every day for a week.

3.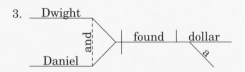

4.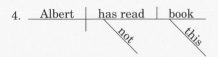

5.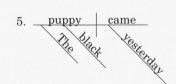

Lesson 113

Aim: To teach the importance of giving precise instructions, and to give guidance and practice in this.

Written Quiz:

1. Write **S** for synonyms, **H** for homophones, and **A** for antonyms.
   a. fair—fare
   b. loudly—noisily
   c. sweet—bitter
2. Write the number of the correct meaning for **pen** in each sentence.

   pen 1. A writing tool. 2. Write with a pen. 3. A fenced-in place.

   a. A calf was in the pen.
   b. This pen writes smoothly.
   c. I will pen him a letter.
3. How can you follow the Golden Rule when you describe a person?
4. Who should be named first when you ar[e] introducing
   a. a boy and a girl?
   b. your mother and another woman?
   c. a boy and your grandfather?
5. What should you do when someone calls an[d] leaves a message?

Quiz Answers:

1. a. H
   b. S
   c. A
2. a. 3
   b. 1
   c. 2
3. Describe the person as kindly as you woul[d] want him to describe you.
4. a. the girl

Boiling an Egg

Get a pan and an egg. Open the faucet and put water in the pan. Put the pan on the burner and boil the egg. Cool and peel the egg before you eat it.

Painting a Wall

Spread the paint evenly on the wall. Stir the paint. Open the can of paint. Sweep the cobwebs off the wall. Do not get too much paint on the brush, or it will drip. Dip the brush into the paint.

1. Which set of directions is easiest to follow?
2. Give three reasons why.
3. Do the directions say how long you should boil the egg?
4. How far apart should you dig the holes?
5. Which set of directions could you not follow? Why not?

> Writing Directions >

Write directions telling how to do something. You may choose one of these if you wish.

How to set the table.
How to wash the dishes.
How to do some other job at home.
How to keep your desk neat.
How to prepare a paper to write a lesson.
How to play a game.

Lesson 113 Answers
Working With Directions

1. the first set (Planting Tomatoes)
2. (Possible answers.) They are in the correct order. They tell how far apart to make the holes. They tell how deep to make the holes. They tell how to put the soil back into the holes.
3. no
4. At least 1 yard.
5. the third set (Painting a Wall); They were not given in the proper order.

Writing Directions
(Individual answers.)

---

b. your mother
c. your grandfather

5. Write down the message right away.

Class: Discuss the rules in the lesson. Then read these sets of directions to the pupils. Pause after each set to identify the error in it.

To bake a cake, put 3 cups flour, some milk, 2 eggs, 1 cup butter, 1 teaspoon salt, 1 teaspoon baking soda, and vanilla into a bowl. Pour this into a pan and bake it. (Important details are missing.)

Get the dishpan and put in soap and water. Put the clean dishes in the drainer. Rinse the clean dishes in clear water. Dry the clean dishes or leave them in the drainer to dry by themselves. Use a scouring pad to scrub the dishes that are really dirty. (Directions are not in proper order.)

Dress warmly. Make a little ball for the snowman's head. Make a big ball for the bottom part of the snowman. If you get cold, go into the house. Use pieces of coal for the snowman's eyes. If you find a stick in the snow, throw it away. Make a middle-sized ball for the middle part of the snowman. Put the little ball on top of the middle-sized ball. You may put a hat on top of the snowman's head. Put the middle-sized ball on top of the big ball. (Directions are not in proper order. Unnecessary details are included.)

Stress the importance of giving clear directions. Show the necessity of thinking things through before starting a project or trying to tell someone else how to do it.

★ **EXTRA PRACTICE**
Worksheet 65 (*Giving Clear Directions*)

> Review and Practice >

Write **H, S,** or **A** to tell whether these pairs of words are **homophones, synonyms,** or **antonyms.**

1. bare—bear
2. smooth—rough
3. little—small
4. tall—short
5. old—aged
6. hymn—him

114. Reviewing What You Have Learned

> Oral Drill >

A. Answer these questions.
   1. What is the purpose of introductions?
   2. How should you introduce someone to your mother?
   3. What should you be sure of before you dial a telephone number?
   4. How should you speak when you use the telephone? How should you not speak?
   5. What are some important things to remember when you tell someone how to do something?

B. Make these introductions in class.
   1. Introduce a new boy in school to your brother.
   2. Introduce your cousin who is a boy to another one of your cousins who is a girl.
   3. Introduce your teacher to your grandmother.
   4. Introduce a friend in school to your mother.

> Written Practice >

A. Write the correct answers.

Review and Practice
| 1. H | 3. S | 5. S |
| 2. A | 4. A | 6. H |

Lesson 114 Answers
Oral Drill
A. 1. Introductions are given to help people get acquainted and feel comfortable.
   2. You should say *Mother* first.
   3. You should be sure you have the right number.
   4. You should speak loudly and clearly. You should not speak too softly, neither should you shout.
   5. Give the directions in the right order. Say everything that needs to be done. Do not add unnecessary details.

B. (See that introductions follow the rules.)

Lesson 114

Aim: To evaluate students' progress and reinforce concepts taught earlier.

Class: Use Oral Drill in the class discussion. Clarify the written exercises as needed.

1. How should you introduce a younger person to an older person?
2. When you introduce a man to a woman or a boy to a girl, whose name should you say first?
3. If someone calls and wants to leave a message, you should (try to remember it, write it down).
4. What should you leave out when you tell someone how to do something?

B. In each set of sentences, one child did not follow the rules for using the telephone. Write what the child should have done instead.
1. Joan wanted to call her friend Sarah. When Sarah answered, Joan said, "Guess who."
2. Mark was trying to call Duane. He let the telephone ring five times and then hung up because no one answered.
3. Marilyn called Kay to plan a birthday surprise for Marilyn's sister Rose. Marilyn spoke very softly so that Rose would not hear.

C. Write **true** or **false** for each sentence.
1. When you introduce people to each other, the most important thing is to be thoughtful and courteous.
2. To introduce a boy and a girl of about the same age, you may say either name first.
3. When you answer the telephone, just say "Hello."
4. You should give the steps in the right order when you tell someone how to do something.
5. You may leave out the steps that the person can figure out himself.
6. Make the directions short, but say everything that needs to be done.

Written Practice

A. 1. Say the older person's name first.
2. the woman's or girl's name
3. write it down
4. unnecessary details

B. 1. Joan should have given her name.
2. Mark should have let the telephone ring longer.
3. Marilyn should have talked loudly enough for Kay to hear easily. (She could have waited until Rose was not around.)

C. 1. true
2. false
3. false
4. true
5. false
6. true

115. The Parts and Form of a Friendly Letter

Perhaps you know someone who lives far away. You probably wish you could visit that person more often. Did you know you can visit that person through the mail? You can do that by sending a letter. Such a letter is called a **friendly letter.**

A friendly letter has five important parts. The first part is called the **heading.** It is in the upper right corner of the paper. It tells the person who receives your letter what your address is and when the letter was written.

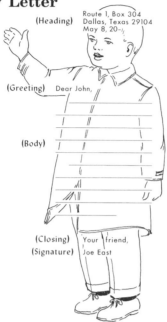

(Heading) Route 1, Box 304
Dallas, Texas 29104
May 8, 20–

(Greeting) Dear John,

(Body)

(Closing) Your friend,
(Signature) Joe East

The first line of the heading contains the writer's house number and the name of his street or road. If he lives in the country, the first line may contain his route and box number. The second line contains the name of the city and state, and the Zip Code. The third line gives the date when the letter was written.

Next comes the **greeting.** When we first meet a person, we often greet the person with "Good morning" or "Hello." In a letter we greet the person with "Dear" and the name of the person to whom we are writing.

Lesson 115

Aim: To introduce the friendly letter and teach its five parts.

Oral Review:

1. How should we write the first line of a paragraph? (Indent it.)
2. Which person's name would you say first if you were introducing
   a. your school friend and your father? (Father)
   b. a man and a woman? (the woman's name)
   c. your mother and your friend? (Mother)
3. What should you say first when you answer the telephone? (You should say "Hello" and give your name.)
4. What should you do if the person who is wanted on the telephone is not at home? (Ask if you can take a message, and write the message down right away.)
5. Give three rules to remember when you tell someone how to do something. (Give the directions in the right order. Say everything that needs to be done. Do not give unnecessary details.)

Class: Ask how many in the class have written or received a letter. Perhaps some have read a letter that another person has received, such as their parents. Do they remember anything that was written in the letter? What made the letter interesting? Was there anything about the letter that made it hard to read?

Discuss the reason for each part of a friendly letter. Point out that the heading especially is important, for the receiver may need it when he writes back to the sender.

Ask for ideas on things to write in a letter. Work together at starting with bare facts and then

The main part of the letter is called the **body.** It contains the message that we want to send. Except for the indenting of paragraphs, the left margin of the body should be straight and in line with the greeting. The right margin should be kept as straight as possible.

The **closing** is like saying "Good-bye" in our conversation. We may write "With love," "Sincerely," or some other suitable closing.

Last of all, we should write our **signature** to show who has written the letter. The closing and the signature are in line with the left margin of the heading.

> Working With a Friendly Letter >

Study this letter. Then answer the questions that follow.

> Route 1, Box 97
> Millersburg, Ohio 44654
> March 4, 20—

Dear Joseph,

The Lord blessed us with a nice shower today. This will really help the crops.

While it was raining today, I worked on my bluebird house. I am almost finished with it. We have many different kinds of birds around here. A great blue heron visits our pond regularly.

We bought two more calves at the sale Wednesday. It seems as though we are getting more and more animals. We now have six calves. The lambs that were born this spring are really growing.

I am looking forward to Grandfather and Grandmother's visit here. I hope you can come while they are here.

> Your friend,
> Jonathan

xpressing them in a more interesting way. Compose
. letter on the board, using thoughts contributed by
he students. If time allows, you may want to make
ome mistakes in the letter and ask the pupils to cor-
ect them.

★ **EXTRA PRACTICE**
Worksheet 66 (*The Friendly Letter*)

1. Who wrote this letter?
2. To whom did he write it?
3. Where does Jonathan live?
4. When was the letter written?
5. Does the writer live in the city or in the country?
6. What do you notice about the first line of each paragraph?
7. How did the writer greet the person he was writing to?
8. Write the closing of the letter.
9. Write the heading of the letter.
10. Write one sentence from the body of the letter.
11. Write the signature of the letter.
12. Write the greeting of the letter.

> **Review and Practice** >

Copy each sentence, adding commas, apostrophes, and capital letters where they are needed.

1. The disciples who went with Jesus were peter james and john.
2. Patsy please set the table.
3. At the zoo we saw lions tigers monkeys and zebras.
4. Johns and Eugenes bicycle tires were flat.
5. We dont know why they didnt come.

Lesson 115 Answers
Working With a Friendly Letter

1. Jonathan
2. Joseph
3. in Ohio
4. March 4, 1988
5. in the country
6. The first line of each paragraph is indented
7. Dear Joseph,
8. Your friend,
9. Route 1, Box 97
   Millersburg, Ohio 44654
   March 4, 1988
10. (Individual answers.)
11. Jonathan
12. Dear Joseph,

Review and Practice

(Corrected items are underlined.)

1. The disciples who went with Jesus were Peter, James, and John.
2. Patsy, please set the table.
3. At the zoo we saw lions, tigers, monkeys, and zebras.
4. John's and Eugene's bicycle tires were flat.
5. We don't know why they didn't come.

116. Rules for Writing a Friendly Letter

In Lesson 115 you learned about the five parts of a friendly letter. These parts help to make it enjoyable for your friends to read your letters. In this lesson you will learn some rules for correctly writing the five parts of a friendly letter.

1. In the heading, usually all the words are capitalized. Put a comma between the route and the box number if there is one, between the city and the state, and between the date and the year.
2. Always begin the first word in the greeting with a capital letter. If the second word in the greeting is a name, capitalize it also. Put a comma after the greeting.
3. Capitalize the first word in the closing. Put a comma after the closing.
4. Capitalize the signature.

> **Writing the Parts of a Letter**

1. Write the letter parts for each letter in the correct form for two letters, as shown in the diagram of the boy in Lesson 115. Leave a few empty lines for the body. Use capital letters and commas where they are needed. Use the present year in the date.
   a. route 1 box 249 amelia virginia 23002
      april 30 20—
      dear daniel
      your friend joel
   b. 210 main street orrville ohio 44667
      may 2 20—
      dear betty
      with love rachel

Lesson 116 Answers
Writing the Parts of a Letter
1. a.   Route 1, Box 249
                  Amelia, Virginia 23002
                  April 30, 20— (present year)
   Dear Daniel,
   _____
   _____
   _____
                  Your friend,
                  Joel

   b.   210 Main Street
                  Orrville, Ohio 44667
                  May 2, 20—(present year)
   Dear Betty,
   _____
   _____
   _____
                  With love,
                  Rachel

Lesson 116

Aim: To teach some rules for writing a friendly letter in correct form.

Oral Review:
1. How do we diagram a sentence with a direct object? (We put a straight line between the verb and the direct object.)
2. What is the purpose of introductions? (to help strangers feel more comfortable)
3. When you use the telephone, how should you hold the receiver? How should you speak? (Hold the receiver about an inch from your mouth and right against your ear. Speak clearly and loudly but do not shout.)
4. When you tell someone how to do something
   a. give the directions in the —— order. (right)
   b. say —— that needs to be done. (everything)
   c. do not give —— details. (unnecessary)

5. Name the five parts of a friendly letter. (heading, greeting, body, closing, signature)

Class: Review the five parts of a friendly letter, and then call attention to the picture in Lesson 115. Ask, "What do you think is the most important part of a letter?" (the body)

Refer to the sample letter in the picture as you point out capitalization, commas, and indentation. Use the following questions.

1. The names of people, cities, states, and months should always be capitalized. Do you remember why? (They are proper nouns.)
2. Why is it necessary to write the date? (So that whenever the receiver reads the letter, he will know when it was written. He may want to read it again years later.)

2. Write your own heading, greeting, closing, and signature in the same form as you did in number 1.

> ▷ Review and Practice ▷

Write the correct word for each sentence.
1. There (was, were) a big crowd following Jesus.
2. We (began, begun) the chores before Father came home.
3. Uncle Henry asked Joel and (me, I) to help him.
4. I couldn't find (anything, nothing).
5. There (is, are) ice on the pond.
6. I have (saw, seen) geese flying north.
7. (Us, We) and our friends played a game.
8. The store didn't have (nothing, anything) to sell.
9. There (was, were) tracks in the snow.
10. Jesus (seen, saw) Nathanael under a tree.
11. The children were happy when they saw Grandmother and (they, them).
12. We didn't see (no, any) deer in the woods.

●━●━●━●━●━●

117. Writing to Share With Others

A letter is not just some words written on paper. It may be a great help to someone who is sad or lonely. Read the following story for an example of this.

> Grandfather rocked slowly back and forth as he sat on the porch. He lived by himself, and he was often lonesome. He thought longingly about his grandchildren as he looked across the fields.

3. Why do you think there is a comma between *May 8* and *20*—? (The comma separates the two different numbers.)
4. Some of the lines in the body do not come as far left as the others. Why? (These lines show where new paragraphs begin.)
5. Which word in the closing is capitalized? (Only the first word.)

Observe that the pattern in the illustration is to be followed in the written exercises.

★ **EXTRA PRACTICE**
Worksheet 67 (*The Parts of a Friendly Letter*)

---

2. (Individual answers.)

Review and Practice
1. was
2. began
3. me
4. anything
5. is
6. seen
7. We
8. anything
9. were
10. saw
11. them
12. any

Lesson 117

Aim: To help pupils see the value and blessing of writing letters.

Oral Review:
1. The word *not* is (a verb, an adjective, an adverb). (an adverb)
2. Before you use the telephone, what should you be sure of? (Be sure you have the right number.)
3. When you tell someone how to do something
   a. in what order should you give the directions? (Give directions in the right order.)
   b. how much should you say? (Say everything that needs to be done.)
   c. what should you *not* give? (Do not give unnecessary details.)
4. Name the five parts of a friendly letter. (heading, greeting, body, closing, signature)

"How I wish they would come for a visit again," thought Grandfather. "But I suppose they are busy on the farm."

Just then the mailman stopped at the gate.

Grandfather slowly got to his feet, picked up his cane, and started walking to the mailbox.

"The usual things," he thought as he looked through some advertisements. Then he saw it—a letter! His face shone as he tore open the envelope and noticed the signatures of his grandchildren. Grandfather was not lonely anymore. Someone cared about him!

When you write a letter, remember to follow the rules you have studied. Ask yourself these questions after your letter is finished.

1. Does it have correct form?
2. Are capital letters used correctly?
3. Does it have correct punctuation?
4. Did I begin a new paragraph each time I wrote about a different thing?
5. Is it interesting and clear? Is it the kind of letter I would enjoy receiving?

5. When writing a letter, where should you use commas
   a. in the heading? (between the route and box, between the city and state, and between the date and year)
   b. with the greeting? (after the greeting)
   c. with the closing? (after the closing)

Class: Read aloud the lesson title. Ask, "What does it mean to share?" (To give someone part of what is yours.) How can we share when we write? (We share our time and our thoughts.) The Bible has much to say about sharing, and writing letters is one way we can do this. Mention Hebrews 13:16: "But to do good and to communicate [share] forget not."

Discuss the incident in the lesson. Read the following paragraphs for another example.

Martha was tired. She had spent the whole day walking from hut to hut, visiting the people in the village. As she trudged up the path, she thought of her family thousands of miles away. She pictured her parents' lovely home, and a great longing filled her heart. Martha was close to tears as she stepped inside the door of her house.

But what was that? A letter! Joyfully Martha snatched it off the table and opened the envelope. A few minutes later she was humming a tune.

Talk about ways to make letters interesting. Instead of saying, "Mother is washing," you could write, "The clothes on the line are flapping in the breeze." Do not just write, "It finally rained"; say, "Yesterday it rained, and the thirsty ground really seemed to drink it in." Add color to chores: "I don't like to wash dishes, but I am thankful that I can work and that we have food to eat." It is the writer's

When you send a letter, you will need to address an envelope for it. Near the middle of the envelope, write the address of the person to whom you are sending the letter. Use clear, neat handwriting. Put our own name and address in the upper left corner of the envelope.

Jonathan Zook
Route 1, Box 97
Millersburg, Ohio 44654

JOSEPH MARTIN
6590 LAKE ROAD
GOSHEN INDIANA 46526

> **Writing to Share**

Think of someone who may be sad or lonely and would be happy to receive a letter. Write a letter to this person. Check your letter by asking the five questions given in your lesson.

> **Review and Practice**

Write each set of choppy sentences as one smooth sentence.
1. I saw a bird. It was big and brown. It was flying over our pond.
2. James has a garden. It is little. It has corn in it.
3. Glenn brought a pencil to school. It is blue. It is sharp.

Lesson 117 Answers
Writing to Share
(Individual letters.)

Review and Practice
(Wording may vary slightly.)
1. I saw a big brown bird flying over our pond.
2. James has a little garden with corn in it.
3. Glenn brought a sharp blue pencil to school.

feelings that make a letter colorful and interesting.

The letters that the children write in these lessons may be saved for the Extra Activity at the end of the unit. Personal letters, of course, may actually be sent to someone.

118. A Thank-you Letter

It is courteous and kind to remember to thank people for things they have done for you or given to you. If they are too far away to tell them "Thank you," you may send them a thank-you letter.

A few words that show sincere appreciation may do much for a person. You should tell the person why you appreciate what was given to you or done for you.

> **Correcting a Letter of Thanks**

Copy the following letter in correct form. Use capital letters and commas correctly. Use the present year in the heading.

121 grant street   bridgewater vermont 05034 march 15 20—   dear rhoda thank you for the kind invitation to take me along with your family to gather maple syrup. That is something I have wanted to do for a long time. my parents say that I may go along, and I am looking forward to spending the day with you. I will try to be ready by 7 o'clock thursday morning. your friend ruth

> **Writing a Letter of Thanks**

Write a thank-you letter to someone, using your address and the present date in the heading. Proofread it for correct form, capital letters, and punctuation.

Lesson 118 Answers
Correcting a Letter of Thanks

121 Grant Street
Bridgewater, Vermont 05034
March 15, 20—

Dear Rhoda,

Thank you for the kind invitation to take me along with your family to gather maple syrup. That is something I have wanted to do for a long time. My parents say that I may go along, and I am looking forward to spending the day with you. I will try to be ready by 7 o'clock Thursday morning.

Your friend,
Ruth

Writing a Letter of Thanks
(Individual letters.)

Lesson 118

Aim: (1) To teach some reasons for writing thank-you letters. (2) To give practice in writing a thank-you letter with correct form, capitalization, and punctuation.

Oral Review:
1. The verbs *seen, done,* and *gone* (need, do not need) a helping verb. (need)
2. When you tell someone how to do something,
   a. give the directions in the —— order. (right)
   b. say —— that needs to be done. (everything)
   c. do not give —— details. (unnecessary)
3. Name the five parts of a friendly letter. (heading, greeting, body, closing, signature)
4. Tell how each part of a letter should be written.
   a. greeting (Capitalize the first word and put a comma at the end.)
   b. closing (Capitalize the first word and put a comma at the end.)
   c. signature (Capitalize it.)
5. Write the kind of letter that ——. (you would enjoy receiving)

Class: Recall the five parts of a friendly letter. A simple diagram on the board will be helpful for this review.

Read the title and discuss what is meant by a thank-you letter. Have the children ever seen one? Discuss comments that could be included other than just, "Thank you for the book." For example, "I like it so much that I am already reading it the second time. My brother really likes it too."

You may wish to show a thank-you letter that you have received, or one that you have written as an example.

119. Reviewing What You Have Learned

> Oral Drill

1. What are four things you should remember when you write a letter?
2. A letter that we send to visit with someone is called a —— letter.
3. Such a letter has —— parts.
4. Name the parts in order.

> Written Practice

A. Write a heading, a greeting, a closing, and a signature for a letter. Use correct punctuation.

B. Draw an envelope on your paper. Address it correctly to one of your friends. Put your own name and address in the correct place on the envelope.

C. Write each letter part correctly. Add punctuation and capital letters where they are needed. Use the present year in the headings.

1. your friend
2. dear jane
3. bethesda ohio 43719
   route 1 box 163
   may 12 20—
4. with love
5. your cousin
6. october 14 20—
   ina illinois 62846
   255 green street

> Extra Practice

Write a thank-you letter to someone who has given you something or has done something for you. Remember to use correct letter form.

Lesson 119 Answers
Oral Drill

1. a. Think about the things you want to sa before you start writing. It may be helpfu to make a list.
   b. Write the kind of letter you would enjo receiving.
   c. Begin a new paragraph each time you te about a different thing.
   d. Write clearly, correctly, and interestingly
2. friendly
3. five
4. heading, greeting, body, closing, signature

Written Practice

A. (Individual answers.)

B. (Individual answers.)

C. 1. Your friend,
   2. Dear Jane,
   3. Route 1, Box 163
      Bethesda, Ohio 43719
      May 12, 20—
   4. With love,
   5. Your cousin,
   6. 255 Green Street
      Ina, Illinois 62846
      October 14, 20—

Extra Practice
(Individual letters.)

Lesson 119

Aim: To review and evaluate concepts taught earlier.

Class: Do Oral Drill in class. Give additional review and drill as needed.

120. Poetry

Poetry is writing put in a beautiful form that is especially pleasing to hear. Good poetry has beautiful word pictures, and it usually has **rhyme** and **rhythm** too. You will learn more about rhyme and rhythm in the next several lessons.

We should learn to read poetry well. Memorizing poetry is even better than reading it. Then we can say it without looking at a book. It is good to be able to recite poetry when someone needs comfort or cheer.

Poetry is written in a different way from other kinds of writing. Only a certain number of words are put in each line. Every line begins with a capital letter, and the poem is divided into **stanzas** rather than paragraphs.

Here are some rules for writing poems. Do you see how they are followed in the poem later in this lesson?

1. Write the title in the center of the first line.
2. Skip a line between the title and the first line of the poem. Also skip a line between each stanza of the poem.
3. Begin each line of the poem with a capital letter.

Lesson 120

Aim: To introduce poetry and teach how to copy a poem correctly.

Oral Review:

1. What are antonyms? (*words with opposite meanings*)
2. Correct this sentence: Them birds are blackbirds. (Those birds are blackbirds.)
3. Name the five parts of a friendly letter. (heading, greeting, body, closing, signature)
4. When writing a letter, where should you use commas
    a. in the heading? (between the route and box, between the city and state, and between the date and year)
    b. with the greeting? (after the greeting)
    c. with the closing? (after the closing)
5. Write the kind of letter that ——. (you would enjoy receiving)

Class: Discuss what makes poetry different from regular writing. Then read several poems from a book like *Poems for Memorization* or a songbook. Point out the structure of poetry as well as the vivid word pictures in a good poem.

Read hymns written by William Cowper, Fanny Crosby, and other writers who experienced affliction. Point out that it is often through the hard experiences of life that a poet writes the most beautiful poems.

> **Thinking About Poetry** >

Write the correct word for each blank.
1. Good poetry has —— word pictures.
2. Poems usually have r—— and r——.
3. It is good to read poetry, but it is even better to ——
   poetry.
4. Poems are divided into —— rather than paragraphs.
5. Each line of a poem begins with a —— letter.

> **Copying a Poem** >

A. Copy this poem according to the rules in the lesson. Write
   only as much on each line as the writer of the poem did.
   Use punctuation just as it is in the poem.

Sowing and Reaping
If you sow good carrot seeds,
　Good carrots from them grow.
You will not gather beans or corn
　As anyone should know.

If you live to please yourself,
　You're sowing harmful weeds.
Bad habits are the harvest from
　These harmless-looking seeds.

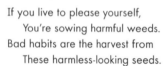
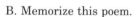

B. Memorize this poem.

> **Review and Practice** >

Write **noun, pronoun, verb, adjective,** or **adverb** for
each sentence.
　1. It describes a noun.

Lesson 120 Answers
Thinking About Poetry
　1.　beautiful
　2.　rhyme, rhythm
　3.　memorize
　4.　stanzas
　5.　capital

Copying a Poem
A. (The poem should be copied exactly as shown.)

B. (Oral work.)

Review and Practice
　1.　adjective

2. It shows action or being.

3. It describes a verb.

4. It names a person, place, or thing.

5. It tells **what kind of, how many, which,** or **whose.**

6. It takes the place of a noun.

7. Its past form may end with **ed.**

8. It tells **how, when,** or **where.**

9. Its possessive form may end with **'s.**

10. It may be a noun marker.

2. verb

3. adverb

4. noun

5. adjective

6. pronoun

7. verb

8. adverb

9. noun

10. adjective

121. Rhyme in Poetry

Rhyme helps to make a poem enjoyable because the words at the end of some lines sound alike. Rhyme is probably the first special thing we notice about poetry.

If a poem has four lines, the last words in lines 1 and 2 may rhyme, and the last words in lines 3 and 4 may rhyme.

> Praise to God, immortal praise,
> For the love that crowns our days;
> Bounteous source of every joy,
> Let Thy praise our tongues employ.

Sometimes the rhyming words are at the end of lines 1 and 3 and lines 2 and 4.

> A certain man of whom we read,
>   Who lived in days of old,
> Though he was rich, he felt his need
>   Of something more than gold.

Lesson 121

Aim: (1) To help students appreciate good rhyme in poetry. (2) To give them practice in using words that rhyme.

Oral Review:

1. On a sentence diagram, where do we put
   a. a direct object? (on the base line after the verb, with a straight line between the verb and the direct object)
   b. adjectives and adverbs? (on slanted lines under the words they describe)
2. Tell how each part of a letter should be written.
   a. greeting (Capitalize the first word and put a comma at the end.)
   b. closing (Capitalize the first word and put a comma at the end.)
   c. signature (Capitalize it.)

3. How can you say "thank you" to someone who lives far away? (by writing a thank-you letter)
4. How should we begin each line of a poem? (with a capital letter)

Class: Read several poems to the class. Point out the rhyming words and discuss the difference between perfect and imperfect rhyme. In a good poem, the thoughts are expressed in such a way that imperfect rhyme is hardly noticed. Here are two examples.

> I am so glad that our Father in heav'n
> Tells of His love in the Book He has giv'n.
>
> Many mighty men are lost,
> Daring not to stand,
> Who for God had been a host,
> By joining Daniel's Band!

On the other hand, a poem without good word pictures and worthwhile thoughts is not a good poem

And sometimes only the last words in lines 2 and 4 rhyme.

> Away in a manger,
>   No crib for a bed,
> The little Lord Jesus
>   Laid down His sweet head.

Working With Rhyme

Work together as a class to supply the missing words. Use words that rhyme.

1. I like to watch the stars at night
   They seem so small but look so ———.

2. I made a snowman cold and tall.
   The sun soon made him start to ———.

3. See the little maple ———
   Swaying gently in the ———.

Using Words That Rhyme

Copy the poems below, and put one word in each blank. Use rhyming words where they are needed.

1. Before we enter each new day,
   We read God's Word and sing and ———.

2. I walked beneath the ——— so blue
   And saw the ——— that sang and ———.
   The ——— were buzzing through the air.
   "Oh, thank You, God," I whispered ———.

Lesson 121 Answers
Working With Rhyme
1. bright
2. fall
3. trees; breeze

Using Words That Rhyme
(Some answers may vary. The following are suggestions.)

1. Before we enter each new day.
   We read God's Word and sing and <u>pray</u>.

2. I walked beneath the <u>sky</u> so blue,
   And saw the <u>birds</u> that sang and <u>flew</u>.
   The <u>bees</u> were buzzing through the air.
   "Oh, thank You, God," I whispered <u>there</u>.

even though it has perfect rhyme.

Working With Rhyme is to be done as a class activity.

★ **EXTRA PRACTICE**
Worksheet 68 (*Rhyme*)

3. Some shepherds watching in the night
Beheld a brilliant, heavenly ———.
An ——— spoke with voice so ———:
"For you is born a Saviour ———."

4. I like to watch the stars at night;
I like to watch the ———.
I think of all the boys and ———
Who now are having noon.

Review and Practice

A. Write **H, S,** or **A** to tell whether these pairs of words are **homophones, synonyms,** or **antonyms.**
   1. new—old
   2. shout—yell
   3. die—dye
   4. ache—hurt
   5. one—won
   6. back—front

B. In each sentence, write the word that gives a better word picture.
   1. A (big, huge) bear was eating the honey.
   2. The spider (scurried, ran) across the floor.
   3. The wren was singing a (nice, cheery) song.
   4. The raindrops (fell, pattered) on the leaves above me.
   5. Thick black smoke (rolled, came) out of the chimney.

Can You Do This?

Write a line to finish this poem. It should end with a rhyming word.

I have a little rabbit;
His house is called a hutch.
I feed him and I pet him,

_____

Review and Practice
A. 1. A   3. H   5. H
   2. S   4. S   6. A

B. 1. huge
   2. scurried
   3. cheery
   4. pattered
   5. rolled

Can You Do This?
(Last line may vary.)

I have a little rabbit;
His house is called a hutch.
I feed him and I pet him,
I like him very much.

---

3. Some shepherds watching in the night
Beheld a brilliant, heavenly <u>light</u>.
An <u>angel</u> spoke with voice so <u>clear</u>:
"For you is born a Saviour <u>dear</u>."

4. I like to watch the stars at night;
I like to watch the <u>moon</u>.
I think of all the boys and <u>girls</u>
Who now are having noon.

122. Rhythm in Poetry

You have learned that rhyme helps to make poetry enjoyable. Rhythm also helps to make poetry pleasing and beautiful.

You know that words have accented and unaccented syllables. Rhythm is made by writing words in such a way that the accented and unaccented syllables follow a pattern. In the lines of poetry below, say the accented syllables with more force than the unaccented ones with the curved lines.

> ⏑ ˊ ⏑ ˊ ⏑ ˊ ⏑ ˊ
> The Lord is my be-lov-ed Friend.
> ⏑ ˊ ⏑ ˊ ⏑ ˊ ⏑ ˊ
> On Him I al-ways can de-pend.
>
> ˊ ⏑ ˊ ⏑ ˊ ⏑ ˊ
> Je-sus loves me, this I know,
> ˊ ⏑ ˊ ⏑ ˊ ⏑ ˊ
> For the Bi-ble tells me so.

▷ Working With Rhythm ▷

A. In the following poem, pairs of words are given in parentheses. Either word could be used, but one gives better rhythm. Copy the poem, choosing the words that give better rhythm.

God's Work and Mine

A (little, small) lassie found a rose
   Unopened yet, and thought,
"I'll open up the rose for (God, Jesus);
   I think He has forgot."

Lesson 122 Answers
Working With Rhythm

A–B.   **God's Work and Mine**

A little lassie found a rose
   Unopened yet, and <u>thought</u>,
"I'll open up the rose for God;
   I think He has <u>forgot</u>."

Lesson 122

Aim: To help students see the need of proper rhythm in poetry. (2) To give them practice in constructing proper rhythm.

Oral Review:

1. Say the eight forms of *be.* (am, is, are, was, were, be, been, being)
2. Choose the correct verb form in each sentence.
   a. The children had (went, gone) outside to play. (gone)
   b. When it started to rain, they (came, come) back inside. (came)
   c. Soon they (saw, seen) a lovely rainbow. (saw)
3. What makes poetry different from other writing? (It is written in stanzas rather than paragraphs. Every line is capitalized. There are rhyming words at the end of some lines.)

4. Give a rhyming word for each of these: *tree, hill, kind, joy.* (Possible answers: me, be; fill, will; mind, behind; boy, toy)

Class: Discuss the meaning of the word *rhythm.* Demonstrate by having everyone clap their hands in rhythm or doing some other activity in rhythm. Also show how rhythm can be spoiled.

Read several poems and discuss their rhythm. As with rhyme, point out that imperfect rhythm does not necessarily make a poor poem. The mechanics of poetry are important, but the real test of quality is the thoughts and feelings expressed in a poem.

★ **EXTRA PRACTICE**
Worksheet 69 (*Rhythm*)

She did not understand God's plan
    And (spoiled, damaged) a rose that day,
For buds need time to (blossom, bloom) out;
    To (hurry, rush) them does not pay.

With patience we should grow and learn
    God's (lessons, instructions) day by day,
And wait on Him to show us all
    That we should (perform, do) or say.

B. In the poem you copied, underline the words at the end of the lines in each stanza that rhyme or almost rhyme.

> Review and Practice >

A. Copy the wrong word in each sentence. If another word should be used in its place, write the correct word beside it.
1. Them rabbits ate the lettuce in our garden.
2. I got this here pen for my birthday.
3. The empty bottles are those there.
4. I would like to pick some of them flowers.
5. Is this here the book you want?

B. Write **good** or **well** for each sentence.
1. Father bought a —— bicycle at the sale.
2. The baby sleeps ——.
3. Abram's herdsmen and Lot's herdsmen did not get along ——.
4. That is —— lumber for making furniture.
5. Sister Edith is not feeling —— today.

She did not understand God's plan
    And spoiled a rose that <u>day</u>,
For buds need time to blossom out;
    To rush them does not <u>pay</u>.

With patience we should grow and learn
    God's lessons day by <u>day</u>,
And wait on Him to show us all
    That we should do or <u>say</u>.

Review and Practice

A. 1. Them, Those
  2. here
  3. there
  4. them, those
  5. here

B. 1. good
  2. well
  3. well
  4. good
  5. well

>━ Can You Do This? ▷

A. Copy these lines of poetry, leaving an empty space between them. Put an accent mark like this ´ above each accented syllable. Put a curved line like this ˘ above each unaccented syllable.

> Lit-tle chil-dren, can you tell
> Who has kept us safe and well?

B. Supply the missing words. Use words that give good rhyme and rhythm.

> Remember your Creator, God,
> Remember while ――― ―――.
> He made your eyes and ――― and ―――;
> He made your ――― ―――.
>
> He watches over you each ―――;
> If you are weak, ――― ―――.
> He helps you in your work ――― ―――;
> He hears your ――― ―――.

◆━◆━◆━◆━◆━◆━◆

123. Reading Poetry

> So they read in the book in the law of God distinctly, and gave the sense, and caused them to understand the reading.
>
> Nehemiah 8:8

This verse gives a good pattern for reading the Bible. It is also a good pattern for reading poetry. We should read

Lesson 123

Aim: To teach that poetry must be read with proper expression, and that the mood of poetry shows what kind of expression to use.

Oral Review:

1. Which sentence part tells who or what does or is something? (the subject)
2. What is the subject of a commanding sentence? (you)
3. When you copy a poem, where should you write the title? How should you begin each line? (Write the title in the center of the first line. Begin each line with a capital letter.)
4. What makes rhyme in poetry? (words whose endings sound alike)
5. What makes rhythm in poetry? (accented and unaccented syllables arranged in a certain pattern)

Class: Read the following stanzas to the class. First read in a sing-song manner, then read with proper expression. Discuss the difference.

> Who taught the bird to build her nest
> Of softest wool, and hay, and moss?
> Who taught her how to weave it best,
> And lay the tiny twigs across?
>
> Who taught the busy bee to fly
> Among the sweetest herbs and flowers,
> And lay her store of honey by,
> Providing food for winter hours?
>
> —Jane Taylor

Explain what is meant by the mood of poetry. The mood of a poem is its general feeling. It may have a mood of joy, sadness, worship, thankfulness, or other moods. Read the following poem and discuss its mood.

in a way that expresses the meaning and feeling of the words. A dull, singsong voice is not pleasant. It sounds as tiresome as the hum of a motor or the dripping of water from a faucet.

The **mood** of a poem helps you know how to read it. The mood is the feeling of the poem. A poem with a joyful mood should be read in a loud, joyful voice. You should not shout, but your voice should express the feeling of gladness that is in the poem.

A poem with a serious or sad mood should be read more softly and slowly. But you should still read loudly and clearly enough to be heard well.

Poems also have other moods. Whenever you read poetry, try to use the expression that best brings out the mood or feeling of the poem.

> To Do Together

Read each poem with good expression. To keep from reading in a singsong voice, put extra force on the words in bold print.

1. Oh, what a **happy child** am I,
     Although I cannot **see**!
   I am **resolved** that in this world
     Contented I will be.
                    —*Fanny Crosby*

2. We were **crowded** in the cabin;
     Not a **soul** would **dare** to sleep—
   It was **midnight** on the waters,
     And a **storm** was one the deep.

Lesson 123 Answers
To Do Together
(Oral work.)

Welcome, welcome, little stranger;
Fear no harm and fear no danger.
We are glad to see you here,
For you sing, "Sweet spring is near."

Now the white snow melts away;
Now the flowers blossom gay.
Come, dear bird, and build your nest,
For we love our robin best.
                    —Louisa May Alcott

Discuss the moods of various other poems, and have pupils read them with proper expression. Most songbooks have a good selection of poetry with different moods.

Use To Do Together for additional practice in class. For Can You Do This? explain that the psalms in the Bible are poetry, but this poetry does not have rhythm and rhyme as we know it.

> Practice With Poetry >

A. Write whether the mood of each poem is **joyful, prayerful, quiet,** or **sad.**

1. Baby sleeps, so we must tread
     Softly round her little bed,
   And be careful that our toys
     Do not fall and make a noise.

2. Good morning, Merry Sunshine,
       How did you wake so soon?
   You've scared the little stars away
       And shined away the moon.

3. Jesus, tender Shepherd, hear me,
       Bless Thy little lamb tonight;
   Through the darkness be Thou near me,
       Keep me safe till morning light.

4. We may not know, we cannot tell,
       What pains He had to bear;
   But we believe it was for us
       He hung and suffered there.

B. Be ready to read the poems in Part A with good expression.

> Review and Practice >

Copy each sentence. Add quotation marks and capital letters where they are needed, and use the correct end marks.

1. are you ready for the hike asked sister susan
2. the children answered, we are ready
3. marvin exclaimed, I can hardly wait
4. remember to stay in one group, said sister susan

Practice With Poetry

A. 1. quiet
   2. joyful
   3. prayerful
   4. sad

B. (Oral work.)

Review and Practice
   (Corrected items are underlined.)
   1. "Are you ready for the hike?" asked Sister Susan.
   2. The children answered, "We are ready."
   3. Marvin exclaimed, "I can hardly wait!"
   4. "Remember to stay in one group," said Sister Susan.

> ⟩ Can You Do This? ⟩

Find these references in the Psalms. Write whether each one has a mood of **comfort, praise, trust, sadness, earnestness,** or **thanksgiving.**

1. Psalm 13:1–4
2. Psalm 23
3. Psalm 121

4. Psalm 136:1–3
5. Psalm 137:1–6
6. Psalm 148

Can You Do This?

1. earnestness
2. comfort (*or* trust)
3. trust (*or* comfort)

4. thanksgiving
5. sadness
6. praise

◆◆◆◆◆◆◆◆◆

124. Writing a Poem

So far in the lessons on poetry, you have been working with poems that other people wrote. In today's lesson you will try to write some poetry of your own. This is easier for some people than for others, but almost anyone can write some poetry if he is willing to learn and work hard.

The songs you sing in church and school are poems with music set to them. Perhaps more  people have the gift of writing poetry, but they never try to do it. So their gift is not used to the glory of God.

Sometimes poetry can give a better picture of something than a story can. See how many word pictures you can find in this poem.

The April skies are bright and clear;
We little think a shower is near.
But soon dark clouds begin to form,
And we expect a sudden storm.

Lesson 124

Aim: To encourage pupils to write poetry, and to provide them with the necessary motivation.

Written Quiz:

1. What is one important thing to remember when you tell someone how to do something?
2. Name the five parts of a friendly letter.
3. What is one way to make a friendly letter interesting?
4. Write whether each of these goes with **rhythm** or **rhyme.**
   a. Accented and unaccented syllables.
   b. Words that sound alike.
   c. load—road, seven—heaven
   d. ˊ ˘ ˊ ˘ ˊ ˘ ˊ
5. What is meant by the mood of a poem?

Quiz Answers:

1. (Any one of these.) Say everything that needs to be done. Give the steps in the right order. Do not give unnecessary details.
2. heading, greeting, body, closing, signature
3. (Possible answers.) Write the kind of letter you would enjoy receiving. Use good describing words.
4. a. rhythm
   b. rhyme
   c. rhyme
   d. rhythm
5. the feeling of the poem

Class: Ask the children if they know what a poet is. (Explain that a girl who writes poetry can also be called a poetess.) Say, "Today each one of us will try to be a poet or poetess. The lesson will help you see how to write poetry."

Soon drops of rain stream from the sky,
And water puddles round us lie.
Then suddenly the sun peeks through,
And we can see a sky of blue.

Again the sky is overcast,
And rain is falling thick and fast.
Once more we see the sun shine through,
But drops of rain are falling too.

At last the raindrops cease to fall;
We hardly see the clouds at all.
Our windows all are washed and dried,
And now we hurry back outside.

▷ Finishing Poems ▷

Work together as a class to finish these poems.

1. Before I eat my food so good,
     I bow my head and pray.
   (Add two more lines.)

2. I love my mother dear and kind;
     She does so much for me.
   (Finish the poem.)

▷ Review and Practice ▷

Write each title correctly.
1. the tiny train
2. inside and outside
3. blackie
4. tony's garden
5. noah and the ark

Lesson 124 Answers
Finishing Poems

(Encourage pupils to give original suggestions.
The following are possibilities.)

1. Before I eat my food so good,
     I bow my head and pray.
   I thank the Lord for blessing me
     So richly every day.

2. I love my mother dear and kind;
     She does so much for me.
   She cares for me both day and night;
     How thankful I should be!

Review and Practice

1. The Tiny Train
2. Inside and Outside
3. Blackie
4. Tony's Garden
5. Noah and the Ark

Point out that to write a poem, we must first have an idea of something to write about. It is helpful to form a good picture in the mind and then express it in colorful language. Practice doing this as you work with the poems to be finished in class (Finishing Poems). You may also wish to ask for ideas to write about and have the pupils help to develop them into one or more original poems. Your enthusiasm will arouse the pupils' enthusiasm.

For the written assignment, you will need to specify how many lines or stanzas the pupils should write. Their poems are to be saved for the Extra Activity at the end of the unit.

★ **EXTRA PRACTICE**
Worksheet 70 (*Helps for Writing Poetry*)

Can You Do This?

Write a poem of your own. Your teacher will tell you how many stanzas or how many lines you should write. You may get an idea from these pictures.

Can You Do This?

(Individual poems. Check for originality, rhyme, and rhythm.)

125. Reviewing What You Have Learned

> **Oral Drill** >

1. What makes poetry pleasing to hear?
2. What makes rhythm?
3. Poems are not divided into paragraphs, but into ———.
4. What three things should you remember when you copy a poem?
5. Why is memorizing poetry better than just reading it?
6. Read the poem below, choosing the best words in parentheses. Say why you think those words are best.

Don't Give Up

If you've tried and have not won,
    Never (stop, give up) for crying;
(All, Everything) that's good and great is done
    (Ever, Just) by patient (trying, working).

If by easy work you (beat, succeed),
    Who the (more, higher) will prize you?
Gaining (success, victory) from defeat—
    That's the test that (proves, tries) you!
            —*Phoebe Cary*

> **Written Practice** >

A. Copy this poem correctly.

the snowbird

when all the ground with snow is white,
    the merry snowbird comes
and hops about with great delight
    to find the scattered crumbs.

Lesson 125 Answers
Oral Drill

1. rhyme and rhythm
2. Rhythm is made by writing words in such a way that the accented and unaccented syllables follow a pattern.
3. stanzas
4. a. Write the title in the center of the first line.
   b. Skip a line between the title and the first line of the poem and between each stanza.
   c. Begin each line of the poem with a capital letter.
5. If we memorize poetry, we can say it without looking at a book. We can also recite it to someone who needs comfort or cheer.
6. *Line 2:* stop (better rhythm)
   Line 3: All (better rhythm)
   Line 4: Just (better rhythm and meaning)
          trying (better rhyme)
   Line 5: beat (better rhythm and rhyme)
   Line 6: more (better rhythm)
   Line 7: victory (better rhythm because of the accent)
   Line 8: tries (better rhyme)

Written Practice

A. (The poem should be copied with the title and the first letter of each line capitalized. You may wish to mention that a snowbird is usually a junco.)

Lesson 125

Aim: To review concepts taught previously.

Class: Follow the usual procedure for reviews. The Oral Drill may be included in the written assignment if desired.

how glad he seems to get to eat
   a piece of cake or bread!
he wears no shoes upon his feet,
   nor hat upon his head.

but happiest is he, I know,
   because no cage with bars
keeps him from walking on the snow
   and printing it with stars.

B. Copy these poems correctly, and add the missing parts.

  1. Dear God, I've had a happy day;
      I tried to do my best.
    And now I thank You for the night
      When children all can ———.

  2. I lifted up my eyes on high.
    God put a rainbow in the ———.
    Its lovely colors I would ———
    With all the children ———.

  3. All the flowers ——— and gay
    Wave around me when I ———.

  4. Ripe red apples big and round
      Grow upon the tree.
    (Add two more lines.)

B. (Underlined words may vary.)

  1. Dear God, I've had a happy day;
      I tried to do my best.
    And now I thank You for the night
      When children all can <u>rest</u>.

  2. I lifted up my eyes on high.
      God put a rainbow in the <u>sky</u>.
    Its lovely colors I would <u>share</u>.
      With all the children <u>everywhere</u>.

  3. All the flowers <u>bright</u> and gay
      Wave around me when I <u>play</u>.

  4. Ripe red apples big and round
      Grow upon the tree.
    <u>I am glad that God above</u>
    <u>Put them there for me.</u>

Review One

> Oral Drill

1. What book can help you to spell and pronounce words correctly?
2. Give definitions for these words. Also give some examples of each.
   a. homophones   b. synonyms   c. antonyms
3. Name some things you should avoid when you give an oral description.
4. What are some questions that will help you give a good description of a place?
5. Give the four rules to remember when introducing people.

> Written Practice

A. Copy all these words in alphabetical order. After each word, write **front, middle,** or **back** to tell where you would find that word in the dictionary.

kernel	mountain	yield
diamond	chariot	upright
winch	obstacle	beautiful

B. Choose words from these pairs of homophones to fill the blanks in the sentences below.

right—write	hole—whole
by—buy	threw—through

1. We did not eat the —— pie.
2. How many epistles did Peter ——?
3. The children —— corn to the pigs.
4. Mother made a —— for each plant.

Review One Answers
Oral Drill

1. the dictionary
2. a. Homophones are words that are pronounced alike but have different meanings and different spellings.
   b. Synonyms are words that mean the same or nearly the same.
   c. Antonyms are words that have opposite meanings. (Individual examples.)
3. Avoid sounding as though your mouth is full of food or as though your jaws are stiff. Do not use too many *ands*. Do not speak in a whiny or tiresome voice.
4. How large is the place? What things do you see? What do you hear? What do you smell? What feelings do you have when you are there?
5. a. To introduce a younger person to an older person, say the older person's name first.
   b. To introduce a man to a woman or a boy to a girl, say the woman's or girl's name first.
   c. To introduce someone to your mother, say *Mother* first.
   d. To introduce two men, two women, two boys, or two girls to one another, say either name first.

Written Practice

A.
beautiful—front	obstacle—middle
chariot—front	upright—back
diamond—front	winch—back
kernel—middle	yield—back
mountain—middle	

B. 1. whole
   2. write
   3. threw
   4. hole

Review One

Aim: To review concepts taught in the last unit in preparation for a test.

Class: Do Oral Drill in class. Remind the pupils that if they have a problem with a certain concept, they should turn back to the original lesson for help.

5. Father will not —— the pony.

6. The boy standing —— the tree is my brother.

7. Jesus passed —— Jericho.

8. Most people eat with their —— hand.

C. The words below have more than one meaning. Use each word in two sentences. Show a different meaning in each sentence.

1. pen   2. rest   3. bat

D. Write a synonym for each word.

1. pretty   3. big   5. happy
2. small   4. broad   6. hop

E. Rewrite each sentence, using antonyms instead of the words in bold print.

1. The **crooked old** oak trees lost **many** of their leaves.

2. The **poor** man drove a **dull old** car.

3. We walked **down** the **winding** path.

4. The children were playing **noisily outside.**

5. The weather was **cold** and **cloudy** when we started.

F. Write **true** or **false** for these sentences about using the telephone. If a sentence is false, write it correctly.

1. If you are not sure about a number, dial the number you think is the right one.

2. If you are calling, give your name when someone answers the telephone.

3. Talk very loudly so that the other person is sure to hear you.

4. Hold the receiver right against your ear.

5. If someone leaves a message, try your best to remember what it is.

5. buy

6. by

7. through

8. right

C. (Individual answers.)

D. (Possible answers.)

1. pretty—beautiful, lovely

2. small—little, tiny

3. big—large, huge

4. broad—wide, roomy

5. happy—cheerful, joyful

6. hop—jump, bound

E. (Possible answers.)

1. The <u>straight</u> <u>young</u> oak trees lost <u>few</u> of their leaves.

2. The <u>rich</u> man drove a <u>shiny</u> <u>new</u> car.

3. We walked <u>up</u> the <u>straight</u> path.

4. The children were playing <u>quietly</u> <u>inside</u>.

5. The weather was <u>warm</u> and <u>clear</u> when we started.

F. 1. false; Be sure you have the right number before you dial.

2. true

3. false; Talk loudly and clearly, but do not shout.

4. true

5. false; Write down the message.

Review Two

> Oral Drill >

A. Say the missing words in these sentences about giving directions on how to do something.
1. Give the directions in the right ——.
2. Say —— that needs to be done.
3. Say —— —— of each thing is needed.
4. Make the directions —— and ——.
5. Do not give —— details.

B. Answer these questions.
1. Name the five parts of a friendly letter in order.
2. When should you begin a new paragraph in a letter?
3. How can you tell someone "thank you" who lives very far away?
4. How is poetry different from ordinary writing?
5. When you copy a poem, where should you write the title?
6. How should you separate the stanzas from each other when you write a poem?

> Written Practice >

A. Name the part of a letter that each of these belongs to.
1. With love,   5. Your cousin,
2. May 4, 2008   6. Ann Yoder
3. Dear Diane,   7. Akron, Ohio
4. Thank you for the book.   8. Dear friends,

B. Show how to address an envelope to a friend.

Review Two Answers
Oral Drill
A. 1. order
   2. everything
   3. how much
   4. clear, short
   5. unnecessary

B. 1. heading, greeting, body, closing, signature
   2. Begin a new paragraph each time you tell about a different thing.
   3. Send him a thank-you letter.
   4. Poetry usually has rhythm and rhyme. Each line begins with a capital letter. It has stanzas instead of paragraphs.
   5. Write the title in the center of the first line.
   6. Skip a line between each stanza.

Written Practice
A. 1. closing   5. closing
   2. heading   6. signature
   3. greeting   7. heading
   4. body   8. greeting

B. (Individual answers.)

Review Two

Aim: To review and reinforce concepts taught earlier in preparation for a test.

Class: Do Oral Drill in class. Have pupils look over the Written Practice and ask any questions they may have.

C. Write the numbers from **1–8**. Copy the words in bold print that give correct rhythm.

> Two eyes to see (1) **nice, lovely** things to do,
> Two lips to smile the (2) **entire, whole** day through,
> Two ears to hear what (3) **friends, others** say,
> Two hands to put the (4) **playthings, toys** away,
> A tongue to speak (5) **kind, loving** words each day,
> A (6) **kind, loving** heart to work and play,
> Two feet that errands (7) **gladly, eagerly** run—
> Make happy days for (8) **someone, everyone.**
> —*Louise M. Oglevee*

D. Copy and finish the following poems.

1. Lions fierce, giraffes so tall,
   Monkeys climbing up the ———,
   Zebras, seals, and kangaroos—
   All these creatures live in ———.

2. God made the flowers that smell so ———;
   He made the birds that sing and ———.
   He looks upon His world so fair,
   And keeps us in His tender ———.

C. 1. nice
   2. whole
   3. others
   4. toys
   5. kind
   6. loving
   7. gladly
   8. everyone

D. 1. Lions fierce, giraffes so tall,
      Monkeys climbing up the <u>wall</u>,
      Zebras, seals, and kangaroos—
      All these creatures live in <u>zoos</u>.

   2. God made the flowers that smell so <u>sweet</u>;
      He made the birds that sing and <u>tweet</u>.
      He looks upon His world so fair,
      And keeps us in His tender <u>care</u>.

Extra Activity

The descriptions, directions, letters, and poetry you wrote in this unit can be saved in a booklet. You may want to gather these materials together now and start making your booklet.

Work together with your teacher to decide the kind of paper you will use for the cover. Decide what kind of lettering you will use and what the title of the booklet will be. Decide what kind of design or picture you want to put on the cover. The pictures on this page may give you some ideas.

You may want to make title page divisions within the booklet. You could have a different title page for the work you did in each kind of writing.

At the beginning of the book, write the number of the year this book was made and the names of all the members of your class.

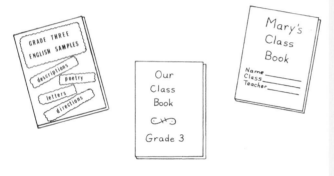

Extra Activity

Aim: To provide the pupils with an organized way of saving their English composition papers.

Class: Point out the value of keeping papers together instead of letting them be scattered around. Also tell the pupils that these booklets will be meaningful to them in later years. You may want to make a sample to give the pupils an idea of how to proceed with theirs.

This activity may be done by each student or as a class project.

A Poem to Enjoy

The Shepherd

The gentle shepherd loves his sheep;
    He watches lest they fall.
And if they wander from the fold,
    He answers when they call.

The heavenly Shepherd loves His sheep;
    He answers every prayer.
And day by day He watches us
    And gives us tender care.

Discussing the Poem

1. Which stanza speaks of an earthly shepherd?
2. Which stanza speaks of a heavenly Shepherd?
3. What adjective describes the earthly shepherd?
4. What three things does an earthly shepherd do for his sheep?
5. Which word names the place where the sheep are kept?
6. Which word means "walk away"?
7. Who is the heavenly Shepherd?
8. Who are His sheep?
9. How are the two shepherds alike?
10. Find the two pairs of rhyming words.

Answers to Discussion Questions

1. the first stanza
2. the second stanza
3. gentle
4. He loves his sheep. He watches lest they fall. He answers straying sheep when they call.
5. fold
6. wander
7. Jesus
8. People who follow Him.
9. Both shepherds love and care for their sheep.
10. fall—call; prayer—care

A Poem to Enjoy

Aim: To give practice in reading and enjoying poetry.

Class: Review rhyme, rhythm, and other concepts taught in the lessons on poetry. Have each pupil read the poem correctly, with good expression.

Name_____

Worksheet 1
Alphabetical Order

1. Put each list of names in alphabetical order.

a. Rome   _____Bethlehem_____

    Jerusalem _____Corinth_____

    Bethlehem _____Jerusalem_____

    Corinth _____Rome_____

    Samaria _____Samaria_____

d. Mahlon _____Mahlon_____

    Mark _____Malachi_____

    Manasseh _____Manasseh_____

    Matthew _____Mark_____

    Malachi _____Matthew_____

b. Zaham _____Zabad_____

    Zaphon _____Zacharias_____

    Zanoah _____Zaham_____

    Zabad _____Zanoah_____

    Zacharias _____Zaphon_____

e. Abishai _____Abiathar_____

    Abimelech _____Abigail_____

    Abigail _____Abijah_____

    Abiathar _____Abimelech_____

    Abijah _____Abishai_____

c. Jonah _____Jonadab_____

    Jonas _____Jonah_____

    Jonathan _____Jonan_____

    Jonadab _____Jonas_____

    Jonan _____Jonathan_____

f. Bethlehem _____Bethany_____

    Bethany _____Bethel_____

    Bethel _____Bethlehem_____

    Bethuel _____Bethphage_____

    Bethphage _____Bethuel_____

2. Read each pair of words. If they are in alphabetical order, write **yes** in the blank. If they are not in alphabetical order, write **no.**

__yes__ a. answer, apostle

__no__ b. clean, chute

__no__ c. descend, depend

__yes__ d. game, garden

__no__ e. leave, learn

__no__ f. monkey, money

__yes__ g. parable, paradise

__yes__ h. recent, recess

__no__ i. starling, starlight

__yes__ j. telegram, telegraph

Name_____   *(English 3, Lesson 4)*

Worksheet 2
Recognizing Sentences

1. Put a period at the end of each group of words that is a sentence. Do not put a period at the end if it is not a complete thought.

   a. Job loved God.   e. Some men stole his cattle.

   b. Lived in Uz   f. Burned up his sheep

   c. He had a big family.   g. His servants were

   d. Satan wanted Job to sin.   h. Job still did not sin.

2. Make a complete sentence from each group of words in number 1 that is not a complete thought.   (Individual answers for *b, f,* and *g.*)

   _____

   _____

   _____

3. The following paragraphs are hard to read because the sentences are run together. Divide them into proper sentences by putting a period at the end of each complete thought.

   God was pleased with Job. He gave Job more than he had before. Job had twice as much. God blesses those who obey Him. Jesus said that if we love Him, we will obey Him.

   God was not pleased with the people. He saw them building a tower. He confused their speech so that they could not understand one another. He caused the people to be scattered from each other.

   God was pleased with Noah. He told Noah to build an ark. He told him how big to make it. God sent a flood, but Noah and his family were safe inside the ark.

Name_____

Worksheet 3
Telling Sentences

1. Write **X** before each sentence that is written correctly.

   X   a. The Lord is my shepherd.

_____ b. let not your heart be troubled

_____ c. come unto me

_____ d. honour thy father and mother

   X   e. He is not here: for he is risen.

_____ f. the grace of our Lord Jesus Christ be with you all

_____ g. he that believeth on me hath everlasting life

   X   h. In the beginning God created the heaven and the earth.

_____ i. my son, if sinners entice thee, consent thou not

   X   j. God is our refuge and strength.

   X   k. God loveth a cheerful giver.

2. Some of these are sentences and some are not. Underline the complete sentences.

   a. <u>A blanket of snow covered the ground.</u>

   b. Many yellow daffodils.

   c. Busy robins and bluebirds.

   d. <u>Everyone was ready for spring.</u>

   e. The cheery, warm sun.

   f. <u>Soon the snow started to melt.</u>

   g. <u>By noon all the snow was gone.</u>

   h. New green grass.

   i. <u>Wrens were singing.</u>

   j. Buds on the trees.

Name_____   *(English 3, Lesson 7)*

Worksheet 4
Simple Subjects and Simple Predicates

1. Underline the two simple subjects or two simple predicates in each sentence. On the blank before the sentence, write **S** if you underlined subjects, or **P** if you underlined predicates.

    __S__   a. <u>Amos</u> and <u>Joel</u> were prophets of God.

    __S__   b. <u>Peas</u> and <u>corn</u> are vegetables.

    __P__   c. Mother <u>peeled</u> and <u>sliced</u> the apples.

    __S__   d. <u>Ducks</u> and <u>geese</u> swam in the streams.

    __P__   e. Jesus <u>taught</u> and <u>healed</u> the people.

    __P__   f. We <u>read</u> and <u>write</u> in school.

    __S__   g. <u>Richard</u> and <u>Thomas</u> were playing outside.

    __P__   h. Father <u>hammered</u> and <u>sawed</u> in the shop.

2. On each line write a sentence as the directions tell you.   (Individual answers.)

    a. One simple subject and one simple predicate.

    _____

    b. Two simple subjects and one simple predicate.

    _____

    c. One simple subject and two simple predicates.

    _____

3. Diagram these sentences.

    a. Paul prayed and worked.

    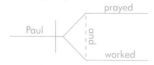

    b. Luke and Mark wrote.

    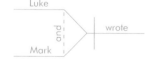

    c. Men and women worshiped.

    d. Jesus healed and taught.

Name_____

Worksheet 5
Asking Sentences

1. Write **A** before each asking sentence, and **T** before each telling sentence. Add the correct end punctuation to each sentence.

____T____ a. Saul was on his way to Damascus.

____A____ b. What did he want there?

____T____ c. A light shone around about him.

____A____ d. Where did the light come from?

____A____ e. What happened to Saul when he saw the light?

____A____ f. Where did the Lord tell him to go?

____T____ g. The light blinded Saul.

____T____ h. Ananias put his hands on Saul.

____T____ i. Saul was baptized.

____A____ j. What did Saul do in the synagogues?

2. Cross out each word that should begin with a capital letter, and write it correctly on the line before the sentence. Also add the correct end marks. The first sentence is done for you.

____The____ a. ~~the~~ big spider scurried across the floor.

____Did____ b. ~~did~~ you see the thick black smoke as you went by?

____Have____ c. ~~have~~ you noticed that a hummingbird can hold almost perfectly still in midair?

____A____ d. ~~a~~ bright flash of lightning zigzagged across the sky.

____How____ e. ~~how~~ do the birds know that they should fly south in the fall?

____The____ f. ~~the~~ hawk was gliding through the air.

____When____ g. ~~when~~ was the rabbit eating lettuce in your garden?

____Why____ h. ~~why~~ does the killdeer act as if its wing is broken?

____Two____ i. ~~two~~ busy squirrels were gathering nuts.

Worksheet 6
Subjects and Predicates in Asking Sentences

1. Underline the subjects once and the predicates twice. Each sentence has a verb phrase, so be sure to underline both verbs.

   a. Did Sarah laugh?

   b. Does Faith smile?

   c. Will Jay work?

   d. Can ice crack?

   e. Do bells ring?

   f. Could Jesus heal?

   g. May David play?

   h. Might wasps sting?

   i. Would Abraham go?

   j. Can wrens sing?

   k. Did Angela clean?

   l. Are bears furry?

   m. Have pupils worked?

   n. Could Paul write?

2. Diagram sentences **a** to **g** in number 1.

   a.

   | Sarah | Did laugh |

   e.

   | bells | Do ring |

   b.

   | Faith | Does smile |

   f.

   | Jesus | Could heal |

   c.

   | Jay | Will work |

   g.

   | David | May play |

   d.

   | ice | Can crack |

Name_____   *(English 3, Lesson 11)*

Worksheet 7
Commanding and Exclaiming Sentences

1. Write **C** before each commanding sentence, and **E** before each exclaiming sentence. Also add the correct end marks.

   __C__   a. Close the windows when it starts to rain.

   __C__   b. Pick up the paper from the floor.

   __E__   c. Mother, Michael cut his leg badly!

   __C__   d. Set the table with the good dishes.

   __E__   e. What a pleasant surprise it was!

   __C__   f. Get your Bibles.

   __C__   g. Wipe the dust off the dresser.

   __E__   h. The neighbor's barn is on fire!

2. Follow these directions for writing sentences.   (Possible answers.)

   a. Write a sentence that you might say if you were excited about receiving a letter in the mail.

   __I got a letter!_____

   _____

   b. Write a sentence that a father might say to his boys when it is time to get up.

   __Get up, boys._____

   _____

   c. Write a sentence that a doctor might say when he tells a sick man what to do.

   __Stay in bed and drink plenty of water._____

   _____

   d. Write a sentence that you might say if a bird came flying into your house.

   __There's a bird in the house!_____

   _____

Name_____   *(English 3, Lesson 12)*

Worksheet 8
Subjects and Predicates in Commanding Sentences

The simple subject of every command is **you.** In the Bible, **thou** or **ye** are often used for **you.**

1. Underline each simple subject that is given. If the subject is not given, write a subject on the blank before the sentence and put parentheses around it. The first two are done for you.

_____ a. Come <u>ye</u> to the waters. (Isaiah 55:1)

_____(you)_____ b. <u>Sing</u> unto the Lord. (Psalm 96:2)

_____ c. Praise <u>ye</u> the Lord. (Psalm 148:1)

_____(you)_____ d. <u>Obey</u> them that have the rule over you. (Hebrews 13:17)

_____(you)_____ e. <u>Have</u> faith in God. (Mark 11:22)

_____ f. <u>Be</u> <u>ye</u> doers of the word. (James 1:22)

_____(you)_____ g. <u>Pray</u> without ceasing. (1 Thessalonians 5:17)

_____(you)_____ h. <u>Follow</u> peace with all men. (Hebrews 12:14)

2. In number 1 above, draw two lines under the simple predicate of each command.

3. Diagram the simple subject and simple predicate of each sentence. If the simple subject is understood, put parentheses around it.

   a. Be careful with that hammer.

   (you) | Be

   d. Wash all the windows.

   (you) | Wash

   b. Write your name on your paper.

   (you) | Write

   e. You and Leon mow the lawn.

   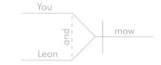

   c. You read the verse.

   You | read

Name_____   *(English 3, Lesson 15)*

Worksheet 9
Names and Initials

Write correctly all the names in these paragraphs. The first one is started for you.

Paragraph 1

The first president of the United States was george washington. His father's name was augustine washington. geroge married martha d custis. One night he awakened martha because he was sick. They sent for his friend james craik, who was a doctor, but george did not get better. He died that day.

George Washington, Augustine Washington, George, Martha D. Custis, Martha,

James Craik, George

Paragraph 2

The fifth president's name was james monroe. His father's name was spence and his mother's name was elizabeth. james took lessons at home until he was twelve years old. When he grew up, he married elizabeth kortright. Their two girls were named eliza and maria.

James Monroe, Spence, Elizabeth, James, Elizabeth Kortright, Eliza, Maria

Paragraph 3

millard fillmore was the thirteenth president. His parents' names were nathaniel and phoebe. They had nine children. His father owned two books. They were a Bible and a hymnbook. millard's wife was abigail powers. They had two children named millard p fillmore and mary a fillmore.

Millard Fillmore, Nathaniel, Phoebe, Millard's, Abigail Powers, Millard P. Fillmore,

Mary A. Fillmore

Name_____   *(English 3, Lesson 16)*

Worksheet 10
Quotation Marks

1. Answer the following questions about this sentence.

    God called from the burning bush, "Moses, Moses."

    a. Who was speaking in this sentence? _____God_____

    b. What are the exact words of the speaker? _____Moses, Moses_____

    c. Why are quotation marks used in the sentence? _____

    ____They are used to show the exact words of the speaker._____

2. Place quotation marks in these sentences wherever they are needed.

    Moses turned to see the bush that was burning. When God called to him, Moses answered, "Here am I."

    God said, "Do not come near. I have seen the hard things that My people are suffering. I will send you to bring them out of Egypt."

    Moses answered, "Who am I?" He thought he was not able to bring the people out of Egypt.

    But God said, "I will be with you."

    Moses was still afraid to go. He said, "I cannot talk well enough."

    God asked him, "Who made man's mouth? Have not I?"

    God sent Aaron, Moses' brother, to go with Moses and speak for him. Moses and Aaron went and talked to the children of Israel and to the king of Egypt.

3. Write two sentences using quotation marks.   (Individual answers.)

    a. _____

    _____

    b. _____

    _____

Name_____

Worksheet 11
Capitalization in Quotations

1. In each sentence, underline one word that should be capitalized.

   a. Brother James announced, "<u>today</u> is the day for the hike."

   b. "<u>oh</u>, good!" cried all the children.

   c. Martha asked, "<u>where</u> are we going?"

   d. "<u>are</u> we taking our lunches along?" asked Marlin.

   e. "<u>how</u> long will we stay?" Rhoda asked.

   f. Richard asked, "<u>will</u> we see any squirrels?"

   g. Brother James laughed and said, "<u>please</u> do not ask so many questions at once."

   h. Brother James told them, "<u>we</u> will start at ten o'clock."

   i. "<u>we</u> will eat our lunches in the woods," he said.

   j. "<u>do</u> not leave any bags or papers lying around," he reminded the class.

   k. He continued, "<u>by</u> two o'clock we should be back at school."

   l. Brother James instructed, "<u>remember</u> to stay together in one group."

   m. At ten o'clock he said, "<u>we</u> will go quietly now."

2. Put quotation marks where they belong in these sentences.

   a. "Where is Abel thy brother?" God asked Cain.

   b. Cain said, "I know not."

   c. "Make thee an ark of gopher wood," God said to Noah.

   d. The angels said to Lot, "Escape for thy life."

   e. "Where is the lamb for a burnt offering?" Isaac asked Abraham.

   f. Joseph asked Pharaoh's officers, "Why do you look so sad?"

   g. Saul said, "The people spared the best of the sheep and oxen."

   h. Elijah said to Elisha, "Ask what I shall do for thee."

Name_____   *(English 3, Lesson 18)*

Worksheet 12
End Marks in Quotations

1. Add the correct marks to these sentences.

   a. "What a beautiful rainbow!" exclaimed Mother.

   b. "Did you know God made the rainbow?" she asked.

   c. "I know He made the rainbow," said John.

   d. "He made the first rainbow after Noah came out of the ark," said Gladys.

   e. "Where does the rainbow end?" asked little Katie.

   f. "There is another rainbow!" exclaimed John.

   g. "Do you think Father sees the rainbows?" asked Mother.

   h. "Do you think Grandmother sees them?" asked Katie.

2. Put quotation marks where they belong in this story.

   "Mother, look! See what we found!" exclaimed Leon and Lily. Two pairs of bright brown eyes sparkled with excitement.

   Mother looked at the tiny bird Leon was holding. It sat quietly on his hand and looked up at them with bright little eyes.

   "Isn't it a pretty little bird, Mother?" Lily stroked it very gently with her finger.

   "A tiny hummingbird!" breathed Mother softly. "Where did you find it?" she asked.

   "Out on the lane," Lily answered.

   Leon said, "It must have fallen out of its nest. I think it's too little to fly. Can we feed it, Mother, till it grows big enough to fly?"

   "What will it eat?" Lily wondered. Then she asked, "Shall I catch a bug?"

   "Hummingbirds drink nectar out of flowers," Mother explained.

Name_____   *(English 3, Lesson 22)*

Worksheet 13
Capitalization

1. Cross out each word that needs a capital letter, and write it correctly on the line below the sentence.

   a. the names of ~~jacob's~~ wives were ~~rachel~~ and ~~leah~~.

   Jacob's, Rachel, Leah

   b. ~~lazarus~~ was the brother of ~~mary~~ and ~~martha~~.

   Lazarus, Mary, Martha

   c. Two of ~~joseph's~~ brothers were ~~reuben~~ and ~~levi~~.

   Joseph's, Reuben, Levi

   d. Jesus called ~~simon~~ and ~~andrew~~.

   Simon, Andrew

   e. God sent ~~moses~~ and ~~aaron~~ to Pharaoh.

   Moses, Aaron

   f. The king held out his scepter to ~~esther~~.

   Esther

   g. The sons of ~~noah~~ were ~~shem~~, ~~ham~~, and ~~japheth~~.

   Noah, Shem, Ham, Japheth

   h. ~~paul~~ wrote letters to ~~titus~~ and ~~timothy~~.

   Paul, Titus, Timothy

   i. The rulers arrested ~~peter~~ and ~~john~~.

   Peter, John

(Individual answers.)

2. After each name, write one more name that begins with the same letter.

   a. Luke _____   d. James _____

   b. Mary _____   e. Betty _____

   c. Smith _____   f. Hart _____

Name_____   *(English 3, Lesson 23)*

Worksheet 14
Punctuation

1. Write the correct letter to match each description.

   c   Used after a sentence that shows strong feeling.   a. period

   a   Used after a telling sentence.   b. quotation marks

   e   Used with **s** to show ownership.   c. exclamation mark

   d   Used after an asking sentence.   d. question mark

   b   Used to show a speaker's exact words.   e. apostrophe

2. If a sentence has a mistake, add the missing punctuation mark. If it is correct, write **X** in front of the sentence.

       a. Isn't that a wonderful rain?

       b. Jesus said, "Come unto me."

  X   c. Mary attended school every day.

       d. "We visited the zoo yesterday," said Alan.

  X   e. Oh, look at all the flowers!

  X   f. Where did Mother get that lovely dish?

       g. John's food was locusts and wild honey.

  X   h. "We won't have school tomorrow," said the teacher.

       i. "Marie fell off the swing!" cried Linda.

3. Put quotation marks where they are needed in these sentences.

a. Father said, "It is a beautiful day."

b. "Let's have a picnic," said Mother.

4. Add quotation marks and the correct end marks to these sentences.

a. The children shouted, "The ball went down the chimney!"

b. Thomas asked, "How can we get it out?"

Name_____

Worksheet 15
Spelling Correctly

Use a dictionary if you need help with these exercises.

1. Write **yes** or **no** to tell whether the words for these numbers are spelled correctly.

   __yes__ a. 20 twenty   __no__ e. 50 fivty

   __no__ b. 19 ninteen   __yes__ f. 90 ninety

   __no__ c. 40 fourty   __no__ g. 18 eightteen

   __yes__ d. 13 thirteen   __yes__ h. 12 twelve

2. Write the plural form of each word.

   a. pony   ponies   e. foot   feet

   b. loaf   loaves   f. bush   bushels

   c. mouse   mice   g. knife   knives

   d. fly   flies   h. match   matches

3. Write the correct letter in each blank.

   a. We rec*e**i*ve instructions from the Bible.

   b. Mark caught his foot in the bi*c*y*c*le wheel.

   c. An ang*e*l told the shepherds that Jesus was born.

   d. We try to be qui*e*t when Mother is resting.

   e. After we had no rain for a month, the ground was qui*t*e dry.

   f. Jonathan and David were good fri*e*nds.

4. Write the past form of each word.

   a. know   knew (known)   e. go   went (gone)

   b. bring   brought   f. ride   rode (ridden)

   c. leave   left   g. sing   sang (sung)

   d. see   saw (seen)   h. buy   bought

Name_____   (English 3, Lesson 26)

Worksheet 16
Nouns

1. In each column, cross out the two words that are not nouns.

a. umbrella	b. chalk	c. lamb	d. truck
tulip	candle	wood	turtle
~~bright~~	cheese	~~pretty~~	basket
napkin	~~throw~~	garden	~~also~~
~~build~~	~~about~~	~~suddenly~~	envelope
deer	tower	boat	~~after~~

2. Write whether each noun names a **person,** a **place,** or a **thing.**

   a. church _____place_____   g. snow _____thing_____

   b. doctor _____person_____   h. school _____place_____

   c. mother _____person_____   i. girl _____person_____

   d. apple _____thing_____   j. flower _____thing_____

   e. home _____place_____   k. airport _____place_____

   f. uncle _____person_____   l. teacher _____person_____

3. Underline the nouns in these verses. The numbers in parentheses show how many nouns there are.

   a. Also he sent forth a <u>dove</u> from him, to see if the <u>waters</u> were abated from off the <u>face</u> of the <u>ground</u>. (4)

   b. And I saw another mighty <u>angel</u> come down from <u>heaven</u>. (2)

   c. <u>Children</u>, obey your <u>parents</u>. (2)

   d. Then he took the five <u>loaves</u> and the two <u>fishes</u>. (2)

   e. When the <u>morning</u> was now come, <u>Jesus</u> stood on the <u>shore</u>. (3)

Name_____   *(English 3, Lesson 27)*

Worksheet 17
Proper Nouns

1. Write **C** before each common noun and **P** before each proper noun. Write each proper noun correctly.

_C_	a. flower	_____	_P_	i. canada	_Canada_
_P_	b. mexico	_Mexico_	_C_	j. sparrow	_____
_P_	c. chicago	_Chicago_	_P_	k. andrew	_Andrew_
_C_	d. church	_____	_P_	l. lake erie	_Lake Erie_
_C_	e. city	_____	_C_	m. morning	_____
_P_	f. idaho	_Idaho_	_P_	n. joanna	_Joanna_
_C_	g. minister	_____	_P_	o. arctic ocean	_Arctic Ocean_
_P_	h. canaan	_Canaan_	_P_	p. ohio river	_Ohio River_

2. Use two of the proper nouns above in sentences of your own.   (Individual answers.)

_____

_____

3. The nouns in these sentences are in bold print. Write **C** above each common noun and **P** above each proper noun.

     P   P   C

  a. **David** killed **goliath** with a **stone.**   _____ _Goliath_ _____

             P   P   C

  b. Young **samuel** helped **Eli** in the **tabernacle.**   _____ _Samuel_ _____

     P   C   C   P

  c. **Jesus** healed a **man** in the **synagogue** at **capernaum.** _Capernaum_

           P   C

  d. In **jerusalem** was a **market.**   _____ _Jerusalem_ _____

     P   P   C   C

  e. **Mary** and **Martha** lived in the **town** of **bethany.**   _Bethany_

     P   P   C   P

  f. **Peter** went to **Caesarea** to the **home** of **cornelius.**   _Cornelius_

4. In number 3 above, one proper noun in each sentence has a mistake. Write that noun correctly in the blank after the sentence.

Name_____   *(English 3, Lesson 28)*

Worksheet 18
More Proper Nouns

1. Write a proper noun for each common noun.   (Individual answers.)

   a. country _____   i. weekday _____

   b. girl _____   j. holiday _____

   c. last name _____   k. state _____

   d. boy _____   l. street _____

   e. disciple _____   m. king _____

   f. teacher _____   n. ocean _____

   g. town _____   g. town _____

   h. month _____   n. ocean _____

2. Fill each blank in these sentences with a proper noun. (Individual answers for letters *a–g.*)

   a. My cousins live in the state (or province) of _____.

   b. The first minister who preached was _____.

   c. They named their baby _____.

   d. On their way to _____, the missionaries sailed across the

      _____.

   e. I live in the state (or province) of _____.

   f. A town near my home is _____.

   g. My birthday is in the month of _____.

   h. Jesus was born in _____Bethlehem_____.

   i. _____Moses_____ and _____Aaron (*or* Joshua)_____ led the children of Israel.

   j. The garden of Eden was the home of _____Adam_____ and _____Eve_____.

Name_____

Worksheet 19
Other Proper Nouns

1. In these sentences, underline each word that is not written correctly. If a sentence has no mistake, put **X** in the blank.

_____ a. A visitor came to <u>calvary christian school</u>.

_____ b. I would like to buy the book called <u>caterpillar green</u>.

_____ c. Elmer named his new dog <u>brownie</u>.

_____ d. We visited the <u>mountain view church</u>.

__X__ e. The children were happy when Jason came home.

_____ f. We parked in front of the <u>jefferson building</u>.

_____ g. Jacob wanted a horse named <u>pete</u>.

__X__ h. Sister Ann has taught at Greenville School for six years.

_____ i. The rabbit named <u>snowball</u> got out of the pen.

_____ j. Michelle got a pretty card from <u>aunt rachel</u>.

2. In each sentence, cross out one capital letter that should be a small letter.

a. Aunt Sarah gave us a pretty Flower in a flowerpot.

b. Our pet Tweety has a new Cage.

c. We got this arrowhead on our Trip to Alaska.

d. Dr. Patrick gave Caleb some balloons and Candy.

e. Please get me a Bible and a Dictionary from the shelf.

f. My cousin Susan gave me a dish for my Birthday.

g. Jenny saw lions and tigers at the Zoo in Pittsburgh.

h. On Tuesday we painted the floor of the Kitchen.

i. A Farmer from Texas bought our property.

j. Saul met the Lord on the Road to Damascus.

Name_____   *(English 3, Lesson 31)*

Worksheet 20
Singular and Plural Nouns

1. Write correctly each plural form that is not correct. If a form is correct, just copy it.

   a. blocks _____blocks_____   g. turkies _____turkeys_____

   b. bunnys _____bunnies_____   h. trees _____trees_____

   c. chairs _____chairs_____   i. flowers _____flowers_____

   d. monkies _____monkeys_____   j. countrys _____countries_____

   e. flys _____flies_____   k. toys _____toys_____

   f. plants _____plants_____   l. cookies _____cookies_____

2. Show the singular or plural forms by filling in the missing words.

Singular	Plural	Singular	Plural
a. day	days	f. match	matches
b. lady	ladies	g. glass	glasses
c. pony	ponies	h. boy	boys
d. berry	berries	i. baby	babies
e. broom	brooms	j. daisy	daisies

3. Rewrite each phrase. Change the noun in bold print to its plural form.

   a. the old **cross** _____the old crosses_____

   b. the little blue **dress** _____the little blue dresses_____

   c. the English **class** _____the English classes_____

   d. the pleasant **porch** _____the pleasant porches_____

   e. Mother's good **dish** _____Mother's good dishes_____

   f. their soft **couch** _____their soft couches_____

   g. our delicious **lunch** _____our delicious lunches_____

   h. the low green **bush** _____the low green bushes_____

Name_____   *(English 3, Lesson 32)*

Worksheet 21
Plural Nouns and Possessive Nouns

1. Read each sentence. If the noun in bold print has a mistake, write it correctly in the blank before the sentence. If it is correct, write **X** in the blank.

_____X_____ a. We sang three **hymns.**

_____aunt's_____ b. My **aunts** house is blue.

_____disciples_____ c. Jesus sent two **disciple's** into a village.

_____donkey's_____ d. The Lord opened the **donkeys** mouth, and it spoke to Balaam.

_____X_____ e. Many **trees** covered the hillside.

_____boy's_____ f. Jesus used a **boys** lunch to feed the multitude.

_____Bears_____ g. **Bear's** sleep through the winter.

_____X_____ h. Jonah was in the **whale's** belly.

_____rabbit's_____ i. A **rabbits** ears are long.

_____X_____ j. The children have new **Bibles.**

_____barn's_____ k. The **barns** paint is peeling off.

2. Write the plural form of each noun in the first blank, and the possessive form in the second blank.

a. robin _____robins_____ _____robin's_____

b. animal _____animals_____ _____animal's_____

c. father _____fathers_____ _____father's_____

d. fox _____foxes_____ _____fox's_____

e. monkey _____monkeys_____ _____monkey's_____

f. visitor _____visitors_____ _____visitor's_____

g. baby _____babies_____ _____baby's_____

h. girl _____girls_____ _____girl's_____

Name_____   *(English 3, Lesson 33)*

Worksheet 22
Plural Nouns Not Ending With *s*

1. Write the correct plural form of each noun.

   a. man   _____men_____   f. ox   _____oxen_____

   b. sheep _____sheep_____   g. deer   _____deer_____

   c. child _____children____   h. woman _____women_____

   d. tooth _____teeth_____   i. foot   _____feet_____

   e. mouse _____mice_____   j. goose _____geese_____

2. Write three singular nouns. Then write their plural forms.   (Individual answers.)

   a. _____   _____

   b. _____   _____

   c. _____   _____

3. In the blank before each sentence, write the correct plural form of the noun in parentheses.

   ____sheep____   a. A flock of (sheep) was grazing on the hillside.

   ____men_____   b. The (man) patched the road in front of our house.

   ____feet_____   c. My new shoes hurt my (foot).

   ___matches___   d. Do not play with (match).

   ___children__   e. The (child) played quietly.

   ____oxen_____   f. Long ago (ox) were used for plowing.

   ___chimneys__   g. That house has two (chimney).

   ____teeth____   h. After dinner I brushed my (tooth).

   ____mice_____   i. The (mouse) got into the house through a tiny hole under the door.

   ____spies____   j. Twelve (spy) searched the land of Canaan.

   ____deer_____   k. Moose, elk, and caribou are (deer).

Name_____

Worksheet 23
Words in a Series

1. Add commas where they are needed in these sentences.

   a. Rubber is used to make erasers, boots, combs, and other things.

   b. Bananas, coffee, and cotton are raised in Africa.

   c. Herons eat fish, frogs, crayfish, and other small animals.

   d. The hippopotamus eats fruit, grass, leaves, and vegetables.

   e. The robin, the catbird, and the hermit thrush lay blue eggs.

   f. Gas, limestone, and coal are taken out of the ground in Indiana.

   g. Monkeys eat birds, flowers, roots, and other things.

   h. Pine, spruce, and redwood are three kinds of needle-leaf trees.

   i. Bumblebees, wasps, and ants are insects.

   j. Angel Falls, Niagara Falls, and Ribbon Falls are famous waterfalls of the world.

2. Complete each sentence with nouns in a series.   (Individual answers.)

   a. Three of my favorite foods are _____

   _____

   b. Four books of the Bible are _____

   _____

   c. Three things in the kitchen are _____

   _____

Name_____   *(English 3, Lesson 36)*

Worksheet 24
The Work of Pronouns

1. Underline the best pronoun to use instead of each noun.

   a. cat (I, <u>it</u>)   d. sister (he, <u>she</u>)

   b. pencil (she, <u>it</u>)   e. book (<u>it</u>, they)

   c. man (<u>he</u>, she)   f. John's (he, <u>his</u>)

2. Write a list of singular and plural nouns. Beside each noun, write a pronoun to take its place. The list is started for you.   (Remaining answers will vary.)

Noun	Pronoun		Noun	Pronoun
a. <u>block</u>	<u>it</u>	f. _____		_____
b. <u>children</u>	<u>they</u>	g. _____		_____
c. <u>Father</u>	<u>he *or* him</u>	h. _____		_____
d. _____	_____	i. _____		_____

3. Complete each sentence with a pronoun that stands for the noun in bold print.

   a. The **girls** said, "_____We_____ are going for a walk."

   b. **Alice** said that _____she_____ did not feel well.

   c. The **boys** were tired because _____they_____ had put away all the hay.

   d. **"Jane,** I want to talk with _____you_____," said the teacher.

   e. **Thomas** smiled when _____he_____ saw the puppy wagging its tail.

   f. The **nurse** said, "_____I_____ will bring you some medicine."

Name_____   *(English 3, Lesson 38)*

Worksheet 25
Pronouns That Tell *Whom*

1. On the line before each sentence, write whether the pronoun in bold print tells **who** or **whom.**

_____who_____ a. **I** played with Robert.

_____whom_____ b. Mary gave the motto to **me.**

_____who_____ c. **He** saw the robin building her nest.

_____who_____ d. **She** made supper for the girls.

_____whom_____ e. I told **him** the news.

_____whom_____ f. Mother talked to **her** on the telephone.

2. These sentences change the meanings of the sentences above. Underline the correct pronoun in each one.

a. Robert played with (I, <u>me</u>).

b. (<u>I</u>, Me) gave the motto to Mary.

c. The robin saw (he, <u>him</u>) under the tree.

d. The girls made supper for (she, <u>her</u>).

e. (<u>He</u>, Him) told me the news.

f. (<u>She</u>, Her) talked to Mother on the telephone.

3. In the blank before each sentence, write the correct pronoun to replace the word or phrase in bold print.

_____her_____ a. Mother said that the pitcher was given to **Mother.**

_____he_____ b. Peter told the teacher that **Peter** had broken the window.

_____me_____ c. Donald said, "Please give the pencil to **Donald.**"

_____them_____ d. The children were happy with the surprise Mother made for **the children.**

_____she_____ e. Martha did not go along because **Martha** was feeling sick.

Name_____   *(English 3, Lesson 41)*

Worksheet 26
Using a Noun and a Pronoun Together

1. Underline the correct pronoun in parentheses.

   a. David and (<u>he</u>, him) hid behind the barn.

   b. Martha and (<u>she</u>, her) welcomed Jesus into their home.

   c. Mother and (me, <u>I</u>) worked in the garden.

   d. Jesus ate with Peter and (they, <u>them</u>).

   e. My cousins and (me, <u>I</u>) played together.

   f. (<u>She</u>, Her) and Salome walked to Jesus' tomb.

   g. Aunt Emma and (<u>we</u>, us) went on a trip.

   h. The baby smiled at Nancy and (I, <u>me</u>).

   i. (<u>They</u>, Them) and the Pharisees tried to find fault with Jesus.

   j. Mother made dolls for Grace and (<u>her</u>, she).

2. Choose one pronoun in each pair and use it correctly with a noun in a sentence.

   Example: she, her

   Answer: The surprise was for Rhoda and her.

   a. he, him   (Individual answers.)

   _____

   b. they, them

   _____

   c. she, her

   _____

   d. I, me

   _____

Name_____

Worksheet 27
Commas With Nouns and Pronouns

1. Put commas where they belong in these sentences.

   a. Mother, Father, Barbara, and I went for a walk.

   b. Mother talked to Leah, Doris, and me.

   c. Please help Thomas, David, and us.

   d. Grandfather, Grandmother, Uncle Nathan, and we had a picnic.

   e. Paul, Nathanael, and I are in the third grade.

   f. The Yoders, the Schrocks, and we are invited to the wedding.

   g. Eleanor, Nancy, and I watched the beautiful sunrise.

   h. Mother said that Miriam, Rhoda, and I may have a little garden.

2. Follow the directions for writing sentences of your own.   (Individual answers.)

   a. Use two nouns and one pronoun in a series.

   _____

   b. Use three nouns and one pronoun in a series.

   _____

3. Write **X** before each sentence that is written correctly.

   __X__ a. Barbara, Mary, and I unpacked the dishes.

   __X__ b. She and Eunice are related to Timothy.

   _____ c. Merlin Mark and I looked at a book.

   _____ d. Father Mother and us like to read.

   __X__ e. Larry, John, and I watched the hummingbirds.

   _____ f. Her, Betsy, and Joanna made dinner.

   _____ g. Mervin, Jonathan, and me have green bicycles.

   __X__ h. Rebecca, Lois, Mary, and I wrote letters.

   _____ i. Ralph Catherine and I walked to school.

Name_____   *(English 3, Lesson 43)*

Worksheet 28
More About Commas

1. Put commas where they belong in these sentences.

   a. Anna, is this your handkerchief?

   b. Father and Mother, may we look at the new book?

   c. Harry, here are your shoes.

   d. Leon and Melvin, you may sweep the porch.

   e. Beth, please get the baby.

   f. Lloyd, please open the window.

   g. Mildred, you may pass the wastepaper can.

   h. Timothy and Lewis, pick up the toys.

   i. Boys, it is time to have devotions.

2. Cross out the commas that are not needed in these sentences.

   a. Dale, you, should let Jonathan, have that book.

   b. Robert, and Rodney, are these your pencils?

   c. Marie, do you know if Ida, and Katie, will be coming?

   d. John, please help Lester, with his boots.

   e. Boys, and girls, I, have a surprise for you today.

3. Put an **X** before each sentence that is written correctly.

   __X__ a. Lord, I will follow thee whithersoever thou goest.

   _____   Lord I will follow thee whithersoever thou goest.

   _____ b. Mother may we have some cookies please?

   __X__   Mother, may we have some cookies please?

   __X__ c. Brother John, here are the screws you ordered.

   _____   Brother John, here are the screws, you ordered.

Name_____   *(English 3, Lesson 44)*

Worksheet 29
Using Pronouns Correctly

1. Cross out the unnecessary words in these sentences.

   a. Lazarus ~~he~~ died.

   b. Jesus ~~He~~ went to raise Lazarus from the dead.

   c. Martha ~~she~~ went to meet Him.

   d. The people ~~they~~ went to the place where Lazarus was buried.

   e. Martha ~~she~~ said Lazarus would rise at the last day.

   f. Mary ~~she~~ came to Jesus when Martha called her.

   g. Jesus ~~He~~ wept when He saw the other people weeping.

   h. Jesus ~~He~~ called Lazarus to come forth.

   i. Lazarus ~~he~~ rose from the dead.

2. In the second sentence of each pair, write the correct pronoun to take the place of the words in bold print in the first sentence.

   a. I got the **Bible** for my birthday.

      I read _____it_____ every day.

   b. **Thomas and Titus** are twins.

      _____They_____ look very much alike.

   c. **The repairman** fixed the pump.

      Then _____he_____ checked the water heater.

   d. **The old people** enjoyed our singing.

      _____They_____ said we should come again.

   e. **Betty** fed **the dog.**

      _____She_____ played with ____it, him, or her____ in the yard.

   f. I talked to **Uncle Joe and Aunt Lena.**

      I told _____them_____ about our trip.

Name_____   *(English 3, Lesson 46)*

Worksheet 30
Possessive Pronouns

1. In each sentence, cross out one or two words that are incorrect. Write those words correctly on the line below the sentence.

    a. ~~Her's~~ is blue and ~~your's~~ is green.

    __Hers, yours_____

    b. The barn with the green roof is ~~our's~~.

    __ours_____

    c. Both of the pencils are ~~my'ne~~, but the pen is ~~Alberts~~.

    __mine, Albert's_____

    d. The house on top of the hill is ~~their's~~.

    __theirs_____

    e. The brown pony is ~~his's~~ and the black one is ~~Marys~~.

    __his, Mary's_____

    f. Is this coat ~~your's~~?

    __yours_____

2. Use each pronoun in a sentence of your own.   (Individual answers.)

    a. theirs _____

    b. his _____

    c. yours _____

    d. mine _____

    e. ours _____

    f. hers _____

Name_____

Worksheet 31
Correcting Poor Speech Habits

1. Cross out the wrong word or phrase in each sentence, and write the correct word in the blank before the sentence. The first one is done for you.

<u>   This   </u>   a. ~~This here~~ is a sweet-smelling lily.

<u>   That   </u>   b. ~~That there~~ is a new fence.

<u> Those *or* They </u>   c. ~~Them~~ look like storm clouds.

<u>   that   </u>   d. This grass is taller than ~~that there~~.

<u>Those, They, *or* These</u>   e. ~~Them~~ are the plants we watered.

<u>   these   </u>   f. Apple pies are sweeter than ~~these here~~.

<u>   this   </u>   g. Is ~~this here~~ the chair that belonged to Grandmother?

<u>   Those   </u>   h. ~~Those there~~ are the books we bought at a sale.

2. Rewrite sentences **a, b, f,** and **h** in number 1, changing the pronouns so that the meaning is different. Be sure to use the pronouns correctly. The first one is done for you.

a. (farther) <u> That is a sweet-smelling lily. </u>

b. (nearby) <u> This is a new fence. </u>

f. (farther) <u> Apple pies are sweeter than those. </u>

h. (nearby) <u> These are the books we bought at a sale. </u>

3. Cross out the unnecessary words in these sentences.

a. This ~~here~~ is a yellow delicious apple.

b. That ~~there~~ is a different kind of apple.

c. The plants we set out last week are these ~~here~~.

d. Those ~~there~~ are the trees with dark green leaves.

e. Is this ~~here~~ the cake you baked today?

f. These ~~here~~ are the kittens we found beside the road.

g. That ~~there~~ is the motto we bought.

Name_____   *(English 3, Lesson 51)*

Worksheet 32
Action Verbs

1. Write **verb** beside the words that are action verbs.

_____	a. moonlight	____verb____	g. run
____verb____	b. pour	_____	h. beautiful
_____	c. beside	_____	i. sweater
____verb____	d. kick	____verb____	j. throw
____verb____	e. cut	____verb____	k. play
_____	f. paper	_____	l. dinner

2. Underline the verbs in these sentences.

   a. Cornelius <u>prayed</u> to God.

   b. Dorcas <u>made</u> clothes.

   c. Noah <u>build</u> the ark.

   d. Abel <u>brought</u> an offering.

   e. Nicodemus <u>asked</u> questions.

   f. Ruth <u>gathered</u> grain.

3. Write an action verb on each line to tell what the subject does or did. (Individual answers.)

   a. Farmers _____.   h. Children _____.

   b. Horses _____.   i. Ministers _____.

   c. Fish _____.   j. Raindrops _____.

   d. Nurses _____.   k. Hummingbirds _____.

   e. Plants _____.   l. Mothers _____.

   f. Boys _____.   m. Carpenters _____.

   g. Bees _____.   n. Clocks _____.

Name_____

Worksheet 33
Past Forms of Verbs Without *ed*

1. Write the past form of each verb.

   a. fly _____flew_____   f. bring _____brought_____

   b. ride _____rode_____   g. come _____came_____

   c. write _____wrote_____   h. go _____went_____

   d. think _____thought_____   i. see _____saw_____

   e. eat _____ate_____   j. throw _____threw_____

2. Write the correct past form of each verb in parentheses.

   _____blew_____ a. The wind (blow) all night.

   _____drove_____ b. Father (drive) the car into the garage.

   _____caught_____ c. The mouse was (catch) in the trap.

   _____ran_____ d. The horses turned and (run) away.

   _____told_____ e. Grandfather (tell) us a good story about long ago.

3. Underline the correct verb in each sentence. If the verb you underlined is the past form, write **past** after the sentence.

   a. Last week we (come, <u>came</u>) home from our trip. _____past_____

   b. The children will (<u>sing</u>, sang) three songs. _____

   c. The robin (bring, <u>brought</u>) some food for her babies. _____past_____

   d. Yellow leaves (fall, <u>fell</u>) to the ground last night. _____past_____

   e. I hope we will (<u>go</u>, went) to the zoo. _____

   f. Aunt Emma (leave, <u>left</u>) her coat here. _____past_____

Name_____   *(English 3, Lesson 56)*

Worksheet 34
Singular and Plural With Verbs

1. Underline the verb in each sentence. In the blank before the sentence, write **yes** if the form is correct for that sentence, or **no** if the form is not correct.

       Examples: ___yes___ The shepherd <u>watches</u> the sheep.

              ___no___ The baby <u>play</u> happily.

___yes___ a. Helicopters <u>make</u> much noise.

___no___ b. Bright flowers <u>blooms</u> in Grandmother's garden.

___yes___ c. Hummingbirds <u>build</u> tiny nests.

___no___ d. Men <u>harvests</u> the crops.

___yes___ e. Crickets <u>chirp</u> in the summertime.

___no___ f. Our teacher <u>teach</u> us how to spell.

___yes___ g. The mailman <u>brings</u> mail to the mailbox.

___yes___ h. The painter <u>paints</u> buildings.

2. In each blank write the correct form of the verb in bold print. Use the present form or the **s** form.

   a. **bake**   My sisters _____bake_____ cookies almost every week.

   b. **walk**   Grandfather _____walks_____ with a cane.

   c. **read**   We _____read_____ the Bible every morning.

   d. **study**   Gerald _____studies_____ well before tests.

   e. **watch**   God _____watches_____ over us all the time.

   f. **build**   A bobolink _____builds_____ a nest of grass and weeds.

3. Write a subject to go with each predicate.   (Individual answers.)

   a. _____ sails.   e. _____ whistles.

   d. _____ roar.   c. _____ climbs.

   b. _____ blink.   f. _____ crawls.

Name_____

Worksheet 35
Using Verbs With *There*

1. Write **X** before each correct sentence.

___X___ a. There were two thieves crucified with Jesus.

___X___ b. There was some glass on the floor.

_____ c. There was several crows sitting on the fence.

___X___ d. There is a big turtle in our pond.

_____ e. There are a firefly in the room.

_____ f. There is some eggs in the nest.

___X___ g. There are two maple trees in our lawn.

_____ h. There was two broken windows in the barn.

_____ i. There is some people walking up the drive.

_____ j. There was some fishermen mending their nets.

2. Five of these sentences have mistakes. Write them correctly on the lines below.

a. There was some baby ducks on our pond.

b. There was two people hurt in the accident.

c. There were twelve boys in Jacob's family.

d. There was twelve disciples who followed Jesus.

e. There is many apples on that tree.

f. There are many different languages in the world.

g. There was six children in third grade last year.

h. There was a piece of pie on each plate.

(a) There were some baby ducks on our pond._____

(b) There were two people hurt in the accident._____

(d) There were twelve disciples who followed Jesus._____

(e) There are many apples on that tree._____

(g) There were six children in third grade last year._____

Name_____   *(English 3, Lesson 61)*

Worksheet 36
Helping Verbs

1. Underline each verb phrase. Draw another line under each helping verb.

   a. Kathy <u>has done</u> her lesson.

   b. Nathan <u>has gone</u> to church already.

   c. That chickadee <u>has come</u> to the bird feeder five times.

   d. All the people <u>have eaten</u>.

   e. Mother <u>had seen</u> her cousin only once.

   f. The girls <u>had taken</u> the dolls outside.

2. Underline the correct verb form in each sentence. Also underline the helping verb if there is one.

   a. Carol (<u>went</u>, gone) to the house for a drink.

   b. Charles <u>has</u> (did, <u>done</u>) that job before.

   c. The Hoovers <u>have</u> (<u>gone</u>, went) on a trip.

   d. The cows <u>had</u> (<u>eaten</u>, ate) all the hay.

   e. The children (<u>saw</u>, seen) a deer on their way to school.

3. Write each sentence, using the correct form of the verb given.

   a. Jesus has (go) to heaven.

   <u>Jesus has gone to heaven.</u>

   b. The firemen have (do) their work well.

   <u>The firemen have done their work well.</u>

   c. The children have (eat) their picnic lunch.

   <u>The children have eaten their picnic lunch.</u>

   d. We had (sing) that song before last night.

   <u>We had sung that song before last night.</u>

Name_____

Worksheet 37
Contractions

1. Write the two words that each contraction stands for.

    a. doesn't   _____does not_____

    b. haven't   _____have not_____

    c. aren't   _____are not_____

    d. don't   _____do not_____

    e. can't   _____can not_____

    f. wasn't   _____was not_____

    g. wouldn't _____would not_____

2. In the blank before each sentence, write a contraction for the words in bold print.

____hadn't____ a. The Israelites **had not** seen manna before.

____didn't____ b. At first they **did not** know what it was.

___couldn't___ c. The wise men **could not** find baby Jesus right away.

___shouldn't__ d. Jesus told His disciples that they **should not** be concerned about

                     who is the greatest.

___weren't___ e. Joseph's brothers **were not** honest when they told their father

                     about Joseph.

3. Underline the verbs in these sentences.

    a. We <u>will</u> not <u>go</u>.

    b. Eve <u>did</u> not <u>obey</u>.

    c. Our baby calf <u>did</u> not <u>drink</u>.

    d. The blind man <u>could</u> not <u>see</u> Jesus.

    e. Some pupils <u>are</u> not here today.

    f. The robins <u>have</u> not <u>come</u> back from the south.

Name_____   (English 3, Lesson 66)

Worksheet 38

Subjects and Predicates

1. Draw a line between the complete subject and complete predicate in each sentence. On the line below the sentence, write the simple subject and the simple predicate.

   a. Faithful old Abraham | believed God's promise.

   Abraham believed _____

   b. Low, dark clouds | moved across the sky.

   clouds moved _____

   c. Fluffy baby rabbits | sniffed at my hand.

   rabbits sniffed _____

   d. Ruth | gathered grain in the fields.

   Ruth gathered _____

   e. The little brown wren | sang a cheery song.

   wren sang _____

2. Add complete subjects to these complete predicates.   (Individual answers.)

   a. _____ ate all the sunflower seeds.

   b. _____ fell from the trees in our yard.

   c. _____ walked slowly down the steps.

   d. _____ pecked busily on the maple tree.

   e. _____ twinkled in the dark sky.

3. Add complete predicates to these complete subjects.   (Individual answers.)

   a. Bushels of bright apples _____.

   b. Happy boys and girls _____.

   c. The little brown puppy _____.

   d. The big white rooster _____.

   e. All the cars and trucks _____.

Name_____

Worksheet 39
Direct Objects

1. Each sentence is about the picture above it. Complete the sentence with a direct object.

a. Robert is leading the _____horse_____ to the water.

c. Sister Darlene rang the _____bell_____ this morning.

b. James and John were mending their _____nets_____.

d. Karen picked some _____flowers_____ for Mother.

2. Write five sentences, using words from this list as direct objects.   (Individual answers.)

car	gate	balloon
Bible	broom	puppy
letter	bread	water

a. _____

b. _____

c. _____

d. _____

e. _____

Name_____   (*English 3, Lesson 68*)

Worksheet 40
Diagraming Sentences With Direct Objects

1. Circle the letter before each sentence that is diagramed correctly.

(a.) Jesus | fed | people   b. Jesus | fed | people

c. Samson | caught | foxes   (d.) Samson | caught | foxes

e. Paul | made | tents   (f.) Paul | made | tents

g. David | wrote | songs   (h.) David | wrote | songs

(i.) Dorcas | made | clothes   j. Dorcas | made | clothes

(k.) Herod | killed | James   l. Herod | killed | James

2. Diagram these sentences.

   a. God made fireflies.

   b. Farmers sell grain.

   Farmers | sell | grain

   c. Pigs eat corn.

   Pigs | eat | corn

   d. Cows give milk

   e. Mary writes letters.

   Mary | writes | letters

   f. Camels carry loads.

   Camels | carry | loads

   g. People gave money.

   people | gave | money

   h. Children eat fruit.

   Children | eat | fruit

Name_____

Worksheet 41
More About Direct Objects

1. Write **yes** or **no** to tell if each sentence has a direct object.

   ___yes___ a. Moses hit the rock.

   ___no___ b. Jesus prayed earnestly.

   ___yes___ c. Lydia sold purple cloth.

   ___no___ d. Paul preached long.

   ___no___ e. Jonah sat down.

   ___yes___ f. Elisha plowed fields.

   ___no___ g. Paul traveled much.

   ___no___ h. Hagar ran away.

   ___yes___ i. Wise men brought gifts.

2. Write direct objects for these sentences.   (Most are individual answers.)

   a. Father painted _____.

   b. Cain killed _____Abel_____.

   c. Mother picked _____.

   d. We raked _____.

   e. Margaret canned _____.

3. Diagram the sentences in number 2.

   a.

   | Father | painted | [direct object] |

   b.

   | Cain | killed | Abel |

   c.

   | Mother | picked | [direct object] |

   d.

   | We | raked | [direct object] |

   e.

   | Margaret | canned | [direct object] |

Name_____   *(English 3, Lesson 72)*

Worksheet 42
Writing Sentences in Correct Order

Write each group of sentences in the right order and in correct paragraph form.

1. The next morning the snow was very deep.

   Father shoveled a path to the barn.

   One night it snowed and snowed.

   _____One night it snowed and snowed. The next morning the snow was very deep._____

   _____Father shoveled a path to the barn._____

   _____

   _____

2. Jesus looked up into the tree.

   Jesus went home with Zacchaeus.

   Zacchaeus climbed a sycamore tree.

   Jesus told Zacchaeus to come down.

   _____Zacchaeus climbed a sycamore tree. Jesus looked up into the tree._____

   _____Jesus told Zacchaeus to come down. Jesus went home with Zacchaeus._____

   _____

   _____

3. We ate it for dinner.

   Mother and Ann peeled the apples.

   Father picked some apples from our tree.

   Mother made an apple pie.

   _____Father picked some apples from our tree. Mother and Ann peeled the apples._____

   _____Mother made an apple pie. We ate it for dinner._____

   _____

   _____

Name_____

Worksheet 43
The Topic of a Paragraph

In each paragraph, underline the topic sentence and cross out the sentence that does not belong.

Paragraph A.

<u>Mother Robin built a nest on a low branch.</u> She used grass, mud, feathers, and bits of string. ~~Cardinals have red feathers.~~ She laid three blue eggs in the nest.

Paragraph B.

<u>A truck brought a big box for Henry.</u> Henry opened the box with Mother's knife. ~~Mother was making dinner.~~ Inside the box was a long toy train. Henry was very happy.

Paragraph C.

<u>Joanna made a bouquet for Mother.</u> She picked red and yellow flowers. She put them in a vase with water. Mother set the bouquet on the table. ~~Aunt Betsy often has vases with flowers in them.~~

Paragraph D.

One day four men brought a crippled man to Jesus. <u>Jesus healed the crippled man.</u> He told the man to rise and walk. ~~Jesus had twelve disciples.~~ The man could get up and go home. Also accept: <u>One day four men brought a crippled man to Jesus.</u>

Paragraph E.

<u>An angel told the shepherds that Jesus was born in the city of David.</u> ~~David had been a shepherd too.~~ The shepherds went to see baby Jesus. They found Him lying in a manger.

Paragraph F.

<u>Duane was kind to Loren.</u> Loren fell and dropped his books and his blue lunch box. Duane picked up the books and the lunch box. He helped Loren brush off his clothes. ~~Duane has a yellow lunch box.~~

Name_____   *(English 3, Lesson 74)*

Worksheet 44
Working With Titles

In each blank, write correctly the best title for that paragraph.

the ants' food	high in the sky
helen keller	the anthill
the baby grouse	food for the ostrich
the eagle's eye	flowers and birds

Paragraph A. __Food for the Ostrich_____

The ostrich has little to eat in the desert where it lives. Its main food is rough grass or thorny plants. It also eats snails, and sometimes it eats lizards or snakes.

Paragraph B. __The Anthill_____

The inside of an anthill is very interesting. Some anthills are as high as a man. They have many winding passages that lead from one part to another. The Bible says that ants do their work without any guide, overseer, or ruler. God gives them skill.

Paragraph C. __The Baby Grouse_____

The baby grouse was two days old. He had been the last of the chicks to hatch. He was eager to be up and going. He peeked from under his mother's warm wing. His dark eyes glistened.

Paragraph D. __Helen Keller_____

When Helen Keller was a little girl, she was so sick that she became blind and deaf. She could not see the beautiful flowers or hear the lovely songs of the birds. Helen's teacher taught her how to read and spell with her fingers.

Paragraph E. __The Eagle's Eye_____

The eye of the eagle is interesting. It has a thin inner eyelid that the eagle can draw over its eye when there is too much light. Because of this eyelid, the eagle can look directly at the sun. Even when the eagle is high in the sky, it can see a small animal on the ground and dive down to catch it.

Name_____

Worksheet 45
Working With Adjectives

1. Before each noun write two adjectives that tell **what kind of.**   (Individual answers.)

a. _____ sky   g. _____ water

b. _____ stream   h. _____ wind

c. _____ trees   i. _____ porch

d. _____ house   j. _____ chair

e. _____ road   k. _____ apple

f. _____ book   l. _____ sunset

2. Write three sentences, using an adjective in each sentence. Draw an arrow from each adjective to the noun that it describes.   (Individual answers.)

    Example: We picked up small shells along the beach.

_____

_____

_____

3. These sentences come from Bible verses. In each sentence underline one adjective that tells **what kind of.**

a. Sing unto the LORD a <u>new</u> song. (Psalm 96:1)

b. With a <u>strong</u> hand shall he let them go. (Exodus 6:1)

c. His meat was locusts and <u>wild</u> honey. (Matthew 3:4)

d. The Israelites passed over on <u>dry</u> ground. (Joshua 3:17)

e. They put on him a <u>purple</u> robe. (John 19:2)

f. There arose a <u>mighty</u> famine in that land. (Luke 15:14)

g. This <u>poor</u> man cried, and the LORD heard him. (Psalm 34:6)

h. I ate no <u>pleasant</u> bread. (Daniel 10:3)

i. There followed him a certain <u>young</u> man. (Mark 14:51)

Name_____   *(English 3, Lesson 77)*

Worksheet 46
Adjectives That Tell *How Many* and *How Much*

1. In each blank write an adjective that tells **how many** or **how much.** (Individual answers.)

   a. That tree has _____ leaves.

   b. We found _____ new kittens under the porch.

   c. Mother baked _____ pies yesterday.

   d. Last year we had _____ snow.

   e. After the poor man paid for his food, he had _____ money left.

   f. Grandmother got _____ medicine from the doctor.

   g. I put _____ spoons on the table.

   h. On one test I missed _____ spelling words.

   i. _____ people from south America were in church.

   j. Not _____ the people knew about the accident.

   k. We gave _____ corn to the chickens.

   l. The doctor said Uncle Ben may eat _____ sugar for a month.

   m. There are _____ people in our family.

2. Draw one line under each adjective that tells **what kind of.** Draw two lines under each adjective that tells **how many** or **how much.** You should underline two words in each sentence.

   a. Jesus taught <u>many</u> <u>good</u> lessons.

   b. <u>One</u> parable was about a <u>rich</u> man.

   c. He had <u>no</u> room to store his <u>bountiful</u> crops.

   d. The <u>selfish</u> man planned to tear down his <u>old</u> barns.

   e. He would build <u>some</u> <u>new</u> barns.

   f. He would have <u>much</u> food for <u>many</u> years.

   g. That night the <u>foolish</u> man died and left <u>all</u> his riches.

Name_____

Worksheet 47
Noun Markers

1. Write whether you would use **a** or **an** with each noun.

a. _____a_____ pear

b. _____an_____ apron

c. _____an_____ Indian

d. _____a_____ daisy

e. _____an_____ owl

f. _____a_____ button

2. Complete each sentence by adding a noun marker and a noun.   (Possible answers.)

   Example: We saw **the mountain** in the distance.

a. Lillian brought _____an_____ _____umbrella_____ because it was raining.

b. Mother gave _____the_____ _____room_____ a good cleaning.

c. We saw _____a_____ _____monkey_____ that could ride a tricycle.

d. Mother peeled _____an_____ _____apple_____ for Donald.

e. When Mother made a cake, we licked _____the_____ _____bowl_____.

f. Father cut down _____a_____ _____tree_____ for firewood.

g. Sister Malinda came to help us with _____the_____ _____work_____.

h. _____A_____ _____truck_____ roared down the road.

3. Diagram these sentences.

a. A long black train carried coal.

c. An apple has seeds.

b. The hungry bears ate fish.

d. An old gray horse pulled the cart.

Name_____   *(English 3, Lesson 81)*

Worksheet 48
Adjectives That Tell *Whose*

1. Underline each adjective that tells **whose.** Draw an arrow from the adjective to the noun it describes. The number in parentheses tells how many adjectives you should find.

   Example: Abraham's servant saddled his camels and left. (2)

   a. The servant was going to find a wife for Abraham's son. (1)

   b. Abraham wanted Isaac's wife to be from his people. (2)

   c. So he sent his servant to the land where his brother lived. (2)

   d. The servant made his camels kneel by a well. (1)

   e. Then he asked God to show him who would be Isaac's wife. (1)

   f. Soon Bethuel's daughter, Rebekah, came to draw water. (1)

   g. She offered the servant a drink and said, "I will draw water for your camels." (1)

   h. Rebekah invited Abraham's servant to her house. (2)

   i. Rebekah's brother said, "There is room for you and your camels." (2)

   j. The servant knew that God had answered his prayer. (1)

   k. The girl's father and her brother said, "Take her and go." (2)

   l. So their daughter and sister went with Abraham's servant. (2)

2. Diagram these sentences.

   a. Leroy's truck was hauling sand.   c. Marlin's bird says his name.

   | truck | was hauling | sand |
   Leroy's

   | bird | says | name |
   Marlin's   his

   b. My sister sews her dresses.

   | sister | sews | dresses |
   My   her

Name_____   *(English 3, Lesson 84)*

Worksheet 49
Adverbs That Tell *How*

1. Read each sentence. If it has an adverb that tells **how,** underline the adverb. If it does not have an adverb that tells **how,** put **X** in the blank before the sentence.

   __X__ a. We started for home early.

   _____ b. The snow fell <u>softly</u>.

   __X__ c. The rabbit dashed across the road.

   _____ d. The sun shone <u>brightly</u>.

   _____ e. Everyone spoke <u>quietly</u>.

   __X__ f. The new desk stood in the corner.

   _____ g. Hold the new baby <u>carefully</u>.

   __X__ h. Sue had blue buttons on her dress.

   _____ i. The breeze blew <u>gently</u>.

   _____ j. The ship moved <u>slowly</u> across the ocean.

2. Here are five action verbs. After each verb, write an adverb that tells **how** that action was done.   (Possible answers.)

   Example: walked slowly

   a. sang   _loudly, joyfully, cheerfully_

   b. studied   _carefully, diligently, eagerly_

   c. played   _quietly, kindly, roughly_

   d. drove   _slowly, swiftly, recklessly_

   e. talked   _loudly, softly, kindly_

3. Write sentences using three of the phrases from number 2.   (Individual answers.)

   _____

   _____

   _____

Name_____   *(English 3, Lesson 85)*

Worksheet 50
Adverbs Ending in *ly*

1. Change these adjectives to adverbs.

   a. slow _____slowly_____   f. rough _____roughly_____

   b. soft _____softly_____   g. cheerful_____cheerfully_____

   c. glad _____gladly_____   h. sweet _____sweetly_____

   d. quick _____quickly_____   i. kind _____kindly_____

   e. sad _____sadly_____   j. joyful _____joyfully_____

2. Make sentences with three of the adverbs you wrote for number 1.   (Individual answers.)

   _____

   _____

   _____

3. Diagram these sentences.

   a. Enoch served the Lord faithfully.   d. Their friends sang joyously.

   b. The girls cheerfully did their work.   e. Hopefully the man watched.

   c. The woman spoke sadly.

Name_____

Worksheet 51
Adverbs That Tell *When*

1. Underline the adverbs that tell **when.**

   a. <u>sometimes</u>

   b. sharply

   c. hard

   d. <u>always</u>

   e. <u>then</u>

   f. simply

   g. merrily

   h. <u>never</u>

   i. <u>usually</u>

   j. noisily

2. Complete each sentence with an adverb that tells **when.**   (Possible answers.)

   a. We _____*often*_____ help to gather the eggs.

   b. Mother is ready to go _____*now*_____.

   c. We were glad when the bus _____*finally*_____ arrived.

   d. Dorothy _____*seldom*_____ traveled in an airplane.

   e. Part of our order came today, and the rest will come _____*tomorrow*_____.

   f. Dinner will _____*soon*_____ be ready.

   g. We _____*sometimes*_____ hear a siren.

3. Draw one line under the adverbs that tell **how,** and two lines under the adverbs that tell **when.** Each sentence has one adverb of each kind.

   a. Penguins <u>seldom</u> move <u>fast</u> on land.

   b. They <u>usually</u> waddle <u>clumsily</u> on their short legs.

   c. They can swim <u>rapidly</u>, but they <u>never</u> fly.

   d. They <u>often</u> leap <u>swiftly</u> out of the water.

   e. Penguins in zoos may die <u>soon</u> because they <u>easily</u> get sick.

Name_____   *(English 3, Lesson 87)*

Worksheet 52
Adverbs That Tell *Where*

1. In each sentence, underline the adverb that tells **where.**

   a. I heard a cheery whistle <u>outside</u>.

   b. George brought the box <u>downstairs</u>.

   c. <u>Inside</u> was a new game.

   d. God took Elijah <u>away</u>.

   e. I know I laid my Bible <u>there</u> last night.

   f. I cannot find it <u>anywhere</u>.

   g. Cheerfully Maria skipped <u>upstairs</u>.

   h. You may leave the baby <u>here</u> while you go.

2. Underline the adverbs that tell **where.**

   a. The jet was flying very (swiftly, <u>high</u>).

   b. Empty the bucket (<u>outside</u>, now).

   c. The sun is always shining (<u>somewhere</u>, steadily).

3. Complete each sentence with an adverb that tells **where.**   (Possible answers.)

   a. We all slept _____upstairs_____.

   b. Bright, twinkling stars were _____everywhere_____ in the sky.

   c. The Klines lived _____there_____ before we did.

   d. We do not allow our dog to come _____inside_____.

   e. _____Nowhere_____ could Mother find the seeds she wanted.

   f. We will put the book _____down_____ till after dinner.

   g. Samuel went _____downstairs_____ to get a jar of peaches.

   h. The killdeer tried to lead us _____away_____ from her nest.

   i. _____Here_____ is where we plan to build a new house.

Name_____

Worksheet 53
How, When, and Where

1. Write the adverbs used in these sentences.

   a. How will Aunt Clara come? _____ How _____

   b. When will she come? _____ When _____

   c. How does she write? _____ How _____

   d. Where will she sleep? _____ Where _____

   e. When will she do her work? _____ When _____

   f. How will she know our names? _____ How _____

   g. When will she go? _____ When _____

   h. Where will she put her things? _____ Where _____

   i. When will she eat? _____ When _____

   j. How does she travel? _____ How _____

   k. Where will she sit? _____ Where _____

2. Diagram sentences **a** to **f** in number 1.

   a.

   b.

   c.

   d.

   e.

   f.

3. Write three sentences of your own using **how, when,** and **where.**   (Individual answers.)

   _____

   _____

   _____

Name_____   *(English 3, Lesson 90)*

Worksheet 54
Adjectives and Adverbs

1. Find one adjective and one adverb in each sentence. (Do not count noun markers.) Underline the adjectives once and the adverbs twice.

   a. The <u>clear</u> stream flowed <u>slowly</u> through the meadow.

   b. <u>Happily</u> the children ate the <u>ripe</u> peaches.

   c. <u>Sometimes</u> Mother makes a <u>yellow</u> cake.

   d. The <u>sly</u> fox could be found <u>nowhere</u>.

   e. I saw <u>Mark's</u> father <u>outside</u>.

   f. <u>His</u> dog <u>always</u> follows him to school.

   g. <u>Much</u> dust settled on the porch <u>yesterday</u>.

   h. Lois <u>never</u> ate <u>green</u> grapes.

2. The words in these lists are adjectives and adverbs. Write each word after the question it answers. You should write three words in each blank.

that	smooth	down	softly	some	seldom	your
four	today	boy's	third	happy	none	gladly
kindly	her	inside	now	these	green	there

Adjectives

   a. what kind of _____ *smooth, happy, green* _____

   b. how many or how much _____ *four, some, none* _____

   c. which _____ *that, third, these* _____

   d. whose _____ *her, boy's, your* _____

Adverbs

   e. how _____ *kindly, softly, gladly* _____

   f. when _____ *today, now, seldom* _____

   g. where _____ *down, inside, there* _____

Name_____

Worksheet 55
Well and *Good*

1. Put an **X** before each sentence that is correct.

   _____ a. Sarah had a fever and was not feeling good.

   __X__ b. The carpenters did a good job.

   __X__ c. Mark could not run well after he hurt his leg.

   __X__ d. Most owls can see well in the dark.

   _____ e. Sharon does good in English.

   __X__ f. Our new vacuum cleaner sweeps well.

   __X__ g. Do not get your good shoes dirty.

   _____ h. The vegetables are growing very good.

2. Use **good** or **well** to complete each sentence.

   a. We each had a piece of _____good_____ homemade bread.

   b. David could use his sling _____well_____.

   c. The baby sleeps _____well_____ at night.

   d. The yellow apples made _____good_____ applesauce.

   e. Because of all the noise, I could not hear _____well_____.

   f. We should be thankful for _____good_____ food to eat.

   g. We hope Brother Victor will soon be feeling _____well_____.

   h. Lonnie works _____well_____.

3. Write two sentences with **good** and two sentences with **well**.   (Individual answers.)

   _____

   _____

   _____

   _____

Name_____   *(English 3, Lesson 93)*

Worksheet 56
The *No* Words

1. Underline the **no** words in these sentences.

   a. <u>Nobody</u> came to the door when I knocked.

   b. There was <u>nothing</u> in the mailbox.

   c. <u>None</u> of the lions hurt Daniel.

   d. The old man has <u>never</u> traveled much.

   e. Cain did <u>not</u> love Abel.

   f. <u>Nowhere</u> on earth is it as beautiful as in heaven.

   g. Harold has <u>never</u> been in Ohio.

2. Complete each sentence with a **no** word.   (Probable answers.)

   a. We planted the seeds, but _____ none _____ of them grew.

   b. There was _____ nothing _____ in the house to eat.

   c. That dog _____ never _____ killed any chickens.

   d. We sold the table because we had _____ nowhere _____ to keep it.

   e. James wanted _____ nobody _____ to see his picture until it was done.

3. Diagram these sentences.

   a. George found no arrowheads.

   c. Penguins never fly.

   b. We went nowhere.

   d. Carol does not sew.

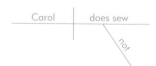

Name_____

Worksheet 57
Using the *No* Words Correctly

1. Write each sentence correctly, using only one **no** word. (Two possible answers are given for each.)

   a. Don't tell nobody about the surprise for Mother.

      Don't tell anybody about the surprise for Mother.

      Tell nobody about the surprise for Mother.

   b. They haven't gone nowhere.

      They have gone nowhere.

      They haven't gone anywhere.

   c. There wasn't nobody there to help Joseph.

      There wasn't anybody there to help Joseph.

      There was nobody there to help Joseph.

   d. Jerry didn't never ride in a boat.

      Jerry didn't ever ride in a boat.

      Jerry never rode in a boat.

   e. The children didn't want to play nothing.

      The children didn't want to play anything.

      The children wanted to play nothing.

2. Write a sentence with a **no** word to answer each question. Use a different **no** word in each answer.   (Wording may vary slightly.)

   a. Was something chasing the chickens?

      Nothing was chasing the chickens.

   b. Can anybody tell me the answer?

      Nobody can tell me the answer.

   c. Did any of the dishes break?

      None of the dishes broke.

   d. Have the children ever seen an ox cart?

      The children have never seen an ox cart.

   e. Did you find the mother rabbit anywhere?

      I found the mother rabbit nowhere.

Name_____   *(English 3, Lesson 96)*

Worksheet 58
Writing a Story From Pictures

1. Study this picture and write a story about it. You may name the girls and use these questions to help you write the story.   (Individual work.)

Do the girls look happy? Why not?

Why are they quarreling?

How are both girls in the wrong?

How was their quarrel settled?

What lesson did they learn?

2. Write a story about this picture. You may name the boy.   (Individual work.)

Name_____

Worksheet 59
Clear Word Pictures

1. Put an **X** before the word that gives the clearer word picture.

   a. _____ jumped   b. __X__ dash   c. __X__ chuckle   d. _____ clean

   __X__ leaped   _____ run   _____ laugh   __X__ scrub

2. Write two sentences using words you marked in number 1. You may change the form of the words.   (Individual answers.)

   _____

   _____

3. Complete each sentence with a noun from this list. Choose nouns that make good word pictures.

creek	animal	soil	flowers	meadow
water	creature	dirt	blossoms	field

   a. A small furry _____creature_____ darted into the tall grass.

   b. Mother brought in some _____soil_____ to start her plants.

   c. We ate lunch beside the cool, sparkling _____creek_____.

   d. Annie likes to read under the trees in the _____meadow_____.

   e. The apple tree was full of sweet-smelling _____blossoms_____.

4. Complete each sentence with an adjective from the list below. Choose adjectives that make good word pictures.

white	good	huge	pretty	sparkling
little	big	tiny	delicious	beautiful

   a. The _____tiny_____ mouse peeked through the hole.

   b. The snowy mountaintop made a _____beautiful_____ picture.

   c. _____Delicious_____ smells came from the kitchen.

   d. The _____huge_____ crane lifted the train car.

   e. The _____sparkling_____ snow almost blinded us.

Name_____

Worksheet 60
Writing Smoothly

1. Put an X before the group of words that is smoother.

___X___ a. Friday morning it rained hard.

_____   Friday it rained. It rained hard. It rained in the morning.

_____ b. We have a horse. It is brown. Its name is Bobby.

___X___   We have a brown horse named Bobby.

_____ c. The lighthouse is tall. It is white. It stands by the sea.

___X___   The tall white lighthouse stands by the sea.

___X___ d. Jeffrey found a big brown arrowhead.

_____   Jeffrey found an arrowhead. It was big. It was brown.

2. Write each set of ideas as one sentence.   (Wording may vary slightly.)

   a. David was reading his book. It was new. It was about birds.

     David was reading his new book about birds.

   b. We watched the bears. They were white. They were in the water.

     We watched the white bears in the water.

   c. Joseph had a coat. It was pretty. It had many colors.

     Joseph had a pretty coat of many colors.

3. Answer each set of questions with one sentence.   (Sentences should follow these patterns.)

   a. Do you have a brother or sister? What is his or her name? How old is he or she?

     I have a brother named Kevin who is two years old.

     or My brother Kevin is two years old.

   b. Did you go to the store? When did you go? With whom did you go?

     I went to the store yesterday with Mother.

   c. Did you play? What did you play? When did you play?

     I played tag this morning.

Name_____

Worksheet 61
Homophones

1. Underline the word in parentheses that has the meaning given.

   a. (<u>sum</u>, some) The answer to an addition problem.

   b. (<u>flour</u>, flower) A powder made from grain.

   c. (ate, <u>eight</u>) A number.

   d. (we, <u>wee</u>) Very small.

   e. (see, <u>sea</u>) A large body of water.

   f. (<u>sun</u>, son) A light in the sky.

   g. (bear, <u>bare</u>) Not covered.

2. Underline the correct homophone in each sentence.

   a. The three Hebrews would not (bough, <u>bow</u>) to the golden image.

   b. The angry king had them (throne, <u>thrown</u>) into a fiery furnace.

   c. The Hebrews did not (<u>know</u>, no) whether they would live or die.

   d. But the fire did not burn them or (there, <u>their</u>) clothes.

   e. Not a (<u>hair</u>, hare) on their heads was singed.

   f. This was a (grate, <u>great</u>) and marvelous miracle.

3. Finish each pair of homophones. The first one is done for you.

a. him,	hymn	h. sent,	cent *or* scent
b. too,	to *or* two	i. inn,	in
c. herd,	heard	j. oar,	or *or* ore
d. so,	sew *or* sow	k. write,	right
e. dear,	deer	l. rode,	road
f. through,	threw	m. heel,	heal *or* he'll
g. for,	four	n. be,	bee

Name_____   *(English 3, Lesson 103)*

Worksheet 62
Words With More Than One Meaning

1. Before each sentence, write the number of the meaning from below that matches the word in bold print.

    __1__   a. The barn burned down **fast.**

    __3__   b. The king of Nineveh told everyone in the city to **fast.**

    __2__   c. We did not **lock** the door.

    __4__   d. This brown **lock** came from Ralph's head.

    __10__   e. The **board** had a meeting yesterday.

    __7__   f. That **board** is five feet long.

    __5__   g. That **type** of cloth does not tear easily.

    __8__   h. I will **type** the letter.

    __9__   i. A robin hopped across the **yard.**

    __6__   j. Mother bought a **yard** of blue material.

1. Quickly.	6. Thirty-six inches.
2. To close with a key.	7. A flat piece of sawed wood.
3. To go without food.	8. To write with a typewriter.
4. A ring of hair.	9. A grassy place around a house.
5. A certain kind.	10. A group of people who direct.

2. Underline each sentence in which a word is used wrong.

    a. A kite eats snails. <u>Plant the kite.</u> The kite has a long string.

    b. A crane lifts heavy things. The children craned their necks. <u>Write a letter to the crane.</u>

    c. <u>Trim the watch.</u> Watch the children. He lost the watch.

    d. Pound the nails well. <u>The ducks are swimming in the pound.</u> Please get a pound of butter.

Name_____

Worksheet 63
Synonyms and Antonyms

1. Match the words on the left with their synonyms on the right.

   a. gift _____present_____ fix

   b. said _____told_____ blossom

   c. sick _____ill_____ told

   d. flower _____blossom_____ ground

   e. stone _____rock_____ ill

   f. lad _____boy_____ present

   g. creature _____animal_____ rock

   h. aged _____old_____ wicked

   i. soil _____ground_____ old

   j. sinful _____wicked_____ boy

   k. fire _____flames_____ animal

   l. repair _____fix_____ flames

2. Underline one or two pairs of antonyms in each verse.

   a. <u>Hate</u> the <u>evil</u>, and <u>love</u> the <u>good</u>. (Amos 5:15)

   b. Thou are lukewarm, and neither <u>cold</u> nor <u>hot</u>. (Revelation 3:16)

   c. Haman was afraid before the <u>king</u> and the <u>queen</u>. (Esther 7:6)

   d. <u>Servants</u>, be subject to your <u>masters</u>. (1 Peter 2:18)

   e. A time to <u>weep</u>, and a time to <u>laugh</u>. (Ecclesiastes 3:4)

   f. They shall come from the <u>east</u>, and from the <u>west</u>, and from the <u>north</u>, and from the <u>south</u>. (Luke 13:29)

   g. The <u>crooked</u> shall be made <u>straight</u>, and the <u>rough</u> ways shall be made <u>smooth</u>. (Luke 3:5)

Name_____   *(English 3, Lesson 107)*

Worksheet 64
Describing a Place

One day I was going through the woods. On one side of me was a high bank. Trees were on the bank. Leaves were on the trees. On the other side of me was a creek. Rocks were in the creek. Fish were in the creek. Grass was on the ground. Flowers were growing. Some parts of the woods were darker than other parts. I sat down and listened to different sounds. I was sorry when it was time to go home.

1. On other paper, rewrite the description above to make better word pictures. The questions below may help you.   (Individual work.)

   • What kind of day was it?
   • Can you think of a better verb than **going?**
   • What kind of trees were there?
   • What color and size were the leaves?
   • What kind of rocks were in the creek? What kind of fish?
   • What are some better verbs to go with **fish, grass,** and **flowers?**
   • What color and size were the flowers?
   • What kind of smell did the flowers have?
   • Why were some parts of the woods darker than others?
   • What did you sit on?
   • What sounds did you hear?
   • Why were you sorry when it was time to go home?

2. Write a good description of the place shown in the picture.   (Individual work.)

Name_____

Worksheet 65
Giving Clear Directions

1. For each set of directions, write **Not complete, Mixed up,** or **Too many details.**

Planting a Garden

Plow or till the soil to get it ready. Cover the seeds with soil. Drop the seeds into the rows. Make straight rows about three feet apart.

a. _____ *Mixed up* _____

Making Lemonade

Squeeze some lemons and pour the juice into a pitcher. Add some water to the juice. Add ice if you want it cold.

b. _____ *Not complete* _____

Canning Peaches

Wash the peaches and put some of them into a pan. ~~Sit down on a chair.~~ Cut the peaches in half. Remove the seeds and peel the peaches. ~~First peel one half, and then peel the other half.~~ Put the peeled peaches into jars, and put lids on them. Set the jars in a canner with enough water to come to the necks of the jars. Boil them for about fifteen minutes. Take the jars out of the water and set them somewhere to cool. When you hear the lids popping, they are sealed. ~~Carry the jars to the basement. When you want to eat peaches, use a jar opener to open the jars.~~

c. _____ *Too many details* _____

2. Cross out two of the unnecessary sentences in the set of directions that you labeled **Too many details.**   *(Any two of the above should be crossed out.)*

3. Write correctly the set of directions that you labeled **Mixed up.**

_____ *Plow or till the soil to get it ready. Make straight rows about three feet apart.* _____
_____ *Drop the seeds into the rows. Cover the seeds with soil.* _____
_____
_____

Name_____   *(English 3, Lesson 115)*

Worksheet 66
The Friendly Letter

1. On the line beside each part of the letter below, write which part it is.

8342 Adamson Lake Road

_____Heading_____   Kaleva, Michigan 49645

_____Greeting_____   Dear Elizabeth

Greetings in Jesus' Name.

Mother is making a new blue Sunday dress for me. While she sewed, I took care of baby Jason till he slept.

In school we are studying about birds. This week we colored a picture of a goldfinch. There is a chart on the wall to write down the names of birds we see. So far, we have seen sixteen different kinds. I like to learn about birds.

_____Body_____   Father, Lewis, and Ray went to help Uncle Roy fix his barn. Part of the roof blew off when it was so windy last week. That day a tree blew down in our yard.

We have three baby kittens. They are very cute. Sometimes they play on the porch.

I hope your family can come to visit us soon.

_____Closing_____

_____Signature_____   Barbara

2. Find at least three mistakes in the letter. Write what the mistakes are. (Any three.)

The heading has no date.

The greeting is not followed by a comma.

In the body, the fourth paragraph needs indention.

There is no closing.

Name_____

Worksheet 67
The Parts of a Friendly Letter

1. Write these parts of a letter correctly. Beside each, write one of your own.

   Example: your cousin _____Your cousin,_____   _____Yours truly,_____

   a. your friend   _____Your friend,_____   _____(Answers will vary.)_____

   b. with love   _____With love,_____   _____

   c. dear mary   _____Dear Mary,_____   _____

   d. john   _____John_____   _____

   e. dover delaware _____Dover, Delaware_____   _____

   f. may 12 2007   _____May 12, 2007_____   _____

   g. walnut street   _____Walnut Street_____   _____

   h. tampa florida   _____Tampa, Florida_____   _____

2. In this letter form, fill in each part with answers that you wrote in the second column above.   (Individual answers.)

   _____

   _____

   _____

   _____

   _____

   _____(Body)_____

   _____

   _____

   _____

Name_____   *(English 3, Lesson 121)*

Worksheet 68
Rhyme

1. Beside each word in Column A, write a rhyming word from Column B.

Column A		**Column B**
a. plant	ant	fish
b. key	tree	tree
c. talk	walk	wing
d. girl	curl	sail
e. dear	hear	far
f. light	might	curl
g. star	far	ant
h. house	mouse	mouse
i. dish	fish	walk
j. pray	stay	might
k. sing	wing	stay
l. preach	teach	hear
m. tail	sail	teach

2. Beside each word, write a word that rhymes with it.   (Individual answers.)

a. shock	_____	h. cheer	_____
b. snow	_____	i. should	_____
c. roll	_____	j. run	_____
d. cat	_____	k. trick	_____
e. sheep	_____	l. cold	_____
f. kind	_____	m. hill	_____
g. wide	_____	n. deeds	_____

Name_____

Worksheet 69
Rhythm

1. Underline the words that give better rhythm.

   a. I saw a (small, <u>little</u>) bird

      Away up in a tree;

    And as I looked (<u>up</u>, upward) at him,

      He looked right down at me.

   b. He looked so very (<u>happy</u>, glad);

      Then he began to sing.

    He (appeared, <u>seemed</u>) to be so thankful

      For (<u>life</u>, being) and everything.

   c. And then I prayed, "Dear (<u>Father</u>, Lord),

      Just help me (also, <u>too</u>), to be

    As very, very thankful

      As birds (<u>up</u>, sitting) in a tree.

   d. "And help me to (realize, <u>remember</u>)

      That I need never fear;

    For You will always (<u>keep</u>, protect) me

      My (<u>Lord</u>, Master) and Saviour dear."

2. In each stanza cross out two words that spoil the rhythm.

   a. A little burn can hurt a lot,

      And, oh, how ~~much~~ it can smart!

    A little cinder in one's eye

      Can ~~great~~ agony impart.

   b. A little leak can sink a ~~large~~ ship,

      But ~~even~~ though it seems absurd,

    The cruelest little thing of all

      Is just an unkind word!

Name_____   *(English 3, Lesson 124)*

Worksheet 70
Helps for Writing Poetry

Supply the missing words for these poems.

1. **My Dear Parents**

    I have a mother kind and sweet;

    She dusts and keeps our house so _____neat_____;

    She washes dishes, irons our _____clothes_____,

    When I need help, she always knows

    Exactly what is _____good_____ and right.

    For her I breathe a prayer each _____night_____.

    I have a father big and _____strong_____,

    Who works for us the whole day _____long_____.

    He always knows a game that's fun;

    He reads to us when day is _____done_____.

    I like to bow my head and pray,

    "God _____bless_____ my father every _____day_____."

2. **The Snow**

    Last _____night_____ when we were sound _____asleep_____,

    The snow fell fast, and snow piled _____deep_____.

    When morning came and we looked out,

    The snow was lying all _____about_____.

    The _____wind_____ was blowing high and low,

    And wrinkling up the pure _____white_____ _____snow_____;

    And everywhere that we could _____see_____

    We found that God made mystery.

    —*Marguerite Church Clark*

    —Adapted

Beginning Wisely

Unit 1 Test   **Score** _____

Name _____ **Date** _____

A. Use a word from this list to complete each sentence.

workbook	friend	three	command	subject
alphabetical	question	two	predicate	topical

1. Your English textbook is your _____friend_____.

2. Words in a dictionary are listed in _____alphabetical_____ order.

3. A sentence must have _____two_____ parts.

4. The _____subject_____ tells who or what the sentence is about.

5. A _____command_____ is a sentence that tells someone to do something.

(5 points)

B. In the blank before each sentence, write **T, A,** or **E** to tell whether it is a **telling,** an **asking,** or an **exclaiming** sentence. Then copy the sentences. Begin and end each one correctly.   (Corrected items are underlined.)

___T___   6. the gray squirrel was busily gathering nuts for winter

  The gray squirrel was busily gathering nuts for winter. _____

  _____

___A___   7. will he need much food for the cold weather

  Will he need much food for the cold weather? _____

  _____

___E___   8. what an interesting creature he is

  What an interesting creature he is! _____

  _____

(9 points)

C. Diagram these sentences.

9. Ducks swim.

| Ducks | swim |

12. Do trains whistle?

| trains | do whistle |

10. Lions hunt and roar.

Lions / hunt / and / roar

13. Moses and Aaron returned.

Moses / and / Aaron / returned

11. Listen!

| (you) | Listen |

(12 points)

D. Write each name correctly. Then write the initials.

14. john quincy adams   John Quincy Adams   J. Q. A.

15. william h taft   William H. Taft   W. H. T.

16. benjamin harrison   Benjamin Harrison   B. H.

(6 points)

E. Write these sentences correctly.   (Corrected items are underlined.)

17. Father asked, are the peas ready to pick

   Father asked, "Are the peas ready to pick?"

18. dinner is ready, Mother called

   "Dinner is ready," Mother called.

19. it is cold outside, exclaimed Mary

   "It is cold outside!" exclaimed Mary.

(10 points)

F. Write a contraction for each pair of words.

20. could not _____ couldn't _____   22. she has _____ she's _____

21. we are _____ we're _____   23. he would _____ he'd _____

(4 points)

G. Rewrite each phrase as a possessive phrase with an apostrophe.

24. the wisdom of Solomon _____ Solomon's wisdom _____

25. the faith of Abraham _____ Abraham's faith _____

26. the miracles of Christ _____ Christ's miracles _____

27. the journeys of Paul _____ Paul's journeys _____

(4 points)

Total points: 50

Beginning Wisely

Unit 2 Test   **Score** _____

Name _____ **Date** _____

A. Copy a word from this list to complete each sentence. You will not use all the answers.

plural	possessive	pronoun	proper
singular	apostrophe	verb	common

1. A word that does the same work in a sentence as a noun is a

   _____<u>pronoun</u>_____.

2. If a noun names more than one, it is _____<u>plural</u>_____.

3. A_____<u>proper</u>_____ noun is a specific name that always begins with a capital

   letter.

4. If a noun names only one, it is _____<u>singular</u>_____.

5. The _____<u>possessive</u>_____ form of a noun tells **whose.**

6. A_____<u>common</u>_____ noun does not name a specific person, place, or thing.

                                                                        (6 points)

B. Put commas where they belong in these sentences.

7. Joseph, it is your turn to pass the wastepaper can.

8. We bought soap, apples, salt, and eggs at the grocery store.

9. Father had a surprise for Thomas, Ann, and me.

10. Grandmother, here are some flowers for you.

                                                                        (7 points)

C. Underline the nouns in these sentences.

11. We set the <u>dishes</u> on the <u>table</u>.

12. <u>Father</u> used an <u>ax</u> to split the <u>wood</u>.

13. The <u>mailman</u> put a <u>package</u> into the <u>mailbox</u>.

                                                                        (8 points)

D. On the line below each sentence, write correctly the words or phrases that need capital letters.

14. On the day after christmas, paul miller traveled through ohio on his way to maryland.

Christmas, Paul Miller, Ohio, Maryland

15. My uncle gave me a puppy in may, and we named it bouncer.

May, Bouncer

16. When our family went to rocky glen church last sunday, we were surprised to meet aunt nancy there.

Rocky Glen Church, Sunday, Aunt Nancy

17. Last summer we visited the zoo in pittsburgh, pennsylvania.

Pittsburgh, Pennsylvania   (1 point for not capitalizing *summer*.)

18. A man was cleaning windows on the tenth story of the edison building.

Edison Building

19. In the catalog I saw a book called the man in bearskin.

The Man in Bearskin   (2 points.)

(15 points)

E. In the blank before each sentence, write the correct form of the noun in parentheses. Use a plural form or a possessive form.

brothers   20. Joseph had ten older (brother).

lion's   21. God delivered David from the (lion) paw.

berries   22. We picked twelve quarts of (berry).

sheep   23. The shepherd had one hundred (sheep).

boy's   24. This looks like a (boy) coat.

(5 points)

F. Read each sentence. If it has a mistake, write the sentence correctly on the line below. If it has no mistake, put an **X** on the blank in front of the sentence.

_____ 25. There were pennies nickels and dimes in the box.

   There were pennies, nickels, and dimes in the box.

_____ 26. These dishes are her's.

   These dishes are hers.

__X___ 27. That is a passenger train.

_____

_____ 28. Uncle Ben and me took a walk through the woods.

   Uncle Ben and I took a walk through the woods.

_____ 29. Abraham he was faithful.

   Abraham was faithful.

_____ 30. This here is the first corn we have had this summer.

   This is the first corn we have had this summer.

__X___ 31. Mother called Betty and me.

_____

_____ 32. Are them your blue boots?

   Are those (or they or these) your blue boots?

__X___ 33. This book is for you and her.

_____

(9 points)

Total points: 50

Beginning Wisely

Unit 3 Test   Score _____

Name _____ **Date** _____

A. Use the correct word from the list to complete each sentence. You will not use all the words.

past	noun	topic	person
was	verb	not	helping

1. A word that shows action or being is a _____ verb _____.

2. Verb forms are changed to tell about the _____ past _____.

3. Some verb forms need a _____ helping _____ verb.

4. The word _____ not _____ is often used with verbs, but it is not a verb.

5. All the sentences in a paragraph must tell about one _____ topic _____.

(5 points)

B. Underline the verbs in these sentences. On the line before each sentence, write **A** if the verb shows action and **B** if it shows being.

___A___ 6. The wind <u>shook</u> the old apple tree.

___B___ 7. The cactus plant <u>is</u> prickly.

___A___ 8. Baby <u>eats</u> by himself.

___A___ 9. The people <u>believed</u> the Word of God.

___B___ 10. The boys <u>are</u> twins.

(5 points)

C. On the blank before each sentence, write the correct form of the verb in parentheses. More than one form may be correct.

___patches *or* patched___ 11. Mother (patch) our clothes.

___goes *or* went___ 12. Rover often (go) with Father.

___made___ 13. Martha has (make) salad for supper.

___fell *or* fall___ 14. The nuts (fall) from the trees.

___teaches *or* taught___ 15. Dan (teach) history in the afternoon.

(5 points)

D. Write **do, does, did,** or **done** to complete each sentence. Use present forms in sentences 16 and 17.

16. Mother _____ does _____ not feel well today.

17. Wild rabbits _____ do _____ not like to be caged.

18. We _____ did _____ the cleaning yesterday.

19. The clock _____ did _____ not run before it was repaired.

20. The children have _____ done _____ their work carefully.

(5 points)

E. Underline each verb form that must be used with a helping verb.

21. <u>taken</u>   24. did

22. went   25. gave

23. <u>grown</u>   26. <u>begun</u>

(6 points)

F. Beside each contraction, write the two words from which it is made.

27. don't   _____ do not _____   30. shouldn't   _____ should not _____

28. haven't   _____ have not _____   31. couldn't   _____ could not _____

29. can't   _____ can not _____   32. wouldn't   _____ would not _____

(6 points)

G. Diagram the simple subject, simple predicate, and direct object of each sentence.

33. Mother washed the dishes.

Mother | washed | dishes

34. The three boys helped Father gladly.

boys | helped | Father

(6 points)

H. Make a good paragraph from these sentences. Write your paragraph on the lines below.

He put it on a post outside the kitchen window.

When he was finished, he had a pretty bird feeder.

Allen got some boards, nails, and a hammer.

Father lost his hammer.

Soon he was busy hammering and sawing.

Soon many birds were enjoying the new bird feeder.

<u>The New Bird Feeder</u>

    Allen got some boards, nails, and a hammer. Soon he was busy hammering and sawing. When he was finished, he had a pretty bird feeder. He put it on a post outside the kitchen window. Soon many birds were enjoying the new bird feeder.

(Count 4 points for correct order, 2 points for straight margins, 1 point for indentation, and 1 point for leaving out the unnecessary sentence.)

(8 points)

I. Write the following titles correctly. Choose the one that best fits the paragraph you wrote for Part H, and write that title on the short line above the paragraph.

35. a boy and a bird   A Boy and a Bird

36. the new bird feeder   The New Bird Feeder

37. a bag of nails   A Bag of Nails

(4 points)

Total points: 50

Beginning Wisely

Unit 4 Test   Score _____

Name _____ **Date** _____

A. Write the letter of the correct word or phrase before each description.

a. adverbs   d. noun markers

b. nouns   e. possessive form

c. verbs   f. adjectives

___b___ 1. Words described by adjectives.

___c___ 2. Words described by adverbs.

___f___ 3. Words that tell **what kind of, which,** and **whose.**

___d___ 4. The words **a, an,** and **the.**

___a___ 5. Words that tell **how, when,** and **where.**

___e___ 6. A kind word that tells **whose.**

(6 points)

B. Underline all the adjectives in these sentences. The numbers in parentheses tell how many there are.

7. We saw <u>our</u> <u>first</u> robin yesterday. (2)

8. <u>The</u> toad has <u>a</u> <u>sticky</u> tongue. (3)

9. <u>This</u> tongue is used to catch food. (1)

10. Vultures are <u>big</u> birds that eat <u>dead</u> animals. (2)

(8 points)

C. Rewrite each phrase, using a possessive noun or pronoun.

11. a palace for a king   _____a king's palace_____

12. the car belonging to him   _____his car_____

13. the coat she owns   _____her coat_____

14. the Word of God   _____God's Word_____

(4 points)

D. Underline the two adverbs in each sentence.

15. <u>Yesterday</u> a train whistled <u>loudly</u>.

16. I did <u>not</u> hear it <u>today</u>.

17. I hurt my food <u>badly</u> <u>here</u>.

18. <u>Today</u> the men worked <u>swiftly</u>.

(8 points)

E. If the word in bold print is an adjective, underline it once. If it is an adverb, underline it twice.

19. Jason tried **hard** to solve the **hard** problem.

20. Speak **right** and say the **right** words.

21. Does a **fast** train always travel **fast**?

(6 points)

F. Put an **X** before each sentence that is diagramed correctly.

_____ 22. Birds | sang | cheerily

__X__ 25. They | have | car \ no

__X__ 23. Lightning | flashed \ suddenly

__X__ 26. boys | chuckled \ The \ two \ softly

_____ 24. motor | did not | work \ The

_____ 27. Ann | seldom | complains

(6 points)

G. Cross out one wrong word in each sentence. If another word should be used in its place, write the correct word in the blank before the sentence.

_____Those_____ 28. ~~Them~~ oranges are really sweet.

_____good_____ 29. Mark did a ~~well~~ job.

_____ 30. This ~~here~~ book is the one I like.

_____well_____ 31. The baby had a fever and was not feeling ~~good~~.

_____could_____ 32. It was so dark I ~~couldn't~~ see nothing. (*or* anything ~~nothing~~)

_____ 33. These apples are ripe, but those ~~there~~ are green.

_____well_____ 34. Robert usually behaves ~~good~~.

_____had_____ 35. Gehazi said he ~~hadn't~~ gone nowhere. (*or* anywhere ~~nowhere~~)

(8 points)

H. In the blank before each sentence, write a verb that gives a clearer picture than the verb in bold print.   (Possible answers.)

climbed, scampered 36. The monkey **went** up the tree.

_____called_____ 37. "Come and help me," **said** Father from the barn.

_____grabbed_____ 38. The hungry child **took** the spoon from my hand.

drew, painted 39. The artist **made** a beautiful picture.

(4 points)

Total points: 50

Beginning Wisely

Unit 5 Test

Score _____

Name _____ Date _____

A. Use one of these words to complete each sentence.

poetry   volume   mood   rhyme

paragraph   stanza   memory   rhythm

1. Writing put in a beautiful form is _____poetry_____.

2. The _____mood_____ of a poem is its feeling.

3. A verse of a song or poem is called a _____stanza_____.

4. The _____rhyme_____ of a poem is made by lines whose endings sound alike.

5. The _____rhythm_____ of a poem is made by a regular pattern of accented and

   unaccented syllables.

(5 points)

B. In each sentence, find and underline a pair of homophones, a pair of synonyms, or a
   pair of antonyms. In the blank before the sentence, write **H, S,** or **A** to tell whether you
   underlined **homophones, synonyms,** or **antonyms.**

   __H__ 6. I could <u>not</u> open the <u>knot</u> in my shoestring.

   __S__ 7. We watched a <u>beautiful</u> sunset one <u>lovely</u> summer evening.

   __A__ 8. The <u>old</u> cat watched as her <u>young</u> ones played in the grass.

   __H__ 9. I want to <u>write</u> a letter to her <u>right</u> away.

(8 points)

C. Write these words in alphabetical order.

straight   still   stamp

steady   stumble   stomach

10. _____stamp_____   13. _____stomach_____

11. _____steady_____   14. _____straight_____

12. _____still_____   15. _____stumble_____

(3 points)

D. Write sentences as the directions tell you.   (Individual answers.)

16. Write two sentences, showing two different meanings for **fly.**

_____

_____

17. Write a sentence to describe a horse. Use good picture words.

_____

_____

(3 points)

E. After each number, write the name of the letter part that belongs on the line or lines with that number in parentheses.

18. _____heading_____

19. _____greeting_____

20. _____body_____

21. _____closing_____

22. _____signature_____

```
                              _____
                                       (18)
                              _____

(19)_____

        _____
_____(20)_____

_____
                    (21)
                    (22)
```

(5 points)

F. Write **true** or **false** before each sentence.

_____false_____ 23. To introduce a younger person to an older person, say the younger person's name first.

_____true_____ 24. To answer the telephone, say **Hello** and give your name.

_____false_____ 25. When you tell someone how to do something, let him figure out in what order to follow the directions.

_____true_____ 26. To introduce someone to your mother, say **Mother** first.

_____true_____ 27. When you give directions, make them as clear and as short as you can.

_____false_____ 28. When you try to call someone, hang up after the other telephone rings four times.

(6 points)

G. Copy this poem correctly on the lines. The poem should have three stanzas, with four lines in each stanza.

my tooth

a tooth fell out

and left a space

so my big tongue

can touch my face.

and every time

I smile, I show

a place where something

used to grow.

I miss my tooth,

as you may guess,

but now I have

to brush one less.

_____My Tooth_____

_____A tooth fell out_____

_____And left a space_____

_____So my big tongue_____

_____Can touch my face._____

_____

_____And every time_____

_____I smile, I show_____

_____A place where something_____

_____Used to grow._____

_____

_____I miss my tooth,_____

_____As you may guess,_____

_____But now I have_____

_____To brush one less._____

_____

_____

(10 points, 1 for title and 3 for each stanza)
Total points: 40

Index